GANG OF EIGHT

The First Tee

Darby Winterhalter Löfstrand

ArTemenos Publishing, LLC
Flagstaff, Arizona

Gang of Eight: The First Tee

Copyright (c) 2014 by Darby Winterhalter Löfstrand

Cover art: Phil Ilirjan Vehap, Creative Director,
THINK Brands, New York
Cover photo: Don Kunkle Winterhalter
Interior photo provided by Patrick Quinn

Lyrics for "The Scotsman"
by Benjamin Michael Cross
used by explicit permission.
Copyright (c) 1974, 1979 Vic-Ray Publishing (ASCAP)
All rights reserved.

All rights reserved. No part of this book may be used, transmitted, or reproduced in any manner whatsoever without written permission from the publisher, except in the case of brief quotations embodied in critical articles or reviews.

For information contact:
ArTemenos Publishing, LLC
P.O. Box 2802
Flagstaff, Arizona 86003

Library of Congress Control Number: 2014943670.

ISBN 13: 978-0-9765643-1-7
ISBN 10: 0-9765643-1-9

Published by ArTemenos Publishing, LLC. Flagstaff, Arizona

Printed in the United States of America.

This is for the men who make up this "almost true" story, and the families who so generously supported them over the years, the miles, and the absences. Clearly, this story wouldn't exist without them, and I am deeply indebted and honored at their trust and confidence.

I am also grateful to my husband, Tobias, for his unwavering love and assistance.

To Mom, my best friend, who encouraged me to prevail when time and the vicissitudes of life got in the way.

To Allene Edwards, my editor, without whom this story would be far less civilized, and to Charles Steadham at Vic-Ray Publishing and songwriter Mike Cross for permission to use his song "The Scotsman."

To my friends, golfers and non-golfers alike, who showed their support by asking – every time they saw me – "Is it done yet?"

But mostly, this book is for Dad ... quite simply, the best human being I know, on and off the course.

"... any one of us could have gone and played these courses alone, but it wouldn't have been nearly as special as how we did it together. Thanks for making this trip so unforgettable."

– Gary Plato, PGA;
Head Pro Emeritus, San Jose CC;
Gang of Eight Founding Member

CONTENTS

The Back Story

Prologue 1
1 June, 1980 - Don Winterhalter and Hank the Starter 12
2 New Year's Eve, 1980 - Patrick Quinn 32
3 August, 1981 - Charlie Quinn 38
4 February, 1982 - Don Ridge 46
5 July, 1982 - Rudy Staedler 51
6 August, 1985 - Don Ridge 92
7 July, 1990 - Chris Clark 102
8 April, 1992 - Gary Plato 109
9 August, 1994 - Don Ridge and Gary Vandeweghe 117
10 May, 1997 - Patrick Quinn 131
11 August, 1997 - Gary Vandeweghe 140
12 August, 1997 - Don Winterhalter 148
13 October, 1997 - Gary Vandeweghe 153
14 October, 1997 - Gary Vandeweghe 157
15 November, 1997 - Gary Plato 159
16 January, 1998 - Gary Vandeweghe 166
17 January, 1998 - Don Winterhalter 169
18 January, 1998 - Rudy Staedler 173
19 March, 1998 - Charlie Quinn 184
20 May, 1998 - Don Ridge 188
21 June, 1998 - Gary Plato 193
22 June, 1998 - Chris Clark 195
23 August, 1998 - Don Ridge 203

The Trip to Scotland

24	August 27, 1998 - Don Winterhalter	209
25	August 28, 1998 - Rudy Staedler	214
26	August 30, 1998 - Patrick Quinn	227
27	August 30, 1998 - Chris Clark	241
28	August 30, 1998 - Charlie Quinn and Rudy Staedler	247
29	August 31, 1998 - Gary Vandeweghe	258
30	August 31, 1998 - Gary Plato	262
31	August 31, 1998 - Patrick Quinn	268
32	September 1, 1998 - Don Winterhalter and Rudy Staedler	281
33	September 1, 1998 - Chris Clark	294
34	September 2, 1998 - Don Ridge	304
35	September 3, 1998 - Patrick Quinn and Gary Vandeweghe	325
36	September 3, 1998 - Charlie Quinn	345
37	September 3, 1998 - Patrick Quinn	351
38	September 4, 1998 - Chris Clark and Rudy Staedler	353
39	September 5, 1998 - Don Winterhalter	394
40	September 6, 1998 - Gary Plato	409
41	September 6, 1998 - Don Ridge and Patrick Quinn	427
42	September 7, 1998 - Charlie Quinn	441
43	September 8, 1998 - Chris Clark	457
44	September 8, 1998 - Don Winterhalter	470
45	September 9, 1998 - Gary Vandeweghe	475

GANG OF EIGHT

The First Tee

PROLOGUE
October, 1977
Gary Plato

The last box snapped open. Inside, gleaming with newness, brightly colored ball caps nested in shiny plastic bags. Red, blue, yellow, green, and brilliant white – they all sported the four-part crest resting atop a banner, which encased the words "San Jose Country Club." Gary Plato ran an appraising thumb over one. Even after all these years, the logo worked. Elegant; distinctive; recognizable.

In one scoop, he snatched the items and placed them on the counter, then nodded toward the far wall of the golf shop. "These can go on that shelf, there," he said to the second assistant professional. "Arrange them by color, with the white in front." He punched through the packing tape on the bottom of the box, then folded it flat. No reason to waste it. It was a good sized box and would come in handy when a member wanted something shipped or gift wrapped.

As Plato slid the flattened box onto a high shelf in the bag room, he heard a chuckle, then the low rumblings of an adolescent male from the other side of the temporary wall, a barrier that sectioned off a small portion of the space to create a junior locker room. Over the three inch gap where the particle board failed to reach the ceiling, a small trail of white smoke mischievously curled through the air. Plato sniffed. Cigar smoke.

Quickly, he grabbed a step stool, wedged it between stored golf bags and a tall stack of paper towels, and peeked over the gap.

Chris Clark and Patrick Quinn sat draped over the small couch, their feet kicked out before them, ankles crossed, their heads thrown back in mock arrogance. Chris's chiseled, tanned face and blond hair were in stark contrast to Patrick's oval face, Irish-white skin, and dark hair. Each wore the acceptable garb of a golfer, though Chris, at nineteen, had a bit more style than his younger compatriot. Each grasped a long, narrow cigar.

Chris leaned his head back and exhaled a stream of smoke. "I think you could have made a single bogey if you'd just used the three iron, like I suggested."

"Naw," Patrick said, mimicking a deeper voice than that of his eleven years. He waved his cigar in the air. "When I try that, half the time I end up hitting it long over the green. No, I think I used the right club. I just didn't hit it hard enough."

Chris sat up and poked his cigar in Patrick's direction. The smoke wafted into Patrick's face, and he coughed.

"You showed no courage, as the pro would say," Chris said emphatically. "You lacked the conviction of your choice."

Plato swallowed his laughter and his head bumped the ceiling. Patrick looked up and Plato ducked, sending a box of used golf gloves tumbling to the floor.

"I just saw the pro," Patrick said, a hint of panic raising both his tone and volume back to that of a child's.

"What do you mean you just saw the pro? Where?" Chris replied.

"He was up there," Patrick said.

Scuffles and a muffled, "Quick! Give me yours!" followed another waft of smoke over the wall. Plato forced the smile from his face, then burst through the door. Patrick stood, hands empty, while Chris crouched over the garbage bin in the corner, frantically attempting to extinguish one of the cigars.

"Okay you guys, give me those," Plato barked, holding out his palm. He hoped he sounded stern. "Come on."

Patrick looked to Chris, panic blanching his face. Chris reached into the bin and retracted the other stogy, then placed both cigars in Plato's outstretched hand. Plato pressed his lips together to keep from laughing. One had clearly not been lit.

"Sorry, Mister Plato," Patrick mumbled, eyes downcast.

Plato thought the poor kid might start to cry. "Apology accepted, but don't let me catch you at this again." He jerked his head toward the door. "Now Patrick, get over to the range and practice. I want you to hit at least two buckets. No, make it three, before you leave. And use all the clubs in your bag, not just the driver."

Patrick bolted for the door, shouldering the taller, lankier Chris aside. Plato then glared at Chris. "And what's your story? He's only a kid."

Chris grinned sheepishly. "Ah heck, Gary. A couple of the guys and I were in here smoking and Patrick came in. He just wanted to be one of us. We wouldn't let him light it. We were afraid he'd burn down the building."

"At least you did one thing right," Plato said. "Now get out there and hit some balls. And make it look like you're sorry."

Chris nodded toward the cigars in Gary's hand. "Don't smoke them both at once," he said, then slipped from the building.

Plato tossed the cigars into the trash bin and chuckled. He wondered whose stash the boys had raided. It was not likely to have been Chris's father, Bill Clark. Plato had never smelled the telltale aroma of any type of tobacco on Bill, much less a cigar. He considered checking the couch for ash or burn marks, then refrained. He'd known these boys nearly their entire lives; they were full of life, not trouble.

He returned to the golf shop to find Rudy Staedler casually leaning against the counter, slender as a rail with a chiseled face that begged to be painted in caricature. Rudy was the moral compass of the clubhouse, and Plato considered him his closest pal.

"Hey Pro!" Rudy called, grinning. "How about a quick nine before the sun sets? I had a great round today and want to make sure it wasn't a fluke." He sniffed. "Is that cigar smoke I smell?" His grin widened. "You been having a little break in the juniors' room?"

Plato removed his golf cap and scratched his forehead. "Naw. I just caught Chris Clark trying to be Humphrey Bogart."

"No kidding?" Rudy chuckled.

"And Patrick Quinn was right there with him, pretending to be eighteen."

Rudy's jaw dropped. "He was smoking? A cigar?"

"Not really," Plato said. "It wasn't lit."

Rudy whistled. "Charlie'll have Patrick's hide if he finds out, along with the Clark kid's. Jeez, and Chris had such a future ahead of him."

"They're good kids, both of them," Plato said. "They'll make something of themselves."

"Well Chris is always saying he wants to try to make it on the tour. Wasn't he on that junior team that won the Bay Cities Golf Championship? And he came within one shot of winning the Club Championship two years ago."

"Yep." Plato nodded. "Only Ernie Pieper beat him, and he's won more Club Championships than anyone here at San Jose, so that was no surprise, really. But I told Chris he was too smart to be a golfer. He's got enough brains to really do something in life. Besides, when was the last time he hit a tee shot down the center of the fairway?"

Rudy grinned. "At least he grew into his bag. I used to laugh every time he'd go out. I'd look up the fairway and there'd be this blue bag, bouncing along. I'd think, where's the kid? It was just a bag with legs!"

"Bill wouldn't buy him his own until he was convinced Chris was serious," Plato said. "Probably did Chris some good – gave him some muscles."

"Well the Quinn boy won't be allowed to have many career options," Rudy said.

"No. I imagine he'll take over at Charlie's family business soon as he gets old enough." Plato glanced through the window. "Speaking of Charlie ..." He nodded toward the man walking slowly toward the golf shop. "Let's keep the cigar thing between ourselves, okay?"

Rudy nodded. "Hey, I saw nothing."

Charlie Quinn, stout and sedate, entered the golf shop with a sand wedge in hand. He nodded a welcome to Rudy, then turned his heavy-lidded gaze on Plato. "This thing needs a new grip, Gary. I can't seem to get anything out of those bunkers lately. It just slips right out of my hands."

"Sure it's the club there, Charlie?" Rudy asked. "I can't get out of those blasted bunkers either."

Plato ran an experienced hand over the dark grip. "Let's try some sandpaper, first, before I regrip it."

Charlie frowned. "I've done that already."

"Have you tried wrapping it with flypaper?" Rudy asked. "I've heard that works real well."

"Funny, coming from you," Charlie said, smiling. "Dawn suggested velcro. I told her you'd have me skinned before the Board."

"Are you kidding? Half of them would claim it a great idea and join you."

Plato chuckled, then quickly crossed to the back room, retrieved a worn patch of sandpaper, and went to work on the shiny grip. Satisfied, he returned to Charlie and held out the club. "Give this a try. I really roughed it up."

As Charlie gripped the club and took a short practice swing, Don Ridge entered the shop. The club face narrowly missed Ridge, who sprung out of the way with a leprechaun's leap.

"Whoa, Charlie!" Ridge said. "You tryin' to ruin Nellie's nights?"

Rudy grimaced. "That's not a picture I even want to imagine, Don."

Ridge waved a rugged hand, dismissively. He turned to Plato. "Did you hear Vandeweghe and I won a bell at the Cravens?"

"I did," Plato said. "Congratulations. That's quite a feat."

"Vandeweghe was all lit up about it today on the course," Charlie said as he leaned heavily on the sand wedge, nodding. "He said you played lights out."

Ridge's cherubic, ruddy face reddened. "Well now, I don't know about that, but we sure got the job done. Think we closed them out three and two."

"It was five and four, Donnny man."

Plato turned and saw Gary Vandeweghe's athletic six-foot-four frame filling the doorway. "We left them crying in the dust," Vandeweghe said. In two strides, he was fully in the golf shop, filling it with an unmistakable aura of command. He rifled through a rack of men's shirts. "Hey Pro, you got any of those nice LaCoste shirts with the San Jose Club logo? I promised a guy at the Cravens I'd send him one."

The other men were grinning. Charlie was shaking his head in bemusement. "You're looking at them," Plato said. "But if you don't see what you want, I'll be glad to order something. I can get it by next weekend."

Vandeweghe pulled a stark white shirt from the rack and raised it, scrutinizing the workmanship. "Aaahh ... this'll do. It's a large. Don't most guys wear a large? I think this guy's a large." He tossed the shirt on the counter. "Go ahead and wrap this up." His gaze swept the counter, then the work space behind it. "You got a card of some sort? Something I can write a note on?" His eyes landed on a pad of paper. "There, that'll work. Hand me a sheet of that note paper." Before Plato could tear off a sheet, Vandeweghe had found a pen and was poised, waiting. He scribbled a few lines on the paper, then tucked it in the collar of the now neatly folded shirt. "Can you get that out Monday? I'll call you with the address when I get home." He glanced at his watch. "Oh, Barb's going to be waiting. Gotta run!" He flashed a big smile at everyone. "See you guys tomorrow!" And he was out the door, the screen slamming in his wake.

Charlie blinked. Ridge sighed. Rudy's chest rumbled with a chuckle. Plato busied himself wrapping the shirt.

Ridge finally broke the silence. "That man's either gonna die early from a heart attack, or die old as a billionaire."

Charlie's eyelids drooped. "I'm betting on the latter."

"My bet is he'll never die," Rudy said. "He's too ornery." He turned to Plato. "So, Pro ... how about hittin' the ball around a few before the sun sets?" He glanced around. "Anybody else?"

Ridge squinted behind his glasses. "I'll go a few with you. Let me go grab a beer for the road." With his signature light step, he exited the shop.

Charlie appeared to ponder the proposition, his jowls puffing outward. He tossed a sideways glance at Rudy. "You going to start on one or six?"

Rudy shrugged. "Whichever will get you on the course, Charlie."

"The back side's got a few more bunkers," Plato said. "Might give you a chance to try out that club." Charlie rumbled into laughter and Plato blinked, then hurried to cover his faux pas. "Not that I think you'll land in any, but we could toss a few practice balls into the sand, see what happens."

Charlie shook his head and moved toward the door. "You three go tear it up. I'm gonna collect Patrick and get home for dinner. Don't know what got into that boy this afternoon. I saw him back on that practice range. Second time today." He waved as he softly closed the screen door behind him.

Plato sighed. "Gosh, I didn't mean to upset him."

"You didn't," Rudy said. "If he'd wanted to play, he'd have come along. Charlie's got that thick Irish skin. Come on. It's getting late."

"I'll meet you and Ridge on the tee," Plato said. "Let me lock up, here."

Rudy adjusted the visor perched on his head. "Back side, then?" Plato nodded. "Don't be too long about it," Rudy said. "I have to get home and work on those plans for the development in Livermore." Then he disappeared.

A second later, a whistled tune faded down the cart path toward the clubhouse and the sixth tee. The phone rang.

"San Jose Country Club, Gary Plato here."

"Hey pal!"

Plato instantly recognized the voice of his longtime friend, Al Braga. Plato leaned against the counter. "Hi there, Al. How are things over at The Villages?"

"Good, good," Al said. "In fact, I thought you might like to pop over next week and hack around a few holes."

"Love to. Wednesday work for you? The club's hosting a big social thing for the county and the course will be closed for part of the day."

"Perfect. Make it about two and we'll have dinner after."

"Okay, shall do. Oh, and Lynea mentioned she'd like to get together with Jan and do some shopping for the kids for the Halloween party."

"I'll let Jan know to give her a call," Al said. "See you on Wednesday."

"Wednesday it is," Plato said, and hung up. He opened the cash register and removed several charge tickets. As a private club, they handled no cash, for which he was grateful. He disliked dealing with money. He quickly sorted the tickets, then reached beneath the counter for the envelope where they were filed until the end of the month. The screen door opened.

"Rudy, I'm almost done," he said without looking up.

An unfamiliar, lyrically resonant male voice said, "Hi, sorry to bother you. Maybe we're too late?"

Just through the door stood a couple, apparently in their forties, dressed for the course in Bermuda shorts and LaCoste shirts. The man's sported a familiar logo – Winged Foot Country Club. Plato came around the counter and held out his hand, smiling. "Gary Plato, Head Professional," he said in introduction. "Can I help you?"

The man took his hand and delivered a firm, secure handshake. "Don Winterhalter," he said, then stepped aside and motioned to the woman. "This is my wife, Penny."

Penny's handshake was pleasantly firm and confident. It matched the look on her pretty face. "Nice to meet you both," Plato said, meaning it, though the immediacy of that feeling surprised him. "What can I do for you?"

Don pulled a tee from his pocket and rolled it between his fingers. "Well, we just transferred here to the Santa Clara area and we're looking to join a club. We thought we'd stop in and ask a few questions, but it looks like we caught you on your way out. Would you prefer we come by another time?"

"Absolutely not," Plato said. "I'd be happy to answer any questions you have. Just fire away." Plato watched the couple's demeanor as he answered the inquiries about membership fees, qualities of the general membership, number of low handicap players, the women's groups, various club tournaments, and the style of the course itself. They were obviously well versed in private membership, and he sensed Don was an avid golfer, probably sporting a fairly low handicap, while Penny was more of a weekend player, albeit a good one. They were articulate and friendly, and Plato was not surprised to discover Don was an executive with IBM, while Penny was a stay-at-home mother of two girls. Their situation would fit right in here. More than that, though, Plato sensed both these people would get involved with the club on a social level. They certainly weren't shrinking violets.

"So when are you looking to make a decision?" Plato asked.

"Immediately," Penny answered, tossing a laconic look at her husband. "He's tearing up the carpet, chipping into the sofa and garbage can."

"Aw, come on now," Don said, smiling. "At least I keep it in the living room. We wanted to replace that carpet anyway."

Plato made a quick decision. "I assume you don't know any of the members, since you've just moved here. Don, let me set you up with one of the guys for a round. We can go from there." He nabbed a pad of paper and a pencil. "What's your number?"

Phone numbers were exchanged, handshakes reciprocated, and last minute questions answered. Then Don and Penny left, and Plato quickly finished closing the shop. He was locking the door when Rudy's voice echoed from the parking lot.

"Hey Pro! You lose your keys or something?"

Plato waved, then shot down the short hill in his cart, careening to a stop next to Rudy. "Jump in," Plato said. "Sorry. I got hung up with a couple that stopped by, asking about membership."

Rudy settled into the cart and Plato stepped on the pedal. "Oh yeah? Who do they know?"

"They've just transferred here from New Jersey. They don't know anyone." On the tee, Plato grabbed his driver, pulled the sock from the head, and tossed a ball onto the ground. "You want to take him out and play a round? See what you think?"

"You're late, Plato," Ridge called from his cart. "Gee, we've already played this hole twice, and Rudy here made birdies both times. You missed it all."

Plato took his stance and set his focus.

"Come on, hit the ball!" Ridge yelled. "Grandma was slow, but she was old!" Without waiting for a response, he steered his cart down the center of the fairway.

Plato watched the cart zip away. "That's tempting," he said with a smile, then sent his ball sailing over the moving target. He picked up his tee and jumped back in his cart beside Rudy. "So what do you say? I think you'd like this guy. Seems real upstanding."

"When?" asked Rudy. "Bev and I are leaving for Tahoe day after tomorrow, spend a couple of days with some friends." When their cart came to a stop beside Ridge, Rudy jumped out, grabbing an iron from his bag, which was tied to Ridge's cart. "We won't be back for a week."

Ridge addressed his ball. "You two wanna have a conference, or can we play some golf here?" Without waiting for an answer, he smashed his ball toward the green.

Rudy quickly sent his ball sliding after Ridge's and Plato reciprocated by sailing his ball to the front fringe. He jumped in his cart and, again, motioned for Rudy to join.

"You gonna ride with him the whole way?" Ridge called as both carts raced up the fairway. "You want your clubs?"

"No, no, I'll ride with you after this hole," Rudy said, then turned to Plato. "I could play with this new guy week after next, if that'll help."

Plato considered, then said, "No. Thanks though. I want to catch him before he gets hooked into Los Altos or Sharon Heights. I think this guy's worth having here."

Rudy jumped from the still rolling cart and headed toward the green. "You really liked him, huh? Why not have Ridge play with him then?"

Plato pointedly raised his eyebrows at Ridge, who tapped his ball into the cup, then danced a victory jig. "Yes-sir-ee! I'm gonna get a birrrrrdeeeee!" he sang, his Southern drawl made more rich by the effort.

Rudy shrugged and a big smile swept his face. "Probably smart to keep the crazy cousins in the closet until the new guy's part of the family," he said.

Plato chipped from the front fringe, then squatted to assess the line of his putt. "I'll find somebody. One of the older members. Someone who's been here longer than all of us combined."

"What's this guy's name, anyway?" Rudy asked, as Plato's ball rolled softly to the cup.

"Don," Plato said, "Don Winterhalter."

"Winner-halter?" Rudy asked, then rolled the name around on his tongue. "Winner-halter. Winner-halter."

Plato had a satisfying sense he'd be hearing that name spoken by other members, soon enough. He'd check with a few of the longtime Club members – Jack Bariteau or Hank Lucente, Doc Burchfiel or, better yet, Ed Schuler. He'd be an excellent choice to take Don Winterhalter out this week, before he had a chance to line up a round at any of the other clubs.

At the seventh tee, Rudy waggled over his ball.

"Rude," Ridge drawled, "where did you get that darn shirt? The color is blinding! Did it come with a battery to get that color?"

Rudy chuckled, then swung. The ball screamed down the center of the fairway. "I don't need no stinkin' batteries," he said with a feigned – and bad – New York accent. "Your turn, you Confederate turnip."

Gang of Eight: The First Tee

Plato leaned on his driver and chuckled as Ridge and Rudy bantered back and forth, trading friendly insults and laughing at them, and each other. The membership here was fun – the men were serious about their game, but most were great pals both on and off the course. Plato thought about Winterhalter and instinctively knew the guy would be well accepted by the other men.

Rudy putted and Plato cringed with disappointment as the ball lipped out.

"Ah hell," Rudy said, "I guess I left my A game on the tee this afternoon." He tapped the ball into the cup. "And maybe my B game as well."

"Well your C game couldn't beat a toddler with a full diaper," Ridge said, then scooted just out of range as Rudy waggled his putter at him in a playfully threatening manner.

Yes, indeed, Plato thought. The Winterhalters would be lucky to become members at San Jose C.C.

CHAPTER 1

June, 1980

Don Winterhalter and Hank the Starter

The sun, having been cursed by at least twenty early rising golfers, pouted behind a low bank of clouds, giving the morning a decisively damp and foggy feeling. Don Winterhalter didn't mind. After last night's party at the club, he wasn't really interested in squinting through bright sunlight. In fact, he wasn't interested in being upright at all, but it was Saturday, and that meant the usual crowd of guys would be meeting in the clubhouse in about forty minutes. If he were late, he'd never hear the end of it, especially since he'd swallowed far less alcohol than anyone else. He could safely assume there were others in worse shape.

He slung his golf bag into the trunk of his car. "Penny!" he called from the garage, "I'm outta here. You bringing the girls out to the club for lunch?"

Penny moved into the doorway, wiping her hands on a kitchen towel, her athletically curvaceous figure hidden beneath baggy sweats. "No, we'll stay here today. I think Darby wants to read by the pool, and Judy mentioned something about going to Santa Cruz with some friends this afternoon."

Don's nose twitched. "Do we know these friends?"

"We should. They're the neighbors' boys." She waved her towel. "Go play and don't worry. I'll make sure to get phone numbers, locations, and specific timetables before she gets in the car."

Gang of Eight: The First Tee

"A mug shot and a social security number would be nice," Don said with a smirk, then waved and lowered himself into the driver's seat. As he turned to look out the back window, his stomach lurched. Okay, he thought, no sudden moves, no fast motion. If I'm lucky, I'll keep my coffee in my stomach until I reach the club. Then get a Bloody Mary and hope for the best.

At six-thirty in the morning, the traffic was light and the drive easy across Santa Clara Valley from Silicon Valley's bedroom community of Saratoga to the club atop the eastern mountain ridge. Well, if one could call it a mountain. After living near both the Cascade Range in western Montana and the Wasatch Range in Utah, he'd developed a different standard for the term. If the peak didn't garner at least ten feet of winter snow, have a tree line, and dominate the horizon, it wasn't worthy of the designation. The "mountain ridge" upon which San Jose Country Club sprawled was certainly higher than any other topography in the immediate area, but it wasn't exactly significant as far as "mountains" went.

Still, it would kick his butt this morning, with that long walk up the first fairway to the green sitting on the plateau. As he drove into the club's parking lot, he decided he might be forced to develop a little respect for this "mountain." The way his head felt, it was going to be a very, very long walk.

Obviously he wasn't alone in his hangover. The twelve men seated around the tables in the upstairs Oak Room weren't as lively as usual. In fact, they were downright dour. Even that flat belly Chris was subdued, though he'd made plenty of noise last night about being able to hold his liquor. Young Quinn was the only one who looked as if he had any life. But heck, he'd been drinking soda all night.

Ignoring the pounding in his temples, Don straightened his spine and lightened his step. "Hey, what is wrong with this picture?" he called. "Somebody die last night?"

Charlie had his face buried in a plate of scrambled eggs and hash browns. Without looking up he said, "Yes. My friends, Jack Daniels and Jim Beam. Died a horrible death."

"We buried them several times over on the practice green," said Vandeweghe.

Ridge slapped the edge of the table with his cotton napkin. "So that's why it was so darn hard to sink a putt last night! I thought that green looked a bit more bumpy than usual."

Don sat down as a waiter approached. "Your usual, Mr. Winterhalter?" the young man asked.

"Not today, Mark," Don said. "Just a side of wheat toast with very little butter, and a Bloody Mary. Stiff on the bloody and easy on the Mary."

Mark frowned. "I'm sorry, Mr. Winterhalter, but the bar doesn't open until eleven. I can get you a tomato juice, if that works."

"Bring the whole bottle," Ridge said, waving Mark away. "And bring some Tabasco sauce, too."

"Jeez, Ridge, I don't think a Virgin Mary's going to help," Don said.

"Who said anything about virgins this morning?" Ridge said. He turned and motioned to Patrick. "Hey, Patrick. You still know where they hide the key to the liquor cabinet?"

Patrick grinned. "You bet. One glass of clear magic, coming up." He slid behind the bar and ducked from sight.

"Always good knowing kids in high places," Ridge said, rubbing his hands together with delight.

The sound of shifting bottles clamored from behind the bar. Don pressed his fingers to his temples. "Easy Patrick, you'll wake the dead with that clatter."

Mark arrived, carrying a large bottle of V8 Juice and a shot glass of dark liquid, along with an extra large glass. Laying beside the toast was a leafy stalk of celery. From behind the bar, Patrick held up a highball glass nearly topped with gin.

Plato chuckled. "I'll just put one Bloody Mary on your lunch tab, Don."

"Better mark me down for two, Gary," Don said, mixing the ingredients together.

"Or even three!" Rudy said. "Damn, Patrick, what else do you supply?"

"Winning money for his pop," Charlie said. "Drink up, Winner-halter. I might actually have a chance to win something off you this morning."

"That's the point, Pops," Patrick said, grinning. "That's the point."

With anywhere from eight to twelve guys, the first tee always got a bit crowded when the Saturday morning group showed up. Hank, the starter, knew better than to look down at his tee-time sheet. None of their names would be marked, though the eight o'clock slot would be crossed off. It was never an issue for the members who had signed up for an eight-ten tee time, though. Despite the small herd of men, it rarely took more than a few minutes for them to hit their drives and head up the fairway, some on foot, a few in carts. This was no polite foursome where the golfers waited silently for each drive, then moved onward en masse. No, this was controlled chaos, where anyone who was ready hit, then took off up the fairway, safe in the knowledge that the guy hitting behind him was good enough not to knock his head off. Once on the greens, the guys ignored protocol – anyone prepared putted out, then headed immediately for the next tee. With these guys, the honor system just got in the way of a good round of golf.

Despite the lack of formality, this Saturday group was sacrosanct, gratis the Head Pro, Gary Plato, who only occasionally played with them, but always supported their weekly game. The format was an anomaly, one Hank assumed was particular to San Jose Country Club, and over the years he had come to enjoy watching the group develop and mutate. The group included some of the club's best golfers, and the rest were nothing to dismiss. The highest handicap amongst them was probably a nine or ten, with most below a three.

This morning, they all looked a bit ragged-around-the-edges. Poor Winterhalter looked like he was going to pass out, sitting on a bench with his chin resting in his hands. Charlie Quinn's eyes had nearly disappeared between his reddened jowls and puffy eyelids, and there was a decisive tremor in his hands. And Vandeweghe's clothing, usually so meticulous, was actually uncoordinated this morning – his teal shirt clearly clashing with the green pants, and a shiny belt with a large "G" as the buckle flashing in the sun.

Hank coughed politely; it wouldn't do to laugh. "Ready, gentlemen?" he said. Several of the men winced and Hank could swear he heard Rudy moan. "Who's up first?"

Ridge stepped up to the tee and quickly hit. "I think us old men should get ahead of the flat bellies. We may be a bit dangerous today."

Chris chuckled. "I have no intention of playing in front of you guys this morning. In fact, Patrick and I just might join the foursome behind you."

Hank glanced down at his clipboard and raised his eyebrows. He motioned for Chris and Patrick to join him, then pointed down at the names. Patrick's face blanched. Chris moaned, then stepped in front of Jack Lovegren, who had just stepped onto the tee box.

"Sorry, Jack," Chris said, placing his ball on a tee. "But I think Patrick and I will jump ahead after all, if you don't mind."

"On any other day, I'd mind," Jack said, glaring at the club in his hand, "but I think you just saved me from a grave mistake. Why in the devil do I have a four wood in my hand?"

Quickly, Chris drove his ball, then turned to Patrick. "Come on, kid, tee it up and let's get going."

Patrick yanked his driver from his bag and stepped onto the tee just as Plato closed in on the box, his driver in hand, signifying his decision to join the game today. Chris emphatically shook his head, and his expression was one of total frustration. "Sorry, Pro," he said, "but Patrick really needs to hit next."

"Why? What's happening?" Plato asked.

"I believe Chris is correct," Hank said quietly. "It would be best if the young gentlemen went ahead and hit. We have a foursome at eight-ten which might be more comfortable following senior members."

Hank held out the clipboard and Plato looked at the tee sheet. Eyebrows raised, he let out a soft whistle.

"That bad, huh?" Vandeweghe said, swinging his club at air.

Plato waved at Patrick, then addressed him by the nickname affectionately given the young Quinn years ago. "P.Q. Hit."

In answer to the questioning looks on the other men's faces, Hank said, "Mr. Hinckley and friends are scheduled."

A round of "Ah's" followed the announcement and Rudy waved his club toward the tee box. "Okay, Patrick, get out of here as fast as you can."

Patrick jogged onto the tee and, without a practice swing, drove his ball, then took off running up the fairway, yelling over his shoulder, "Someone bring my clubs! Better yet, I'll just play every shot with my driver!"

"Keep going! We old bucks've got your back!" Winterhalter yelled, then winced.

Chris grabbed both his and Patrick's bags and jogged up the cart path. The clubs made a terrible racket as they clinked and clanked together.

"Don't you worry," Vandeweghe called after Patrick. "I won't let that old geezer on this tee until you're safely on number two green!"

Patrick turned and jogged backward up the fairway. "Make it three!"

The men burst into laughter. "I'll tell your mother you'll be home early!" Charlie called after Patrick, then drove his ball ten yards from his son's feet. "Move faster!"

Vandeweghe looked at Charlie. "So Hinckley's still harassing P.Q. about that broken French door?"

Charlie leaned on his driver. "I thought we'd cleared it up when I paid for the repairs, but Patrick came home last week and said the old man had chased him right out of the clubhouse, yelling about how 'children shouldn't be allowed to play the course'."

"Hinckley's the grinch incarnate," Vandeweghe said. "Someday his skin'll turn green."

"He was yelling at Patrick through the back fence at the house two days ago," Charlie said from his cart. He motioned to the passenger seat. "Get in, Ridge. Let's go play some golf."

"Amen to that," Ridge said, and was barely seated before Charlie had the cart careening up the right side of the fairway.

"Hank," Plato said, and motioned for the tee-sheet. He jotted a note on it, then handed it back with a nod. "Put that on my desk when you're done, and I'll take care of this. Patrick has every right to play here."

"Heck, the kid plays better in his sleep than Hinckley does on his best day," Vandeweghe said, leaning on his driver.

"Hey Vandeweghe, what *are* you wearing?" Don waggled his club toward Vandeweghe's belt. "You going all designer on us, now? You're going to blind us with that glitz."

Vandeweghe looked down at his belt. "What? It's a monogram belt. And what's wrong with trying to have a little class around you bums?"

"And here I thought the 'G' stood for Gucci," Don said.

Vandeweghe rolled his eyes. "It stands for Gary, you knucklehead."

"Well, Mr. Gucci, er, I mean Gary, you're up," Hank said.

Don chuckled. "Mr. Gucci. That's gonna stick, you just know it."

Vandeweghe hit his drive, and retrieved his broken tee. "Not if you don't tell anyone," he joked. "Jeez, aren't there any secrets around this place?"

Don stepped up to the tee box. "You think we can keep it a secret, when you're wearing *that*?"

"Well, do you want me to take it off?"

"No!" Don and Plato exclaimed simultaneously, then Don added, "Your pants will fall off, and then who *knows* what will blind us." He swung and the ball leapt down the middle of the fairway, then he hefted his bag onto his shoulder and starting walking up the fairway. "Come on, Gooch," he said, waving for Vandeweghe to follow. "Get your shiny belt moving."

Hank laughed as Vandeweghe trudged away, grumbling about his new nickname.

Plato shook his head as he teed up. "Gucci. That's never going away. Poor guy." He wiggled, swung, and sent his ball in a wild hook. "Ah, rats!"

Fifty yards up the fairway, Don waved, signifying the ball had bounced over the fence, out of bounds. He yelled back over his shoulder, "Hey Pro, looks like ol' Jimmy Beam's come back to haunt you!"

Hank politely coughed away another smile as Plato teed up a second ball, cursing under his breath. The ball screamed up the fairway in Don's direction.

"Duck!" Plato yelled, grinning like a Cheshire cat. To Hank's amusement, Don continued to walk, simply flipping "the bird" back at Plato as the ball flew over his head.

Plato hefted his bag onto his shoulder. "See you in a few hours, Hank," he said, and trooped up the hill after his friends.

Yes, Saturday mornings at eight were always amusing.

It was a little over an hour later when Don finished putting out on the fifth green. Today, he was glad the course was oddly laid out, with "the turn" happening at the sixth hole, not between the traditional ninth and tenth. He

Gang of Eight: The First Tee

needed coffee now, though it appeared most of the group were feeling much better. Ridge and Vandeweghe were leading the pack. He and Charlie were one stroke behind, matched by Patrick, Bob Cracolice, and Hank Lucente. Chris, Rudy, and Jack brought up the rear, but only by two strokes. Plato had managed to overcome his unfortunate beginning at the first tee. Don noticed the pro was actually smiling when they all congregated on the sixth tee. Chris stepped up to drive first.

"Okay, gentlemen," Plato said. "Fire in the hole!"

"And dud in the air," said Patrick, as they watched the ball slice in mid-flight and land under in a group of young eucalyptus trees huddled together on the right side of the fairway.

"It went exactly where I aimed it," Chris said.

"It's a safe shot for you, Chris," Ridge said as he arranged his ball between the markers. "Since you've hit plenty of balls over there, you're bound to know how to play it."

The men chuckled, and Don found himself humming. One by one they hit their drives, then walked or carted down the fairway, a small herd working their way around the course. Only a few minutes later, Don stood beside Rudy on the seventh tee, situated a hundred feet above its kidney-shaped green. This little par three was deceptively difficult, and Don leaned on his club and watched Ridge, Chris, and Patrick struggle on the green below him.

Rudy whistled as Ridge's two-foot putt teetered on the lip, then settled back, refusing to drop. "You know," Rudy said, "I played a member-guest over at Carmel Valley Ranch. Their clubhouse dining room is real nice. Made ours look like a dump. Maybe you guys on the Board should round up a renovation committee or something."

Don scraped the ridges of his iron with a tee. "Yeah, it's starting to look used."

"Used and abused," Rudy said.

The three golfers below vacated the green and moved to the eighth tee. Don turned his attention to Plato as he addressed his tee shot.

Whack. The ball landed softly behind the pin, then back spun to within two feet of the hole.

"Good one, Pro," Rudy said. He turned to Don. "So what kind of direction should we go? Ultra modern? Rustic California? French Provincial?"

Charlie teed up his ball. "How about Classic Clubhouse Dining Room?" he said, then swung. "Dawn and I would like that one."

Don teed up next. "That sounds good, but what does it look like?" He swung.

"I don't care what we do," said Vandeweghe, "but I'd like something with a little class. None of this trendy stuff. And no plaid." He motioned toward Rudy's tartan slacks. "We got enough of that around here."

Don joined Rudy and Charlie as they laughed and marched down the stairs from the elevated tee. "Maybe a warmer color?" Don asked. "Burnt oranges, reds, plumbs?"

"Yeah, the winter white stuff we have now is for the birds," Charlie said. "One dinner and half the chairs were ruined by stains. Whoever chose that stuff in the first place?"

"Ah, let me think … Oh, yeah! You did," Rudy said, smiling, "a decade ago, or so I'm told. But I've never believed it. Looked more like a hundred years ago."

"At least," Charlie agreed, and went to clear off the leaves that lay between his ball and the cup.

Don looked over his line. "This looks familiar," he mumbled.

Vandeweghe came up behind him. "Isn't this the putt you missed that cost you last year's Club Championship?"

"Thanks for the reminder," Don said.

"Always a bridesmaid, never a bride," Rudy declared. "What is it now – four championship games, four second place finishes?"

"Ah, but he's got five club Master's trophies on his shelf," Vandeweghe said. "That's no small fry."

Don motioned for Rudy to pull the flag. He settled in over his ball, glanced back at the hole, then putted.

The ball rolled dead straight for the cup then, six inches from the lip, found an indentation and veered just off the left edge. It came to a stop two inches from the hole.

Gang of Eight: The First Tee

"I have a whole closet of dresses," Don said, lightly pounding the green with his putter. "And none of them white."

Vandeweghe tapped his ball. "That's okay. It's a bad color on you, anyway."

Three members stood in the middle of the eighth fairway, waiting as their guest aligned his shot with the flag, 180 yards away.

"You want to land it just slightly left of the flag," the first member whispered to the guest. "Or you'll be working against the slope of the green."

The guest nodded. The second member hit and the third stepped up to his ball.

"So you going to Cancun or the Bahamas this year?" the first again whispered. The guest golfer paused in his answer, waiting for the third to swing.

Whack.

"Jenny prefers the Bahamas, so we'll probably head there," the guest said, moving to address his own ball. "The problem is the twins. What to do with them while we're gone."

"Leave them with us," the third member said. "Carrie would love to have playmates for a few weeks this summer."

"*Fore, please!*" Jack Lovegren's voice reverberated from the tee box behind them.

The guest ducked, frantically looking around. "What the hell?"

"Lovegren" the third member said, and chuckled. "Impatient goon."

"Where'd his ball land?" the guest asked.

"Oh, he hasn't hit yet. It's just his way of announcing his intentions," the first member explained to his guest.

"The Saturday league is looking to play through," the third mumbled.

A light "thud" marked the arrival of a ball. It rolled to a light stop not three feet from the now rattled guest.

All four men looked back at the tee. It was circled by a large group of golfers, with one very tall, slender man standing center, obviously just completing his drive. The tall man waved.

The guest golfer shook his head in amazement. "Were we playing that slow? How did –" He did a quick count of the men on the tee "– three foursomes come up on us?"

The first member removed his cap and scratched his head. "We aren't playing slow. And it's one big, damn clique. They all play together every Saturday." Another "thud" announced the arrival of a second ball, which had landed twenty yards to their left.

The second member turned and waved his club in the air. "Yeah! Yeah! We see you!" he yelled back to the group on the tee. "Let us finish out this hole!"

The four men hefted their clubs and began moving to the green. "Best to let them play through," the first member said, as a third ball landed to his right ten yards ahead of him.

"Sonofabitch, who drove that one?" the guest asked, looking back at the tee.

"That'd be Quinn."

"Young Quinn. That kid can hit a ball."

The guest glanced back. There was now a shorter golfer on the tee, and six men marched down the sides of the fairway, along with a kid who didn't look to be more than fourteen. All were chatting away as if they were in a park. Whack! The man on the tee swung, and the ball sailed down the center, landing close to the long drive. The golfers walking never even glanced up.

"Wow," the guest said. "Doesn't your pro have something to say about this? Ours would have been all over this with a raging rule book."

Another thud announced the landing of another ball. The four men turned and, walking backwards, saw Plato step off the tee and follow the large group of men. It was quite a sight – several men walking, two carts darting about, and four golfers waiting by their balls, obviously anxious to hit.

The first member snorted. "Yeah, our pro has something to say."

"Fore!" the third said, and laughed.

———•◦•———

Don retrieved his ball from the cup and followed Plato and Patrick to the thirteenth tee, where Rudy and Vandeweghe were preparing to drive. Behind them, the last four of the Saturday group were just chipping onto the twelfth green, while ahead, Ridge, Chris, and Charlie were already out in the fairway, walking to their drives.

Don shaded his eyes from the sun. The fairway stretched out four hundred yards, with a slight dogleg right. It would have been a simple hole, except for the mighty eucalyptus tree dominating the left side of the fairway, perfectly situated to grab balls at the apex of their flight. It was the last standing soldier in what had been a small army of eucalyptus, and Don always found its presence challenging.

"Where'd Ridge land?" he asked.

"Down the right," Rudy said.

Don grabbed his driver. "Okay, let's tickle his toes." He teed it up, swung, and watched as the ball shot out, low in the air, then faded toward the right, safe from the eucalyptus. It landed three yards behind Ridge, then rolled past him. Without looking back, Ridge waved, walked to where his drive had come to rest, and hit.

"How do you do that?" Vandeweghe asked. "Get so much distance when your ball is just scootin' across the fairway?"

"It gets up high enough to pass you like a freight train," Don said.

Plato stretched as he walked onto the tee. "Thanks for the lesson, Mr. Winterhalter. I needed that." He teed his ball.

Rudy laughed. "Yeah, that tree is starting to shake already, just seeing you walk onto the tee."

"Look at it shake!" Vandeweghe chimed in.

Rudy waggled his club at Vandeweghe. "You aren't one to talk," he said with a big smile. "Between you and Plato there won't be any goddamn trees left on this fairway."

"It is starting to look a little thin," Patrick said.

"Thin, heck," Rudy said. "A tree company couldn't do as good a job as these two."

Plato started to laugh and stepped away from his ball. "Hey, don't be getting on me right now. I'm gonna knock it right down the middle this time."

"Just look at that eucalyptus shake already!" Rudy continued. "It's a quaking-euk, shaking in its roots."

Don shook his head as moans of humorous disgust filled the air. He so enjoyed the banter between these guys. Plato finally stepped up to his ball and swung, and the moans changed to laughter as the ball sliced through the outer edges of the branches of the eucalyptus.

"Oh, oh, oh! Just missed it!" Rudy called.

"Only because the tree was all shriveled up," Vandeweghe said, a crooked smile on his face.

They all shouldered their bags and began hiking up the fairway.

"That's the first time you've missed it this year!" Rudy said.

"That tree was all scrunched over," Vandeweghe said. "If it'd been sitting out there the way it was supposed to, like a real tree –"

"Hey," Plato said, "Come on now. I thought I hit a foul."

Rudy turned to Patrick and pointed up the fairway. "You may not remember this, but years ago there were about a dozen trees up there, and they've all slowly died off from fright."

"Well, if you can't cut them, knock 'em down with a golf ball," Plato said, shrugging.

Patrick's eyes twinkled. "So that's what happened. They died from blunt force trauma."

The four men approached the tree. On the side facing the tee, the bark hung ragged from the massive trunk, while small dents marked where balls had slammed into it.

"Look at all those hits, there," Don said, surveying the tree.

Patrick nodded. "We keep bruising the poor thing."

"It's like Phil Harris, you know?" Plato said, walking toward his ball. "Bing Crosby and Phil Harris were in Ireland – Hey Rudy! Tell Patrick that joke about Phil Harris and Bing Crosby."

Don leaned on the tree. Rudy grinned. "Okay. So Phil Harris said he and Bing Crosby were playing in Scotland, and late one night they were driving from one town to another, trying to get to the next golf course for an early morning tee time, and they passed a distillery. All the lights were on and the smokestacks were going and the workers' cars were in the lots. Everything was just as busy as if it was the middle of a workday. And Crosby turns to Harris and says, 'Hey look, Phil, they're making that stuff faster than you can drink it.' And Harris turns back to him and says, 'Yeah, but I got 'em working overtime'."

Ridge burst into laughter while Patrick continued on to his ball, a look of confusion on his face.

"Got 'em working twenty-four hour shifts!" Plato said, to which Rudy added, "Working overtime!"

Patrick grabbed an iron from his bag and took a practice swing. "You know," he said, "I have no idea who those guys are or what that joke has to do with the eucalyptus tree."

Rudy doubled over with laughter. Plato addressed his ball and said, "That's good, P.Q. 'Cause neither do we." Then he swung and sent his ball neatly flying toward the green.

Don stood on the sixteenth tee and surveyed his options. It was a decent par five, but you could cut out some real estate if you leaned toward the right side. Too much, though, and you were dead under the trees. Five other balls lay safely to the left. He took aim and leaned into his drive. What the heck. You didn't win by always playing it safe.

"Oh, oh!" Rudy exclaimed. "There it goes again, skimming under those trees. Jeez, you are one lucky rat!"

"Scootin' along, as usual," Vandeweghe said, then grinned mischievously. "Maybe because he's so low to the ground himself."

Rudy waggled his index finger and squinted. "Hey, there are lots of good things at this altitude."

"Yeah, like smog," Patrick mumbled. "Or prairie dogs."

Don retrieved his tee. He'd always hit the ball low. It was just his game.

"Come on, Scooter," Vandeweghe said as he shouldered his bag and headed up the fairway.

"Scooter?" Patrick said, and began to laugh. "That's perfect!"

Don hummed. "If the shoe fits." All these years, he hadn't really had a nickname. "Scooter" was fun. He liked it.

"Scooter, Scooter, golf ball booter," Rudy sang. "Lootin' all the birdies!"

Patrick playfully slugged him, and they harassed each other as they walked to their tee shots. Don followed. It was a good nickname, but only if he continued to make his low ball flight work for him.

He stopped by his ball. It was perfectly situated to give him a shot at the green.

"Nice work, Scooter!" Vandeweghe called from where his ball lay, some twenty yards behind Don.

"Thanks!" Don waved. Yep, he had a feeling the moniker would stick.

Minutes later, having made birdie on seventeen, he trudged up the eighteenth fairway, then paused beside Plato.

Vandeweghe stood behind his ball, glaring at the wall of treetops that reached up from deep in a ravine which sliced across the fairway. He fingered his eight iron, then the nine iron. "Neither of these feels right," he mumbled.

"I'd aim about three trees to the left there, Gary," Plato said, pointing. "That's the line."

Vandeweghe sighed and chose the nine iron.

Don knew it was the wrong club the moment Vandeweghe hit the ball.

"Aw, come on!" Vandeweghe yelled, and stuffed the offending item back into his bag. "Blasted wind, always gets me on this hole."

Don smiled. There wasn't any wind.

"Get legs, baby, get legs," Plato said.

The sound of the ball thrashing through branches and greenery announced its arrival in the ravine.

"Good program, Gary," Rudy said, "It just never quite got there."

The men hoofed it to the edge of the ravine, then fanned out and began searching.

Rudy scoured the edge. "Get on down there, P.Q.," he said, motioning to the bottom of the ravine, fifty feet below. "You're young."

"Yeah, and destined to stay that way if I have to keep risking my life for you guys," Patrick said. But he slogged on down through the dried and dying bushes with delight.

Don smiled. He knew Patrick would brave anything – cactus, rose bushes, probably quicksand for that matter – for anyone in the group. It was why they all liked the kid so much. That, and he could pound a ball a mile and still keep it in the fairway, which was quite impressive.

Vandeweghe and Plato crossed to the narrow wooden bridge and Vandeweghe pointed. Don saw a ball lying in the center of the bridge, resting between two planks of wood.

"Found it!" Vandeweghe announced.

Don remained at the edge of the ravine, standing beside Rudy. "Are you in the hazard? You're out of the hazard, aren't you?" he asked.

Plato walked up beside them. "No, the hazard's up here," he said with authority.

Vandeweghe frowned. "Where?"

"Up here," Plato said, "on the edge of the ravine."

"Up here," Don echoed, then hefted his bag on his shoulder and descended to the bridge. Vandeweghe stood in the middle, contemplating his predicament. Don dropped his bag. Might as well watch the fiasco.

Vandeweghe shrugged and looked down the bridge toward the cart path that led to the green. "I wonder if I can get relief..." he said, sounding wistful.

Patrick hiked out of the ravine. "You know they change that rule a couple of times a week, I swear."

"Hey, Gary, you get relief from the top of the bridge in hazard, but not from underneath it," Rudy said, reading from a small rule book. He waved it in the air. "Always carry one, just in case."

Patrick chuckled. "And I thought he had the darn thing memorized."

"From the top, but not underneath. That's what I thought." Vandeweghe looked back at the fairway. "But then I'll have to drop it in the hazard."

Plato shrugged. "Well, drop it in the hazard. Or do you want to go a little further back onto the fairway? You can do that."

Vandeweghe's expression belied his rising frustration. "Well, I know, but then I'm dead in terms of yardages."

"You can go back as far as you want from the point of entry," Plato said patiently.

"I can, but I have to get all the way back to where I have any sort of a shot." Vandeweghe sighed as he looked up to the top of the plateau. It was at least another twenty yards before it flattened out significantly enough to give Vandeweghe a decent shot.

Rudy trotted down, stopping beside Don. With an iron, Rudy circled a dry patch of dirt before the bridge's entrance. "You can drop it over here by the hazard near the cart path, and hit it down the bridge."

Vandeweghe's face turned red. Rudy must have noticed it too, because he quickly followed his comment with, "But then again, you may not want to …"

Vandeweghe glared at Rudy. "But I'll be lying three there –"

"No, there's no penalty for dropping it off the bridge," Rudy hastened to explain. "If you get a free drop here you can hit it down there and be three."

Plato joined them, and stared down the bridge. "Place it carefully and the ball isn't going to roll."

Rudy shrugged. "Personally, I'd hit if off the cart path. Hit it down the bridge."

Vandeweghe's expression became puzzled, then he laughed. "Yeah, I can use that putter of Plato's. Nobody cares if that gets all beat up."

Don joined in the laughter.

Plato feigned indignation. "Are you complaining about my putter?"

"He wants to use it for the shot, is that okay?" Rudy said, smiling. He pointed at the dry patch of dirt. "Gary, put it right here."

"No, no, I want it up the bridge!" Vandeweghe waved his hands. "Get outta here," he said with a grin. "I'm gonna putt it up the bridge. Leave me alone."

"Putt it?!" Rudy asked. "What are you gonna putt it up the bridge for?"

"Well, how else am I gonna hit it?" Vandeweghe exclaimed.

"Hit it!" Rudy yelled back.

"With what?"

Rudy yanked an old wedge from his bag. "Here."

Watching the exchange, Don struggled not to burst into outright laughter.

Vandeweghe's voice softened. "I'm not hittin' it with your club. Just leave me alone."

Don shifted his weight. Rudy shrugged, carefully stepped over the contested ball and crossed the bridge to the green-side. He paused beside Patrick, then dropped his bag and crossed his arms over his chest. He and Patrick shared a look that seemed to say, "Oh well."

Plato walked back twenty feet, to a spot on the downward slope of the fairway. "Put it right here. You take your three wood, choke up on it and you knock it on the green."

Vandeweghe threw his hands in the air. "It'll ricochet off the trees and I'll kill myself!" He grabbed his nine iron and stood behind his ball. "Crazy guy," he mumbled, then smiled. "Friend. Huh."

"Right down your bridge," Rudy called.

Vandeweghe swung. The club struck the wooden handrail on the follow-through, and Vandeweghe let out a small yelp of pain, but the ball sailed cleanly off the bridge.

Don grimaced. He hoped Vandeweghe hadn't done any significant damage to his wrist or hand.

Plato jogged down to the edge of the ravine, squatted, and peered across. "Beautiful! Beautiful!" He yelled.

Rudy looked up to the green. "All riiiight! You're dancing!" Shouldering his bag, he headed toward the flag. "You didn't hurt that path or the bridge, did you, Mister Gucci?"

"I heard that," Vandeweghe said, and shook his left hand.

"Regulation par, coming up!" Rudy called back over his shoulder.

Vandeweghe crossed the bridge, grumbling about the ravine and his shot from the bridge. Don allowed himself a quiet chuckle. It wasn't often Gary Vandeweghe, now "Mister Gucci," got ruffled. It made the whole round worthwhile.

Don was the first one to putt out at eighteen. He grabbed his bag and began walking toward the clubhouse. "I gotta hit the can. I'll catch you guys in the grill."

"Yeah, yeah," Vandeweghe said. "You just don't want to witness my fabulous par, that's all."

Don waved. He knew he'd shot two above par, and wondered if anyone had done better. Given the way they all had felt at the top, he'd be surprised if any of the group shot sub-par. It'd be a minor miracle.

Once in the grill room, he sat at the long table which was always prepared for the return of the Saturday group. He ordered a Coke. The first guys in were busy wolfing down nuts and sipping on various beverages as they watched a tournament on the television. Within minutes, Rudy, Plato, Patrick, and Vandeweghe hustled up the stairs from the men's locker room.

"So, net four on eight?" Plato asked, a golf pencil poised over a score card.

"No, no," Vandeweghe said, looking back at Rudy, "It was the Linda Vista Country Club–"

"So what'd you get then?" Plato said.

Rudy stopped. "What? You talking to me?"

"No, P.Q.," Plato said.

"–And it wasn't until nineteen-ten, or maybe twelve–" Vandeweghe said.

"But I thought the Club was started in eighteen-something," Rudy said.

"Oh, me? I thought you were talking to Gary," Patrick said, bringing up the rear of the group. "Uh, I think I got five on nine."

Plato nodded and his pencil worked furiously. "You had a net three on ten?"

"Hey, Gary, Gary," Vandeweghe motioned to Plato. "When did the Club start?"

Plato busily scribbled on the scorecard. "What club?"

"Don't I get a stroke on sixteen?" Patrick asked, peeking over Plato's shoulder at the card. "I'm just a kid, after all."

"San Jose!" Vandeweghe said, and rolled his eyes. "What do you mean, 'what club'?"

"A four on eleven, net four on thirteen," Plato said, and sunk into a chair that seemed to materialize beneath him.

Vandeweghe tossed his hands up in the air and grinned. "The year, Plato, the year!"

"Naw, give it up, Gooch," Ridge drawled from his chair at the end of the table. He motioned for Mark, the waiter. "That card's got him mesmerized."

Don waved a handful of nuts in the air. "See, I told you the name would stick. So how'd y'all do?"

"And a net four on eighteen," Plato said, and punctuated his words with the pencil.

"Saved your ass," Vandeweghe said, pointing at Rudy. He turned to Don. "And it's 'G' for Gary, not Gucci. I told you."

Don shrugged. "Might as well have stood for 'glue.' You're stuck with it now!"

"Okay. Now we've got Charlie Quinn and Ridge," Plato said, grabbing another card from the pile on the table.

Don listened to the groans of his friends. He munched on more nuts.

"Forget it. Forget it. We got seventy-seven 'n seventy-eight," Ridge said, nodding in thanks as Mark produced a bottle of beer and a frosted glass.

So a few of the guys had obviously not fared well, after all. Don wasn't surprised.

Charlie smirked and tossed a pretzel in Don's direction. "What are you laughing at, Winner-halter?"

"Just the usual, Charlie, just the usual," Don said, and ate the pretzel.

Charlie threw him another. "So what'd you shoot?"

"Seventy-three."

"Dammit, Patrick, I thought you spiked that Bloody Mary this morning!" Charlie slumped back into his chair.

"I brought gin, not diesel fuel," Patrick said, grinning. "I didn't know you wanted me to kill the guy."

"It's about the only way to stop him," Charlie said, and tossed two dollar bills on the table. "Here's for the pot. No doubt Winner-halter here will be taking it home." He sighed. "Again."

"You had four on eleven, you had five on twelve..." Plato chanted.

Don turned his attention to the television. He knew he didn't carry the day that often, but it was a nice reputation to have, nonetheless. It was awfully nice, indeed.

CHAPTER 2

New Year's Eve, 1980
Patrick Quinn

The room glittered with the play of lights from the many chandeliers. The band bobbed to their own creations, and dozens of club members swayed on the dance floor. Patrick sat in a chair at a table tucked neatly in the back of the room. It wasn't "his" table – originally he had sat at the table for which his parents had paid, closer to the front and center – but this one had been vacated by its patrons, and it afforded the best view of both the room and the distant lights of San Jose through the large bay windows.

He watched the dancers. How was it that so many athletic people could be so awkward on the dance floor? Even Chris, who certainly was no slouch in any sport, looked like a newborn duck just out of his shell. And there was Vandeweghe, who had played college basketball with enough success that he was nearly drafted, yet watching him dance you couldn't help but wonder how the guy got out of bed in the morning without falling on his face.

Of course, Patrick knew he was sitting there, nursing his soda, because he wasn't any better. In fact, he was pretty sure he was even worse, if that was possible. But at least he had the good sense not to demonstrate it. What was it the pro was always saying? "Better to keep your mouth shut and be thought a fool than to open it and be known for one." Well, he'd just sit here and keep people guessing.

The music stopped with a light crescendo. "Thank you, folks," the guitarist mumbled into his microphone. "We'll take a quick break and be back in ten. Don't go away now."

Like any of this crowd was leaving their chardonnay and champagne any time soon.

Chris and his fiancé, Hally, followed the Vandeweghes to two tables that had been shoved together near the big windows, where the other members of the Saturday group were bunched together, along with their wives. Patrick noted that Al Braga and his wife were also there. Though not able to play with the group on Saturdays, Al was a regular on other days, and he always treated Patrick like one of the guys.

Chris stood at the table and looked around. Uh oh, Patrick thought, and tried to slump further into his chair, but Chris found him and waved, beckoning for him to join.

"P.Q.!" Chris yelled over the din. "Stop hiding!"

Patrick picked up his drink and wove his way to the group, nodding hello en route to various partying couples.

"Hey!" Don Winterhalter said, raising his hand for a shake. "Happy New Year, P.Q.!"

Patrick returned the handshake. "Careful there, Mr. Winterhalter," he said, stretching his fingers in mock pain. "You'll ruin my golf swing."

Don smiled. "Ack. It's your right hand. You don't need it."

"Well the left hand doesn't do him much good," Charlie said, grinning.

"Pull up a chair, there, P.Q.," Rudy said, motioning for his wife, Beverly, to make room. There was precious little of it, with the tables so close and members sprawled out in their chairs.

Patrick planted his feet. "Don't worry about it, Mrs. Staedler. I've been sitting all night. I think the blood has pooled in my –" He caught himself, and felt his face redden.

Everyone at the table laughed, including – much to his surprise – his mother, Dawn. "At least not *all* of it has left your brain," she said.

Vandeweghe stood. "I'm heading to the bar." He motioned to include the crowd at the table and said, "Refills, anyone? Rudy, want another Coke?"

"Naw, I'm set," Rudy said, then looked to his wife. "Bev?"

She shook her head. "Thanks, Gary, but I've had enough sugar for tonight."

"I'll take another chardonnay," Charlie said, waving his empty glass.

"Well, okay, me too," Dawn said, and drained the last swallow from her glass.

Don nodded toward his wife. "We'll have one."

"One for each or are you sharing?" Vandeweghe asked.

The group laughed.

"Bring a whole case," Don said. "We'll all share them."

"Yeah, yeah, of course," Vandeweghe agreed. "Only white? Or do some of you lushes want to switch to red?"

"I wasn't serious, Gary," Don said, standing. "Come on, I'll help you cart over a few glasses."

"Sit down, Don," Barbara Vandeweghe said with polite authority, then gave her husband a piercing look. "Get a few bottles. Three chardonnays and two cabs." She glanced around. "Anyone want a merlot?" Shaking heads punctuated the silence. "No? Okay, then just the cabs."

Vandeweghe nodded and strode off toward the bar.

"Jeez, Barb, I hope you have enough room for all of us at your house," Don said, breaking the silence. "We're none of us going be driving home after all that wine."

"You can stumble down to our house and sleep on the back lawn," Dawn said. "There's plenty of patio furniture and cushions."

Don smiled. "I've seen your lawn, Dawn. We won't need cushions."

Patrick shifted his weight and sipped his soda. He could have stayed at home tonight, or gone to a party with school friends. But there was something really compelling about hanging out with this group. Even the wives were cool. None of them ever seemed to mind the many rounds of weekend golf, the hours on the practice range, the time spent at the "nineteenth hole" hashing out the last missed putt. In fact, with the exception of his own mother, most of the wives spent as much time at the club as their husbands, and some of them played nearly as well.

He glanced around the table. Barbara Vandeweghe. Now she could play. Probably better than her husband on any given day. He'd heard she had competed in the North South Cup at Pinehurst. Had he heard correctly she'd won?

"P.Q. Hey, Patrick!" Vandeweghe waved two bottles in his face. "Place these over there by your pop, would you?"

Don read the label on the bottle placed before him and Penny. "Jeez, Gary," he said with a crooked smile, shaking his head with appreciation. "Why'd you get the cheap stuff?"

"Only the best for my buds," Vandeweghe said, pouring chardonnay. "Only the best." He turned to Patrick and waved an empty wine glass. "Come on, come on. It's New Year's Eve for chrissake. Have some."

Dawn waggled a finger. "One swallow and I'll burn your woods."

Charlie grunted. "They're metal, dear."

"Then I'll melt them," Dawn said.

Patrick took the glass, avoiding looking at his mother as he was sure she was giving him that "do as I said" frown. Vandeweghe poured an inch of wine into Patrick's glass.

"That won't kill him, Dawn," Vandeweghe said, then quickly added, "A toast!" He raised his glass and looked everyone at the table in the eye. "A toast to the best golfing buddies a guy could ever want." A groan went up from the women at the table. "And their fabulous women!"

There was a chorus of "Here, here!" and "I'll drink to that!" and "Amen!" Patrick took a sip of the wine. He'd never been fond of the stuff, preferring beer. Not that he'd had much chance to become a connoisseur, at his ripe old age of fifteen, but he'd tasted enough at formal dinners and barbecues to know what he'd be ordering, once he turned twenty-one.

Vandeweghe raised his glass in Patrick's direction, then glanced around his friends and said, "Now, P.Q., I hope to be saying this same toast someday to this same group at St Andrews!"

Don nodded. "Now *there* would be a toast."

"Wouldn't that be just great?" Rudy said, leaning forward conspiratorially. "All of us playing the Old Course?"

Ridge pulled at his necktie. "That's just a pipe dream, that's what that is. I hear they dole out tee times like Plato here doles out gimme's."

When the laughter died down, Vandeweghe said, "They're even harder to get than Plato's gimme's. It's a lottery, nowadays. But if one of us became a member..." He leaned back, gazing at the others, and Patrick felt a chill go up his spine when Vandeweghe looked at him.

"Now who'd want to go and do a thing like that?" Charlie said sarcastically. "What? Fly all the way over there once a month, have lunch in the clubhouse ... gee, you'd get bored after a year, playing that rusty Old Course."

"You'd do it in a minute," Patrick said.

"I'd do it in a second," Charlie said, leaning back and laughing. "Where do I sign up?"

"Anyone have a piece of paper?" Don asked. "Let's all sign up."

Ridge swirled the wine in his glass. "To play, maybe. But I don't want to be a member."

"Really?" Jack Lovegren's brow wrinkled. "Why not?"

"Ah, heck," Ridge said, his southern drawl thick with the night. "I'm real happy right here. Why do I need another membership at another club?"

"To play it!" Rudy said. "And this isn't just some other club. This is the St Andrews."

"Well, this is the San Jose Country Club," Ridge said, gesturing at the course outside the bay windows. "If you're not happy with that, then by jeez, go somewhere else and leave the rest of us to better company."

Plato poured more chardonnay into Ridge's glass. "Now, now. Nobody here's leaving the club. Not if I have anything to say about it."

"But you gotta admit," Chris said, "it'd be pretty special, playing the Old Course."

Nods and murmurs of consent were drowned out by the first chords of a song, signifying the band had returned.

"Someday you'll get there," Jack said, standing and clapping Chris on the shoulder. "Someday." With outstretched hand, he invited his wife to the dance floor.

"You know, I'm not giving up on being a member of the R & A," Vandeweghe said, pouring himself more wine. "I'm working on it."

Patrick sat in the chair vacated by Jack. Casually, he reached for the closest chardonnay bottle.

"Don't even consider it," Dawn said, moving the bottle out of reach. "You've had twice what the law allows, and more than you should."

"Ah, the kid's walking home," Charlie said, but then nodded to the bar. "Go get yourself another soda, Pat."

Patrick shrugged. Soda didn't sound so tasty, after the wine. "I'm okay. Thanks, Pop."

"Heck, why not stay close to home," Don said to Vandeweghe. "Join Spyglass or shoot for the moon and join Cypress Point."

Barbara nodded. "That does make more sense, Don."

"Yeah, yeah, of course it does," Vandeweghe agreed. "And I'd certainly be honored to be a member at either of those courses. Don't get me wrong about that. But there's just not the same..." He paused, searching for the word.

"Honor?" Don suggested.

"Esteem?" Plato added as Rudy said, "Dignity?"

"No, that's not it," Vandeweghe said. He paused again, and the group waited, watching. "Elegance. That's it. There's a simple elegance at St Andrews, an ancient beauty. Being a member – that would be beautiful."

Charlie chuckled. "Yeah, well, none of us who are wearing pants at this table are beautiful enough."

"Oh, well that goes without saying," Vandeweghe said, laughing. "So I guess it's up to the girls." The band swung into a snappy tune. "Come on, let's go burn up the floor!"

Patrick sunk deeper into his chair as the group vacated the table. He eyeballed the wine, considering, then shrugged and wandered out onto the balcony, closing the sliding glass door behind him. Before him spread the course, dark and quiet under the small sliver of moon. Beyond that lay a vast bowl of twinkling gems – the lights of San Jose as it celebrated the ending of one year and the beginning of another.

Patrick wondered what the upcoming months would bring. A hole in one? A steady girlfriend? A new set of clubs? All of those were possibilities, but the one thing he knew wouldn't happen was a trip to Scotland, and a round at the Old Course. That would just have to wait.

If it ever happened at all.

CHAPTER 3

August, 1981

Charlie Quinn

Charlie stood before the mirror in his bathroom. His dark suit looked crisp, the tie subtle, the white shirt pressed and stiff against his skin. He felt like he was going off to a business meeting.

He looked at his hands; they were trembling. What was he thinking? He should stay at home, send a card, flowers. He had no business going. He wasn't sure he could get through it without falling apart, and that would be ... embarrassing. For everyone.

"You'll be late," Dawn said from the door.

He grunted in response, but didn't move.

"You sure you don't want me to come along?" Dawn asked. Her tone was kind, but matter-of-fact. Charlie loved that about her – his wife was no weak, simpering woman. Especially at a time like this.

He rolled his shoulders, shrugging under the jacket. Dawn stepped forward and adjusted the collar.

"Better?" she asked.

He slumped. "Damn jacket weighs a ton today," he mumbled.

Dawn straightened his tie, loosening it a bit in the process. With a curt nod, she preceded him down the hallway.

When he arrived in the kitchen, his feet turned to lead. "Where're my keys?" he said, standing limp beside the sink. Dawn snatched them from the small desk near the entrance and placed them in his hand. "Thanks," he said, then shuffled through the laundry room to the garage. He took several deep breaths as the garage door rose, then he lumbered into the car.

Dawn was standing at the house door, arms crossed, a thin smile on her face. "I'll have dinner ready when you return."

Charlie nodded. He backed the car into the circular driveway, then stopped. He felt exhausted. Maybe he should make a phone call to Winterhalter, tell him to send his condolences.

A breeze gently caressed the rose bushes that edged the drive, and the flowers leaned toward the road, bobbing their petals as if to say, *there's the way, Charlie. There's the way.*

He placed the car in gear and eased onto the street. A young boy on a bicycle careened out of a driveway. Charlie jerked the car away from him and slammed on the brakes.

"What are you doing?!" he yelled, frantically thumbing for the button to lower the car windows. "Do you want to get yourself killed?"

The boy ferociously peddled down the street, turned a corner, and disappeared. The car windows remained up.

Charlie thought of Patrick at that age; remembered how his son used to bolt from the driveway on his bike, riding pell mell for heaven-knew-where. Now Patrick was almost sixteen. Not yet able to drive. Not yet able to be in any danger … Ridge's daughter hadn't been much older, maybe eighteen? Twenty? Charlie remembered her from some dinner at the club – bright, witty, pretty in a summer-blue dress.

Panic swelled in his chest, the emotional tide turning against him. She'd been driving home from the beach, with friends. Why hadn't she been wearing her seat belt? Why hadn't the ambulance arrived sooner? Why did things like this happen to children?

He rammed the car into park and got out. Slowly, he walked around the car, keeping one hand on the gleaming metal. The cool sturdiness of it under his hand settled him. The gentle rumble of the engine beneath the hood soothed him.

He got back into the car and glanced at this watch. Now he would be late.

Taking deep breaths, he continued down the hill, keeping a watchful eye for future daredevils. Once he was on Alum Rock Road, the volume of traffic demanded his attention, and he was able to stop thinking. Just drive.

Two miles down the hill, he braked for a red light. Through the closed windows he could hear the thump, thump of a rock song. He glanced to his right. Beside him, seated in a small Toyota, were two young women, maybe in their twenties. They were head-dancing to the music, singing at the top of their voices, laughing together when they missed the words. The driver had a cigarette dangling from her fingertips. She was blonde. The other brunette. They were pretty, in that same way all young women were – filled with a vibrancy, an innocence, a self-assuredness.

The driver glanced at Charlie, smiled brightly, then drove off through the intersection. Behind him, a car beeped. The light had turned green.

He continued down the hill. There was now a sizable lump in his throat, and breathing had become difficult. Maybe he should pull over again.

Maybe he should turn back.

The highway entrance sign loomed ahead. Charlie steered the car toward the ramp, his foot off the gas pedal. An old truck passed him quickly, then cut in front of him and careened down the ramp. He gasped. Had that been Ridge? How could that be? Why would he be over here, in San Jose?

Charlie sped up, wove his way into traffic, and searched the cars ahead for the truck. There it was. He pressed the gas pedal, anxious to catch up to the vehicle. But when he did, his heartbeat slowed. The license plates were from Oregon, and the truck was much more beat up than the one Ridge drove.

It wasn't Ridge, after all.

Charlie gritted his teeth. Of course it wasn't Ridge. Not today. Maybe not tomorrow, or next week, either. Or the week after that.

Charlie put the car in the right lane and drove along deliberately. He thought of Ridge, of the day they met at the club, their first round, how Ridge had been so anxious to be accepted as a good golfer. Charlie gripped the steering wheel. Ridge was a good golfer. He had nothing to prove.

"What will this do to his game?" Charlie said, and instantly felt asinine for even thinking such a thing. Ridge would have much more to contend with than his golf game. Still, the atmosphere, the Saturday group, the focus demanded by the game itself – these things could be a balm for life's difficulties, a momentary haven from tragedies.

The exit to Morgan Hill was coming up, and Charlie maneuvered into the correct lane. As he headed south along Highway 101, he felt less emotional. The rolling hills of golden grass, the small homesteads, the occasional fast food restaurant came and went. It had all been here the last time he drove down to Ridge's place; it would be here next time, too.

Too soon, though, the exit he needed loomed ahead. At the light off the highway, he rolled to a stop and took a deep breath. A blue Cadillac with a white top pulled up behind him. Through the rearview mirror, he looked closely at the driver, then felt relief wash over him in a relaxing wave.

Winterhalter.

Perfect timing.

The light turned and Charlie made his way onward, a little faster and more confidently now, knowing Don had his back, literally.

Several miles and many turns later, Charlie saw the sign marking his destination. He pulled into the parking lot and looked for two spaces together. As he maneuvered his car across the lot, he noted many cars he knew from the club, including that of Vandeweghe, which surprised Charlie, since he knew Gooch had planned an overseas trip for this week. Charlie then passed Rudy's car, which was also surprising, since Rudy had made the cut at Lahontan's club championship, and should have been playing today. Well, it appeared the whole Saturday group was here, except Patrick.

Charlie sighed. He wouldn't, couldn't, have brought Pat. It would have been too much.

"Hi, Charlie," Don said, climbing from his car. "Glad we're not late."

Charlie again felt the weight of the jacket as they walked toward the single-story ranch style building. "Looks like someone's house. I guess I expected something more formidable and imposing."

Don paused at the foot of the stairs that led to a covered porch. "Wouldn't be Ridge or Nellie. I think their church recommended this place."

From inside, soft music could be heard. Don pursed his lips. "Oh boy," he said. "I'm always better when they don't play music. Easier to stay unemotional."

Charlie agreed. He hadn't listened to music on the drive down, for just that reason. "I hear you. I'll hold your hand if you'll hold mine."

Don chuckled a little, then walked up the steps and grabbed the door handle. "That'd give them something to talk about around the grill room, wouldn't it?" He pulled the door open, motioning for Charlie to proceed.

Charlie stepped into the foyer and paused. Dozens of people graced the softly lit viewing room before him. Some stood, others sat in folding chairs, still others leaned against the cream-colored wallpaper. In the center of it all huddled the Saturday golfing group, shoulder to shoulder, surrounding Ridge and his wife Nellie ... and a light-colored coffin.

Without a word, Don brushed past him and crossed to the group. Vandeweghe and Plato stepped aside to make room for Don, and Charlie caught a clear look at the coffin. It appeared too severe, too clumsy to gently hold a young woman, a beloved daughter, a precious life.

Then the Saturday group closed tight, like a barrier against the world, a fortress against the impending reality of tomorrow. Charlie tugged at his ear.

He wouldn't have to ask how Ridge was holding up, or worry about how he would handle the days and months and years to come. Those surrounding shoulders would help carry those burdens. Silently, unobtrusively, but ever-present.

He wove his way through the small crowd and joined his circle of friends.

"Charlie," Ridge said, reaching forward to shake his hand, his voice strained and weak. "Glad you could make it."

"Wouldn't have missed it for the world." Charlie squeezed his friend's hand just a little tighter than usual. "Not for anything." And the weight of his jacket was forgotten.

Charlie trotted up the steps from the men's locker room to the grill. He'd had a decent round, but he was hungry and cold. The October winds had gone right through him those last few holes. A burger and a beer sounded great. At the usual table, Chris, Plato, Don, Vandeweghe, and Rudy hunched over score cards, comparing notes and apparently bickering over something Chris had done on eighteen. With a sigh Charlie noted Ridge was still not in attendance.

"No, it was in the hazard," Vandeweghe said. "I saw it, right there over the line."

Rudy rolled his eyes. "Fine, but he didn't ground his club, and I saw *that*."

Charlie pulled out a chair. "What are you guys yammering about, now?" He caught Mark's elbow as the young man passed. "Mark, could you get me a cheeseburger, coleslaw, and one of those newfangled beers you guys are carrying now? Thanks."

"Sure thing, Mr. Quinn," Mark said, and trotted off toward the kitchen.

"Newfangled beers?" Plato said, grinning. "I don't think I've ever seen you drink a beer, Charlie."

Charlie shrugged. "Times they are a changin'." He looked over at the chair Ridge always seemed to frequent. It was conspicuously empty.

Don followed his gaze. "I can't imagine he'll come out for the rest of the season. He's taking time with Nellie and his other daughter, Rhonda."

Charlie nodded. He thought of Patrick, who had gone up to the practice putting green. "A round might get his mind off things, but family comes first. Absolutely."

Vandeweghe snapped a pretzel in two. "I can't even imagine what I'd do if one of my girls..." The pretzel crumbled in Vandeweghe's big hand.

Don tapped a red golf tee on the table. "I gave Darby the lecture on wearing her seat belt."

"And let me guess," Rudy said, "she rolled her eyes and said 'I know, Dad'."

Don's grin was fleeting. "Yep, you got it, to which I said I'd sell her car and ground her for life if she didn't pay attention."

"I think I'll just never let my girls drive," Vandeweghe said. "Hire a limo driver."

Charlie leaned heavily on the table. "Make sure he's a she, and old and ugly, if you catch my drift."

A light chuckle rippled around the table, and Charlie was pleased he'd been able to lighten the mood a bit.

"It's tough," Plato said. "We can't lock them up for the rest of their lives."

Rudy's eyebrows went up. "Why not? Sounds like a reasonable response to me."

Don twiddled the tee, rolling it through his fingers. "You know, I almost killed a kid when I was young. I was playing with a BB gun and shot his ear. If it had been two inches to the left, I'd have spent my life in a penitentiary." He shrugged. "Life isn't safe. Sometimes we just have to have faith."

"It's like a round of golf, lads," Plato said. "Day to day, we never know what the course will bring us, or what we'll shoot." He quickly nodded toward Don with a smile. "No pun intended."

The room went quiet around them. Charlie looked over his shoulder. Ridge was walking toward them, a look of uncertainty on his face. His clothes hung limply on his normally solid frame. Charlie suddenly felt vulnerable.

As one, the golfers around the table stood. "Ridge!" Plato said enthusiastically. "You're just in time for lunch and a newfangled beer!" He winked at Charlie.

Ridge stood uncomfortably, his hands stuffed in his jacket pockets. "I thought I'd come hear the tales you've concocted from your sorry rounds," he said. "But if there's beer to be had, I'll take one. There's nothing at home…" His voice drifted off in sadness.

Charlie wanted to rush over and hug the man, to assure him, to make him smile. Damn, the guy looked like he hadn't ever smiled. Charlie thrust out his hand. "Glad to have you back," he said, and was rewarded when Ridge returned the shake by grasping with both his hands.

The other men followed, each gripping Ridge's hand with strength and meaning. Charlie motioned to Mark and ordered a round for everyone at the table.

Without missing a beat, Plato tossed a score card at Ridge and said, "Check it out, my friend. Rudy was four under par in this wind."

Ridge snatched the card as if it was a life preserver. "No kidding?" he said loudly. "On which holes did you cheat?"

"Only the even numbered ones," Rudy said.

Vandeweghe shook a finger at Ridge. "And you would have been proud of Chris, today. He managed to keep it in the fairway on six!"

Chris waggled a french-fry. "Yeah, by driving into the fairway bunker."

"Which is the only reason he double-bogeyed the hole," Don said with a chuckle.

Charlie's food arrived, and he settled in to the burger with gusto, watching Ridge all the while. The conversation became comfortable and easy, and focused solely on golf. Ridge relaxed, a bit of color returned to his face, and soon he was harassing them with gibes about their game.

Yes, Charlie thought, life was like a round of golf. But he couldn't think of anyone better with whom to share life's bogeys and birdies than those sitting right here at this table. He felt very blessed, very blessed indeed.

CHAPTER 4

February, 1982
Don Ridge

Seated at a round table in the grill room, Don Ridge glanced at the cards in his hand, then at the faces of the three men seated with him. Ed Schuler looked worried and Neil Woodruff appeared crestfallen; only Hank Lucente's visage looked hopeful. Ridge repressed a smile and waited for Neil to make his move. Then Ridge slapped down his cards.

"Gin!" Ridge said.

A moan escaped Neil and Ed. Hank simply glowered from beneath his bushy eyebrows.

"Okay, that's enough torture for one afternoon," Neil said, then stood and stretched. "You been spanked enough, Ed?"

Ed sighed. "This is why I don't play this game. Damn, Ridge. You ever lose?"

"We should make you strip to your shorts when you sit at a table," Hank said, then grinned. "I swear you cheat."

Ridge clutched his chest over his heart in feigned injury. "Now I'm truly hurt by that, Hank. Especially since you're the one who taught me all the tricks."

Neil and Ed laughed, then waved as they shuffled out of the grill room.

Ridge shifted in his seat. The large bay windows that overlooked the sixth tee and eighteenth green were streaked with rain, which was still pounding the course. No point in leaving now.

"Miserable day," Hank said, then tossed a handful of peanuts into his mouth.

Ridge shrugged. "Could be worse. Could be snow."

"We should all escape to Florida or Hawaii," Hank said. "Get in a few rounds of sunshine. My swing's gonna go to the dogs if this keeps up much longer."

Ridge snapped a pretzel in two and waved one end in the air. "Maybe we should go to Arizona. I hear they've got some sunshine in February."

Hank grunted. "Some? It's still a hundred down there, I'll wager."

"I wouldn't be wagering today if I were you," Ridge said, taping the small bundle of bills he'd collected. He tucked them into his wallet, then motioned for Diane, the waitress. "How about a couple of gin and tonics, will you, Diane? One for me, and one for this sad gent."

Hank shook his head and stopped Diane with his gnarly hand on her arm. "I don't need your charity, Don. Keep your damn winnings. You'll need them for next week." He looked up at the waitress. "I'll have a cabernet. The house is fine."

Diane nodded. "Sure thing, Mr. Lucente. One gin 'n tonic for you, Mr. Ridge. Anything to eat beyond pretzels and peanuts?"

Ridge glanced back at the rain and sighed. "Sure, I'll have one of your fine burgers. Medium rare, extra mustard."

"Nothing for me," Hank said and patted his bulging belly. "I'm still trying to keep my svelte waistline."

Diane laughed and headed for the kitchen.

Ridge snapped another pretzel. "You know, Hank, the idea of taking off isn't such a bad thing. I've been thinking ... maybe we should get a group and head for Scotland. I've never played St Andrews. Wouldn't mind taking a whack at her."

Hank pursed his lips and nodded slowly. "Not a bad idea. Who you got in mind to go with you?"

Ridge studied the course. It was blurred by sheets of rain and reminded him of a watercolor painting he once saw in a Carmel gallery. "Gotta be the guys from the Saturday game. Charlie, Vandeweghe, Winner-halter, Cracolice –"

"You have to take Rudy, maybe Woodruff, Clark," Hank added.

"Of course," Ridge agreed. "Do you think Plato would want to go? He's been there, hasn't he?"

"I would think so," Hank said. "He's been everywhere. Hell, is there a course he hasn't played?"

"Something in China, no doubt," Ridge said.

Their drinks arrived and Ridge took a long pull on his. The rain continued in a steady gray sheet. Puddles dotted the green and fairway, and the trees appeared to droop. A trip abroad really did seem to be an excellent idea. Brought a little excitement into this gray winter.

"When do you want to go?" Hank asked.

"Now," Ridge said emphatically, then allowed himself a chuckle. "Though I guess Scotland's not much better than this right now. Maybe we should try sometime in the summer."

"How about August? I'd guess that's a good time to be there."

Ridge nodded. "Tell you what, I'll check into what it takes to get tee times at St Andrews. You check with the guys and see who's interested."

"Okay," Hank said, then took a long swallow of his wine. "Check into cost, too. That'll be an issue with some of these guys who still have families."

A small jolt of pain shot through Ridge. He took several swallows of his drink. Would he ever stop thinking of his daughter? He turned his attention to Diane as she delivered his hamburger. "Excellent! Perfect!" he said loudly. "Just what I need. Thank you, darlin'."

"Sure thing, Mr. Ridge," she said. "Can I get you anything else?"

"How about a big bowl of that chili you have hiding in the kitchen?" Hank said. "Still got it warmed up? I guess I could use a little indigestion, after all."

Diane nodded. "One bowl of chili, coming up," she said, and bounced back to the kitchen.

Ridge swallowed a bite of burger, then said, "Well, if you think of anyone else we should invite, let me know."

"Sure, sure," Hank said. "Same goes for you."

Ridge nodded and turned his attention to his burger. It was large, and he hoped it was enough to fill the empty pit in the bottom of his stomach.

Two weeks went by and Ridge had not made much progress at organizing the trip overseas. He'd been particularly busy at his office at IBM, and with the time difference between California and Scotland, he'd not been able to find an opportune moment to call. No one around the club seemed to know much about costs and procedures for tee-times at St Andrews. Even Vandeweghe was uncertain of the details, much to Ridge's surprise.

After their round on Saturday, Hank informed him that few of the men in the Saturday group were able or willing to take such a journey.

"I've been able to speak with most of the guys," Hank said as he changed from golf to street shoes in the locker room. "But of those, only Charlie's interested, and then only marginally. For most, the cost would be prohibitive at this time."

Ridge frowned. "Ah, heck. It can't be that much, can it?"

Hank shrugged. "That's your department."

"Yeah, yeah," Ridge said, then headed for the grill room.

February rains gave way to March showers and eventually to April sunshine. Ridge had twice made contact with St Andrews, and the news had not been good. A single round on the Old Course was only £16.50, which – with the British pound weakening by the day – was very inexpensive, but getting a tee time for more than a single foursome was problematic, at best. There was a lottery system for the Old Course, and he'd be lucky to get tee times on consecutive weeks, let alone on the same day.

Hank had not been much more successful, receiving only lukewarm responses from Charlie Quinn, Gary Vandeweghe, and Neil Woodruff. The others all agreed it sounded like a good idea, but either had responsibilities that precluded overseas travel, or felt the cost was simply more than they could justify to themselves, let alone their wives and families.

"Well, maybe we should just go ourselves," Ridge said to Hank as they stood on the eighth tee, waiting to hit. Beyond, the fairway teemed with activity as the Saturday herd trampled through their round.

"Or I could keep asking around," Hank said, then glanced behind him. Brian Lawther stood at the back of the tee, arms crossed with his club dangling from between his elbows. Hank looked at Ridge with eyebrows raised in question.

Ridge shrugged. He liked Brian as a pal – heck, the guy had a huge heart – but ...

"You planning to play? Tee it up," Hank said to Brian.

Brian shook his head. "No, you two go ahead. I'll hit last."

Ridge narrowed his eyebrows. "Ah, come on Brian, just hit the ball!"

"No, no, I'll wait," Brian said.

Hank grunted and stepped up to the tee. Ridge puffed out his cheeks. Brian was only an occasional golfer with the Saturday group, but Ridge always found his "must hit last" posture annoying. Ridge was sure Brian did it just to throw everyone else off their game, and received confirmation of this as his badly struck ball sliced out of sight.

Ridge cursed under his breath then joined Hank on the walk down the fairway. "You can hit now!" Ridge yelled over his shoulder. He sighed. The trip to Scotland seemed as far away as the location itself, and as much as he wanted to go, he certainly didn't want to go there alone.

Someday he'd get there. Someday.

CHAPTER 5

July, 1982
Rudy Staedler

Rudy felt a little chill run up his spine as Vandeweghe steered the car through the gate of Seventeen-Mile Drive. It was the first time since Vandeweghe had become a member at Cypress Point Club that Rudy had been able to join in any of the guest rounds. Over the past year, Gooch had been very generous at inviting members of the Saturday group to play, but Rudy had always been out of town, or in finance meetings, or wrangling with contractors. This time, when the invitation came, he cleared his calendar.

He glanced at Don Winterhalter, who sat beside him in the back seat of the sedan. Don smiled and made the single note "happy hum" which had become his signature sound. That hum always made Rudy smile, at the very least. Plato, in the front seat, looked back at them both and gave a thumbs up.

Vandeweghe drove along the coast and Rudy glanced out the rear window. Immediately behind them, in a big sedan captained by Charlie, were Ridge, Chris, and Patrick. Six of the Saturday group had accepted the invitation to play, with Patrick coming along only to walk. As Cypress required each foursome to include a member, Patrick had been sacrificed to make room for one Mr. Percy Blane, a longtime member who had volunteered to suffer through the ordeal of playing a round of golf in paradise. Rudy felt bad that P.Q.

wouldn't be able to actually play, but heck, at least he got to see the course. That was more than the majority of golfers in the world ever experienced.

Vandeweghe parked in the nearly empty lot and Charlie wedged the sedan beside him. Rudy was the first out of either car, then the others followed, some groaning with stiffness in the early morning chill. Plato's expression was one he didn't see often – a fleeting but unmistakable look of sadness. Well, Plato had played courses as good or better when he was on the pro circuit. Maybe this trip was stirring up some memories.

"Welcome, gentlemen, to Cypress Point Club," Vandeweghe said. "Let's go play some golf."

Charlie pulled on a sweater vest. "Did you order this fog to hide the imperfections of this place?"

Rudy looked around. Indeed, it was foggy. He hadn't even noticed. There was little wind, and the unassuming white, two-story clubhouse was softened by a thin veil of mist. The few sounds of the golf course were muffled and distant. It was a bit like stepping into a dream.

"Typical summer morning," Vandeweghe said. "Don't worry, ladies, it'll clear up just about the time we're done."

Several young caddies dressed in formal golf attire arrived at the cars. "Can we take your bags, gentlemen?" one of them asked.

Vandeweghe turned to his friends and motioned toward the range. "Shall we hit some balls first?" Rudy's nod was punctuated by a round of agreeable sounds from the others. "Okay," Vandeweghe said, "grab your shoes. Locker room's over there. The boys will take the clubs up to the pro shop. Then we'll go warm up."

Within minutes they were on the practice range, lobbing balls onto the carpet, which Vandeweghe tried to convince them was really grass. Rudy suppressed the urge to giggle. Damn it was fun to hit a ball onto a nearly empty range. There was just something virginal about it, as if he was the first one to land a ball in that particular spot of grass. It was absurdly extravagant.

Fifteen minutes later they were standing on the first tee. Rudy looked out over the four-foot hedge that protected passing automobiles from the occasional errant low-ball. "Do you hold steeplechases here, too? I'm just waiting for a bunch of racehorses to gallop by."

"Don't even joke about that," Vandeweghe moaned. "The equestrian center isn't that far away. A few months ago some girl fell off her horse and the beast went blasting down the second fairway. Men who wouldn't put their lives at risk for their own children were standing in front of the green, waving their putters and yelling, trying to ward it off before it galloped across the putting surface. It was wild."

Ridge chuckled. "Well, my Nellie would sure be pleased as punch to ride one of her horses down these fairways. I'd probably never see her again."

Charlie grinned lopsidedly. "Maybe because she'd be in the local jail."

"Along with her horse," Patrick added.

A tall, slender, distinguished-looking man with silver-gray hair strolled up to the group. "Good morning!" he said and Rudy thought he detected a slight accent of some sort. "Gary, looks like you brought a handsome group of golfers with you."

Vandeweghe smiled, shook the man's outstretched hand, then turned to the group. "This is Percy Blane, the member who'll be joining us this morning." He then proceeded to introduce each of the men from San Jose. When handshakes and pleasantries were complete, Vandeweghe handed a score card to Plato. "Pro, you'll play with Rudy, Scooter, and me." He handed another card to Percy, then one to Charlie. "Percy, it's you, Charlie, Chris, and Ridge." Vandeweghe then turned to the small group of men who hovered on the edge of the first tee, guarding the army of golf bags. "These are the caddies for today. They'll introduce themselves as we get going."

The next few moments were filled with polite organization, as Rudy joined the first group in laying claim to their bags and the attending caddies, and the second group melted to the back of the tee box.

Vandeweghe pointed at a stand of trees in the middle of the first fairway. "Okay, you want to drive just to the left of that first tree. It's reachable, so for Pete's sake don't aim at it." He turned to Rudy. "You're up, Rude."

Rudy fought the urge to stare at the fog-softened scenery long enough to strike the ball. It sailed up and away in a perfect arc, landing somewhere beyond the tree. He turned to his buddies. "I feel like I just had a wet dream."

"Well, go clean yourself up," Vandeweghe said. "There's a lot of this dream still ahead of you."

Plato grinned. "And if you're not careful, it'll quickly become a nightmare."

After the third hole, Rudy knew what his pal meant. He no longer had the urge to giggle. Cypress Point was no picnic ground; the course was demanding, with the fog not making it any easier. No wonder they played a round here during the Bing Crosby Pro-Am "Clambake."

As they stood on the fourth tee, Rudy whistled. Ahead, just beyond the reach of a normal drive, lay a siege of bunkers. "Those look real friendly," he said.

"Ah, the disappearing bunkers," Vandeweghe said. He turned to Don. "Get your camera out, Winterhalter. Take a picture from the tee, then take another from the green. It'll look like two different holes. Those bunkers just disappear."

Don exchanged his driver for a five iron. "The only way I'm gonna make them disappear is by not driving into them." He teed up and sent the ball slicing into the heavy rough along the right.

"You won't see them much from over there, either," Rudy said with a grin, and stepped up to the tee.

The hole played them like a clown at a carnival, taunting and teasing, briefly turning fun into mild torture. When they finally finished, each with a bogey, Vandeweghe pointed back up the fairway. "So there's MacKenzie's design signature. When you started this hole, you thought there were bunkers everywhere. See any of them now?"

Rudy marveled. From this perspective, the fairway was unmarred, not a bunker in sight, just ripples of green rolling like waves back toward the tee. "Well I'll be flogged," he said. "Those damn bunkers did disappear!"

"That was his plan!" Vandeweghe said, and led them toward the fifth tee.

At the ninth hole, Rudy found himself buried in the bottom of a severely sloping front bunker. He stuffed his hands into his pockets, and glared at his ball.

"Damn," he said under his breath. He jogged closer to the green and peered through the gray mist. Looking between his ball and the flag, he tried to figure out how best to get up and down.

Plato stood on the other side of the green, surveying his birdie putt. "What are you doing over there?" he asked, smiling.

Rudy shook his head. "I don't know, but I'll let you in on it when I figure it out."

Don chuckled. "Well, it's a little tiny hole. Just aim for it."

Rudy returned to the bunker. He truly couldn't see the hole from where he stood, a fact he found oddly humorous. The fog seemed to have settled on the green like a felt blanket. "There's a flag up there somewhere," he yelled. "Isn't there?"

"You want me to heft Plato onto my shoulders and stand over the hole so you can see where it is?" Vandeweghe asked.

"Maybe we could send up smoke signals," Don said.

"I left the cigars back at the clubhouse," Vandeweghe said. "For later."

"Ah, heck with it," Rudy said. He waggled his club above the ball, then closed his eyes and swung. Sand showered him, and it was a full two seconds before he dared open his eyes.

"Whoa, whoa, whoa!" Vandeweghe said, then joined in the shout of triumph voiced by Don and Plato.

Rudy ran up to the green. "Where is it? Where'd it land?" He counted the balls around the pin. There were only three, and he knew them to be those of the other players. "Damn! Did I fly the green?"

Plato calmly walked to the hole and reached in. "More control than a fraction," he said, and pulled a ball from the cup.

Rudy shook his putter over his head. "Birdie!" he yelled, then clamped his hand over his mouth. The guys laughed. "Sorry," he said, though he didn't really feel it.

Vandeweghe stood over his ball and prepared to putt. "No problem." Stroke. "The only other golfers around are the guys behind us." He retrieved his own ball from the hole. "Easy bogey for me!"

While Don and Plato putted out, Rudy returned to the bunker and raked his mess back to a semblance of order. As he left the bunker, a ball landed nearby and neatly bounced into his newly raked sand. He looked up the fairway. Through the fog he could just make out the shape of Chris, waving his club. Rudy waved back. He'd not bother to inform Chris of his lie in the bunker. Let him have a few more moments of joy.

Rudy followed his playing partners to the tenth tee. "You're up, Rudy-my-man," Vandeweghe said.

Don pointed to a big tree just off the back of the tee. "Isn't that the place where Mary Pickford supposedly posed for a photo?" His brow wrinkled in thought. "I'm pretty sure that's what I heard."

Rudy wrinkled his brow. "Seems like a funny place to take a photo. Wouldn't there be more convenient places?"

"I don't know if a photo was taken," Plato said, "but she might have played here. She was a friend of Marion Hollins, who helped develop this course and Pasatiempo."

Don frowned. "Marion Hollins? MacKenzie was the architect."

Plato nodded. "Yes, but lore has it he was invited by Hollins. She was a socialite from the East, came out here in the late twenties, and worked for the guy who was developing this area."

"Is that the same Hollins who won a U.S. Women's Amateur Championship? Around 1920 or 21?" Vandeweghe asked as he leaned on his driver.

Plato nodded. "I believe she was also the first Captain of America's Curtis Cup Team."

"Now that's a new one even for me," Vandeweghe said. "I'll have to dig around and do some research."

"Something new for you to discover," Rudy said as he watched his ball disappear in the direction of the right rough.

"Yep. Like how it feels to hit out of a small, dense forest," Don said with a chuckle. "I know. I discovered that myself on the second hole."

"I think I'm gonna prefer discovering the story of Miss Hollins," Vandeweghe said, and drove his ball right down the center.

At the eleventh green, the fog lifted. Rudy found himself admiring the view whenever possible. It wasn't like he hadn't played his fair share of beautiful and famous courses. Heck, he'd been a member of Spyglass Hill since seventy-seven, and that was certainly one stunning course. And yes, he'd walked Cypress Point often enough as a gallery member during the Crosby Pro-Am, but being on the course was entirely different.

He liked it. He liked it a lot.

He watched a large buck graze on the sea grass between fairways as a seagull sailed over him and headed out toward the ocean. Rudy took a deep breath. Somehow he'd get himself invited to play the Crosby Pro-Am. Somehow.

Someday. Just to play this course again…

The holes along the ocean proved to be even more challenging than the inland holes. Rudy experienced a wide a range of emotions as his ball bounced around the course. Vandeweghe and Don seemed to be going through the same thing. Of their group, only Plato had Cypress by the tail, at one-under-par as they stood on the thirteenth green. Behind them, Charlie was struggling, but Chris and Ridge were one over par, and were demonstrating their delight by hitting into Rudy's group whenever possible.

"We're not anxious or anything, are we?" Rudy said as a ball landed on the front fringe of the green, took a hard bounce and rolled close to his heels.

Only a hundred yards back, Chris waved, then cupped his hands around his mouth to stymie the effect of the ocean wind and yelled, "Fore!"

Rudy had to laugh at his friend. "Some things aren't better late than never!" he yelled back at Chris, then he followed the other three men as they hurried to the safety of the fourteenth tee.

"Chris is hustling us so we can get another round in before we leave," Vandeweghe said.

"I'd be up for that," Don said.

"You'd get no complaints from me," Plato said. "I feel like I'm just starting to get the hang of this baby."

Rudy pulled a ball and tee from his pocket, grabbed his driver, and stepped up to the fourteenth tee. They had reached the part of the course where the ocean came into play and, again, he was struck by the sheer beauty of the place. Every tree, every bunker, every blade of grass seemed sculpted into perfection. It was almost too impeccable. It made his teeth hurt.

"You gonna stand there and gawk, or hit the ball?" Vandeweghe said, a sideways smirk on his face.

"Gawk," Rudy said. "You got a problem with that?"

"Buy a postcard," Don said. "I think they sell them at the 7-11 just outside the gate."

"Five for a dollar," Plato added.

"Printed in China," Vandeweghe said.

"All riiiight, all right," Rudy said, and teed up his ball. "I'm going." Waggle, wiggle, swing. The crack of the club against the ball was muffled by the steady wind that came in from the sea.

"Going, going..." Don said, as the ball sliced and disappeared into a small stand of cypress trees.

"Ah!" All four groaned.

"...into the woods!" Vandeweghe completed the sentence.

They handed their clubs to their caddies and began walking. "Hey, isn't that the name of a musical or a famous play?" Rudy asked as they marched down the fairway. "Into the Woods?"

Vandeweghe nodded. "Sondheim."

"Any famous songs I'd know?" Rudy asked.

The four of them paused and regarded the trees where Rudy's ball had last been seen. The old cypress's branches bent low and, tangling with dozens of roots and trunks, created an octopus-like mess.

"Yeah," Plato said, then smiled and sang, "Oh where, oh where did my little ball go?"

Laughing, Rudy dove into the tangle, quickly followed by his pals as they hunted in earnest for the missing ball.

On the fourteenth hole, errant shots played by all four men caused some slow play. As a result, Chris, Charlie, Ridge and Percy caught up with them on the fifteenth tee.

Rudy stood beside Patrick, and they both admired the ominous scenery that made this hole so special.

"Now that's ... it's just..." Patrick shrugged and tossed his hands in the air.

"Amazing," Rudy said.

"A boring choice of words, but if that's the best you can come up with, okay," Patrick said.

"No, not the view," Rudy said, chuckling, "you. I don't think I've ever heard you at a loss for words."

"Oh, I've heard him go silent," Plato said, "once." He winked at Patrick, and Chris laughed.

Ridge and Charlie joined the group. "Amazing, isn't it?" Charlie said, and that sent everyone but Ridge into a fit of laughter. "What? What did I say?" Charlie asked, his jowls puffing out, pink in the ocean wind.

"Nothing special, Pop," Patrick said, and that made them laugh even more. It became infectious and Ridge joined in, then Charlie gave up and laughed along. Soon enough, however, the view from the tee sobered them and they stood together in admiration.

The short par three had no fairway. Instead, a deep chasm filled with the raging waters of the ocean stretched from the open sea on the right around and out of sight to the left. Beyond it, the green lay surrounded by jagged bunkers. The finishing touch was a tall backdrop of menacing cypress trees. Rudy could hear the ocean surge in the chasm as it pounded against the rock walls, and the mist of the ocean spray created mini rainbows that were here one minute, gone the next. The rhythm of the water gave the distinct sensation he was at the mercy of a living monster – one that fed on golf balls and players' dreams.

"Ooooh, baby!" Vandeweghe sang. He seemed to grow to seven feet tall as he stared down the monster.

Don's face glowed with anticipation. He hummed his little happy sound and motioned toward Plato. "You're up, Pro."

Plato teed it up, then stepped back. With a solid, square stance he watched the rhythm of the sea. He ripped a small handful of grass from between his feet and tossed it into the air. It blew directly over his head. A small smile spread across his face. Quickly he exchanged clubs then, without a word, addressed the ball and swung. It flew low and flat toward the green.

Rudy squinted. Beside him, Charlie shaded his eyes. "See it?" he asked.

The ball landed on a narrow stretch of grass between two bunkers and, like a rock on clear water, skipped across the green and came to a sudden stop.

"It's just at the edge of the back fringe, maybe twenty feet from the hole," Rudy whispered. They held their breath, waiting for the ball to slide back down into the valley of the green. But it stayed there, gleaming with hope.

Plato grinned. "Next," he said and exited the box.

Don stepped forward. He, too, gave the hole a longer look than normal, and Rudy noticed he had a wedge in his hand. Was Don really going to try to fly that wind?

Whack.

The ball screamed into the air, disappearing into the background of billowing clouds, then reappearing slightly lower. It hovered as the wind grabbed it and hung on. Then it dropped, landed hard maybe three feet from the hole, and sat, seemingly indignant.

"Hey, hey!" Rudy yelled.

"Excellent shot!" Vandeweghe said as Chris yelled, "What a guy!"

"Beautiful!" added Plato and Charlie together.

"Al-riiiiiiight," Ridge crowed.

Don hummed loudly. "Who's next?" he said, and stepped aside.

"Let me at it," Rudy said. He took a deep breath and moved between the markers. He had made his decision to duplicate Plato's plan, and he just hoped he'd get enough height to avoid that monster. You go, ball, he thought, then pulled his club back.

The ball went. Hooking a bit over the chasm, it looked like it was aiming toward the big left bunker. Then a strong gust of wind pushed the ball even further left, and it landed in a nice shallow bowl of neatly trimmed grass. Rudy laughed. "Well that's an easy chip."

"Oh, yeah, piece of pie," Vandeweghe agreed, and mirrored the shot.

"I'd sure love to give it a whack," Patrick said.

Vandeweghe and Percy exchanged looks. Vandeweghe handed Patrick his club. "Here, get a ball from your Pop and go for it."

Patrick didn't argue. He caught the ball tossed at him by the caddy and quickly teed it up, then hit. "Oh yeah, oh yeah!" he said.

"Keep going, baby!" Charlie called.

The ball dropped neatly onto the center of the green. Chris chuckled. "Maybe you should buy that club from Gooch."

Patrick smiled broadly. "That was worth coming for," he said, then turned to the others. "Thanks, really."

"It was worth watching," Percy said. "Now you gotta putt it."

Patrick chuckled. "Gee, that's some punishment." He turned to his father. "I can't wait to see you go for it, Pop."

Charlie waved absently at the green across the chasm. "We'll hit after you sink your birdie."

"Go ahead and hit, Charlie," Percy said. "Give your son a show."

Charlie's eyelids drooped as he concentrated on the green. "I might if I could see the damn thing," he mumbled. "Is that the flag, to the right?"

Don nodded. "Yeah, behind that horseshoe shaped bunker."

Charlie squinted. "Horseshoe-shaped? Where do you see that."

"Well, you can't, from here," Don said. "I've know it's there because I've seen aerial photos."

Charlie's eyebrows went up. "I knew it. You're one of those prepared guys. Got to do your homework before you play."

"You going to hit?" Vandeweghe said. "Because I think P.Q. here is itching to see you make a hole in one."

Charlie addressed his ball, took a hard look at his line across the water, then drove the green. He was rewarded with a high-five from Patrick.

Charlie grinned. "Now get out of here and putt so the rest of us can play this beast. This isn't San Jose, after all. Eight-somes not allowed."

Vandeweghe motioned to Plato, Don, and Rudy. "We're all invited to the party," he said. He pointed at Patrick. "You might as well bring your dance shoes."

Patrick nodded. "The shoes I have. It's the partner I'm missing."

"I'll lend you mine for good luck," Vandeweghe said, and Don hummed in acquiescence.

Plato turned to Charlie. "We'll mark your ball, unless you want to drive another one."

Charlie shook his head. "I'm not tempting fate twice in ten minutes." He tossed a penny at Plato. "Use this, and place it heads up, will ya?"

Plato dropped the coin in his pocket. Rudy took one last look at the frothing monster in the chasm, then followed his friends as they marched around it. When they reached the green, he realized Don's ball was even closer than it had appeared from the tee, resting a mere foot from the hole. Don grinned widely. "You boys want me to get this out of your way?" he asked, holding his putter over the ball.

"Gee," Vandeweghe said. "You think you can manage that distance in one shot?"

"Get it out of there," Rudy said. "It's insulting my ball."

Don tapped his and it disappeared into the cup.

Plato gave Don a pointed look. "You know that's rare, that birdie?"

Don gave the ball a little toss, then stuffed it into this pocket. "Don't know why," he said, and went to stand at the ocean side of the green. As Rudy waited for Gooch to chip, he noticed Don was staring out into the ocean, arms crossed, his putter jutting out from between them in an odd angle. He looked like he was contemplating the laws of life. And no wonder, Rudy thought, since he just broke the one that says, "Thou shalt not birdie Cypress Point fifteen."

Rudy realized he and his pals had all miraculously made par behind Don's birdie, including Patrick with the putter he borrowed from Vandeweghe. It felt special, somehow, that all five of them had dodged a bullet together. Then they addressed the sixteenth hole, and he could almost hear another trigger engage.

"Oh boy, this is fabulously formidable," he said, nodding toward their target. The short, rocky cliffs of the mainland jutted out into the ocean, creating a small cove filled with undulating currents. Added to the natural cliffs were three tiers of rock wall, built to protect the gentle green, which sat perched upon the tiny peninsula. Bunkers crawled up a slope beyond the green, ready to swallow any ball hit long in desperation, while thick ice plant covered the areas left and right of the green. From this perspective, it reminded him of an ancient fortress – merciless and oh, so tempting.

Vandeweghe pointed to a narrow fairway which ran along the cliffs to their left. "So, if you'd rather play it safe, you can aim just to the right of that dead tree, then take your second shot straight into the green, across those two bunkers."

Rudy turned and stared at Vandeweghe. Out of the corner of his eye, he noted the others were following his lead.

"You are kidding," Plato said.

"That makes it a one-putt option," said Don.

"Well, yes, of course it would," Vandeweghe said. "But you run less of a risk of losing your ball in the ocean and taking the penalty, in which case you're better off with a bogey than a double bogey, or possibly worse."

Don chuckled. "Thanks but no thanks. No guts, no glory."

Patrick's face twisted into a crooked grin. "Just a walking lexicon of original sayings, today, aren't we, Mr. Winterhalter?"

Don smiled and hummed, then wrinkled his brow. "It's two-twenty to the flag? Roughly?"

"To the front of the green. Over the ocean," Vandeweghe said. "But add ten or so for the wind."

"But the flag's down front," Rudy said, "so there's nothing added there."

"Here's another original saying for you, P.Q.," Don said. "Make it or break it." He took a warm up swing, then shot a cannon at the rock wall. "Make it," he said, and the ball landed safely on the left side of the green.

"Easy two-putt," Vandeweghe said, and put his ball almost in the same spot.

"You two have no imagination," Plato said, as his ball came to a rest in the very center of the green.

"Yeah, well, it's hard not to imagine the ball sailing off into the Pacific," Rudy said, then groaned as his nearly did, slicing toward the ice plant. "Get back! Get back!" he yelled. And it did that too, hooking hard left as a gust of wind ripped across the peninsula.

"Where'd you land?" Vandeweghe asked, squinting.

"Not sure," Rudy said. "I lost sight of it over the left side of the fairway. But I'll take that over the initial option."

"Which was scuba diving," Don said.

"I've always wanted to take up that sport," Patrick said, "but maybe not today."

"Why not?" Vandeweghe asked, then handed him the driver. "Go on, you might as well give this hole a shot, too."

Rudy chuckled. "You're getting spoiled."

"Happy as a rotten egg," Patrick said, and swung.

Rudy watched as Patrick's ball landed high on the green, then spun back toward the hole.

Yells of "Oh, no!" and "Sit down!" and "Bite!" followed as the ball picked up speed and hurtled toward the ocean.

"Is it in the rough?" Patrick asked. "I don't see it."

Rudy motioned with his chin. "I think it's hanging on by its teeth, off to the right just in front of the rock wall."

Vandeweghe retrieved his driver from Patrick and handed it to his caddy. "Well, one way to find out," he said, and led the group around the cove.

To Rudy's delight, they found Patrick's ball wedged into the coarse grass, only a foot from the edge of the cliff.

"Anybody got a rope?" Patrick called to the men fanned out across the green. "I may have to tie it around me, and you can all hang on so I don't swing out into the ocean."

"You'd just take us all with you," Rudy said as he hiked toward the far side of the fairway. "Hey, any of you lucky stiff's wanna help here? I think I'm down in that little beach."

"Yeah, yeah," Vandeweghe said, and he, Don, and Plato marked their balls and joined Rudy. A small idyllic cove nestled twenty feet below them. Protected by tall, jagged rocks, the water lapped in and out gently, teasing but not quite reaching Rudy's ball, which lay nestled in a handful of dark seaweed.

"Staedler, you are one unlucky chump," Vandeweghe said.

"Well, you can hit it," Plato said, "or you can get relief back there." He pointed back along the edge of the fairway.

Rudy sighed. "And a stroke." He took the wedge pro-offered by the caddy, then headed down the rock stairs into the cove. Once there he surveyed his lie. The seaweed lay flat behind the ball. He glanced around. "There ought to be a mermaid laying around down here," he yelled up to the guys.

"Word is there used to be," Vandeweghe said with a chuckle. "Until Crosby brought Harris out to play."

Plato waved his hand. "You gonna play it or do you want relief?"

Rudy surveyed the lie again. "You know, I think I can hit it," he said quietly, then looked up at Vandeweghe, Don, and Plato. "Hey! Somebody show me the direction of the flag."

Plato grinned. "You're gonna hit it, aren't you?"

"Ah, heck, you only live once," Don said.

"There you go again," Patrick said as he joined the others at the edge of the cliff. "Creating those memorable one-liners."

Don grinned and Rudy thought he heard a hum. "So?" Rudy yelled up. "Which direction am I aiming?"

Plato stood between Rudy and the flag. "This way, Rudy," he said, and checked his bearings. "Yep. Just fly it right over me."

Rudy lined up his shot, then looked up at Plato. All he could see was Plato's glasses and cap. "Well you're gonna move, aren't you?"

Plato nodded once. "Don't you worry about me. Open your stance and hit for the other side of the green," he said. "Otherwise it's likely to skim into this heavy stuff up here, and then you'll be digging it out of there with a rake."

"Anybody got one?" Rudy asked.

"Sorry," Don said, "I left mine at eleven."

"Run back and get it," Rudy said. "I'll wait."

Vandeweghe, Don, and Patrick stepped aside, out of any possible range of a ricocheting ball. Rudy glanced up and saw they were all chuckling.

"What are you all lookin' at!" Rudy yelled. "This ain't no circus!"

"Too bad," Patrick yelled back. "'Cause we were just about to start selling tickets!"

Rudy brushed them off with his hand, and set his focus on the job before him. He cautiously moved into position, being particularly careful not to disturb the length of seaweed stretched out behind his ball. He checked his line to Plato's cap, then locked his club onto the trajectory, and swung. The sound of a wave on the sand behind him was quickly followed by a dull thud as the club face met the rubbery seaweed, then the ball. Sand and seaweed and bits of shells flew up into his face, and Rudy closed his eyes tightly.

Above him, the sound of the others yelling was dampened by the ocean.

He peeked. Well, the ball was no longer at his feet. That was a good sign. Maybe.

Wiping the sand from his face, he trotted up the stairs. Plato was still rooted in his line, a big smile on his face. Now on the green, Patrick was three feet from the flag, pointing in an exaggerated manner at a little white spot.

"That's me?!" Rudy yelled, and joined Vandeweghe, Don, Patrick, and Plato on their way to the green.

"You are the God of the Wedges," Patrick said, then stuck his elbow out. "Here, rub some of that magic off onto me, will ya?"

On the green, ball markers were circling the flag, none of them closer than ten feet. Rudy marked his own ball then stepped back to watch. Don placed his ball at the furthest marker.

"Is that for birdie, then?" Rudy asked.

Don nodded. "Yep." He crossed to his ball and took a practice stroke. "This is going right in the hole."

"Another million to one chance that you birdie both fifteen and sixteen," Vandeweghe said. "Especially from that distance. Heck, the pros can't do it."

"You know there's only been eleven hole-in-ones in the history of this hole?" Plato said. "Bing Crosby has one and, believe it or not, his priest has one." He grinned. "So, Don, you said your prayers lately?"

"Before every shot on this course," Don said. He took another practice stroke. "Right in the hole," he said firmly.

"Get that thought out of your mind, Winterhalter," Plato called from the front of the green. "I do not like what you're thinking. Rudy and I need this hole."

Don set up over the ball.

"That's a bad thought," Plato teased. "You wouldn't dare, would ya?"

Don glanced up. "Okay with you that I putt? Any time?"

"Fire away," Rudy said.

The wind died, and the distinct *ping* of the putter against the ball echoed across the green as the ball sprung forward and arced neatly toward the cup.

"Don't you dare, don't you dare!" Plato hollered as the ball sped closer to the hole. Five feet. Three feet. One foot ... Without even losing pace, it fell in with an irrefutable *clunk*.

"Get out of that hole!" Plato yelled, then joined the rest of the guys in laughter and cheers.

"How 'bout that!" Vandeweghe said, picking the ball from the cup and tossing it to Don. "Never in doubt. It could have been up a mountain!"

Plato reached out and shook Don's hand. "Oh, that was bad," he said, but he was all smiles. "I mean, that was *really* bad. Congratulations!"

"Just another day on the golf course," Don said. But his eyes looked awfully bright.

"MacKenzie was one sick bastard," Rudy said as he stood on the seventeenth tee and surveyed his options.

"One sick *brilliant* bastard," Vandeweghe said with a smile, then nodded. "Okay. You want to air the ball out over the water, about there." He pointed to the right of the coastline. "The wind'll push it back onto the fairway." He shifted to point at a small clump of cypress trees that stood tall in the center of the fairway. "Your optimum shot is just to the right of those trees, in that narrow lane that runs along the ocean."

"Or on the cliff," Patrick said. "That'll make for a great photo, if nothing else."

"You said it, P.Q.," Plato said. "Nothing else."

Rudy turned to Don. "Lucky you. By virtue of your now famous birdie on the sixteenth, you get to show us the yellow brick road."

Patrick chuckled. "Well, well, Dorothy. Do ya' feel like the cowardly lion standing in front of the Wizard's throne?"

Don nodded and joined in the laughter. "Hiding behind my tail and shaking in my fur."

"Just remember that the lion found his courage in the end," Plato said.

Don swung his club in practice. "But only after he melted a witch or something."

Vandeweghe pointed at the green, off in the distance. "Well, there she is!"

Rudy leaned on his driver and watched the surf pound the rocky fingers of cliff that jutted out along the entire length of the fairway. There was a lot of room to get into trouble. A lot.

Crack!

Rudy's eyebrows rose. Don had aimed the ball at least thirty yards off the coast. A gutsy call, to say the least.

"Go ball, go," Don said.

"Come back," Vandeweghe added.

The ball hung high over the water, then curved gently to the left, dropped to the grass, and stuck.

"Wow," Rudy said. "That's some wind."

"You're off to see the wizard," Patrick sung.

"Let's hope those ruby red slippers fit everyone here," Plato said, and stepped onto the tee.

The good witch smiled on them, and everyone managed to make the fairway, though Vandeweghe had a tough lie, directly behind the stand of cypress trees.

"See that," Vandeweghe had said as his ball rolled to a stop. "That's where you *don't* want to be."

They walked along the coastline as they made their way down the fairway, and Rudy was mesmerized by the scene. No wonder this was one of the most photographed holes in golfdom.

Patrick walked up alongside. Rudy pointed to a spiked rock upon which sat dozens of birds. "Looks like a magazine ad."

Patrick nodded, "A scratch and rub."

Gang of Eight: The First Tee

The wind carried the pungent odor of soggy bird waste. Rudy wrinkled his nose. "Yeah, they are a bit smelly. Someone ought to take a fire hose to that rock and wash it down every now and then." He and Patrick paused as Don, twenty feet away, swung.

"Nice shot," Patrick said.

Rudy turned his attention back to the ocean. "Pat, look," he said and pointed. A flock of pelicans pressed out toward open water. With an exaggerated southern twang, he said, "They're perty as a picture, ain't they?"

Patrick nodded, then did a little hop. "Oh, blast! A picture!" He rifled through his jacket pockets. "I brought my camera and haven't taken a single picture!" He turned the pockets inside out. "Where did I put it?"

"I thought you gave it to your dad's caddy while we were on the driving range," Rudy said.

Patrick threw his head back and groaned. "Oh, blast. You're right. I did."

"No great loss," Vandeweghe said. He waved at the vista and grinned. "A camera can't capture this anyway. Just take a mental picture."

Rudy nodded in agreement. His mental photo album was going to be stuffed full after this trip.

Vandeweghe's behind-the-tree lie turned out to be even worse than expected, and when he gambled and tried to smash the ball through the branches, it found a solid trunk instead and ricocheted neatly back into his face. He ducked, just in time, and felt the ball crease his hairline.

"Take a lesson, gentlemen," Vandeweghe said as he rubbed the top of his head. "This *really* isn't where you want to be."

Minutes later, the seventeenth green held them all captive. Rudy and Plato had seen their balls land on the back of the green, then roll off onto the fringe. Don's rested on the left edge, and Vandeweghe's was resting on the right.

"Okay, boys, we've got it surrounded," Plato said as he surveyed the four balls. "Don, I think you get to lead the attack."

Don punched his putter and the ball bounced awkwardly toward the hole, then stuttered to a stop a mere four inches from the cup.

"Nice charge," Rudy said. "Just needed a little more horse."

"When I grow up, I wanna be just like you," Patrick said.

"What?" Don said. "Fat and lazy?"

"Yeah, gee, that describes you perfectly." Patrick rolled his eyes. "No! Short but mighty!"

Vandeweghe stood over his putt, then said, "You'll probably get the mighty down, but we'll have to cut you off at the knees to get the short part."

"Not so good for the game," Don said, smiling. "Good putt, Gary. Knock it in."

"Okay, so I'll make do with mighty," Patrick said.

"Mighty good, or mighty fast," Vandeweghe said, then knocked his putt just past the rim. "Well, misery loves company," he said as he tapped his ball back into the cup.

"Then stay over there, away from me," Plato said as he addressed his ball. "I don't want any part of your miserable company." He groaned as his ball rolled left of the hole.

Vandeweghe laughed. "Well, it looks like you're going to suffer it anyway!" He waved at the ball. "That's good, Pro, pick it up."

"Yea, it's in the circle of friendship," Rudy said, and placed his ball before his marker.

Plato waggled his putter at Rudy. "Ah, not with me, it isn't."

Patrick chuckled, then, with a cartoon pirate voice, said, "Yeah, we plays our rounds with a different circle o' friends."

Plato knocked his ball into the cup and retrieved it. Then he smiled. "The circle of friendship is that thing that goes deep down under the green. It's got roots."

"And now for the philosophical part of our program," Patrick said.

"It's not philosophy," Plato said. "It's fact. Good friends nourish each other, grow together."

Rudy backed off his putt. "Ah, man, that brought back a really funny memory," he said.

"Can't you remember while you're putting?" Vandeweghe said.

"Only one program on that channel," Patrick said.

Rudy putted and the ball rattled in the cup. "My philosophy professor at college. He used to say" – he switched to a deep voice – "'You're all animals. All you want is food and sex.'"

"And he's right!" Vandeweghe said. "Emphasis on the food! Come on, let's putt this thing out and get through eighteen. I want to eat lunch."

When all the putts had dropped, Vandeweghe led his friends toward the eighteenth tee. Rudy lagged behind. He walked back to the cliff and looked down at the rocks gleaming beneath the foam of the ocean, then he turned his gaze to the coastline. It really was beautiful, with the deep emerald of the fairways giving way to the rust red and shiny green of ice plant dangling over the craggy cliff. Rudy looked back at the majestic stand of cypress trees jutting up from the neatly cut grass, and he thought of what Plato had said, about the circle of friendship and those deep roots.

He felt dampness well up behind his eyes. He'd only known these guys for six years now, but he felt he could trust them for just about anything.

"Hey! Staedler! Did ya get lost?! Need a map?!"

Rudy pinched the bridge of his nose and chuckled. "I'm coming! I'm coming!" He could especially trust them not to let him get all sentimental on a golf course. Still, he stole one last look at the scene along seventeen. Another mental photo for that burgeoning album...

When he reached the eighteenth tee, Rudy blew out a low whistle. "I'm having a sincere Grimms Brothers moment," he said. He pointed at the clubhouse chimney, which poked its way above the thin forest of cypress trees. "Doesn't this just look like something from a fairy tale?"

Patrick laughed. "You mean you're finally catching up? The big bad wolf joke was back on seventeen."

"Hey, now," Plato said with a big crooked grin, "Don't go giving us old folks a hard time." He pointed his driver at the chimney. "Eight ball, in the hole." He swung and his ball screamed low beneath the cypress trees, heading straight for the white bricks.

"Beautiful!" Vandeweghe said. "Perfect shot, Pro."

"You've been saving that all day, haven't you?" Rudy said.

"I didn't need to pull it out of the bag until just now," Plato said. He winked at Rudy. "Got an answer for that?"

"Let me see what I can compose off the top of my head," Rudy said. He glanced at the chimney, aligned his club slightly to the right, then let it rip. The ball sliced over the tops of the cypress trees and continued in that direction, out of sight. He turned to Vandeweghe. "Well?"

"You're okay over there," Vandeweghe assured him. "So long as it doesn't clear the thin trees and end up in the denser forest."

"Really dangerous," Patrick said. "Little red riding hood lives over there."

"Well, then, maybe that's exactly where I want to go," Rudy joked, and stepped off the tee.

"Now, now," Plato said, and nodded toward Patrick "In our midst we have a young man who is most impressionable."

"So was the big bad wolf at one point in his life," Vandeweghe said, and drove his ball far left of the chimney. "Oh, blast!"

Patrick clucked. "You're no longer in a fairy tale, Gary."

"More like a Stephen King novel," Don said, and Rudy joined the others in an appreciative chuckle.

As far as Rudy could tell, all four balls landed somewhere in the safety zone. He followed Vandeweghe and surveyed the trees that lined the fairway. One had a thick trunk, possibly ten feet across, but the branches had twisted and leaned out so badly they needed support, and were being held up by large, well-placed poles of cypress wood. As he passed beneath it, he glanced up at the canopy. Cypress trees were so fascinating, so much more interesting than any tree he'd seen, anywhere else. They sure added to the mystique of the place. And, he decided as he glared at his ball – which rested near a jutting hump of cypress root – the difficulty.

"That you, there, Rudy?" Plato asked as he hiked toward a more pleasantly placed ball. "How'd you end up under that tree?"

Rudy looked closely at the ball. Dumb luck, it had his markings. "Yeah, it's mine," he grumbled, and eyed the green. It started low and rose up toward the clubhouse and parking lot, with a slight lean to the left. "Hey, Gary!" he yelled across the fairway. "Does that thing slope as much as it appears to?"

Vandeweghe nodded. "More," he said.

Rudy watched as Don neatly laid his ball into the front right bunker.

"Forgot to say your prayers," Rudy said.

Don grunted. "Gotta be careful what you wish for. I just prayed not to go over the green and land on the cement."

"You didn't," Vandeweghe said, and swung. His ball went high and the wind carried it past the back of the green. "But I sure did." He looked around at the other golfers. "Anyone else have a prayer?"

Rudy took a slow practice swing and bumped the trunk of the tree under which he was stuck. "I sure don't," he said.

"Maybe you should knock it back onto the fairway," Plato suggested. He pointed back toward the tee. "Knock it that way a few yards, just to give yourself a chance."

Rudy wrinkled his brow. "Go backwards?" He pointed his club at the flag. "But the green's that way!"

"So?" Plato said. "With that lie, you don't have a swing, and you may end up burying the ball into that shelf of long grass. It doesn't make sense." He waved his hand. "Go that way, just a few yards."

"I'm not going backwards," Rudy said. "That's just against the nature of golf." He wiggled his feet into the sand at the base of the cypress and prepared to hit.

"Rudy, don't be so pigheaded," Plato said. "You've got no shot!"

Rudy gritted his teeth and swung. The club smacked into the trunk on the backswing, then seemed to twist in Rudy's hand in the downswing. The ball went forward a foot, hit another exposed root, and popped straight up. He had the instantaneous desire to swing at it, using his club like a baseball bat. The ball dropped back onto the dirt.

He sighed.

"And what prayers are you saying now?" Patrick said with a chuckle, then headed for the green.

Rudy looked over at Plato. "Don't say it!" *Don't you say a thing.*

"I'm not saying a word," Plato said. He leaned on his iron and waited. "Just hoping we can get to the green before dinner."

"That's not saying nothing!" Rudy said, then took a mighty swing at the ball, hoping to just muscle himself out of the predicament. The ball took off, low and fast. "Fore!" he yelled.

Everyone hit the grass, while the nearest caddy crouched, covering his head with Don's bag. The ball smacked into the bag with a tremendous *thwack*, ricocheted toward Patrick and hit him in the back of his head. Patrick yelped, dropped to the grass, then lay still. The ball landed a perfect ten yards from the front of the green.

A bolt of panic blazed through Rudy. "Oh my God, Patrick, you okay?!" He raced toward the young man.

Patrick slowly sat up and began vigorously rubbing the back of his skull. The caddy trotted over, his face white.

Vandeweghe materialized out of the woods. "Wow, P.Q.! You alive?"

Patrick turned, and Rudy could see he was laughing, hard. Patrick waved. "Never better! I think I just had my first near-death experience!" He reached for Don's bag and inspected it. "Sorry, Don. Looks like your bag has seen the proverbial light." He looked up at the silent caddy. "Are you okay?"

The caddy nodded, then smiled weakly. "I didn't realize I'd given Mr. Staedler such bad reads that he'd go aiming for me," he said, and everyone laughed.

Patrick stuck his fingers in the main pocket of the bag, where the zipper had been smashed apart.

"Shot it right between the eyes!" Plato said as he leaned over to take a look.

Rudy's knees were weak, but he felt the adrenaline rush abate. He hadn't killed Patrick. He inspected the bag. "Jeez, Don, I'm really sorry. When we get back home, I'll lend you my other bag and we'll send that in to get it fixed."

Don shrugged. "Time for a new one, anyway." He pointed at the broken pocket. "Pat, dig around in there. I think you'll find a pin or something to keep it closed."

Patrick dug around in the pocket, then removed a large safety-pin. He grinned. "You thought this might come in handy some day, eh?" he said, then pinned the pocket closed.

"I'll bet you just assumed it would be for your pants, not your bag," Vandeweghe said.

"Well, if that ball had hit the zipper of your pants, you'd be needing more than a safety pin to hold things together," Rudy said.

They all laughed, as much from relief as from the humor of the moment. Rudy looked over to his ball. "P.Q., thanks to you I have a shot at bogey."

Patrick stood and stuck his hand out for Rudy to shake. "Patrick Quinn, ball placement specialist," he said. "We aim to get in the way, any time we can."

Plato readjusted his cap. "Your mom'll be happy to know you finally found a useful way to use that hard head of yours." He motioned toward the trees. "Come on, let's go watch this Houdini from a safe distance."

Rudy waited until everyone was settled off the fairway, then chipped his ball up onto the green. A surprising feat, given that his hands were still shaking. When he got to his ball, he realized he'd probably have a double-bogey on this hole. He marked his ball and stepped off to wait for Don and Vandeweghe to chip up. So he'd double bogey. Heck, after that initial lie, he should feel lucky. It could have been a lot worse.

Patrick stood near Don, whispering and grinning with delight as he absently rubbed the back of his head.

Yep, it could have been a lot worse.

Rudy stood with his foursome on the edge of the eighteenth green, watching as Charlie, Ridge, Chris, and Percy finished their round. One of the caddies had brought a cold, wet towel for Patrick, and he sat – at a safe distance – holding the towel to his head.

Charlie marked his ball on the green and, with a concerned look on his face, crossed to his son. "What happened to you?"

Patrick shrugged. "Nothing, Pop. Just cooling off my thoughts."

Charlie grunted. "Did somebody finally have enough of your wisecracks and clock you with a nine-iron?"

"It'd take a driver to make a dent in that thick head of his," Plato said, smiling.

"Charlie! You're up!" Chris called from the green.

Charlie waved acknowledgment, but didn't move. He watched his son. "You feel dizzy? Nauseous? Are you bleeding?"

"Pops, I'm fine," Patrick said warmly. "Pro's right – it would take more than an errant golf ball to do much damage."

"Especially one hit by me," Rudy confessed. "God knows I don't get much on them anymore."

Charlie shot Rudy a look and headed back to his ball marker. Rudy wasn't sure what to make of it. Certainly Charlie had to know he hadn't meant to hit Patrick.

"Don't worry about him," Patrick said, seeming to read Rudy's mind. "He'll see the humor in it when he realizes I really am okay."

Charlie putted out, then shook hands over the cup with the rest of his foursome. Rudy hoped Patrick was right. He liked Charlie, a lot, and he certainly didn't want something like this to come between them. He looked back down the eighteenth fairway. This place was too beautiful to facilitate a broken friendship. What was it Plato had said earlier? That friendships had deep roots?

"Oh! My camera!" Patrick exclaimed and lurched to his feet. "Hey Pops, is my camera still in your bag?"

The caddy held the bag as Patrick checked several pockets, finally locating it. "Great! Photo time!"

Rudy glanced around. Only he, Charlie, Patrick, and the caddy were still there. The rest of the guys were heading toward the lockers.

"Hey! Fellas!" Rudy yelled, waving. "Photo time!"

Percy waved from across the driveway. "You guys go ahead without me," he yelled. "I gotta hit the head."

"I wondered if you were ever gonna use that thing," Charlie said. "You made such a fuss over bringing it."

"Gee, Pop, you could've reminded me," Patrick said, gently elbowing his father in the ribs. "Or were you afraid you'd actually have to be in a picture?"

"Didn't want to break your camera," Charlie said with a crooked smile.

Patrick waved toward the ocean. "Okay, gentlemen, stand over there. Then I can get both the eighteenth hole and the water."

"And us," Rudy added. "Don't forget that."

"How do you want us?" Vandeweghe asked.

Patrick paused. "Oh, well, how about by height." He pointed toward the edge of the green. "Gary, you stand over there, and..." He looked from man to man, sizing everyone up. "Don, I think you're on the other end."

"Duuuhhh," Don said in a goofy voice. "Just don't call me shorty."

Rudy joined the others as they laughed, arranged themselves, looked at each other, then rearranged themselves, looked, and rearranged themselves again.

"Jeez, you guys were killers in grade school, weren't you," Patrick said with a smirk.

"When was that?" Ridge asked as he slid between Chris and Plato. "I don't remember."

"Well, you've grown a bit since then, Ridge," Plato said, moving closer to Don.

"Yeah, sideways, not up," Ridge said, and patted his stomach. "And it's all Nellie's fault."

"Don't go blaming that good woman for what you brought on yourself," Plato said. "She doesn't make you drink all that beer."

"No, but she keeps buyin' it, all the same," Ridge said, and his cheeks turned cherry red.

Finally they settled into a line. Rudy noted he was near the end – the short end. He caught Don's eye and flashed a smile at him. "Keeping good company, are you Winner-halter?"

"Now," Patrick said sternly. "I want each man to look to their left, then look to their right, and remember who's standing there."

"Why?" Ridge asked. "You planning on making this a regular thing?"

Patrick nodded and brought the camera to his face. "At least once a year. Now smile!" he barked, and snapped the photo.

"Well that'll be the one and only," Chris said. "Because I'm sure I heard the camera crack."

"Hey wait, wait," Percy said as he returned to the group. "Let's get Patrick in there. Give me that camera, Patrick. Now go stand there next to your father."

Patrick wedged his way into the line next to Charlie.

"Hey, now," Vandeweghe said, "He's not in order."

"Just kneel down, Patrick," Percy said.

Patrick squatted down and checked to make sure he was equal height to Charlie. "So, hurry and take the photo," he said, "my thighs are burning."

The line of men burst into laughter, and Percy pushed the shutter-button.

As the camera was handed back to Patrick, Rudy had the distinct feeling he'd be doing this again. Many, many times.

Rudy walked in the middle of the pack as they made their way across the parking lot to the men's locker room. Since Cypress Point required coat and tie in the dining room, they had brought appropriate clothing. Rudy rubbed his hands together. Despite the brisk walk around the course, he was still chilled from the morning fog. For once, a jacket didn't seem an imposition.

"So what's on the menu today?" Don asked.

"It's flank steak with mushrooms, grilled salmon, and chicken something," Vandeweghe said. "Buffet style, as always."

Don made a quick funny face. "Humph. That's a bit heavy. Don't they have salads?"

"Yeah, yeah. Sure they have salads," Vandeweghe assured him.

"Blue-blooded salads, funny lettuce, and odd ingredients," Ridge said, grinning. "Not a tomato or cucumber in sight. But count me in!"

"I'll take the salmon," Charlie said, then winked at Patrick. "You think they fished it out of the ocean this morning?"

"Of course," Vandeweghe said. "Anybody else?"

"The steak's always good," Percy said, then pointed at Patrick and Chris, "and it'll fill up you youngsters."

Patrick and Chris nodded. "Sounds good," they said in unison.

Plato chuckled. "I'll just be happy if the food's edible. That's fancy enough for me."

Vandeweghe motioned toward several tables, and Rudy chose a seat that offered a view of the ocean. He just couldn't get enough of it.

"Order what you want to drink," Vandeweghe said. "I told Barb I'd call her when we got in. Be right back."

Drinks were ordered and served, and the buffet was assailed with vigor. As a general rule, Rudy had never enjoyed buffets, but this one was a definite exception. The presentation was simple yet elegant, and the aromas that rose from each dish promised tantalizing tastes. He glanced at the plates held by his friends. Given the volume of food on each, it seemed they agreed.

Conversation became sporadic as the food was consumed. What little talk there was turned to tournaments played in Pebble Beach, and at Cypress Point in particular.

"...No, it was Crenshaw's *second* pro win," Vandeweghe said between bites of sautéed mushrooms. "And I'm darn sure it was in nineteen-seventy-six."

Plato nodded. "Yes, yes it was," he said, putting down his fork and carefully wiping his mouth. "I think he was the leader going into the fourth round –"

"And he won by two strokes," Rudy said.

"But his final score was six under, right?" Don asked.

"Seven," Rudy said. "He beat Mike Morley with a seven under par, two-eighty-one."

"He's won a few tournaments since, but nothing really notable," Vandeweghe said.

Don reached for his Coke. "With that putting stroke, I'm guessing he'll win a major one of these days."

"He almost won the PGA in '79," Plato said. "Lost to David Graham in the playoff. Rather heartbreaking to watch."

Rudy waved his fork in the air. "Hey, changing subjects, do you all know that story about the match played during the Clambake between Hogan and Nelson, and Venturi and some guy named Warren or –"

"Ward," Plato said. "Harvie Ward." He nodded emphatically. "Yes, I know the story. Amazing history."

"I don't know about history," Ridge said, "but I can tell you Venturi's advice to a sandbagger when asked how to get more distance between himself and the ball..." He paused for dramatic effect, then grinned. "Venturi told him, after you hit the ball, run backwards."

Rudy joined in the laughter. He wished, for the umpteenth time, that he could deliver a joke as well as Ridge.

"So back to the changed subject," Don said, his forehead creasing in concentration. "Didn't somebody put Venturi and Ward, who were amateurs at the time, right?, up against the pros, on a bet?"

Rudy swallowed. "Eddie Lowry, Francis Ouimet's old caddy."

"The Ouimet that won the U.S. Open early in the century?" Charlie asked.

"1913," Vandeweghe added with a nod. "Over –"

"Harry Vardon!" Chris interrupted, smiling. "I actually know that!"

Patrick's face pinched with disbelief. "You're kidding, right. Since when did you become a walking golf encyclopedia?"

"Yeah, that's Rudy's job," Ridge said, and chuckled. "I swear, Rudy, you know things that aren't fit for a golfer to know."

Everyone laughed. "Well! It's true!" Ridge said, waving a fork full of lettuce at them. "Rudy knows useless things, like who was runner-up at the Masters in nineteen –" he stabbed an Italian olive onto the fork – "oh, I don't know, pick a year."

"Sixty-five," Don said, and winked.

"Easy," Rudy said with a smile. "Gary Player to Jack Nicklaus, by nine strokes." He winked back at Don. "And, Arnold Palmer, who matched Player's score, though not on the final day."

Ridge poked his fork in the air. "See! I told you! Now who really needs to know this stuff? Isn't that what encyclopedias are for?"

"Golf magazines, at least," Patrick said, and chewed on a bite of broccoli.

"I seem to remember that Nicklaus shot a record seventeen under par for the tournament," Vandeweghe said.

Ridge chuckled. "Well, now, you're an ah-ter-nee," he drawled for effect. "You're supposed to have a brain like a big book."

Rudy wrinkled his brow. "And developers just have little book brains, eh Ridge?" He chuckled to keep the mood light as he looked around at the men at the table. "'Cause I can probably spout off a few more –"

"No, no," Ridge said and waggled his head back and forth. "I know you're smart, Rudy. Don't get your knickers all in a twist."

The table exploded with laughter. Rudy joined in, thoroughly appreciating the ribbing.

"Ridge, only you could get away with saying something like that," Charlie said above the din.

"Well I suppose you Yanks are just too proper," Ridge said, and chewed another forkful of salmon with vigor.

"So who won?" Patrick asked, once the laughter had died down. "The Venturi, Ward thing. Who won?"

"Hogan and Nelson won, with Hogan having to birdie the last hole to hold the win. Hogan shot sixty-three, Venturi shot sixty-five, and Nelson and Ward both shot sixty-seven," Plato said. "Between the four of them they made twenty-seven birdies and one eagle. Hogan tied his own course record of sixty-three. To stay one up in the match he had to get the birdie, and to do that he had to make a not-very-easy, twenty foot putt on eighteen."

Don grinned. "I'll bet that was one nerve-wracking putt."

Plato nodded. "Hogan was not the slightest bit interested in losing to two amateurs. He was still a playing pro, though Nelson had retired a few years earlier but still played a lot of golf."

"Wow, sounds like somebody should write a book about that," Chris said.

"I imagine someone will, someday," Vandeweghe said. He drained his ice water. "Everyone done? Should we go get the cars?"

"So instead of caddies we use cars?" Charlie asked, and winked at Patrick.

Ridge snorted. "Only if it's a Mer-caaa-deees," he drawled.

"Or a Rooooooolllllllssss Rooooyce," Rudy said, mimicking Ridge's accent. The men laughed, and Rudy noticed Charlie was laughing the hardest. Rudy felt relief wash over him – bygones were bygones, after all.

Chris glanced at his watch. "Gee, Gary. I don't have to be back until ten or eleven tonight..."

"I could just camp out on that little beach at sixteen," Patrick joked. "Wait for Rudy's mermaid."

Percy scratched his ear, then smiled up at Vandeweghe. "Sixteen?" he said, "You'd drown at high tide. I suggest we go scout the course for a better place than that."

"You game, Percy?" Vandeweghe asked. "I know you were planning on driving back to Los Angeles tonight."

Percy flicked his hand dismissively. "Tonight. Tomorrow. Whenever. This is more fun. After all, I don't often get a chance to play with a pack."

Chris and Patrick laughed. "A pack!" Chris said. "That's one way to put it."

"Penny called us a herd," Don said.

"Makes more sense, since we're stomping around on grass," Rudy said. He had a vision of buffalo running down the fairway at San Jose. "We're just not as destructive."

Vandeweghe snorted. "I don't know about that. Any one of you tears up a course pretty good sometimes." He stood and motioned for them to remain seated. "Let me go set up a second round. You guys meet me out at the first tee in fifteen." He strode away.

Ridge rubbed his hands together. "Ah yes! A chance at that hole in one!"

Plato raised his glass toward Don. "And a chance for you to find out just how special those birdies were on fifteen and sixteen."

Don grinned and hummed, and Rudy caught a special twinkle in his friend's eye. There was something in the air that suggested Don might make Plato eat those words.

After shedding their jackets and ties for newly purchased golf shirts, Rudy and the others gathered in the usual manner, milling about the first tee, ribbing each other. They agreed to mix the groups a bit for the second round, with Patrick again tagging along. Rudy watched as Percy took Chris, Plato, and Ridge off the first tee with style, each man having a spectacular drive.

To his utmost pleasure, Rudy discovered the course played better in the afternoon. The sun had baked the greens to a firmness that made putting more of a challenge, and the cold wind off the ocean was a welcome balance to the strength of the sun on his face. He also enjoyed being able to actually see the first few holes.

"So that's what this fairway looks like!" he said as he stood on the second tee and looked down at the dogleg left, a small valley of gorse gleaming in the sun. "Now I know where to aim."

"Not that it will help you much," Patrick said, receiving a round of laughter as reward.

When they arrived at the eleventh tee, Vandeweghe nodded toward the small hut that housed the restrooms. "Gentlemen, in the afternoon there are usually freshly baked cookies and some fruit down there, if you want some sugar."

Don's face lit up. "Cookies? Did you say cookies? Come on, Patrick, let's go see."

Rudy took his driver from his caddy. "Gooch, you may have found a way to successfully knock ol' Winner-halter off his game."

"You wish!" Don called over his shoulder as he hiked off toward the hut, with Patrick at his side.

"Bring me one!" Charlie hollered.

Rudy leaned on his club and waited to drive. Several minutes went by, then Don and Patrick trotted back to the tee, cookies in hand, and passed them around. Don was chuckling.

"Didn't take long for that sugar to hit you, did it Don?" Rudy said.

Don's eyes twinkled. "It's not the cookie." He motioned to Vandeweghe. "Who put up the artwork?"

Vandeweghe laughed. "It's been there for years. Pretty good, huh?"

Rudy looked from Don to Vandeweghe. "Artwork?"

Don waved his cookie toward the hut. "Go see for yourself. And bring back another chocolate chip, will ya?"

Rudy grunted. "Anything to get you high on sugar and give you a few putting yips."

He crossed to the men's room, entered, and was struck by the clean elegance of the place. Not a speck of dirt or a spider web to be seen on the tiled floor and walls. Heck, it was nicer than most bathrooms at five star restaurants. Then he saw it – hanging over the urinal was a framed black and white, hand drawn original cartoon of a buck standing on his hind legs, using a urinal, below which as written, "The Eleventh Tee At Last." Rudy grinned and shook his head. This was Cypress, after all. He grabbed the door handle, then changed his mind. Might as well make use of the facility. It was a long way back to the clubhouse.

On the twelfth tee, Tom, one of the caddies, leaned close to Rudy and pointed into the distance. "Okay," he said, "you want to thread the needle between that big tall tree on the right, and the left chimney of that white house with the two chimneys."

Charlie stepped up beside them. "Can I aim between the right chimney of the white house and the third bushy tree to the right of the cart path that's to the left of the house?"

Patrick joined them and scratched his chin. "Or maybe aim for the left tree of that row of pompom trees just to the right of the bushy tree to the right of the last chimney on the white house with the two chimneys?"

Rudy pursed his lips together hard, but the laughter shook his whole body. Tom paused, a look of concern on his face, then he burst into laughter. Charlie was quick to join, but Patrick looked pointedly from man to man.

"What?" he asked, raising his hands and shrugging. "It seems like a good line to me!"

"Okay, okay," Rudy said, trying hard to regain control. "The man's trying to help you poor sots, and you're giving him a hard time."

The rest of the group walked up to the tee. Hands on his hips, Tom stared down the fairway, turned to Patrick and, with the utmost sincerity, said, "If you were playing, really, I'd say you need to aim for the small rectangular window that's just to the right of the four narrow windows beneath the right chimney of the white house with the red roof and the two chimneys, but don't go as far as the cypress tree that leans out to the right away from the house, and make sure you stay well left of those other pine trees and definitely right of the cart path." He beamed, eyebrows raised as if asking, "do you understand?"

Vandeweghe glared at the caddy. "You want to repeat that?"

The whole group burst into laughter, including Tom and the other caddies. Vandeweghe's brow creased, then he tossed his head back. "Oooh! I get it, I get it." He laughed along. "Well! It sounded like a good line!"

Finally, things settled down enough for Charlie to drive. The ball sailed slightly right, over the natural sand dune that forced the fairway into a hard dogleg right.

"Jeez, Charlie, what did they put in those cookies?" Rudy asked.

Charlie turned to Tom. "Do you think it cleared the sand?"

"Well, it was heading for the fourth pine tree," Tom said with a grin, "so I think you're okay."

Rudy again leaned on his club. "You don't even know your own strength, there, Charlie."

"You put it right where Hogan would have," Vandeweghe said, preparing to drive. "You know, this was Hogan's favorite par four hole, on any course."

Whack.

His ball hooked and disappeared into a section of sea grass. He shook his head and waggled his club. "I think he liked this hole because it was torturous to the rest of us."

Charlie slid between Rudy and Don, and whispered, "I didn't think I hit it right. I didn't think I had a clue on how to get it there."

Don hummed. "That's a horrible feeling, isn't it? To have no clue."

Charlie chuckled. "That feeling of desperation. Of wanting to walk back to the clubhouse."

"Yeah," Don said, "a feeling that you want to say 'get out of the way, I'm going in and get a turkey sandwich'."

Rudy stepped forward and teed up his ball. "Well, let's hope I'm not looking for a turkey sandwich after this." Five seconds later, he watched his ball disappear into a bunker.

"How about liverwurst?" Don asked, and Rudy left the tee once again enjoying a good laugh with his friends.

When they turned back toward the ocean, the placement of the sun in the sky made the water glisten like a mirror ball. By virtue of Chris's errant drive on thirteen, which caused a lengthy search and rescue, both foursomes, with Patrick in tow, again clustered together on the fourteenth tee. They all looked down the fairway toward the open expanse of the Pacific. It was quite a sight.

"Oh!" Patrick pounced on Charlie's bag, almost knocking over the caddy. "Another photo op!" He waved toward the front of the green. "Okay, gentlemen, over there. Here's your chance to prove you have memories."

Rudy waggled a finger at Patrick. "You couldn't figure out by the way we played the first thirteen holes that our memories are failing?"

"Speak for yourself," Ridge said, then looked left and right. He nudged Chris in the ribs. "Weren't you over there by Plato?"

Chris nudged him back. "Nope, but you were."

Percy held out his hand. "Pat, give me the camera. This is your photo." The group shouldered each other into place. "Say cheese!" Percy said.

A chorus of "beer!" and "steak!" and "coffee!" followed. No one said cheese, but Rudy knew they had somehow managed to smile at the appropriate time.

Percy handed the camera back to Patrick. "That was a beauty. One for the album."

"Too bad this place isn't more photogenic," Charlie said, a crooked smile on his face. "Almost a shame to waste the film."

Percy turned to Plato. "Sir, I think you're up." Within minutes, the first foursome of Percy, Plato, Chris, and Ridge was down the fairway, but Rudy was still enjoying the view too much to notice.

Somehow he played the hole in par, then stood on the fifteenth tee and watched as Don took a few practice swings. The wind had really picked up, and they'd all clubbed up in an effort to combat it. The chance of a par was slim, and Rudy thought a birdie was highly unlikely. Still, there was something in that look on Don's face...

Don addressed the ball. He waggled the club once, pursed his lips, then leaned into his left side just a bit before pulling his club back. The sound of the club face hitting the ball was drowned out by the wind and the crash of the ocean on the rocks, and Rudy glanced at the ground, just to make sure there wasn't a ball still sitting on a tee. He looked up. The ball seemed destined to sail out into the water. Then it curved and plummeted to the green, landing on the back. Rudy exhaled. He hadn't realized he was holding his breath.

"Go, ball, go go go!" Vandeweghe yelled. They all stood, unmoving, as the ball began to roll toward the flag, picking up speed as it went.

"It's going in!" Charlie said.

Then as one, the group moaned as the ball suddenly stopped, just short of the hole.

The rest of the guys hit their tee shots, but none were as successful as Don. "Mark it down," Vandeweghe said with a huge grin. "Only one guy on the green."

When they walked onto the putting surface, they instantly discovered the reason Don had been denied a momentous hole-in-one.

"Oh, man, what a bum break!" Patrick said, staring down at an unrepaired divot into which the ball had settled. "You got ripped-off, Don."

"Call the greens police," Charlie said. "File a complaint. Someone should be arrested."

Don marked his ball and fixed the divot. His face was stern, emotionless. Rudy couldn't decide if he was fighting the urge to curse, or the urge to cry. Heck, either one would have been appropriate. What a way to be denied a place in the history books. Still, it was an easy birdie, and moments later, when Don rammed the ball home, everyone congratulated him.

"Two in one day," Rudy rested his hand lightly on Don's shoulder. "That's extraordinary!"

"Not a bad way to leave this hole," Vandeweghe said, shaking Don's hand, "I haven't heard of many who have birdied fifteen once, let alone twice." Don gave him a little smile. "Still," Vandeweghe continued, "bum rap on the divot. I'll have to do some gentle reminding of a player's responsibilities when I get back to the clubhouse."

Don shrugged. "There are many dimensions to this game, other than just hitting the ball."

"Amen to that," Charlie said, joining the group which had now congregated around the sixteenth tee. "So how about getting that hole-in-one on this hole? Eh, Winner-halter?"

"You are some dreamer, Charlie," Vandeweghe said. "But I believe in dreams, so Don, let'er rip!"

Don swung. The ball played over the ocean, then claimed the green, took a heavy bounce and rolled to a stop. "So much for the hole-in-one," Don said. "But I'll take that putt for birdie."

Vandeweghe laughed. "Oh, how he plays a game with which I am not familiar! Nice shot, Don."

Charlie stepped up to the tee and sized up the wind.

"This hole is gonna punish you," Patrick mumbled.

Charlie turned to Patrick and grimaced. "Now I don't suppose you could be just a bit more positive, could you?"

Patrick chuckled. "Just giving that ball of yours a heads up, that's all. 'Cause I know you're gonna do some damage getting it to that flag."

Don waved at Charlie. "Just commit and hit. Nothing ever happens if you don't commit."

"Amen," said Vandeweghe.

Charlie grinned. "I'm committed to getting through this round without taking too big a bath. Now, do you mind?"

"No, no, hit away, please," Vandeweghe said as he leaned on his club, ankles crossed.

Rudy adjusted his cap. "Well, you do kind of forget about golf out here. You look at that view and you can put it all behind you. But gee, it'd be awfully nice to get to the green and see the view from there, too."

"Just watch and enjoy this shot," Charlie said. He stood over his ball, wiggled, then swung. The ball hooked sharply and disappeared over the thin throat of grass at the entrance of the green. Charlie leaned on the driver and stared at where the ball had gone. He sighed. "It's so hard to care about this game."

Rudy stepped up to the tee. "Pro's always saying when you don't care, that's when you hit well." His ball sailed high, landed short of the green, then took a fortuitous bounce and shot off across the putting surface, finally coming to a rest on the far side, against the fringe. "Hey, I'm putting," he said with a big smile. "Just what I wished for."

Don smiled. "Yeah, you're putting. Just too bad the putt is forty feet long."

Rudy handed his club to his caddy. "Better than chopped liver!" He leaned on the crooked fence made from downed cypress branches and watched Vandeweghe drive. Poor guy managed to pick this moment to find a swing Rudy had never seen before.

"Hey, hey," Vandeweghe said as the ball disappeared over the cliff. "I'm on the beach, right where you were Rudy!"

"Well, grab a swimsuit, a blanket, a few beers and settle in," Rudy said.

"That doesn't sound bad," Vandeweghe said. "Better than what I'm doing now, with this lousy shot of mine and this bunch." He pointed at his pals and smiled.

"I can tell you all about that shot," Rudy said, as they began the hike around the cove to the green. "Maybe we should go get the pro, so he can stand in the line of your shot. I think aiming at his head brings you good luck."

"Or a jail sentence," Patrick said.

Rudy hovered behind his ball, assessing his line. Vandeweghe had opted to take a drop back up on the fairway, as the tide had risen and he would have had to risk standing in the surf to hit.

"Forgot my bathing suit," Vandeweghe had said, and climbed out of the tiny cove.

"I brought mine!" Patrick had said, then held up a golf towel. "Wanna use it?"

Vandeweghe had smirked. "Only to hang myself with if I get in any more of these predicaments."

Now Vandeweghe's ball was safely on the green, along with all the rest. Ball markers dotted the putting surface like pins on a Master's jacket lapel. The closest was Don's, and Rudy realized it was right in his line. He pointed at it with his putter. "Hey, Don, do you mind?"

"Oh, yeah, of course," Don said, and quickly moved his marker to accommodate Rudy.

"This for par," Rudy said, and firmly nudged the ball to the hole. A seal on a nearby rock barked, and was quickly joined by several other seals. The ball rolled past the hole, toward the ocean.

"Those darn seals," Charlie said as Rudy tapped in, "they just call these balls right to them, like candy."

Rudy tossed his golf ball to Tom. "They can have this one," he said. "It's not being so sweet right now." He walked up to stand between the back bunkers and watch. Most of the guys two-putted, and Rudy began to feel uneasy. Don's birdie putt wasn't a gimme, lying at least four feet from the hole, and Rudy really wanted him to get the birdie. Four birdies on two of the hardest holes in the world. That would be a story for Bev when he got home.

Don waited at the edge of the green. He leaned on his putter, ankles crossed, surveying his ball with care. Rudy noticed Don never looked up while the others were putting. Maybe the guy didn't want any false reads.

Finally it was Don's turn. With no fuss, he moved the marker to its original position, placed his ball, took one last quick look at the line, then settled in to his stance.

Rudy held his breath. He felt like he was watching the determining putt at a Major. A gust of wind slammed the green just as Don released the ball. Rudy could tell the guys were verbally coaxing it along, but from his vantage point on the back slope, with the wind in his ears, he couldn't hear the exact words. Rudy clenched his fist as the ball drew to within an inch of the hole. Then he rolled his head back and cursed. The ball had rimmed out, stopping a mere inch from the cup. Don had been denied his second birdie on Cypress Point sixteen.

Tom replaced the flag as the guys filed past Rudy on their way to the seventeenth tee.

"What a rip," Rudy said.

Vandeweghe nodded. "Just bum luck, that's all."

Rudy waited for Don, who had placed his ball back on the green and was standing over his original putt. Tom pulled the flag just as the ball sprung off Don's putter. The ball toppled into the cup, and stayed.

Rudy sighed. Golf was like any sport – it demanded skill, perseverance, and occasionally, the kiss of lady luck. Too bad she was often out having tea just when she was most needed.

"Good par," Rudy said as Don joined him.

Don nodded. "Yep, it was. A good par."

For whatever reason, sixteen seemed to take some of the punch out of the group, and the last two holes were played quickly, rather quietly, and without incident. When they arrived back at the men's locker room, Rudy glanced at his watch. It was nearly six, and they still had a long drive home.

Vandeweghe strode in, his Cypress Point member tie swinging beneath his jacket. He smiled. "Okay! Everybody back into their formal duds. Drinks and snacks on the verandah, then we all head home. Good for everybody?"

A round of "excellent!" and "sounds good to me" and "perfect" resounded in answer.

"Good, then," Vandeweghe said. "Just leave the rest of your stuff in here and we'll collect it before we leave."

Knotting his tie, Rudy joined Vandeweghe as they crossed to the clubhouse. "Hey, Gary," he said, "thanks for all this. Really. It's been fantastic."

Vandeweghe shrugged and smiled. "All for my buddies. After all, what good is having a place like this if you can't share it?"

Rudy nodded. Gooch was right, but it took a generous man to want to share a place like Cypress Point.

As he stepped out onto the verandah – a soda in hand, the view of the Pacific below radiant in the sunset – Rudy felt blessed beyond belief. Not just about being here, though that was certainly tremendous, but again about having such great friends.

"Hey, Rudy, ya gonna share that view?" Ridge said as he bounced out onto the verandah, followed by the rest of the men.

Rudy raised his soda in salute. "That's what we do best, eh?" he said. And meant it. Yes, this was all exceptional, but without these guys to share it with, the glow would be far less.

Far less, indeed.

CHAPTER 6

August, 1985
Don Ridge

Don Ridge adjusted his golf cap and squinted. The sun was low and the clouds forewarned a rare, late afternoon thunderstorm. A stiff wind had been blowing into their faces since sixteen. How fitting. Even the weather was threatening to ruin his game. And this on a day when he needed his game to be at its best. This was, after all, the San Jose Country Club Championship – a once-a-year chance to prove himself.

A particularly strong gust of wind bent the trees along the fairway. Ridge ducked, grabbing the bill of his cap just in time to keep it from sailing into the next county.

Across the fairway, Chris stood near his ball, surveying his shot. Beyond him stood the guys from the Saturday group, surrounded by dozens of other members from the club. He hit. The wind suddenly died. From deep in the ravine, the trees reached for the ball, but it avoided their clutches and disappeared from sight onto the fairway beyond.

Ridge sighed. His ball looked tiny, laying in the divot which some rat had forgotten to fill during the last three days of the Championship's match play. "I just can't get a break here," he mumbled. He knew he shouldn't take it personally, but he did.

He aimed and swung. The club face rammed through the edge of the divot but twisted just enough to send the ball sliding to the left. A strong gust of wind bent the trees after it.

"Ah, get outta there!" Ridge yelled.

The sound of ripping leaves and branches was immediately followed by a loud clap of thunder.

"Blast!" Ridge said and glared up at the sky. "It isn't funny, so you can stop laughing."

"Nobody's laughing, Ridge," Charlie said, joining him.

"Ah, I'm not talking to you guys," Ridge said. They began walking up the fairway. "I just really wanted this match, and that blasted wind isn't helping."

"Neither did that lie," Patrick added, sliding up beside them.

Ridge glanced behind. The Saturday guys followed closely, leading the main crowd. Ahead, Chris was crossing the bridge to the far side of the ravine. Ridge had no doubt Chris's ball was near, if not on, the green. "Rats," he grumbled. He was going to be out of the championship match tomorrow. He'd place a lousy third this year. Again.

"Tough luck, that lie on the top of eighteen," Chris said, shaking Ridge's hand.

"Yeah, well, that wasn't the only problem," Ridge said. "You played real good, Chris. Even without the lie, you would have won." They vacated the eighteenth green, surrounded by club members all heading the same direction – to the clubhouse.

"Thanks, Ridge," Chris said.

"You're playing Vandeweghe, right?" Ridge said, hefting his clubs onto his shoulder. Chris nodded. "Well, just get him thinking about women and he'll buckle at the first tee."

Chris chuckled. "I beat him in 'eighty, remember? And I don't think the subject of girls ever came up."

"Oh, that's right, you did beat him back then," Ridge said, nodding. He opened the door to the men's locker room and motioned for Chris to go ahead. "Well, then, he'll be gunning for this win."

Chris unlaced his golf shoes and slipped into his loafers. "He won the next year, in eighty-one. He came back from two down to beat Rudy."

Ridge shook his head. "How do you remember these things? I can't remember who won last year."

"Dave Larsen," Chris said, grinning. They entered the grill room. "Memory is one of the advantages of youth."

Ridge grunted. "That, and a swing that looks like a darn windmill."

The grill room was packed. Ridge paused and searched the room. "There they are," Chris said, and pointed toward the lower section of the room, where the tables were crowded with both men and women.

Congratulations to Chris and "better luck next time" comments to Ridge were passed around the table. Vandeweghe handed Chris a glass of chardonnay.

"So it's you and me tomorrow," Vandeweghe said, clinking their glasses together. "A final match repeat. Bring your 'A' game to the ballpark. I want to have some fun."

"My money's on one of you guys to win," Don said, smiling. "Nobody else seems to be able to get the job done this year."

"That's not much of a bet," someone called from across the room. "My money's on Clark. Any takers?"

Ridge wasn't surprised when he discovered who had made the comment. "You'd better pay up on your other bets, before you go laying down good money on another," he said, loud enough for the entire room to hear.

Plato kept his eyes down as he said, "He still owes P.Q. for the match on July fourth."

"The man lacks integrity," Don said, and took a large bite from his hamburger.

"On and off the course," Plato said. "He keeps up this kind of behavior, and the Board'll move to have his membership revoked."

"And good riddance, I say." Ridge raised his glass, saluting both Vandeweghe and Chris. "Here's to both of you," he said loudly. "May the best round win."

"Not the best man?" the member called.

The room itself seemed to hold its breath. Ridge felt his face redden beneath his beard. Everyone was still.

Plato stood, his plate in hand. "If it was determined by who was the best man, I'd have to buy a hundred trophies. I don't have that big of a budget." His gaze rested firmly on the offensive club member before sweeping the room. "How's everybody enjoying the buffet? Eat up! The chef's worked hard to please you."

Ridge felt the collective exhalation, and the volume in the room rose as laughter released the tension. He took a swallow of his wine and scanned the room. There were smiling faces, lively conversation, and Plato leading a long line at the lunch buffet.

"I love that guy." Patrick nodded toward Plato. "He's just the coolest."

The offending club member stood, stretched with a loud belch, and left the room.

"And now there isn't anybody here who'd argue with you, Pat," Ridge said. "Nobody at all."

The following day arrived, bright and hot. Ridge hung back as Hank, the starter, stepped onto the first tee. At least sixty members were spread out along the box and fairway. Ridge noticed all of the Saturday group were in attendance, along with most of their wives. He smiled. Of course they'd be there.

Hank surveyed the crowd. "First up, Mr. Gary Vandeweghe," he announced, then stepped aside.

A polite applause followed Vandeweghe as he moved into place. Within seconds, his ball was winging its way down the fairway.

Hank returned. "Next up, Mr. Chris Clark."

The young man towered over his ball, swung, and neatly out drove Vandeweghe by twenty yards, but left it on the far left edge of the fairway. Ridge nodded in satisfaction. It was going to be a very keen match.

The two were tied at the sixth hole. Ridge fingered his plastic cup and blew on the foam that bubbled over the rim. He really needed to teach those guys at the bar how to pull a decent beer.

The crowd had grown to at least a hundred people. He wove through them and made his way to the Saturday group cluster, stopping next to Don. "Who do you think's gonna do it?"

Don's eyebrows went up and down, but he gave no other indication of how he felt. "No matter who wins, it couldn't happen to a nicer guy."

Vandeweghe moved onto the tee, went through his routine, and smiled mischievously as the ball sailed neatly down the center of the fairway. The crowd showed its appreciation with a round of polite applause.

Chris marched up, placed his ball, and swung.

Ridge shaded his eyes and saw the ball head directly into the eucalyptus trees on the right. "That's your shot, Chris. You wouldn't know how to play any other."

Chris grinned as the crowd laughed. "Just where I aimed it," he said, and followed Vandeweghe down off the tee.

Two holes later, they were still tied. Vandeweghe stood in the center of the fairway, surveying his choices. Chris, twenty yards ahead but off in the rough, pulled first one club, then another from his bag, then exchanged it again for the original choice. Vandeweghe continued to mumble to himself and stare down to the green.

Ridge leaned over to Patrick. "I think our friend Mr. Clark is beginning to feel the pressure."

Chris once again switched clubs.

"I'll see what I can do." Patrick slid up beside Chris and glanced at his club. "I just want to see what you got there," he said, grinning.

"Making sure I'm legal?" Chris asked, changing clubs once again.

"No, I know you're not legal," Patrick said. "I just want to see what club you decide on so I know what not to use next time I'm in this spot."

Chris chuckled, shook his head, and took a deep breath – and settled upon a club. Vandeweghe swung and produced a great shot which landed softly within a few inches of the stick. Ridge joined the other members in applause, but kept his attention upon Chris. Had Patrick's gibe relaxed him enough?

"Thanks," Chris said, throwing a sideways smile at Patrick before addressing his ball.

Patrick shrugged. "Just curious, you know."

He returned to stand beside Ridge, who gave him an appreciative wink. "Good job, P.Q. We don't want him collapsing so soon in the game."

"Or ever," Patrick said quietly.

Chris hit. "Run up. Run up!" he said. The group collectively nodded as the ball landed twenty feet from the hole, then rolled to within three feet.

Ridge walked to the green, joined by Don and Charlie.

"This could go on to sudden death if they both keep this up," Charlie said.

"That it could, Charlie," Don said. "They both want it pretty bad this year."

"This is different from any other year?" Ridge said with a chuckle.

"I think Gooch's got more riding on it, though," Don said.

"How so?" Charlie asked.

Don slowed his step. "He hasn't done as well as he'd like since eighty-one, and some of the guys were giving him a hard time about it."

"Our guys? Who?" Ridge felt himself bristle at the thought. He took a sip of his beer.

"No, no, not any of our guys from the Saturday game," Don said, waving his hand dismissively. "No, some of the high handicappers. Telling him he's washed up. Crap like that."

The crowd had reached the green and Ridge paused, surveying the members who stood, shoulder to shoulder, surrounding the two players.

"That's a load of bull," Charlie said quietly. He eyed the group of members ahead, and Ridge knew he was trying to guess which had the nerve to say such a thing.

"Leave it be, Charlie," he said. "Vandeweghe's big enough to take care of himself."

"That isn't the point," Charlie said. "It isn't right, and if I find out who said it –"

"You'll what?" Ridge said. "Kick 'em in the knee? Let it be. It'll sort itself out."

Don nodded. "No doubt with this match. Chris is tough to beat. If Gooch wins, that'll silence any talk."

On the green, both men surveyed their lines, and Vandeweghe moved cautiously to avoid stepping into Chris's. "Nice shot, Chris," he said.

Chris squatted and stared at the hole. "Project Green Light."

Vandeweghe nodded and moved out of his sightline. "Drill it," he said, then rolled his eyes as Chris did just that. "That'll teach me to be more careful about what I ask for," he said as he crossed to his own ball. "Especially when you're involved."

"I won't be insulted if you make it," Chris said, and retrieved his ball from the cup. A minute later, Vandeweghe dropped his ball in for a birdie.

"Okay, three-man," Chris said, hefting his bag and nodding in appreciation, "you're on the tee."

"That makes two of us, my man," Vandeweghe said, following closely behind.

Ridge smiled as he, Don, and Charlie tailed the crowd up to the ninth tee. It was all square, but there was a lot of golf yet to be played. A lot of golf.

Ridge stood at the edge of the eighteenth green and held his breath. Vandeweghe positioned himself over his ball, fifteen feet from the pin. If he made this, it was over. The Championship would be his. Miss it, and it could get interesting, since Chris was on the fringe. No doubt Chris had been putting well today, but it was a tricky line from the fringe, and with the pressure of the Championship riding on the putt ... well, it wasn't a gimme, that's for sure.

Ridge hadn't realized, until this very moment, that he actually wanted Vandeweghe to win it. Maybe because the guy was closer to his age. Win it for the old boys. And silence anyone who questions Vandeweghe's capabilities.

Vandeweghe drew back the putter.

Tap.

Calls of "Come on, ball!" and "In the hole!" and "Turn, turn!" came from the gallery. The ball ignored the comments, rolled past the edge of the hole, and went another three feet before coming to a rest. A collective moan went up from those watching. If Vandeweghe had an emotional response, he hid it well. He stepped back.

Chris bit his lip, shook his head, then went to work. He rechecked his line, moved to the ball, and paused. Someone in the crowd sneezed, a large man by the sound of it, and Chris stepped back, rechecked, then returned to the ball. Ridge focused on Chris's hands. They weren't shaking, and they weren't gripping the club for dear life.

Ridge stuffed his own hands into his pockets.

Tap.

There was a repeat of the calls from the crowd, then a crescendo of "Oh, no!" as the ball picked up speed and, for no apparent reason, veered from the hole. It finally came to a rest a full four feet from the hole.

"Ah!" Chris wailed, leaning back. "Come on! Where did that come from?"

Ridge exhaled. So this was it. Vandeweghe once again had the advantage.

The tall man stalked his ball, circling the line like a tiger circling its prey. He settled on an attack, took his stance, and smacked the ball.

Ridge almost yelped. Too hard, too hard!

"That's going to Toledo!" someone yelled, echoing Ridge's impression, as others in the crowd voiced numerous similar sentiments.

The ball shot to the hole then disappeared inside, rattling around with a definitive clatter. Ridge called out in delight along with the other members, drowning out Vandeweghe's own triumphant yell. Across the green, Chris was staring at his putter as it forcibly tapped the ground at his feet.

Vandeweghe retrieved his ball and kissed it lightly. "Oh, baby!" he said. "Thank you!" He turned toward Chris and the crowd immediately settled to an attentive quiet. If Chris made this putt – and it was almost a sure bet he would – the two golfers would go to a sudden death playoff.

Chris squatted down and, leaning on his putter, contemplated his move. He took several deep breaths. Ridge smiled. Maybe the kid was finally feeling the pressure.

After what seemed to be an eternity, Chris stood, walked to his ball, and without hesitation, putted.

"Go, go!"

"Turn!"

"Get in there, ball!"

The ball bounced along the trajectory, hit a repaired divot, leaned left, hit a miniscule pebble, turned right, settled into a steady roll straight for the hole ... and ran out of steam one inch from the lip.

The crowed roared equal parts approval and disappointment, and Ridge laughed with relief. Vandeweghe's face broke into a huge grin. Chris stood there in his putting stance, staring at the ball, willing it to grow legs and crawl those last millimeters.

"Excellent effort, Chris!" Rudy called from the fringe.

Charlie nodded. "Any other day, kid."

With a sigh, Chris gave up. He met Vandeweghe over the cup and the two shook hands vigorously. "Great game, Gary," Chris said.

"Same to you," Vandeweghe said. "You really had me on the defensive, there."

"There's always next year," Chris said.

Satisfied, the crowd lumbered toward the clubhouse. Ridge followed Chris and Vandeweghe. When did Chris get so tall? He was now the same height as Vandeweghe, though not quite as lanky. Vandeweghe reached over and squeezed Chris's shoulder with affection, and Ridge felt a swell of pride. It was so wonderful to see camaraderie in the midst of competition.

Winterhalter slid up beside him. "Great match, huh?"

Ridge nodded. "I remember when that kid was just, oh, this high." He held his hand up to his waste.

Don's smile softened. "They grow up quick," he said, then looked away.

"Well, this'll quiet any comments about Vandeweghe," Ridge said. He looked closely at Don. "Who was it, anyway?"

Don looked confused. "Hm? Oh! The comment." He glanced down at his shoes, then squinted toward two men walking along the back of the clubhouse. He nodded toward them.

Ridge followed his gaze. An older, heavyset man walked beside a tall, pale man with dark, highly styled hair. Ridge made a face. "It isn't Larry, that's for sure."

Don shook his head. "No, no, certainly not."

Ridge grunted in disgust. "So it was –?" he nodded emphatically toward the tall man, and Don pursed his lips and nodded once.

"Come on, I need a drink," Ridge said. He headed across the green with Don by his side.

"I'm buying," Don said.

The grill room door flew open and Charlie stuck his head out. "Hey! You two!" He raised a glass above his head. "Hustle up! Vandeweghe's providing the goods!"

"We got lucky, Winner-halter!" Ridge said. "Come on, beer's getting warm."

He jogged up to the clubhouse, Don closely at his heels, humming. It was a sound that always warmed his heart, and the repugnant club member was quickly forgotten.

CHAPTER 7

July, 1990
Chris Clark

Chris steered the golf cart to the end of the ninth fairway at Spyglass Hill and pulled to a stop alongside several other carts. Rudy stood beside one. He waved.

"Just leave it there, Chris," Rudy said. "No one will bother it."

Chris nodded. He tossed his glove onto the cart seat, then joined Rudy as he walked up the steps to the wraparound porch that hugged the Founders Room.

"Did you see Ridge's drive off the fourth tee?" Chris asked as he leaned his shoe into the electronic shoe scrubber. "I swear it had a jet engine attached to it."

Rudy grinned. "Just screamed up the fairway, huh?" He nodded and traded places with Chris to knock the grass and grit from his shoes. "When he gets hold of the ball, it needs a flight pattern filed with the FAA."

Chris laughed and reached for the door handle. A small sign on the door read, "Members Only" and Chris paused.

"You're with one," Rudy said, grinning.

Chris grunted and jerked the door open. "Several, in fact," he said. "And hope to be one myself, someday."

Rudy nodded. "We'll have to work on that, Chris. I think you'd be a great addition to Spyglass." He motioned toward the back of the room. "And heck, this course might knock some sense into your game."

Chris chuckled. "Always does."

A television tucked in a corner broadcast an advertisement for Titleist balls.

"Hey Peter, is The Open on?" Rudy asked as he sauntered toward a man standing behind a small bar in the back of the open room. "I thought it wasn't supposed to start for another hour."

Peter wiped his hands on a towel. "I didn't think so either, but there it is," he said. "So what can I get you, Mr. Staedler? Mr. Clark?"

Chris smiled. He hadn't been a guest at Spyglass in six months and yet the man remembered his name. "You still have those fabulous hamburgers, Peter?" he asked, then popped a few pretzels from a glass on the bar into his mouth. The salt tasted good.

"You bet," Peter said, nodding. "Medium rare?"

"Perfect," Chris said. "With cheddar, if you have it."

Peter nodded again, then looked at Rudy with eyebrows raised.

"I'll have a turkey sandwich," Rudy said. "Easy on the mayonnaise."

Chris eyed Rudy's slender frame. "You on a diet again, Rudy?" He grinned. "I mean, you look like you gained an ounce or two over the summer."

Rudy laughed. "Naw, just don't need all the grease."

"And to drink, gentlemen?" Peter asked.

"Coke for me," Rudy said. "Chris?"

"Same," Chris said. "Only make mine a diet."

Rudy grunted. "Like you need a diet, either."

Voices at the door made them both turn. Don, Plato, Patrick, and Charlie entered, all laughing. They were immediately followed by a very animated Ridge.

"Everything was going fine," Ridge said. "Then Harry had a heart attack and died on the tenth tee. Well, that's awful! his wife said. You're not kidding, the guy says. For the whole back nine it was hit the ball, drag Harry, hit the ball, drag Harry." The four men laughed harder. From across the room, Chris found himself chuckling in response.

"Hey, Ridge," Chris said, "You find more jokes? I thought we wore you out at the club last week."

Ridge stroked his newly grown beard. "Naw. There's no such thing as running out of jokes. Life just wouldn't be worth living."

"Guys," Don called over his shoulder as he stood before the television. "Stewart is only two behind Faldo."

Chris joined the others at the large round table astutely arranged for optimum viewing of the television. Conversation stopped as the men absorbed the scenes coming from St Andrews. Finally Rudy asked the question Chris assumed they all were thinking.

"So, has Faldo fallen, or is Payne charging?"

Peter walked up, carrying a platter of sodas, water, and iced teas. "Stewart's been charging. Baker-Finch isn't having a good day, and I think Faldo's six shots up on him now." He set down the last of the drinks. "But Stewart's on fire."

"Any eagles?" Chris asked.

Peter shook his head. "No, but he's birdied five, six, and then ten, right before you walked in. Faldo's just trying to keep his head above water."

"Yeah, well, did you see the eagle he made on eighteen on day one?" Don said.

The door flew open and Vandeweghe exploded into the room. "Oh, man, Faldo's eagle? That was tremendous!"

Chris chuckled. The man never entered a room, he possessed it. Chris loved the fact that he did so without meaning to – his charisma was natural, guileless, and infectious.

"Hey! Mister Van-de-waaay!" Ridge drawled, a big smile on his face. "Did you come to see your new club on 'the tele'?"

Vandeweghe shook hands all around. "No, no, I bugged out of a boring meeting and just drove down. We got a notice there had been a small brush fire in the forest behind the Pebble Beach house and I wanted to make sure we didn't have any damage." He dismissed the inquiries of concern with a wave, then slid into a chair and kicked his long legs out, ankles crossed. "I knew you guys would be coming in right about now and thought I'd hop over and see how it's going."

Chris set down his nearly empty soda. "So about this eagle. What happened?"

Vandeweghe leaned forward on the table. "Faldo lands his drive just short of the Valley of Sin, then grabs what looked like a wedge and hits this fancy little chip 'n run right across it, through this double break, and bam! Right into the hole." Vandeweghe threw his hands in the air and sat back in the chair. "It was just beautiful. The crowd went wild!" A crooked grin creased his face. "Which is saying something, since they're Brits. You know, stiff upper lip and all."

"It's going to get stiffer when they see you're now a member of the ol' Royal 'n Ancient," Charlie said with a twinkle in his eye. "Congratulations, by the way."

Chris joined as beverages were raised in unison and the men voiced various toasts. "Yeah, yeah, thanks," Vandeweghe said, and looked genuinely embarrassed. "I get to go over for the induction ceremony next month. Really exciting. Barb's excited, too."

"Formal ceremony?" Plato asked.

Vandeweghe nodded. "From what I understand, yes it is. I don't mind, just so long as I don't have to make a big speech or something."

"They don't want to hear what you have to say," Charlie again teased. "You're a Yank."

On the television, a lengthy pan of the twelfth fairway at St Andrews' Old Course silenced the group. For several minutes, they sipped their drinks and gave full attention to the battle for the Claret Jug, as the broadcast shifted from Nick Faldo to Payne Stewart, with intermediate shots of other contenders as filler.

When Payne drove into a center bunker on thirteen, Chris joined the men in a communal moan.

"That doesn't look good," Charlie said.

"Those bunkers are called The Coffins," Vandeweghe said. "They're aptly named."

"Nothing like landing in a coffin to commence your demise," Patrick added.

"Now, now," Ridge said. "Give the guy a chance. You watch –"

"What was that?" Rudy interrupted as Stewart's sand wedge failed him, leaving his ball begging for a bogey, if not a double.

"That was the first nail in the coffin," Don said, which garnered a chuckle from the men around the table.

Chris figured any one of those bunkers could bring the grim reaper to your game.

Their hope for an American win dwindled as Payne Stewart struggled, barely eking out the bogey to slip to three behind Nick Faldo. "Meanwhile," the broadcast commentator whispered, "Faldo continues to churn out par after par. Nothing fancy, but certainly safe."

Peter arrived with food in hand, and though the men charged into their lunch, their attention was clearly on the tournament.

"All good?" Peter asked. "Anyone need anything else?"

Chris nodded first "yes" then "no" as a mixture of mustard, ketchup, and grease ran down his chin. "Is fabulous," he mumbled through his napkin. He really liked the Founders Room here at Spyglass Hill. Simple building; simple decor; simple food. All designed to make the members feel comfortable.

"Where's Jacobsen?" Rudy asked. As if on cue, the broadcast jumped to Peter Jacobsen, standing knee-deep in the rough. "Oh, man. Sorry I asked."

"Bananas, look at that stuff!" Ridge said. "How do you get outta that?"

"Ah, yes," Vandeweghe said, "the Road Hole, number seventeen. Wicked. The first time I played there I hit the road and the ball bounced about thirty yards away from the fairway. Never did find it."

They watched as Jacobsen whacked away at the tall grass, his ball barely moving ten yards before dropping back into the rough. Hamburger in hand and eating forgotten, Chris watched, mesmerized. He'd seen photos of the Old Course, but watching the rough punish Jacobsen made his toes curl. This was golf as he'd never played it.

"I have to go there someday," he said quietly.

Jacobsen hammered the ball and, again, it hopped ten yards and dropped straight back into the junk.

"Y' think?" Patrick said, grinning.

Charlie pushed back from the table and patted the crumbs from his face. "He wants to drive the lawn mowers."

Chris laughed. "No, no. But look at the place. It's where it all started."

"And where it's all ending for Jacobsen," Don said, nodding toward the television.

Chris chewed on the remainder of his hamburger as Jacobsen took another swing at the ball, finally knocking it into the fairway. "What a hole. It just demands you be right off the tee."

Ridge laughed. "It demands you be right everywhere, not just off the tee. You'd have one heck-of-a time."

"You got that right," Vandeweghe said. "It's a much more difficult course than it first appears."

Chris nodded, eyes glued to the screen as the picture shifted back to Faldo, swinging from the fairway, humps of scruffy rough behind him. The terrain intrigued him. He pushed his empty plate aside.

"I'm serious," he said, glancing around the table. "Don't you think about playing that?" He nodded toward the television, where Craig Parry sailed a shot from deep inside one bunker to deep inside another, a measly ten yards away. Chris shrugged as the guys chuckled. "Okay," he said, "maybe not *that*, but *there*, anyway. Where it all began."

Vandeweghe nodded. "Well, yeah, it is the birthplace of the game. What golfer doesn't want to play there?"

Don's lips were pursed, his eyes bright. "I've thought about it since I knew it existed, about forty years ago."

"Me, too," Rudy said. "I even planned a trip once, but had to cancel it when one of our projects went south." He paused to watch Stewart miss a birdie putt. "I figure one of these days I'll get there."

"One of these days, we'll all get there," Vandeweghe said. "It'll happen."

Rudy looked at Plato. "What about you, Pro? Ever play there?"

Plato nodded. "Many years ago." He pointed at the television. The picture showed a ball sliding to a stop, maybe nine feet from the pin. "Will you look at that? Faldo's managed to slip a six-iron to give himself a chance at birdie on fifteen. That's some shot, there."

The conversation lagged as they watched Nick Faldo secure his place in history, the putt disappearing into the hole with a flourish, giving him a five stroke lead. Chris sighed. His career in the insurance industry was going well, and he had no reason to complain, but every now and then he wished he had stood just a little longer by his childhood dreams of becoming a touring pro.

He glanced at Plato and found the pro staring at him with a small, warm smile.

"You made the right decision, Chris," Plato said. "It isn't all about playing courses like St Andrews."

Chris shook his head. "You're just uncanny, sometimes," he said. "Scary uncanny."

Rudy pushed off from the table and stood. "Hey! Are we going to sit here all day, watching these guys? There's nine more holes of golf out there..." He nodded at the view through the large, bay windows. "And I, for one, don't feel like wasting 'em."

"Here, here," Don said.

Vandeweghe stood. "Okay, you guys go tear it up. I'll head back to the house and keep an eye on this." He nodded toward the television. "When you're done here, come on over and we'll throw some steaks on the barbecue."

"You have enough?" Plato asked. "Need us to pick up anything?"

Vandeweghe waved dismissively. "Barb stuffed the freezer last time she was down. There's more food than we'd eat in a month."

As the guys filed out, Chris lagged behind, watching the television coverage of The Open. Plato was right, he knew, and maybe it wasn't the tournaments he missed, though he still enjoyed the competitive nature of playing with the Saturday group. As Jacobsen walked down the tough, brown seventeenth fairway at the Old Course, Chris knew it was that he yearned for: the challenge of a course ungroomed, unparalleled, unmatched by any other.

He drained the last of his soda and waved at Peter. "Thanks, Peter. Greatest hamburger in town, once again."

"You're welcome," Peter said. "See you again, soon, I'm sure."

Chris nodded. He was sure of it, too.

CHAPTER 8

April, 1992

Gary Plato

Plato hung up the telephone and sighed. He wasn't prone to worry, especially about any of the guys here at San Jose C.C., but this conversation had him deeply troubled. He looked at Hank, the starter, who was fretting over tomorrow's tee time sheet, and made a decision.

"I'm going to go hit some balls," he said. "Cover the shop, will you Hank?"

Hank nodded and waved, but didn't look up.

Plato grabbed his clubs from the bag room and marched out to a cart, then decided against it. He could use the exercise. Work off some of this concern.

The driving range was across the big parking lot, and Plato waved at a few members who were coming or going. He was glad he was not compelled to speak with any of them.

He chose a spot at the far end of the range and dumped a bucket of balls onto the grass. Instinctively, he grabbed a short iron, then leaned it against the rack and yanked his driver from the bag. He wanted to take a full swing, to hammer at the ball.

The first two went wild, one slicing into the netting that protected the fourth fairway from just these kinds of shots, and the other hooking into the trees. He squinted, pursed his lips, and teed up a third. This time he forced his focus onto the ball, and it sailed straight. For the next half hour he enjoyed the rhythmic release of tee, focus, hit, tee, focus, hit. Only once did he alter, to exchange his driver for a three iron.

Finally he was out of balls. He glanced down the line and noticed there were several partially filled buckets. He went to retrieve them.

"Hey, Pro."

Plato turned. Rudy and Ridge were sitting in a cart.

Plato waved, but continued to collect balls. Once he had two full big buckets, he started back toward his bag. Rudy drove the cart ahead of him, then both he and Ridge walked up to the range. Plato made a sound of resignation. They were not going to go away.

"We just came from the pro shop," Rudy said, his hands stuffed into his pants pockets. "Hank said you were down here."

Plato nodded and dumped the balls on the ground. "Yeah." He really didn't feel like chatting. He pulled his seven iron from the bag.

"You talk to Penny?" Ridge asked. He had his arms crossed over his considerable chest, and from behind his glasses he looked serious. Plato felt his resolve melt. Ridge didn't often look serious.

"Yes, I spoke with her about an hour ago," Plato said. He leaned on his iron. "It doesn't sound good. Don's still bedridden, can't even sit up. I guess he's lost a lot of weight, since he can't keep anything down."

"Have they finally determined what the problem is?" Rudy asked.

Plato shrugged. "I guess they've decided it's a virus he picked up while they were in the Bahamas. They think it's eating at the coating around the nerves in his brain. It may take up to six months for him to recover." Plato scratched at the head of his club. He didn't add the "if ever" he'd heard Penny whisper.

Both Ridge and Rudy made a face of disgust, and Plato felt a small smile play on his lips. "Yeah, that's pretty much how I reacted. Sounds horrifying. Like something from *Twilight Zone*."

"Six months?! Well, what can they do for it?" Ridge said. "Anything?"

"Probably not, if it's a virus," Rudy said.

"That's exactly what Penny said," Plato said. "It's a waiting game. Don's immune system has to fight it off on its own, though they've given him anti-nausea pills. I guess he's so dizzy he can't stop throwing up."

Ridge tugged his beard. "Don – dizzy. Now there's a new one."

Another golf cart zipped across the parking lot and came to an abrupt stop beside Rudy's. Chris and Vandeweghe leaned out and waved.

"Hey!" Chris called. "You guys got a convention going?"

Rudy beckoned them up to the range. "Pro talked to Penny."

Chris and Vandeweghe joined them. "So what's the news?" Vandeweghe asked. "Is he on his feet yet?"

"No, and it looks like he won't be for a while," Plato said.

There was a short silence, as the small group absorbed the implications of the news. Don had been ill for almost two months now. It seemed impossible, given the man. Don rarely caught a cold, let alone a major illness. Plato felt oddly vulnerable.

"Anything we can do?" Chris said.

Plato shrugged. "I don't know that there's anything any of us can do."

"I know what we can do," Ridge said. He stood solid, his stance wide, his shoulders back, arms firmly crossed. He looked sure of himself, full of resolve. "We can pray," he said with a nod. "That's a good man, there. We just need to remind the ol' guy upstairs, and he'll get to working on it. You watch."

"From your lips to God's ears," Rudy said.

Plato felt his spirit rise a bit. If God was going to listen to anyone, he was sure it would be Don Ridge.

The ringing of the phone shattered the late afternoon silence in the pro shop. Plato paused, waiting to see if his assistant picked it up. On the third ring, he snagged the phone from the cradle.

"San Jose Country Club, Gary Plato speaking," he said in his professional tone.

"Gary, it's Penny."

Plato felt his pulse jump. It had been over five weeks since he'd last spoken with her, and even longer since he'd seen her. Caring for Don had kept her at home. With a concerted effort at hiding his concern he said, "Penny, how's Don doing?"

"Well, that's what I'm calling about," Penny said, and Plato was relieved to hear a renewed brightness in her voice. "He's sitting up and had his first solid meal in I-don't-know-how-long." She laughed lightly. "Best of all, he's cranky."

Plato chuckled. "Always a good sign. Gosh, I'm really glad to hear this. We've been worried over here. All of us."

Plato could almost hear Penny nod her head. "I know," she said. "That's why I wanted to call and give you the update. Also, I have a favor to ask."

Plato sat back in his chair. "It's a yes, whatever you need."

"Well, this may be difficult, only because of the timing," she said. "Don was asking about the Masters tournament. I didn't bother to record it, since my mind was elsewhere. But he'd like to see it. Did anyone tape it, by chance? I know it's been several weeks, but I thought maybe you, or someone else recorded it?"

Plato pursed his lips. "I didn't, but I'll ransack the roster to find someone who did. I'll get back to you tomorrow."

"Thank you, Gary," Penny said. "Maybe it'll keep him quiet for an afternoon." She laughed again. "Gosh, I never thought I'd hear myself say that, after all the silence of the past few months."

Plato chuckled. "Different kind of silence, I know. Let me go make some phone calls."

"Thank you. I'll talk to you tomorrow."

Plato pushed the plunger down on the cradle, disconnecting the call, then immediately dialed a number. After two rings, Rudy's voice came on the line.

"Rudy, good news," Plato said, and proceeded to explain his conversation with Penny, and the request.

"Gosh, I didn't tape it either," Rudy said. "But I'll ask around and see if someone else did."

"Good. You cover Spyglass, and I'll cover San Jose," Plato said.

"Okay, I'll call you soon as I find it," Rudy said, and hung up.

Plato made the same call to both Charlie and Patrick, then Chris, Bob Cracolice, and Neil Woodruff. None of them had recorded the Masters, but all vowed to track down a copy, somewhere.

"Gooch, it's me," Plato said after Vandeweghe picked up the phone. "I'm hoping you recorded the Masters. Winterhalter's up and feeling better, and he'd like to see it."

Vandeweghe whistled. "That's good news. Always a good sign when he's talking golf. But the Masters..." He paused. "Gee, I didn't bother to tape it, since Barb and I were there. But I think I know someone who can get me a copy. Let me make a phone call. I'll get right back to you."

"Thanks," Plato said. He hung up, stretched, then glanced at his watch. Two hours had gone by since his conversation with Penny. It was getting late, and the rumble in his stomach reminded him he had personal responsibilities, too. He crossed to the clubhouse and ordered dinner. Lynea was out with 'the girls' this evening, so he had no reason to head home early.

When he returned to his office, the message light on his answering machine was unlit. He stared at it, willing it to blink. With a silent curse, he pulled the phone close and began thumbing his way through the club roster. Another two hours passed, during which he made twenty phone calls. None of them proved fruitful.

The phone rang and Plato snatched the handpiece. "Yes?"

"My, my, we're casual tonight," Lynea teased. "You finally relaxing the rules around there?"

Plato scrubbed his face with his hand. "Sorry, honey, I was just expecting a call from one of the guys," he said, then filled her in on the news and the search.

"Well, come on home," Lynea said. "It's past nine and you shouldn't be calling people this late. You can find it tomorrow."

"You're right," Plato said warmly. His wife held to a specific code of social conduct, and it suited him perfectly. She was the quintessential pro's wife. "I'll lock up and be right home."

"See you then," she said. "Oh, and I'm baking peanut butter cookies, so don't stop for ice cream."

Plato licked his lips. "Excellent. See you soon." Within minutes he was in his car, the problem of the videotape set aside for the moment.

At seven in the morning, sharp, Plato placed his teacup in the sink and snagged his keys from the kitchen hook.

"Honey, I'm heading out now!" he hollered down the hall. "See you tonight!" Her muffled response came from deep within the bedroom.

He had the car halfway down the drive when he heard Lynea yell his name. He stopped.

"Phone!" Lynea said, waving him back. "It's Vandeweghe!"

Plato pulled back in the garage and trotted to the phone. "Gooch, good news?"

"I got it," Vandeweghe said. "I'm having it couriered over to Scooter today. He should have it by this afternoon."

Plato turned to Lynea and gave a thumbs-up. "That's fabulous," he said into the receiver. "Thank you so much. I'll call Penny and let her know."

"Good, good," Vandeweghe said. "Okay, gotta run. See you on Saturday."

Plato hung up, hugged Lynea, and swung her around in a circle. She laughed, and kissed him on the cheek. "I'm glad he was able to find it," she said after being returned to her feet. "Now you can focus on your job."

Plato chuckled. "Taking care of my members is the job. Especially members like Winterhalter."

"Give Penny my best," Lynea said.

Plato waved and hopped back into the car. This was one phone call he was really looking forward to making.

The sun was beginning to rest on the horizon, its rays searching out the mountain sides in an effort to prop itself up just a little bit longer. Plato stood in the pro shop, sorting through receipts. He glanced out the bay windows, toward the parking lot. A man was coming up the hill beside the first tee.

His step was slow, but included a bowlegged bounce that Plato immediately recognized.

He quickly tucked away the receipts and stepped to the door, just in time to open it for Don.

"Hey, hey!" Don said, then hummed a very happy sound. He thrust his hand out. "Pro, you're still here? They haven't driven you away yet?"

Plato grasped the outstretched hand warmly. "Don, good to see you. So good to see you." He knew he was smiling as much from joy at seeing his friend, as to dissolve the sudden lump in his throat. He hadn't realized the depth of his concern until this moment.

Don nodded. "Good to be seen. I was beginning to wonder there, for a while." He leaned lightly on the counter and picked a white tee out of a box.

"Tough go, huh?" Plato said. Don's clothes hung on him limply, his belt tightened at least two notches.

Don rolled the tee between his fingers. "It felt like it could have gone either way," he said. "They told Penny I was in no danger of dying from the virus itself, but it sure didn't feel that way." His face grew grim. "I'm not proud to say, there were days I certainly wished I would die."

Plato nodded, then smiled. "Not your time yet. You still have to win a Club Championship!"

"Oh, don't remind me!" Don laughed. It was sound Plato was deeply relieved to hear. He'd missed that robust laugh over the past four months, even though it wasn't heard often enough in the best of times. Don was more of a smiler ... and there was that hum.

"So you ready to start hitting some balls?" Plato asked.

"I think so," Don said. "Just lob a few onto the range, nothing strenuous. I just want to see if I still have a swing."

"Well, you know where the range is," Plato said. "Nothing's changed."

Don twiddled the tee between his fingers, and Plato was reminded of the first time he ever laid eyes on him. What, fifteen years ago? It seemed like yesterday.

"By the way," Don said, "I want to thank you for your part in getting me the tape of the Masters. That was really special."

Plato shrugged. "It was just a tape recording. Vandeweghe found someone who had it."

Don's eyebrows rose. "You didn't hear the story, did you?"

"Story?"

Don balanced the dimpled end of the tee on his finger. "The tape came from ABC," he said quietly.

Plato was bemused. "Well, yes, they were the broadcasting company."

"No," Don said. "It didn't come from some guy who recorded it off the television. It came from ABC studios." He gave Plato a piercing look, then continued. "Vandeweghe must have contacted someone high up, because they sent an official tape, minus ads. It was hand-delivered by a guy from the local ABC studio. Even he was impressed."

Plato nodded. Just like Vandeweghe – to solve a problem in a unique and unparalleled manner, all done silently, without desire for fanfare, approval, or laurels. The man just had class, which many said was expected, given his upbringing. Plato knew it was a personal trait, not an inherited one. Vandeweghe could have been born to shepherds in Switzerland and he'd still be a gentleman with integrity.

Don flipped the tee back into the box. "Well, enough said. I'll go see if I have anything left."

Plato held a hand up. "Wait, wait, I'll head down with you. I could use some oiling of the old joints, too."

He quickly grabbed a few clubs from his bag, locked the office, and ushered Don from the pro shop. "Ready?"

"Ready as I'll ever be," Don said. "And really, thank you for keeping tabs on me. Penny told me how often you called."

Plato shrugged. "Aw shucks, just part of the job, you know." He gave Don a crooked smile. "But let's not make a habit of it, okay?"

Don laughed. "Good idea, Gary, good idea."

CHAPTER 9

August, 1994

Don Ridge and Gary Vandeweghe

The cards in Ridge's hand felt electric. He hadn't been dealt this good of a hand in a while, and he could hardly contain his delight. He discarded a deadwood. Hank Lucente had on his best "poker face," but this was gin, and Ridge knew he was bluffing.

Carlo Caralli balanced his chair back on two legs and twirled the ice in his glass. He'd lost to Hank earlier, and was now just hanging out and being annoying.

Ridge worked hard not to smile. He rubbed his chin, squinted, and tried to make it look like he was thinking hard about his decision. Carlo grunted and tossed back the last of his drink.

"Do what you're gonna do, and get on with it," Ridge said to Hank. "There's a party upstairs with an open bar that's waiting to be visited."

Carlo waggled his empty glass. "I agree, Don. All these hands have sucked me, and my glass, dry. I'm ready to head back up to the fun." He leaned over to look at Hank's hand. "You should, as well."

Hank's scowl deepened. He glared at Carlo. "You gonna stop giving away my secrets?"

Carlo shrugged and attempted to look innocent. "I'm not saying anything!" He looked at Ridge. "Did I say anything?"

Ridge chuckled. "You don't need to open your big mouth. It's written all over your mug."

Hank slapped a card face down on the discard pile and laid out his hand. "Read it and weep."

Ridge grinned. "My eyes are dry as the desert, Hank." He laid down his cards – three perfect runs.

"Woohoo!" Carlo whooped, and tossed the ice from his glass as his hands flew up in the air.

Hank cursed with a few choice words, leaned back in his chair, and shook his head. "You are one lucky sonofabitch. There's no way my hand should have been beaten."

Ridge pointed at his cards. "There's the way!" He scooped up the money resting on the table. This was definitely his most lucrative night ever. Best to stop while he was ahead. "Come on. Your wives are probably wondering where you went." He stood. "Drinks are on me."

"That's not gonna put much of a dent in your winnings," Carlo said. "It's an open bar."

"Tomorrow, then," Ridge said, and bounded up the stairs. "I'm buying after the game tomorrow."

Hank grunted. "If we don't win it all back on the eighteenth hole."

The noise from the wedding reception being held in the dining room was alluring and joyous. Ridge paused at the entrance. He was never fond of going to parties without Nellie, but they had a pregnant mare ready to give birth at any moment, and Nellie had refused to leave her side. He appreciated his wife's dedication to her horses, but looking around at the festivity, he also knew she would have truly enjoyed this celebration. He spotted Lynea, Penny, and Barbara at a table nearest the band. Several bottles of wine were in attendance, but none of their husbands.

"Ridge!"

Don Winterhalter slapped him on the back, and yelled over the music, "Where you been? You're missing all the fun."

Ridge raised his eyebrows. "Clearly *you* haven't been missing any of it," he joked.

Don laughed, a bit too loudly. "The band is great, and the booze even better!" He steered Ridge toward the bar. "What're ya drinkin'?" He flapped a hand toward the bartender. "George, George, ol' Ridge here is missin' something."

George slapped a bar towel over his shoulder. "What'll you have, Mr. Ridge?"

"Scotch, neat." Ridge turned to Don. "Where are the others?"

Don motioned toward the eighteenth green. "Putting contest. You're needed. And don't worry about not having your putter. Plato raided the ones he had in the shop." George pushed the drink toward Ridge. Don pulled a bill from his pocket and tucked it into a tip jar on the bar. "Come on. Game's on."

Following Don, Ridge slipped out the glass doors to the patio. The air felt cool after the afternoon's blistering heat, but it was probably still seventy-five degrees. Most of the Saturday golf group stood on and around the green, illuminated only by the full moon and the blaze of lights emanating from the dining room. A golf cart was parked on the edge, and as he passed it, Ridge noticed it held two large coolers, well stocked with bottles and cans.

"Hey, hey!" Vandeweghe called, motioning for Ridge and Don to join him. "About time you joined us, Ridge. Perfect timing. We're about to start a new game." He hoisted his glass in the direction of the cart. "Go get yourself a putter, and you're in."

Ridge looked over the small assortment of putters, then caught sight of one tucked behind the others. He slid it back and forth across the grass. It felt good – nicely weighted and balanced.

"Good choice," Plato said, reaching into the cooler and retrieving a bottle of wine.

"Isn't this a Bobby Grace?" Ridge asked. "Looks like that putter Nick Price was using last week at Southern Hills."

Plato nodded. "The 'Fat Lady Swings' putter. Price putted his way to the top of the world ranking with that beauty. This one isn't exactly the same, but very similar. You'll like it."

"Just not enough to buy it," Ridge said. "If I brought home another club, Nellie would tan me. Besides, I do well enough with my Ping, thank you."

"Ridge! Plato!" Vandeweghe's voice rose above the general laughter and banter. "What are you waiting for? An engraved invitation? You're missing all the fun!"

Ridge followed Plato down to the green. Sipping his Scotch, he continued to swing the putter, getting the feel of it. He had to admit, he liked it. He wondered how it would feel against a ball. Would it feel as springy as his Ping?

"Okay, do we all have our tools?" Vandeweghe asked, and placed a bottle on the green, twenty feet from the hole. "Here's our starting point, and our prize."

Ridge squinted. "What's in the bottle?"

Rudy swiggled his hips and slid across the green in a slick dance move. He sang a few notes of an instrumental song, then blurted, "Tequila!" He swiggled his hips a few more times and, with an impish smile, said, "And I like the song much better than the drink."

"Where'd you get that bottle?" Ridge asked, looking to Vandeweghe. "Nobody here drinks Tequila, you know that."

Vandeweghe's eyes twinkled with mischief. "Which is why it's here on the green. Our hosts in Mexico gave it to us when we were down there a few weeks ago, which was really nice of them, but if one of you coconuts doesn't take it home with you tonight, it's going in the trash. Neither Barb nor I like the stuff."

Charlie rolled his eyes. "Not exactly incentive to putt well."

"You can use it to make margaritas on a hot summer day," Vandeweghe said.

"Hey, Rudy!" Patrick said. "Sing that song again. What's it called? I love that song!" He pointed at Charlie. "You and Mom used to play it all the time on the back patio."

"You were supposed to be too young to notice," Charlie said, grinning from beneath his eyebrows.

"*Tequila*," Rudy said.

"No, no, not the drink," Patrick whined. "The song!"

In unison, several men called out. "*Tequila!*"

"That's the name of the song, you pup," Vandeweghe said.

"1958, by The Champs," Rudy said, then wriggled some more and sang a few more bars.

"Really?" Chris asked. "I thought it was from *Happy Days.*"

Vandeweghe placed the bottle twenty feet from the hole. "Enough, you guys. Line up your balls here and let's get playing!" He pointed at a bucket resting on the edge of the green. "Ridge, go get a range ball."

Ridge did as he was instructed. He dropped it beside the others. "Do I get a practice putt?" He shook the Bobby Grace. "I have no idea what this will feel like."

"Hell, no!" Bob Cracolice joked. "None of us got that advantage, either."

"Okay, a point for every ball that drops in the hole," Vandeweghe said. "Half a point for the closest if no one goes in. Furthest from the hole loses a point, or goes in the red. First man to twenty gets the goods." He pointed at the bottle. "And believe me, it's good, for tequila anyway."

Ridge sipped his Scotch. With those rules, they could be here all night. Sure enough, twelve men putted, and twelve balls missed the hole. Ridge underestimated the Bobby Grace, and sent his ball whizzing ten feet past the cup – by far the furthest.

Vandeweghe shook his putter at the shiny white dots on the moonlit green. "Scooter, you're closest, so half a point. Ridge, you're out, so minus a point." He moved the tequila bottle to another location on the green. "Okay, line 'em up!"

Ridge putted four more times, slowly getting the feel for the Bobby Grace but never getting close enough to win a half point, let alone drop the ball in the hole. As he watched his fourth putt slide by and come to a rest eighteen inches from the cup, he had decided the putter was not for him. Nellie would be happy.

"Hey Ridge!"

He turned toward the clubhouse. Ed Schuler stood on the balcony, gesturing.

"Come on up!" Ed called. "We got a gin game going and we need a fourth!"

To Ridge, that sounded like much more fun than putting in the dark with a strange club. "I'll be right up!"

Handing the Bobby Grace to Plato, Ridge excused himself and trotted up the stairs to the dining room. The reception was still going strong, with the bride and groom leading some sort of line dance across the floor. With a jolt of surprise, he saw several of the Saturday golfer's wives in the line, kicking and twisting in tandem. He paused at the top of the stairs. "Ed, give me a minute. I want to check in with Nellie."

The tall, elderly man smiled warmly and clapped him on the shoulder. "Of course, go ahead and do that. And give her my best. We'll be in the grill room."

Ridge stepped into the club office and dialed the phone. It was a little after ten, and he hoped the mare hadn't foaled and Nellie was in bed, sleeping.

"Hello?" Nellie's voice was strong and awake.

"Hello darlin'," Ridge drawled. "Just checking in. Do we have a new member of the family yet?"

Nellie sighed. "No. Ginger's drooping in the corner of her stall, but doesn't appear to be close to foaling. How's the reception? Is the bride beautiful?"

Ridge chuckled. "Aren't all of them? She's in white, and smiles a lot, if that means something."

Nellie yawned. "Are you having fun?"

"Oh yeah, of course I am. Food was great, bar's open, went putting with the guys on eighteen for a while. Now I'm heading down to play some gin with Ed and some strangers."

"Well don't win *all* the games," Nellie said, gentle teasing in her tone.

"I already won the vet's fee from Hank and Carlo. Now I have to go win enough to feed the new critter."

Nellie laughed. "Her mama'll do that for a while. But go have fun, and try to get home before dawn."

"Okay, I'll do that," he said, and hung up. He rubbed his hands in glee. It appeared he'd have plenty of time to win more.

The flashing lights lit up the truck's cab with grim authority. Ridge cursed under his breath, but continued to focus on the road ahead. He was struggling to keep the truck from leaning onto the gravel shoulder, and decided he'd have to check the alignment this week.

The "whoop whoop" of the sirens startled him, and he involuntarily jerked the wheel. The truck swerved heavily onto the gravel, sending rocks spitting out from beneath the tires. He yanked the wheel to the left, and the truck leapt into the oncoming lane.

"Dag nabbit!" He straightened the truck into his own lane, hitting the brakes in an effort to slow the swaying truck. He really needed to do a thorough check on the truck's steering and braking system.

The cab lit up with swirling blue and red, and the siren sounded again, much closer. Suddenly the police car sped past him, and Ridge let out a sigh of relief. He was having enough trouble controlling the truck without distractions.

Abruptly, the tail lights glowed, and Ridge found himself standing on the brakes to keep from slamming into the police car. He swerved to avoid the collision, and to his utmost frustration, the car swerved in front of him, closer now. He twisted the wheel to the right, and the truck skidded to a stop. The police car came to a stop as well, blocking the road. Ridge mopped the sweat from his brow. His hands were trembling.

The policeman walked stiffly toward the truck, his hand on his firearm at his side, a flashlight sweeping the ground, the truck, and then the cab. Ridge squinted in the glaring light. Damn that thing was bright.

"Sir, I need you to step out of the vehicle."

"What?" Ridge reached across to his glove box. "Don't you want my registration?"

The policeman reacted swiftly, blinding Ridge with the flashlight as he opened the truck door. "Get out of the truck, sir. Now," he commanded. "And keep your hands where I can see them."

Ridge shook his head and blinked. Didn't the guy want the truck's registration and insurance card? Wasn't that what they always wanted? And why was he waving around that flashlight?

"Sir, can you get out of the vehicle?"

The policeman sounded more concerned than angry, and Ridge relaxed. He slid out of the cab.

"Okay, that's a good start," the policeman said. "Now, where are you going?"

"I'm heading home from a reception," Ridge said. "I live right up the road."

The policeman smiled. "Some reception if you're just getting home at three in the morning."

Ridge shrugged. "We were playing gin, me and some of the guests."

"So you've had a few drinks?"

The policeman played the flashlight across Ridge's face, and he ducked reflexively. "Jeez, can you cut that thing?" He raised a hand to block the light. "It's awfully bright."

The policeman ignored him. "What'd you have to drink? Been smoking? Take anything?"

Ridge's head snapped back as if he'd been slapped. "What? Like drugs? Are you nuts? I only had a regular drink or two. And I don't smoke."

The policeman lowered his flashlight. He stood rooted to the pavement, solid and steady. Ridge suddenly felt very small and weak. He slumped against the truck.

"Wait here," the policeman commanded. "Don't move." He walked to his car and disappeared behind the wheel.

Ridge slid onto the truck's seat, dangling his feet out the door. His head was swimming, and he felt nauseous.

Suddenly the policeman was back. "Okay, sir. I'm going to ask you to stand up, and put your feet together."

Ridge leaned on the truck's door. He was really having difficulty steadying himself, and the nausea was getting worse. He waved his hand weakly. "I don't feel so good. I think I need to get home."

"Yeah, well, you probably should have done that a few hours ago. But now we're in this together, so step away from the truck, put your feet together, and look up at the sky. If you can do that, maybe we can let you go home."

Ridge wanted to argue, but didn't have the energy. He stepped away from the truck, placed his feet in what he thought was an acceptable stance, and tilted his head back. The motion was enough to send his stomach into a lurch. He stumbled three steps to his left, and retched. He coughed, and retched again. He waved back toward the policeman. "Kleenex. In my cab..."

A few seconds later, a wad of tissue was stuffed into his outreached hand. He wiped his mouth, then the sweat from his face. His hands were trembling terribly. Hell, he knew he shouldn't have mixed his alcohol. Now, he just wanted to lie down on his couch. Nellie would bring one of her herbal concoctions. He'd feel better by dawn. Thank heaven the policeman was here, to help him get home.

"Thanks," he mumbled. But the policeman was now standing by the police cruiser, talking into a wired microphone.

Leaning on the truck, Ridge shuffled to the seat and slumped. He closed his eyes, and the darkness spun. He leaned on the steering wheel, and the world went black.

Gary Vandeweghe woke with a start, eyes struggling to focus and senses oddly alert. He listened for whatever had awakened him, but the silence was reassuring so he closed his eyes. The phone rang again, a scream of peril in the stillness of the early morning. Barbara stirred beside him, and yanked her pillow over her head.

"You gonna get that?" she mumbled.

The phone rang once again and Vandeweghe yanked the handle from the cradle. "What?" he barked and glanced at the clock. Five-ten in the morning. Too early to have missed a tee time.

"Gary, it's Nellie. Nellie Ridge. I'm so sorry to wake you ... "

Her voice was tiny and strained, and Vandeweghe sat up, swinging his feet onto the plush rug. "It's okay, Nellie." He scrubbed his hand across his face. "What's wrong?"

"Don asked me to call you," she said. "He's ... he's at a hospital in Gilroy. They've taken him there for alcohol testing."

Vandeweghe was suddenly very awake. "A D.U.I.? Was he picked up last night?"

"Yes, well, no," Nellie said. "It was at three-something this morning. I waited to call you."

Vandeweghe sighed. "You should have called earlier, Nellie. By now he's probably at the county facility."

"The county...? Would they really take him to the jail?" Nellie sounded angry and strong, ready to do battle. "He can't be there. I mean, he's not a criminal. He's a father, a good man. And he only had a few drinks, I'm sure."

Vandeweghe wanted to reach through the phone and hug her. "Don't worry, Nellie. He's just being held, not imprisoned. We can post bail and have him out in a jiffy."

"Bail? Then, don't I need to be there with our check book?"

"Don't worry about that. I'll take care of it, if necessary. But it will be a few hours before they release him, anyway." He reached for his robe. "Get some rest, if you can, and I'll have him home as soon as I can. Probably around noon."

"Okay," she said, and the anger left her voice. "Thank you. I'll talk to you when you get here, then."

Vandeweghe hung up and sat, rubbing his face. Barbara was out from under the pillow, calmly watching him.

"So...?" Barbara asked quietly. "I gather not everything is okay."

Vandeweghe shook his head. Client-attorney privilege took effect immediately, so as much as he wanted to talk to her, he couldn't. She'd already heard more than she should, he realized. But he still wished he could send Barb over to help Nellie. He wished he could call a few of the guys from the club who had also gone through this, to help Ridge understand what was going to happen. Damn, he really wished it wasn't happening at all.

"I gotta go," he said, and padded to the bathroom to shower the cobwebs from his brain.

Ridge sat in the passenger seat of Vandeweghe's Lexus. His head was pounding, and his arm was sore from where they'd stuck a needle in it at the hospital, to draw blood for the test. Was the nurse young and in training, or did she just like to torture drunks? Supposed drunks, he corrected himself. There had to be some other reason he'd driven as erratically as they said he had.

Beside him, Vandeweghe sat relaxed, driving slowly around turns and keeping the air conditioning running at full blast and the radio silent. He also wasn't chatting, and Ridge appreciated that more than anything. He feared if he opened his mouth to speak, he'd either start screaming in anger, or crying. Neither would be dignified, and clearly he'd been undignified enough.

They pulled into the drive. At the far end of their pasture, Nellie stepped from around their gelding and waved. Ridge felt a lump choke him. Heck, it was more of a baseball.

The car came to an easy stop under a large tree. Vandeweghe turned and, with a warm smile, said, "Okay. Go get a shower and some sleep. I'll check in with you tomorrow and we'll decide how we're going to tackle this. In the meantime, I'll make some phone calls."

The baseball became a bowling ball. Ridge nodded and watched Nellie climb between the fence rails, pulling her gloves off as she went. Her hair was tumbled and her shirt untucked, both not the norm. She waved again, her smile tremulous.

"How am I going to talk to her?" Ridge whispered. He wanted Vandeweghe to spin the car around, gun it down the highway, drive as far and as fast as possible.

"Nellie?" Vandeweghe said, his voice quizzical yet kind. "Ach, she's a trooper. She'll handle this with no trouble. Your wife has a lot of grace, Don. And she loves you, that was clear last night when she called."

Much to his horror, tears welled up in Ridge's eyes. Good God, now he was going to cry on top of everything else.

Vandeweghe placed a hand on his shoulder. "You've had a rough night, my friend," he said quietly. "Go get some sleep. This too shall pass."

Like a bad round of golf, Ridge thought. Only this score was going to be a doozy, and perhaps damage his life's handicap for a long while.

Nellie yanked open the car door, and the smile on her face was angelic. "Hey! There's the man-about-town." She grabbed his hand and helped him from the car. "I thought you said you were going to be home before dawn," she joked. She leaned into the car. "Thank you, Gary. I'll take it from here."

"I have no doubt you will," Vandeweghe said. "We'll talk again soon. Get him something decent to eat. They only had a candy machine at the facility."

Ridge allowed himself to be led to the house, then paused at the door. Vandeweghe had backed the car out of the drive, and was now creeping past the house, waving. Ridge waved back, and the Lexus sped off.

"Come on," Nellie said. "You smell like a bad bar and look like you've been in a fight." She gave him a gentle nudge. "Go get in the shower, and I'll make some lunch. And don't you fall asleep in there. I can't carry you to bed."

Ridge pulled her into an embrace and again felt tears sting his eyes. How could he have let her down like this?

Nellie gently pushed his chest. "Go on. You'll be fine. Gary will make sure of that."

Ridge just nodded and headed for the shower, unbuttoning his shirt as he went. He dreaded the days to come, but he had help. That was for sure. He had a vision of Nellie standing on his left, and Vandeweghe on his right. Two formidable warriors, one armed with a frying pan and the other with a pen.

He stepped into the shower and let out a sigh as the water enveloped him. Then the tears came, and he leaned against the tile and succumbed.

Vandeweghe sat back in his office chair and tapped his knee with his pen. Four months had passed since the night Ridge had been arrested, and they'd finally reached a livable conclusion with the court. Oh, Ridge would have his license suspended for a while, but they'd managed to get an order allowing him to drive to work, and to drive the truck around town for farm errands. There were other concessions as well, and Vandeweghe felt relieved for his friend.

A knock on his door was quickly followed by the entrance of his secretary, Betsy.

She laid a folder on his desk. "Here are the papers."

He tucked them into his briefcase. "Good. Two things – draft a thank you to Judge Bruno, and include an invitation to play Cypress Point, then make the adjustments with accounting on the Ridge bill."

Betsy nodded. "Already done. Court and filing fees only. No hourly."

He nodded. She was always at least one step ahead of him. "Thank you."

"My pleasure." She stepped back and, arms folded over her chest, raised her eyebrows. "The conference call with Miller and Miller has been rescheduled for Thursday, so your calendar is now clear for the day. Don't you have some sort of follow-up meeting with Ridge, on the golf course?"

Vandeweghe chuckled. "Absolutely. Make the call for me, will you?" He yanked his jacket from its hanger. "See you tomorrow."

Half an hour later he pulled into Ridge's driveway and tapped the horn. Nellie opened the door and waved, dish towel in her hand. "He'll be right out, Gary!" she called, and disappeared.

Vandeweghe was struck by the sheer virtue of the place. The quaint house, the barns, the pastures, the big shade trees, and Nellie: ranch girl, cook, and wife extraordinaire. It was all very Norman Rockwell, in a vibrant, affectionate way.

A knock on his trunk pulled him from his reverie. He popped the latch and felt the golf bag land inside, then the trunk slam shut. Ridge slid into the passenger seat.

"Thanks for the call, Gary," Ridge said. "And for coming all the way out here again. Stop at the local gas station and let me fill you up."

Vandeweghe steered the car onto the main road. "Don't be a nut. I don't need your gas. Save your money." He moved into traffic, which was, thankfully, light. "Speaking of which, you're getting a bill from the firm, and you'll have to pay it. It doesn't have any time billed, but the court costs are plenty."

"What do you mean?" Ridge asked. "Of course I need a bill from you that includes your time."

"Nah. You'll get one for court expenditures, but I lost the billable hours."

"Ah, come on!" Ridge said. "You can't do this for free. It was hours and hours. I can't ask you to do this. No."

Vandeweghe shifted gears and sped around a semi-truck, then ducked back into the right lane. "No you can't, and you didn't. But I did, so stop your whining. I might just change my mind."

"But Gary –"

"You can buy me a drink, for chrissake. Now, let's talk about the Cravens. I'd like to go a few days early, if that's okay with you. Maybe play a few other courses in the area."

Ridge was silent. Vandeweghe stole a look at his face. It was red and tight, the lips a thin line.

"You okay with that?" Vandeweghe said.

Ridge nodded. "I don't know how to thank you," he almost whispered.

Vandeweghe grinned. "I do. Win us the damn tournament. I want another bell!"

Ridge laughed. "Okay, okay. I'll get Nellie to drive me out to the club more so I can hit the rock pile. Puttin' around the living room isn't doing me any good."

"Ask the other guys for a lift."

Ridge's voice was soft, but stern. "I won't do that, Gary. I don't want anyone to treat me any differently than before." He paused, then in a stronger voice, said, "And I want my darn bill. Everyone has been very helpful. Too helpful, really. Especially you. I mean, I hit an ugly hook when I got behind the wheel that night. And hell, when you hit it out of bounds, you deal with the stroke penalties. No matter who says 'just grab another ball from the bag'."

"Fair enough," Vandeweghe said, and meant it. But he also knew he wouldn't be including his hours.

CHAPTER 10

May, 1997

Patrick Quinn

Standing in his parents' kitchen, Patrick poured the bottle of Guinness into a frosty mug, grabbed his plate of barbecued ribeye, corn on the cob, and fruit salad and headed out into the backyard. A round of laughter met him as he stepped onto the deck.

Ridge, sitting at the large table amidst many of the Saturday morning golfers, waved a hand in the air, and continued with a joke. "... Then he turns to me and says, 'There's only one way to make this shot – aim for that boulder, bounce it at a ninety degree angle onto the cart path above the green, ricochet it off that big oak tree, then land ten feet above the pin, below that hump. It'll roll right into the cup.' So I turn to him and I say, 'You're kidding, right?' 'Nope,' he says to me, 'But that shot's so difficult I've only once been able to get it done right. So good luck!'"

"Sounds like my last round at Cypress," Vandeweghe said.

The group laughed and Patrick joined, nearly choking on a mouth full of corn. He doubted Vandeweghe had ever had that kind of shot in his entire life, let alone at Cypress Point.

"My favorite joke is that Bob Hope quote," Charlie said.

Rudy leaned forward in his chair. "Which one's that, Charlie?"

"I'd give up golf if I didn't have so many sweaters," Patrick said, winking at Charlie. "Right, Pop?"

Charlie raised his glass of chardonnay. "Right you are, Pat. That's the one."

Vandeweghe turned to Don, who was seated at the head of the table, sporting a pink paper party hat. "What's your favorite golf joke, Don? As honored guest of the party, give us a good one."

"Playing in the club Championship," Patrick mumbled.

He received a hearty round of guffaws from all, including Don, who raised his wine glass in salute and said, "How right you are, Patrick."

Vandeweghe pushed his empty plate back. "So I guess with this move to Terravita you've given up chasing that particular trophy, eh Don?"

"Gee, Don, you could just stop entering the tournament if you want to avoid the humiliation of second place," Rudy said, grinning. "You don't have to go to the trouble of *moving*."

Patrick's throat suddenly clenched, making it difficult to swallow his beer.

"Just following your example," Don said.

Charlie stabbed a finger in Don's direction. "At least you chose Arizona sun instead of Tahoe snow." He turned to Rudy. "I don't know how you stand those winters up there."

"Bev loves to ski," Rudy said, shrugging. "I gotta keep my number one gal happy."

"Aha!" Chris said. "So you do have a number two gal. I always suspected you led a double life."

"My second gal's the same one you were singing to on the fifteenth tee this afternoon," Rudy said.

"Who? The Greek Goddess Nike?" Chris said, eliciting laughter from around the table.

"No!" Rudy said, "Lady Luck you two-timing tomato! Lady Luck!"

"So that's why we haven't seen much of Hally lately," Ridge said. "She's finally catching on to your philandering ways."

"Like she didn't know what she was getting into before we got married," Chris said, grinning. "Pretty hard to hide my affair with golf when I had to be home no later than nine on a Friday night so I could get up and beat you guys on Saturday morning."

Al Braga shifted in his chair. "Why Terravita, Don?" he asked. "Why not The Boulders, or why Arizona at all?"

"Yeah, it's so blasted hot down there in the summer," Rudy said.

"Which is why we'll be at Spyglass an awful lot," Don said. "Actually, the only way I convinced Penny to move was to promise her an escape every summer."

Charlie chuckled. "Reverse snow bird."

"Precisely," Don said, then took a swallow of his wine.

Vandeweghe tapped his fingers on the table. "And Terravita? I mean, The Boulders is right there, it's established, has a nice course, good restaurants..."

Don wrinkled his nose. "Some of those reasons are why we didn't get serious about it. That, and the houses are older. If you want a nice one, you pay dearly for it. If you find one that's decently priced, it needs a quarter million in work. This way we're building from the ground up, making choices as we go."

"And Arizona?" Chris asked. "There are so many other places in the U.S. with great courses."

Patrick drained his Guinness. Personally, he couldn't think of another place in the world he'd rather be than the Bay Area.

Don nodded. "True, true, Chris. But Phoenix has some history for us. Penny and I met at A.S.U., back in the fifties. Both girls were born there. My first years with IBM..." He shrugged and grinned. "A little nostalgia to keep us young as we grow old."

"Well, now you know what they say," Ridge said with a distinctive twinkle in his voice. "Golfers never get old; their putters just don't work as well."

To the sound of more laughter, Patrick carried his now empty plate and glass into the kitchen. Dawn, his mother, leaned over the sink, paring the tops from strawberries. Patrick sighed.

"What's up, dear?" she said, sliding a bowl filled with strawberries across the counter. "Here, sprinkle some powdered sugar on these."

Patrick retrieved the sugar from a nearby cupboard and began to sprinkle the berries. Suddenly he remembered a moment with Don during a round at Pebble Beach, years ago. The two of them were standing on the seventh tee, waiting to hit. Don had nodded toward the ocean, from which rose several large, rugged rock formations, all topped in white.

"If you didn't know it was bird shit, it could look rather pretty," Don had said.

Patrick had nodded in agreement. "They look like they're topped with snow."

"Or powdered sugar," Don had added. "Like chunks of chocolate sprinkled with powdered sugar. Gee, I must be getting hungry."

"Or desperate," Patrick had concluded.

Don had grinned. "That's par for this course, Pat."

Patrick replaced the box of powdered sugar to the cupboard. He felt the lump return to his throat. He frowned. For heaven's sake, the man was moving to Scottsdale, not Siberia.

"Okay, Patrick, what's bothering you?" Dawn said.

"Nothing," Patrick answered reflexively.

His mother frowned then thrust the bowl of strawberries into his hands. "Then stop moping and take these out to the deck. You look like someone just shot your dog."

"I don't have a dog," Patrick said.

"Maybe you should get one," a man's voice said from behind him.

Patrick turned and found Plato standing in the door jamb, his hands filled with empty plates and stacked glasses. "Dawn," he said, "I think your dinner was a huge success. The guys nearly licked the plates clean."

Dawn swept the clutter from Plato's arms and dropped them into the sink. "I'm glad to hear it, Gary. Ice cream and strawberries coming up for dessert."

Patrick waggled the bowl in his hands. "Example A."

Plato looked past Patrick to Dawn. "I imagine the guys would love to have you deliver them, Dawn. We haven't seen much of you all evening."

"How could you miss me?" Dawn said with a chuckle and a motion to her ample girth. She snatched the bowl from Patrick's hands. "Here, give me those. I can read between the lines." She winked at Plato and left the kitchen.

Patrick opened the refrigerator. "Want another beer?"

"I haven't had one yet," Plato said. "But I'll take another 7-Up if you have that."

Patrick nodded and rummaged a can from the bottom shelf, then frowned as he realized there were no more bottles of Guinness beer.

"You're gonna miss him, aren't you?" Plato asked, nodding toward the patio.

"Who? Don?" Patrick said lightly. "Naw, he's a total pain in the ass. Always messing up my chances to win tournaments."

"Well, I know I'm going to miss him," Plato said. "I suppose I should have assumed he'd move on someday, given his career path with IBM, but I sure never let myself think about it."

Patrick smiled. "Well, you know what it stands for, don't you? I've Been Moved." His smile melted. "He told me that once, right before I putted to win a match at Spyglass. Completely shot my concentration." Patrick stuck his head in the refrigerator and shuffled items around. "Why would I possibly miss him?"

Plato shrugged. "Don's definitely left his mark on the club, what with being President, and redecorating the dining room, and winning so many tournaments out there."

"Not to mention releasing that manager, what's-his-name, and hiring Howard in his place." Patrick popped open a Pepsi and gulped a third of it in one swallow before continuing. "That'll have repercussions for years."

"I think we'll all see the wisdom in that choice sooner than later," Plato said.

Vandeweghe stepped into the kitchen, his head narrowly missing the top of the door jamb. "You guys waxing philosophical in here?" He jerked open the refrigerator and began inspecting the contents. "T.Q., your pop got any more chardonnay in here? We're out."

"No on both accounts," Patrick said. "But I think there's some cabs in the bar in the family room." He squeezed between the men and headed for the adjoining room. "I'll go look."

Crossing to the bar, Patrick glanced through the large bay window onto the patio. Don was still wearing his pink hat of honor, though it had slipped slightly to one side, making him look particularly ridiculous. Rudy, Chris, Charlie, Ridge, Bob, and Al all sat around the table, fully engaged in the conversation. His mom stood beside Don, the bowl of strawberries still in her hands, her face very serious. What are they talking about? Patrick wondered. He found several bottles of cabernet sauvignon, chose two he thought his dad would approve, then began to uncork them. As his hands performed the mechanical action, Patrick watched Don Winterhalter.

He'd known the guy most of his life, Patrick realized. What had he been when Don and Penny became members? Eleven? Well, he turned thirty-one this year so yes, the majority of his life had been spent in the shadow of these men, with Don one of the cornerstones of the group. Patrick felt his throat tighten.

He popped the cork on the first bottle and set it aside. The lump in his throat felt like a golf ball.

The group had been together for so long, it just never occurred to him that something could change it. The Saturday morning games just wouldn't feel the same. Neither would the club tournaments.

He began to pull the cork from the second bottle, but it stuck fast. Putting the bottle between his knees, he jerked hard on the corkscrew. With a loud "pop!" the cork snapped from the bottle, slamming Patrick's hand into the underside of his chin.

"Ow!" he yelped. "Son of a –" He looked at the instrument in his hand. A small chunk of cork hung precariously from the tip. The cork had broken before exiting the bottle, leaving half of it still stuck in the neck. Patrick quickly tore the broken end from the corkscrew then began twisting the metal screw into the offending cork. To his utter dismay, the cork resisted the metal and slid deeper into the bottle. A few choice words slipped past his lips. He routed through the bar drawers for a sharper corkscrew. An olive pick stabbed him in the thumb, drawing a bead of blood.

"Blasted mother of a turnip!" he yelled, then stuffed the bleeding thumb into his mouth. He jerked the olive pick from the drawer and threw it into a nearby garbage can, then shoved the contents of the drawer around a bit. A smaller corkscrew appeared. He snatched it up and slammed the drawer shut. He began to maneuver the tip of the corkscrew into the cork, then realized he couldn't see well enough as the bar blocked the light from the window. He moved to the other side, then renewed his efforts. The corkscrew twisted in easily. Good.

With even pressure he pulled upward on the corkscrew. At first nothing happened, then there was a smidgen of motion.

"Come on, come on!" he uttered tightly, and pulled on the corkscrew.

The cork gave way swiftly. Patrick's hand flew straight up, this time missing his face but whacking into the edge of the bar. Patrick yowled in pain. The bottle twisted from his grasp, sending red wine splashing all over his slacks, shirt and, to his horror, his mother's favorite reading chair. A wave of nausea washed over him, quickly followed by anger. A string of expletives exploded in his brain, but he bit his lip to keep them from escaping.

Rap. Rap. Rap.

Patrick looked at the bay window. Standing on the other side, watching intently, were all the men, along with his mother, clutching the bowl to her chest. Their expressions varied from raw concern to amazement to humor. Rudy and Charlie were laughing, but it was Don who caught Patrick's attention. He stood firmly planted, his nose pressed flat against the glass, his eyes crossed, his thumbs up in that ageless sign of positivity, the silly pink hat sideways over his ear.

Patrick burst into laughter. He clutched the bottle as the laughter overtook him, freezing his face into a mask of emotion. Tears spilled down his cheeks.

"What are you doing, kid?" Don said as he entered the room.

Patrick waved his hand in answer, unable to articulate a response through the laughter as tears streamed onto his face.

Dawn burst into the room, several dripping towels in her hands. "Patrick. Put down the bottle before you spill even more," she said, and Patrick noticed the absence of temper in her voice.

Don took a wet towel and joined Dawn in dousing and mopping the chair. Charlie entered, but held his ground near the door to the patio. His eyes seemed to have sunken into his ruddy cheeks, but they held an unmistakable mirth. He shook his head slowly, a smile deepening as he watched the progress of the cleanup.

"What a waste," Charlie mumbled.

"It's just a chair," Dawn said. "It needed a reupholstering anyway. I was getting tired of that plaid."

"I didn't mean the chair," Charlie said. "I meant the wine." He stepped forward and took the bottle from Patrick, who was trying desperately to hold on to some semblance of decorum. "It's my bottle of Opus One," Charlie said as he held it up against the light. "Well, at least you saved half of it."

Patrick wiped the moisture from his cheeks. "I'm sorry, Pop. Really I am. Here I go, raising the value of the wine while simultaneously lowering the value of the chair." He grabbed a small towel from the bar and soaked it in the sink. "Don, let me take over." He shouldered the guest of honor out of the way. "You don't need to be cleaning up my mess."

Don smiled and hummed – that happy, silly hum that Patrick had come to recognize as his sign of joy. The chair blurred before Patrick, the towel became slick in his hands. He rubbed his shoulder against his face, quickly, hoping no one would notice.

"Come, come, now Patrick," Dawn said quietly. "It's just a chair."

The lump in Patrick's throat grew exponentially. He scrubbed the chair vigorously.

Don patted a wine mark on the arm of the chair. "This is nothing," he said. "Darby once dumped an entire can of bright green paint on the kitchen carpet. We spent hours mopping it up."

"Green paint?" Dawn exclaimed. "As in paint for the walls? On the carpet?"

Don nodded as he continued to scrub. "She was painting tack trunks for her barn, back when she was riding hunters. I guess she came into the kitchen to get something and the can slipped from her arms, landed on the floor, and the top came off. Bright green paint everywhere."

"Penny must have been furious," Charlie said.

Don grinned. "Let's just say she was less than pleased. But we managed to get most of it out. And heck, it was a green patterned carpet. You could hardly tell when we were done."

They all stood and surveyed their handiwork. Dawn gave a final pat at the seat. "Rather like this," she said. "This plaid just absorbs the color of the stain."

Charlie nodded. "Call an upholstery cleaner on Monday and they can probably get the rest out with no problem. Just don't mess with it more."

"Thank you, Don," Dawn said. "But you should be out with the rest of the guys. It's your party, after all."

Don shrugged. "No sweat. Now, any chance we can get that ice cream you were promising before this happened?"

"Did someone say ice cream?!" Vandeweghe leaned into the room from the patio. "Now that's what's missing here. Hey Don, you gonna come out and join us one of these days?"

"Yep," Don said, waving. "Just making myself useful, you know."

Vandeweghe clapped Don on the shoulder. "One last time for old time's sake, eh?" He steered Don toward the door. "You know we're all gonna miss you around here. Who's gonna clean up all the messes everywhere we go?"

Patrick leaned against the bar and watched as Don, Vandeweghe, and his father rejoined the rest of the men on the patio. Such an unlikely grouping of friends. A motley bunch in their dissimilarities, but so perfectly matched in their passions for golf and life. It just wasn't possible for Don to move, to leave this behind. Somehow he'd have to remain a part of this gang, a part of the club, a part of Patrick's life. Somehow …

Patrick smiled as a premonition of good times to come swept over him. "Mom, where's that ice cream?" he said, crossing into the kitchen. "We have some celebrating to do!"

CHAPTER 11

August, 1997
Gary Vandeweghe

Gary Vandeweghe leaned heavily upon the split rail fence surrounding the fourth tee, which hung on a precipice, providing an unencumbered view of Santa Clara Valley. Below, the city of San Jose sprawled across the valley, red roofs separated by the bushy tops of mature trees which gave way to steel and concrete gray before disappearing into the smokey blue of the Santa Cruz Mountains on the far west side. It was early evening and the sun had shifted far to the west, making the mountains dark and featureless. Vandeweghe stared at them.

Winterhalter's old house is over there, he thought, gazing across the valley toward Saratoga. I wonder what he's doing right now, down in Arizona? Vandeweghe smiled a little. What am I thinking? He's on the practice tee, pounding through a bucket of balls. Or two.

"Gary, you're up."

Charlie's baritone voice cut into Vandeweghe's thoughts. He absently waved acknowledgment and continued to look across the valley.

Charlie came up beside him. "What's so special? Eavesdropping?"

Vandeweghe grunted. "Yeah, listening to Don clean his clubs in his backyard."

"That's mesmerizing," Charlie said. "Kind of like listening to snow fall. In Alaska."

"Or sand blow in Arizona," Vandeweghe said, then teed his ball and drove, letting it hook slightly. He slung his bag over his shoulder, then headed down the fairway as Charlie slid into his cart and rolled alongside him.

"Have you heard from Don lately?" Charlie asked.

"Oh, yeah, he calls once in a while, just to check up on me," Vandeweghe said. "Or I'll call him, just to do the same to him."

"How's S.C.O. treating him?" Charlie asked.

Vandeweghe shrugged his shoulders. "They gave him an office down in Scottsdale. Fancy little suite in one of those office complexes, a secretary, the whole thing. But it's a half hour commute one way, so he's trying to move to a little box closer to Terravita, dump the secretary, and just do the one-man-band thing."

Charlie chuckled. "He should just work from home. Then he could work in his pajamas. Wouldn't even have to get dressed."

"That's probably his ultimate plan," Vandeweghe said, "but one step at a time." He stood over a ball. "This yours? Or mine?"

Charlie pointed to the right side of the fairway. "I'm somewhere over there in the forest," he said, and drove off.

Vandeweghe checked a nearby sprinkler head for yardage. Charlie was standing over his ball, his stocky legs appearing to sprout from the rough like sapling trunks. He swung, and the stumps became springs, helping to catapult the ball out of the tall grass toward the green.

"Nice, Charlie!" Vandeweghe yelled. He chose a six iron and sent the ball sailing down the hill. Charlie waved and motored on.

As Vandeweghe headed toward the green his thoughts wandered back to Don. Damn if he didn't miss the guy. Maybe he could find an excuse to head down to Scottsdale, play a few rounds at this new course of Don's.

The next few holes were played in a blur as Vandeweghe muddled over dates and possible reasons in his head. Could he organize a business meeting? Should he just take a few days off from the office? Not that his firm would miss him, what with the junior partners being as capable as they were. Would Barbara want to come? What was she doing in the next few months? And when would be a good time for Don? For the weather? Heck, Scottsdale was no picnic in the summer, and he really wasn't fond of the heat.

He walked off the fifth green, still contemplating a possible trip. Patrick and Chris exited the men's grill, laughing.

"Hey, Vandeweghe!" Chris said, "Care if we join you?"

Vandeweghe looked at Charlie, who shrugged. "You young bucks go ahead." He motioned toward the sixth fairway. "We'll wait."

They stood on the sixth tee, waiting for Patrick and Chris to forge ahead. Chris had, again, found the eucalyptus trees along the right side.

"Maybe we should put up a net," Charlie mumbled as he leaned on his driver and watched the two search the woods. "Or scent the balls and hire a bloodhound to find the damn things."

Vandeweghe chuckled, then turned his attention to the view beyond the fairway. They were lower here than on the fourth tee, but if he looked out past the green he could see a wedge of the city and the mountains beyond.

Behind him, a sliding door opened. Music poured out and Vandeweghe looked up. Bagpipes! A flash of St Andrews ... the evening bagpipes along the eighteenth fairway ... musicians downtown near the golf museum ... Scotland.

Don Ridge stood on the upper deck of the clubhouse. "Hey Van-da-waaay, you coming in for a nip after your round, or you heading out right quick?"

"What are they playing up there?" Vandeweghe hollered back. "Who's got the music turned up?"

Ridge motioned behind him. "They're getting ready for some wedding. The bride wanted bagpipe music for her first dance. Can you imagine?"

Vandeweghe grinned widely. "Yes. Yes I can, Ridge. And yes to your question. I'll be in after the round. Will you stick around? I have something I want to discuss with you."

"Sure, sure, I'll wait." Ridge waved and returned through the sliding door.

"They're done," Charlie said. "Chris must'a made a deal with the devil to get out from behind that tree and get the ball where it landed on the green."

Vandeweghe waited until Charlie's drive was safely in the air, then he pounced. "Why don't we all go to Scotland? Play St Andrews, Turnberry – you know, where they played the ninety-four Open – Carnoustie, whatever. Let's get a bunch of the guys, invite Scooter, and go play for a week or two?"

Charlie squinted. "Scotland? St Andrews?" He rubbed his jaw, then said, "But you're a member of the R & A. You play it all the time."

"Naw," Vandeweghe said and waived his hand dismissively. "Maybe twice a year, if I'm lucky."

"Still," Charlie continued, "you'd really want to go there?"

"Sure! Why not?" Vandeweghe swung and didn't even watch his ball. He hefted his bag onto his shoulder with exuberance, and hiked alongside Charlie's cart. "This could be great! You, me, Staedler, and Plato. Of course, he'd want to come. Chris maybe. Cracolice…" He paused long enough to assess his fairway lie, then swung at his ball and sent it flying over the back of the green. "I can probably get us all on the Old Course, and I'm sure we can make arrangements at several other courses. We'll just drive around and play golf like we've always done here on Saturdays. And it'll be kind of a homecoming for Winterhalter!"

"A homecoming ten thousand miles from home." Charlie scratched his chin. "Do you think he'd want to go? Why not just invite him up here?"

"That's no fun, Charlie," Vandeweghe said, then paused to wait for Charlie to hit his second shot before continuing. "It's unlikely he'd come up for anything except a Member/Guest tournament. That's gonna happen, anyway, right? And we'd be distracted by social events – dinners and whatnot. No, this is perfect! No distractions, just golf and golfing buddies. And I know he'd go. He's been dying to get to St Andrews. I mean, what true golfer doesn't want to play there? At least once."

Charlie parked his cart and grabbed his putter. "Didn't he and Penny go over a couple of years ago? Play some courses?"

Vandeweghe nodded. "Yeah, yeah, but they didn't make the draw and couldn't get on to play the Old Course, which is, of course, really what you want to play. They just stood with the crowd and watched. And maybe walked a hole or two." He made his way down the slope at the back of the green and located his ball.

"How's it look?" Charlie asked from where he stood near the pin. "Got a shot?"

"Well, we'll see," Vandeweghe said as he waggled his club over the ball where it nestled in the thick grass. He took two strides up the slope, lined up his ball with the hole, then returned back to his ball. "You can pull the flag, Charlie."

Charlie dropped the flag stick to the side as Vandeweghe chipped up, landing the ball on the fringe. It rolled gently toward the favored destination.

"Giddy up!" Charlie said, waving his hand.

The ball stopped just short of the hole and Charlie moaned. "Aw, another three inches! Tough break, Gary."

Vandeweghe didn't even hear him. "We could go in July or August, or maybe September." He tapped his ball in, then snatched it from the hole. "Check with the guys and find out what's best with them. Doesn't matter with me, and probably won't with Plato or Rudy. What do you say, Charlie?"

Charlie looked up from his putting stance. "I say you're crazy, and I, for one, am not sure I'd follow you over that ledge." He putted, left it short, and moved to finish out. "But heck, maybe the other guys would like to go."

Vandeweghe felt his enthusiasm wane. Maybe playing the Old Course wasn't everything he thought it was. Maybe he was one of the few who found excitement in its ragged edges and oddities. Charlie surely didn't seem to find it very interesting.

He jerked his bag to his shoulder and motioned toward the clubhouse. "I'm heading back. You going on?"

Charlie motioned with his chin toward Patrick, one hole ahead. "I'll go join my son on this miracle tour he's managed to get involved with. You go ahead."

"Thanks," Vandeweghe said, and hiked back up the sixth fairway toward the glowing clubhouse. When he reached it, he looked through the windows and saw Ridge playing cards with Carlo Caralli. Fully deflated by Charlie's lackluster response, Vandeweghe skirted the clubhouse and headed for his car. He tossed his bag into the trunk then leaned on the bumper to change his shoes. The sound of footsteps made him glance up. Plato was crossing the lot, most likely done for the day and heading home.

"Hey Pro," Vandeweghe called. "Got a minute?"

Plato waved and changed his course. "Absolutely. What's up?"

Vandeweghe looked up at his friend's face. "Would you ever go over and play the Old Course?"

Plato's face flashed first surprise, then assurance. "St Andrews? In a caddy's breath!" His head tilted. "Why do you ask?"

"I was thinking we should get a bunch of us and head over for ten days or so," Vandeweghe said. "And invite Winterhalter, rejoin with the old codger and see if Arizona's ruined his game yet, but do it somewhere special."

Plato's eyebrows rose. "The Old Course would be special, and I know for a fact Don would love to go. He's always speaks of it with great reverence." He smiled. "I also know at least two dozen of the members who would follow you over in a heartbeat."

Vandeweghe felt his spirits rise. Maybe this would work.

"When would you want to do it?" Plato asked. "A year, two?"

"Next summer, maybe in August or September," Vandeweghe said. "After the mass rush to play, but before the weather turned to garbage."

Plato nodded. "That sounds excellent." A small smirk twisted his lips. "You want company? Someone to keep you all honest?"

"Of course you'd come with us!" Vandeweghe said, throwing his golf shoes into the trunk. "What, do you think I'd talk to you about this then not invite you? What kind of a heel do you think I am?"

Plato planted his stance and crossed his arms, looking ever so much like a professor. "Now don't get all blue-blooded on me." His tone was soft but firm. "You know I don't think you're a heel. I'm just making sure before I go getting all excited. I'm not one to jump to conclusions. You know that."

Vandeweghe ran his hand through his hair. "Ah, hell, I'm sorry. But of course you'll be invited. Wouldn't be much of a trip without you. Let me ask around and see who else would be interested."

He slammed the trunk and motioned for Plato to join him as he walked to the clubhouse.

"Make sure you ask Rudy," Plato said. "I know he'd go back. He's always talking about how it terrific it was. Oh, and Al Braga. I know he'd be keen to go."

"Sure, sure, Al and Rudy have to be asked," Vandeweghe said, pausing beside Plato's car. "And Ridge. He's in the clubhouse making back his money at gin. I'll go speak with him."

Plato nodded and slid into the driver's seat. "Count me in! And let me know how I can help."

Vandeweghe waved as he headed back to the clubhouse. Scotland, with his buddies. With Winterhalter. How many guys should go? Eight? Twelve? Could he get three tee times if there were twelve? Probably eight would be safer.

Winterhalter, Plato, Staedler, and definitely Ridge. He'd heard Ridge had tried to organize a trip some years back. Ridge would go. And Braga. Even though he didn't play the Saturday game because of his responsibilities at The Village, he was known and liked by all.

Vandeweghe entered through the main door and bounded down the stairs to the men's grill. Hell's Bunker. The Road Hole. The Valley of Sin...

A hearty laugh was his compass and he found Ridge, still sitting at the card table with Carlo Caralli.

"Hey, Ridge," Vandeweghe said, clapping the man on the shoulder. "Fold that lousy hand of yours and come to the bar with me. I've got a much better proposition than that mismatched mess you're holding."

Carlo laughed and Ridge moaned loudly. "Aw, Van-da-waaay, what did you do that for?" He tossed his cards on the table. "All right. I'm out, thanks to this guy." He jerked his thumb toward Vandeweghe. "Remind me not to ask you to Vegas any time soon," he said, then allowed Vandeweghe to steer him to the bar.

"I wouldn't go anyway," Vandeweghe said. "Waste of time. Now, what's the first thing you think of when I say 'the Swilcan Bridge'?"

Ridge made a face and said, "That's not much of a riddle. The Old Course. This why you cost me twenty bucks at the card table?"

Vandeweghe smiled. "The next clue will cost you much more," he said. "The Swilcan Bridge with you, me, Plato, Scooter, and a bunch of others all standing on it."

By the look on Ridge's face, Vandeweghe knew he'd hit the mark.

"Now that's a riddle I'd pay dearly for!" Ridge said. "When?"

Vandeweghe clapped Ridge on the shoulder. "Soon, my friend. Soon!" As he headed across the grill room, he heard Ridge call after him. "Where you going? You owe me more than this for that crack at the gin table!"

Vandeweghe waved without turning around, his mind racing with lists of things to be done, information to be garnered, and friends to be contacted. And first on that list: Winterhalter.

The bagpipers in the main dining hall struck up a rendition of Amazing Grace. Vandeweghe paused, letting the memories from St Andrews wash over him like waves from the Scottish coast.

"Scooter, you are gonna love this!" he said, and nearly ran out of the clubhouse. "You'd better be off that practice tee by now!"

CHAPTER 12

August, 1997
Don Winterhalter

Don Winterhalter looked up from his magazine as his youngest daughter, Judy, shuffled into the living room and tossed herself onto the leather couch.

"What's up?" he asked.

Judy stuffed a decorative pillow under her head and sighed. "Just tired. Traveling with a toddler is a lot of work."

"Is Kolton down for the night?" Don asked. His first, and likely only, grandson had been lurching all over the living room for most of the day, entertaining Penny and him with his one-year-old antics.

Judy nodded. "He was asleep before his head hit the mattress," she said. "Oh, sorry, but I stole all the pillows in the house to surround him on the bed."

"Including ours?"

"Yep," Judy said, pursing her lips as if to ward off any argument. Not that Don had any intention of arguing the loss of his pillow. Kolton's safety was a higher priority than his sleeping comfort. Heck, he'd just stuff a pillowcase with sweaters.

The decorative clock in the kitchen read eight-fifteen. Plenty of time to digest sugar before going to bed.

"You want to hop into the golf cart and head to Albertson's for some ice cream?" he asked.

Judy gave him a look of incredulity. "It's a hundred degrees outside" she said, "Are you nuts? It'll melt before we get home."

"Who said anything about bringing it home? They have tables outside where we can eat it from the carton. Besides, the sun's behind Black Mountain, there's a breeze, and you'll be sitting in the cart."

Judy snorted lightly. "A breeze. Like standing in front of a blow drier."

"Come on, go change into shorts, and tell your Mom we're going."

Judy rolled off the couch and headed to the second master bedroom. Don followed her, pausing in the formal family room as he realized all the cushions to the couch were gone. Judy must have built a wall around Kolton. He hoped the kid could breathe.

He peeked in through the second master's door, looking for his grandson. Sure enough, piles of cushions and pillows lined the outer parameter of the bed. From behind them, Penny's head popped up.

"Oh, it's you," she said. "Close the door. I want to make sure he stays asleep."

"Judy tell you we're heading for ice cream?"

Penny nodded, then whispered, "Have fun."

The phone rang and Penny frantically waved him out of the room. Don trotted into their bedroom and lunged for the portable phone on the nightstand.

"Hello?" he said, his usual lyrical notes lost in a moment of temper.

"Hey Scooter, that you?"

Gary Vandeweghe's voice was always recognizable. "Yep, it's me," Don said, his tone softening. "How ya doing, Gary?"

Vandeweghe sounded out of breath as he said, "Well, I have a proposition for you. Got a minute?"

Don glanced at his watch. "A minute is about it. Judy and Kolton are here for a visit while their condo is having some roof repairs done."

"Good, good," Vandeweghe said. "I won't keep you then. One question..."

Vandeweghe paused, and Don wondered if there was something amiss. "What's up?" Don asked, sitting on a lounge chair in the corner of the room. "Everything okay?"

"No, no, everything's fine," Vandeweghe assured him. "Just wondering if you'd be up for a little golf trip."

Don furrowed his brow. All the tournaments at San Jose Country Club and Spyglass Hill were over for the summer. "What do you have in mind?"

Vandeweghe seemed to choose his words carefully. "Well, you know it's just not been the same around here since you headed for the desert. So a couple of us were thinking we ought to get together, play a few rounds of golf. On a really nice course, one that matters."

"You want to play the Carmel courses?"

Vandeweghe chuckled. "Even better, my friend. How about you, me, Plato, Rudy, Ridge, and maybe a few others heading overseas? Brush up on our Scottish…"

Don's eyebrows rose of their own accord. He shifted to the edge of the chair. "Are you suggesting what I think you're suggesting?"

"If you think I'm suggesting a game on an old links course along the Scottish coast, then yes, I am," Vandeweghe said. "I don't suppose you'd be interested?"

Don felt as if he'd stepped onto a cloud. "Are you kidding?! When?"

"Well, that's still up for debate," Vandeweghe said. "Why don't you look at your calendar for next summer and shoot me some dates. We're looking at about 10 days, not including travel time."

Judy and Penny entered the bedroom, mixed looks of frustration and query on their faces. Don thrust a fist forward, thumb up, and they both perched on the edge of the bed, listening. "Of course, sure, I'll look at it tonight," he said into the phone. "Anything else you need me to do?"

Vandeweghe chuckled again. "Start saving your money. We won't go first class, but it still won't be cheap."

"I've been wanting to do this my whole life," Don said. "Cost isn't an issue."

"Okay, I'm holding you to that," Vandeweghe said. "Now go play with your daughter and grandson. All well with them? Scott there too?"

"No, Scott stayed in Park City to supervise the repairs. But Kolton's growing like a weed. I'll have a set of clubs in his hands by the end of the year."

"Poor kid doesn't have a chance," Vandeweghe said. "Give Penny my best. I'll talk to you again soon." And before Don could respond, he'd hung up.

Don returned the handset to its cradle then turned to his wife and daughter. He hummed a lively note and grinned from ear to ear.

"Well?" Penny asked. "You gonna tell us or do we have to play charades?"

Don stuffed his hands into his pockets. "That was Gary, uh, Vandeweghe," he quickly added. "He's organizing a trip to St Andrews and I've been invited."

Judy clapped her hands. "That's great, Dad! When do you go?"

"Are you going to be able to get on the course? Isn't there a lottery for tee times?" Penny asked, a note of worry clear in her voice.

Don hummed warmly. "Gary's a member of the R'n'A. I'd think that has some weight where tee-times are concerned."

"I hope so," Penny said, then smiled broadly. "How wonderful, Don! So when is he thinking of going? And how many is he taking?"

"It sounds like it'll be a group of at least four, maybe more," Don said, slipping into the walk-in closet to change into an old pair of shorts. "Gary asked me to look at dates for next summer."

"Remember we're heading to Pat and Bill's for Fourth of July," Penny warned. "You're not getting out of that one."

"Don't worry," Don said, rolling his eyes in the safety of his closet. "I'm not going to stiff your sister and my brother-in-law. I'd end up with another horrible velvet painting at Christmas."

He came out and motioned for them to follow him to the kitchen. "Check your calendar for sometime after we return from Pat's, and if we have anything else going on, I'll add that to the calculation." He motioned to Judy's slippers. "You wearing those?"

Judy glanced down and laughed. "Oh, gee, I guess not," she said, and ran back to the bedroom for flip-flops.

Penny planted a quick kiss on Don's lips. "I'm really happy for you. How wonderful that they remembered you."

Don allowed himself a tiny smile. "Gary said they'd arranged this as a way to play with me again. Pretty special."

Judy joined them, carrying her flip-flops. "Okay, ready?"

Don nodded. "You bet! Let's go get some ice cream."

"Have fun and be safe!" Penny yelled after them.

Don motioned for Judy to take the wheel. "I'm too revved up to drive," he said. Judy steered them through the development, scooting along the edge of the golf course, past saguaro cactus and mesquite trees still young and struggling. Don thought about his years at San Jose Country Club: the tournaments, the parties, the decisions as President. That all mattered; it was all wonderful. But he thought about Vandeweghe, and Plato, and Rudy ... about the Saturday morning games, the camaraderie amidst the competitiveness and personal differences, the events that changed them. His eyes went moist. They had all been through a lot together these past twenty years.

He pointed to the right. "Turn here." Judy careened around the corner. "Hey, take it easy Andretti," he said, only half serious. "I'd like to live long enough to make it to St Andrews."

Judy just laughed and screeched to a stop before the privacy gate exiting to the strip mall just outside the boundaries of Terravita.

Don shook his head in mock disgust. "If I don't make it, send your sister in my place, will ya?"

Judy tossed him a look of indulgence, then stepped on the "go" peddle and the golf cart lurched into the parking lot.

Don grabbed the roof of the cart to keep from falling out, and laughed. He would be sixty in November, and life just kept looking better and better.

Scotland, watch out. His "A" game would be in the bag, and his best buddies would be there to join.

CHAPTER 13

October, 1997
Gary Vandeweghe

Gary Vandeweghe walked into the pro shop and looked around. Plato was thumbing through a rack of golf shirts, several in his hand, a look of concentration on his face.

"Hey, Pro," Vandeweghe said, crossing to him. "You gotta help me figure out who to invite to this Scotland thing. There's just too many guys I should invite, and we can't have that many along for the ride."

Plato continued thumbing the shirts, but his face softened into a smile. "Well, that shouldn't be too difficult." He folded another shirt onto the pile over his arm. "Who's less likely to cause trouble? Who's difficult?"

"Besides me?" Vandeweghe said, and was pleased when Plato grinned. "Yeah, yeah, I know what you all say about me."

Plato shook his head, dropping the pile of shirts on the counter. "Okay, since we clearly can't eliminate you, who else can we eliminate based upon their contradictory personality?"

Vandeweghe wrinkled his forehead. "Well, that's everyone. Except for you." He waggled a finger at Plato. "You put the rest of us to shame."

Plato grinned. "You haven't talked to the members on the Greens Committee lately, have you?"

Vandeweghe cocked his head in frustration. He needed Plato's help, not his humor. Plato seemed to sense the moment, and became more serious.

"All right. Who've you got so far? Committed."

Vandeweghe ticked them off his fingers. "Scooter, of course. Rudy immediately. You. Ridge. I asked Charlie but he had played the Old Course a few years ago and didn't like it much."

Plato nodded "I don't imagine he would. It wouldn't suit his style of play very much."

"No, apparently it didn't. But he's still on the fence. So that's six. Chris Clark is interested, but he has those young boys at home and he's afraid to leave Hally alone with them for too long."

"Did you check with Al?" Plato asked.

Vandeweghe nodded. "Yeah. He's real interested, but hedging, since he just bought that driving range in Monterey."

"Can't blame him for that." Plato began folding the shirts, and his forehead furrowed. "I wouldn't leave a new business so soon after purchase. You're just asking for trouble."

Vandeweghe continued with several more names, each with their own set of issues and problems, or with obvious personality conflicts with other members who were already committed. Finally, Vandeweghe shrugged. "That's it. Eleven guys we could consider. What do you think?"

Plato gazed off in the distance, and Vandeweghe wondered if he was listening to some divine guidance. Then Plato grabbed a scrap of paper and scribbled some words.

"Okay, of those guys you just mentioned, these are the ones I know get along well with each other." He read from the list: "You, Rudy, Charlie, Ridge, Chris, and either Cracolice or Braga. Oh, and me. I don't think any of them would object to my being along."

Vandeweghe waved his hand dismissively. "We'd be disappointed if you didn't go. So do I ask these eight, well nine with me included, and see who doesn't want to go? Or do you think I should just ask eight and then move on if someone declines or backs out?"

"Invite only eight," Plato said, quite emphatically. "Don't put yourself in the position of having to back out on someone."

Vandeweghe thrummed the counter with his fingers and stared out the window at the first tee and fairway. He somehow had to get Charlie to join. And between Cracolice and Braga... well, either way, he couldn't go wrong. They were both nice guys. He turned back to Plato.

"You've known Braga for ages, haven't you." It was a statement, not a question. He'd heard they'd gone to high school together.

Plato nodded. "We met when we were sophomores at Alameda. I certainly count him as one of my longest and dearest friends." He pointedly glared at Vandeweghe. "And he's a darn good golfer."

That cinched it for Vandeweghe. He slapped the counter and turned to go. "All right. Thanks, Pro. See you around."

"You bet," Plato said.

Vandeweghe paused at the door. "Oh, and what are you doing with those shirts? Big sale for someone?"

Plato patted the shirts piled before him. "These? They're going to the Golf Over Guns Foundation. I figured I'd buy them and send them over as a donation. It's a good group."

Vandeweghe agreed. "How many you got there? Twenty? Thirty?"

"Twenty-seven."

"Put fifteen of them on my tab," Vandeweghe said, and quickly left the shop before Plato could argue.

When he arrived at home, he dialed Charlie. He simply wasn't going to take no for an answer.

"Hello, Quinn residence."

Vandeweghe leaned back in his chair. "Dawn Quinn, you have the voice of an angel. Where's that devil of a husband of yours? Home?"

"And you, Gary, are a scoundrel," Dawn said, teasing. "No wonder you and my husband get along so well. I'll go get him."

Several moments later, Charlie's voice came over the phone. "Gary, what's up?"

"I'm about to mail out the invitation letter to the guys we're inviting to the Scotland trip." Vandeweghe wrinkled his forehead. "I'm not sending one to you unless you tell me you're going. I have too many guys in contention to waste my paper on someone who doesn't like the game."

"Well aren't we being feisty," Charlie said, and chuckled. "Now I don't like the game, huh? Just because I don't drool all over your precious patch of Scottish weeds and sand."

"That's it," Vandeweghe said. "You're off the list."

Charlie chuckled, and Vandeweghe realized he just adored that deep rumble. The man just had to join them. "Don't make me do this, pal," Vandeweghe said. Then he played his last card. "I know Scooter would be very disappointed if you weren't with us. You're his partner in almost every team event we have, for Pete's sake."

He held his breath. Would Charlie bite? The silence seemed to linger far too long. Vandeweghe felt like he was standing midstream without a fishing pole.

"Oh, all right, all right. You win," Charlie said. "I'll go, but only if I don't have to room with you." That rumble of a laugh came through the phone again. "You take too long in the bathroom."

Vandeweghe pumped his fist in the air in triumph. "No problem. I'll make sure you room with someone else. And I don't take too long in the bathroom. You have me confused with Chris."

"You'd be impossible to confuse with anyone," Charlie said.

Without further discussion, Vandeweghe finagled a firm commitment from him. Heck, he almost made Charlie sign a contract.

"You done now?" Charlie asked. "'Cause I'm beginning to feel like I just bought one of those time share condos. I'm already having buyer's remorse."

Vandeweghe couldn't resist. "Save your remorse for the gorse," he said, and was rewarded with a loud groan from Charlie. Then, laughing, they said their good-byes and hung up.

Vandeweghe retrieved a glass of chardonnay and returned to his desk. Pulling out a small tape recorder, he began dictating the letter he would send. He hoped they would all accept. It would be one helluva ride.

CHAPTER 14

October, 1997
Gary Vandeweghe

Gary S. Vandeweghe
San Jose, California 95127

October 7, 1997

Dear Rudy,

In about a year, a group of eight of us, including you, is going to Scotland to play golf. We will leave on the Wednesday night before Labor Day (September 2) and return on the second following Monday (September 14).

We will fly into Glasgow, pick up two vans, and should be in our hotel in Ayr by Thursday mid-afternoon. Golf that day will be optional. Over the next few days we hope to play Turnberry, Prestwick, Troon, and Western Gailes on the west coast. On the next Tuesday we expect to travel to the east coast, south of the Firth of Forth and play Gullane, North Berwick and Muirfield. On Thursday we then hope to go up to St Andrews for dinner at the R & A Clubhouse, and incidentally, to play the Old Course, the New Course, Jubille, Carnoustie, and perhaps Elie, and Lunden Links.

Darby Winterhalter Löfstrand

The plan is to ask each person to take on one aspect of the trip, such as arranging golf, air travel, vans, driving, hotels, don't-miss restaurants (if there are any in Scotland), company banking, etc. Volunteers are encouraged.

The trip should cost less than $5,000, using $1,500 for airfare, $100 per day for room and the same for golf, $80 per day for meals, and about $20 per day for the vans. Successful gaming might reduce the total cost.

Please express interest immediately and plan to commit right after the first of the year. There is an anxious waiting list, but the plain fact is we don't want to go without you.

Yours very truly,
Gary

GSV:	*bkb*
GV	*DR*
GP	*CQ*
RS	*DW*
CC	*AB*

CHAPTER 15

November, 1997
Gary Plato

Plato looked up from his ledger when he heard the door open. Chris Clark filled the doorway, nearly tall enough to hit his head. When did he get so big? Plato thought, remembering the lanky kid he taught to putt oh-so-many years ago. Where had the time gone?

"Hey, Pro," Chris said, scattering Plato's thoughts. "You coming?"

"Oh, right, right." Plato quickly closed the ledger and stashed it in his top drawer. "Thanks for reminding me; I almost forgot." Chris smiled. "Don't you make some wisecrack about age, young man," Plato chastised. "I can still outplay you."

Minutes later, Plato led Chris into the Clubhouse, where they were met by a round of laughter coming from a small, open room to the left of the entrance. Rudy, Charlie, Ridge, Vandeweghe, and Al Braga were casually sitting around a table.

Plato joined in the hello's and handshakes and "How've you been this fall?" directed to Al, then ordered a drink and settled in beside Rudy. Almost immediately the group got down to business.

"Okay, fellas," Vandeweghe said as a legal pad materialized on the table before him. "We're talking Scotland. We need volunteers for the various assignments."

Rudy swirled his soda. "What's on the list, Gary?"

"And are you sure you want to relinquish control?" Charlie asked, then winked at Plato.

Vandeweghe frowned. "If you think I can do this all on my own, think again. Now, we need someone to arrange the tee times." Vandeweghe scribbled on his pad. "That should be me and Winterhalter." He glanced around the table. "Anyone disapprove?"

Plato grinned as the men mumbled "No, no" and "Of course not." So much for relinquishing control.

"Good," Vandeweghe said. "Now someone needs to look into booking rooms and finding restaurants in all the towns where we're staying. We don't want to be hunting for food after a punishing round of golf."

Chris pointed at Rudy. "I motion we put Rudy in that role. He's been to some of these places before."

Ridge guffawed. "Are you kidding? Look at the man! If his weight is any indicator, we'd be eating sprouts and leafy green vegetables the whole trip. We'll waste away to nothing!"

"Not that you couldn't use some of that wasting," Charlie teased. "A few green beans might be good for you."

Rudy interrupted the banter. "Gary, you've been to more of these places than I have. Can you give me a list of possible hotels? Don't you already know the restaurants?"

"Well, yes, some of them," Vandeweghe said, then shrugged. "But times change and not all the places Barb and I went to were decent. It'd be nice to have some alternatives."

"Okay. I'd be happy to look into it," Rudy said. "Sign me up."

Vandeweghe scribbled on his pad, then waggled his pen at Al. "Brag, you're in charge of pairings. We'll get you the list of courses as we know them."

Plato quickly found a miniscule piece of lint on his pant leg and focused hard. He'd rather hoped he'd be in charge of creating competitions. Then Al suggested they all play at gross and Plato decided to retie his shoe.

"We need a company banker," Vandeweghe said. "Someone we can rely on to keep the books, handle the money, make the tips."

There was a slight pause as everyone turned to Charlie Quinn. "What are you looking at me for?" Charlie asked, sitting back in his chair. "I'm the biggest crook amongst you!"

"Only on the green," Ridge said. "Stealing all those long putts."

Charlie waved his hand. "I don't want to handle all your money. You're big boys; figure it out yourselves."

"That won't work, Charlie," Vandeweghe said in what Plato had come to call his "courtroom voice." "It'll be easier if we all put funds in a pot, and all our expenses are paid from there. Someone has to manage it. You're the only one for the job."

Charlie grunted and receded behind his drooping eyelids. Plato waited and watched, as did everyone. Finally Charlie sighed. "Oh, all right." He smiled. "But I'd better have a bodyguard."

"You're going to have seven of them!" Ridge said.

"I don't need protection from a stranger," Charlie shot back. "I need someone to save me from you guys!"

Plato joined the others in laughter, and there was a slight pause in the business as drink orders were refilled.

"What can I do?" Ridge asked, bringing them back to the activity at hand.

Vandeweghe pointed at him with the pen. "Ridge, seems to me you have to be in charge of organizing the vans we'll need to get around Scotland."

"Why?" Ridge asked. "'Cause I like cars? That's supposed to make me good at organizing transportation?"

Vandeweghe's pen scratched furiously across the pad. "Well, okay then, you can do hotels and restaurants and Rudy, would you mind handling vans?"

"Now, now," Ridge said. He leaned back in his chair and locked his hands behind his head. "Don't go getting all fussy on me. I do like those metal ponies, after all."

"That had nothing to do with it," Vandeweghe said. Plato took a sip of his soda to hide a smile.

Ridge chuckled. "Well it should have. I have a whole stable of them, rusting away in the garage." He scratched his chin. "Come to think of it, maybe I'd be better off staying home and working on them."

A discernible jolt crossed the table. Plato glanced around. There were concerned looks on all his friends' faces.

Ridge sat up and winked. "Had y'all going, didn't I?" Grumbles and laughter fused into one collective release. Ridge waved his thick hand in the air. "Put me down for rustling up the transportation, Vand-da-waay. You just have to tell me where we're going."

Plato quickly tallied up the jobs. "What about Chris?" he asked. "What's he doing?"

Vandeweghe's eyes narrowed and he sat back in his chair, his pen bouncing off his knee. "Chris, Chris, Chris," he chanted, and his hand bounced from left to right. "The man who plays a course as if it was an arcade game. Ping! Ping! Ping! Down the fairway."

Plato waited in anticipation with the rest of the men, including Chris, who seemed to be eating up the attention with sheer delight.

Vandeweghe spread his hands wide and said, "Who else, other than our young Mr. Clark, would be capable of navigating his way around Scotland, bouncing from coast to coast?"

Chris laughed. "Hally says I can't find my way around the kitchen. You expect me to find my way around Scotland?!"

Ridge slapped his hand on the table. "You won't be needing to find a kitchen in Scotland. You're in luck!"

"Unless, of course, he lands a ball in one of those sky-high bunkers," Plato said and raised his glass in salute. "Then you'll be needing a soup ladle!"

"Or a paring knife to slit his own wrists," Al added, to which Chris responded "I'll drink to that!"

"And Pro," Vandeweghe said, "can you organize the air travel to and fro? I don't have time to sort out flight schedules for this crowd."

Plato nodded. "I suppose Don's finding his own way from Phoenix?"

Vandeweghe shrugged. "Makes no sense for him to fly up here just to join us, so yes, I assume that's correct. Still, I'll make sure before you reserve seats."

Plato smiled. Getting this group to Scotland on the same day would be a bit like running a golf camp for young juniors. One had to take into consideration all sorts of personal schedules, foibles, and demands. Not quite as much fun as creating a series of competitions, but a terrific challenge.

"Okay, ladies," Vandeweghe said as he reviewed his notes, "are we forgetting anything?"

A thoughtful silence descended upon the group. Plato ticked off a list in his head and nothing struck him as missing. Then Ridge's voice broke the silence.

"Our nerve," he said with mock seriousness. "I'm already quaking in my boots, just thinking of that first tee on the Old Course."

Laughter and return banter flowed from man to man, friend to friend. Plato sat back, sipped his soda, and watched. It was nearly a year before the trip, and he already couldn't wait. He knew the time would fly by – the summer months at San Jose Country Club always did. But September just couldn't get here fast enough. Not fast enough at all.

Plato left his office and headed to the Men's Grill. It was a gray, dismal, December afternoon three weeks after the initial meeting; fitting for Plato's attitude. He found Ridge and Vandeweghe seated at a window table, devouring lunch. The look on his two friends' faces didn't help to lighten his mood.

Plato frowned. "Did I interrupt something?"

"No, no, of course not," Vandeweghe quickly answered. Too quickly, Plato thought.

Ridge chewed on a french fry. "We been having a discussion on the trip."

"And this causes you two to become grumpy?" Plato said, sliding into a seat.

"Well, yes, dammit," Vandeweghe said. "Ridge here wants to do all sorts of sight-seeing around Scotland." He tossed his hands in the air. "We're there to play golf! Not see old rocks!"

"They're castles, not old rocks!" Ridge said. "And if we're going, we might as well see some of them."

To Plato's relief, Sarah, the waitress, arrived. "What can I get you, Mr. Plato?" she asked.

"Turkey sandwich, hold the mustard. And a diet soda. Thanks, Sarah."

"And what's chewing on you, Plato?" Ridge asked. "You look as dumpy as the day."

"I feel it," Plato mumbled, then leaned forward on the table. "Guys, I'm having the devil of a time getting travel arrangements for Scotland. Trying to get seven tickets on one flight, at times we can agree upon, is nearly impossible."

Vandeweghe chuckled. "And this is a surprise because...?"

"Like herding cats," Ridge said, nodding. "We're all running in opposite directions, I suppose."

Plato nodded. "Exactly." He glared at Vandeweghe. "And some of you run faster than others."

Vandeweghe's eyebrows rose. "Don't look at me! I'm easy. Just tell me when to show up and I'll be there."

Ridge grunted his obvious dissent of this proclamation. Plato waggled a finger at Vandeweghe. "You are the busiest person I know, outside Staedler. Trying to lock down your schedule is a nightmare."

"Well don't try to!" Vandeweghe exclaimed. "Just tell me when you want me to go and I'll clear the calendar."

"I got an idea," Ridge said. "Nellie and I have this terrific friend, Tony. He owns a travel agency. Maybe he'd be willing to take us on. Might make your life easier, Play-toe."

"Definitely worth a try," Vandeweghe said, nodding. "A good travel agency is worth their weight in gold."

"Well, they'd take that weight off my shoulders." Plato instinctively shrugged, the pressure already falling away. "Send me this guy's number and I'll give him a call tomorrow."

Ridge smiled. "So, that leaves you without an assignment, my friend."

"I've already one in mind," Vandeweghe said, then gave a humorous but pointed look at Ridge. "Managing you. Someone has to make sure you don't get lost on your way to some damn ruin."

To Plato's amusement, Ridge and Vandeweghe continued their squabbling. After several moments, Plato interrupted. "You two sound like an old married couple. Why don't you just kiss and make up?"

"'Cause he's had onions," Ridge said without missing a beat. "And I don't even kiss Nellie when she's had onions."

"Well you had garlic!" Vandeweghe said, then stabbed a finger at Ridge. "And brown mustard. And some of it's stuck in your beard! You think I'd kiss you like that?! Go clean yourself up."

Plato was suddenly aware the room had gone profoundly quiet. Ridge and Vandeweghe obviously noticed it, too, for they paused and glanced around. Twenty or so men were seated at nearby tables; all of them were gawking at Ridge and Vandeweghe with looks of bemusement.

"What are ya' looking at?" Ridge exploded, gesturing at them. "Haven't you ever heard a lover's quarrel?"

His answer was unanimous laughter from everyone in the room, interrupted only by calls of "When's the wedding?" and "You make a darling couple!" and "Who wears the dress?"

Both Ridge and Vandeweghe returned the banter, and Plato watched the sunshine return to his two friends' faces. He rewarded Sarah with a wide smile when she delivered his sandwich. Outside it was raining hard and the wind whipped the oak trees into a wild dance. Still, the sandwich was tasty, Ridge and Vandeweghe were now chatting about their latest rounds, and for the first time in a week there was hope he could shed the responsibility of getting them all to Scotland.

Despite the rain, the day looked a whole lot brighter.

CHAPTER 16

January, 1998
Gary Vandeweghe

Gary Vandeweghe flipped through the pile of incoming faxes on his desk. Work, client, work, client ... ah, there it was: a fax from Plato with "Trip to Scotland" handwritten in bold letters. He pulled the three-page fax from the pile.

> *Gucci, check over the following from Tony at the travel agency. I'd prefer the Edinburgh return, and Charlie, Chris, and Ridge do as well. Let me know. Also, note the last comments. GP*

Vandeweghe scanned the travel schedule – from San Francisco to Heathrow to Glasgow, overnight flight. Good, good, he thought, that'll work. Reading the two return options, he agreed with Plato; the return from Edinburgh seemed to work better, and wouldn't they be closer to that part of Scotland, anyway? The fare seemed high at over $1000, but most of the guys would be using mileage anyway, so it really didn't matter.

He flipped to the second page and skimmed the last paragraph, which discussed hotel and room options. Then he read the last few sentences, scrawled in Tony's thin penmanship.

We can talk about the hotels more when I get back. We don't want to wait very long, however, as this will be a big year for Scotland and things will get booked out. Whoever is getting your tee times better move very very quickly.

Vandeweghe felt a slight chill run up his back. He chuckled. It was golf, for heaven's sake. Just golf. Still, to go all that way and not be able to play the courses worth playing...

He grabbed the phone and dialed a number he now had memorized. The call was promptly answered.

"Don Winterhalter's office."

"Carol. Gary Vandeweghe here. Is Don around?"

"He's on the other line with a sales rep right now, Mr. Vandeweghe," she said. "Let me tell him you're on the phone."

The line went quiet for several seconds, then clicked twice. Winterhalter's voice popped through the line.

"Hey Gary, I was just about to call you," he said. "Your ears must have been burning."

"Or my fax machine," Vandeweghe said. "Did you get Plato's note?"

"Right in front of me," Don said. "And I agree with the last statement. I've contacted several of the courses we decided on, and so far we have confirmed tee times at both Turnberry courses, but Prestwick is still a maybe. However, Gullane and North Berwick are booked solid for the two weeks we're in Scotland, and Muirfield only has a single tee time on the fourth. If we wanted to stay another day in Ayr, they could get us all on—"

Vandeweghe interrupted. "But that messes with our tee times at the Old Course. I can't rearrange those."

"Understood," Don said. "So Gullane, Northern Berwick, and Muirfield are out. The other issue is Carnoustie."

Vandeweghe pursed his lips and waited. Carnoustie was a must play.

"The only day we can get all eight of us on is the fourth," Don continued. "Otherwise, we're flipping a coin to see who plays and who doesn't."

"Well that's not an option," Vandeweghe said. "Either we all play, or no one does."

"I agree," Don said. "So I took the two tee times on the fourth."

Vandeweghe chuckled. This was certainly one of the things he liked best about Don: his decisiveness, on the course and off. That also meant he would be safe to book his surprise round, and a flight, earlier in the week.

Vandeweghe refocused as Don completed a sentence. "...what happens with Western Gailes."

"We won't be able to get on there, either?" Vandeweghe said.

"I don't know yet. They gave me two options and I faxed them back. I've yet to get a confirmation."

Vandeweghe sighed. Well, no one said this was going to be easy. "Let's come up with some plan B courses, just in case." He scribbled a note to himself. "I'll make a list tonight and you do the same. We'll put our heads together tomorrow. I'll give you a call when I'm off the course."

"I don't think that's necessary, yet," Don said, "but I'll string together some options." Through the phone, Vandeweghe could hear a door open and Carol's voice mention someone's name. "Gotta go, Gary," Don said. "Talk to you tomorrow."

"You're on," Vandeweghe said, and hung up the phone. His fingers formed a teepee. Too bad about Muirfield. He'd really wanted to share that with the guys. He'd be disappointed if Western Gailes didn't work out, either. He glanced at his clock, then calculated the hour in Scotland. Four-fifteen in the evening. Maybe they'd still be open.

He snatched the phone from the cradle and punched a button.

"Angela, would you put a call through to the pro shop at Machrihanish? In Scotland. And hurry; it's already late over there. Thanks." He recradled the phone. No matter what else happened, he'd get the guys on the Old Course, and Machrihanish.

The phone buzzed.

"Machrihanish golf shop, Gary," Angela said.

"Good, put them through." He waited for the connection, then pounced. "Hi, this is Gary Vandeweghe calling from California. ... Yes, in the United States..."

CHAPTER 17

January, 1998

Don Winterhalter

Saturday.

Don Winterhalter stood in his kitchen and quickly dialed Vandeweghe's number. It was picked up on the third ring.

"We got Western Gailes," Don said. "First foursome off at three-ten on the first. Second group right behind."

"Good, good," Vandeweghe said. "Barassie confirmed an afternoon tee-time on the third."

Don wrinkled his brow and quickly flipped open his brief case. "Hang on, Gary." He rifled through the Scotland folder. "Shoot," he said, running his finger across the grid on the paper. "The Old at Royal Troon is at three-fifty and four on the third."

"Oh, damn," Vandeweghe exclaimed. "I forgot we changed that to the third. Okay, I'll get back to you."

Don nodded. "Will do," he said and hung up.

Tuesday.

The phone rang. "Don Winterhalter here."

Vandeweghe's voice nearly jumped through the line. "Lunden Links confirmed for the morning of the first."

Don grabbed the tee-time grid and penciled it in. "I have a call in to Panmere. Have you heard from Barassie?"

"Still waiting," Vandeweghe said, and Don noticed the frustration in his tone. "I know a couple of other rounds hinge on their call. I'll let you know as soon as I know."

"I got a call coming in." Don hovered a finger over the blinking red light on his phone. "Talk to you later."

Simultaneously, they hung up.

Wednesday.

"Scooter," Vandeweghe said. "I've got something cooking for the second. Block out the entire day."

Don groaned. "I just confirmed with Letham Grange for the second. And Panmere gave us the option of the afternoon."

"Let's change those," Vandeweghe said. "I can't call these people again."

Don pursed his lips, then sighed. "This mystery round worth that much?" He heard Vandeweghe chuckle, then say, "More. News from Edzell?"

Don tapped his mechanical pencil against the grid. "Still waiting. Still ... waiting."

Vandeweghe chuckled again and signed off.

Saturday.

Don slammed on the car brakes and leapt out. He pushed the garage door button and waited just long enough to ensure no rogue snakes wiggled in, then he jogged into the house. Penny stood in the kitchen, the phone against her ear. She waved and mouthed, "Vandeweghe." Don grabbed the phone.

"Scooter! I thought maybe you'd abandoned me," Vandeweghe said. "I thought we had a noon phone meeting."

Don grinned. "Sorry, I had a last minute game with a friend at the Boulders." He sat down on a kitchen chair and focused on business. "So, I had a call from Barassie this morning. Eight-thirty on the first."

Vandeweghe paused. "But isn't that –"

"Lunden Links," Don said. "Already moved them to the afternoon of the fifth." He found a tee in his pocket and began twiddling it between his fingers. "As for Panmere –" he nodded as Penny held up a diet soda, her eyebrows raised in question. "Waiting. Still waiting."

Tuesday.

"Moved Panmere to the seventh," Don said. "Lunden to the third."

Thursday

Vandeweghe's voice crackled through the long-distance line, making Don wince. "Scooter! Our tee-times at both the Old and New courses have been moved to the fourth, fifth, and sixth. Sorry about that, pal. I just got the call."

Don's hand reached for the file holding the schedule and course contact numbers. Then he said goodbye to Vandeweghe and punched another button on the phone.

"Carol. Clear the next 3 hours. I'm gonna be busy…"

Monday.

"Gary, we're in luck!" Don said. "Carnoustie had an opening on the seventh at nine. Panmere agreed to take us at two-fifty that afternoon. I just canceled Lunden Links and figured we could walk on if we have time someday." He tapped the grid. "And Edzell gave us a two-fifteen on the last day we're in Scotland."

There was a discernible sigh of relief from Vandeweghe. "Wow, Don, I think we've done it," he said. "We have Turnberry—"

"Both Ailsa and Arran," Don interjected.

"Yes, yes," Vandeweghe said. "Barassie, Western Gailes, the mystery round, Portland, then the Old at Royal Troon —"

"They're next door to each other," Don said, "but what about the drive from Troon to St Andrews? Have we left ourselves with a midnight drive?"

"We should be all right, if we don't turn into hacks all of a sudden," Vandeweghe said. "So St Andrews." He paused, then, "I have two definite tee-times on the fourth, but currently only one slot for the fifth. I'm still working it, trying to get a second time."

"We'll play it by ear," Don said. "Maybe that's a day we can hoof it over to Lunden Links."

"Sure, sure," Vandeweghe said. "But then we play the New Course on the sixth, and that's all of us."

"Carnoustie on the seventh," Don said, checking it off on the grid, "and Panmere that afternoon. Letham Grange on the eighth, with Edzell after – our last round."

Vandeweghe grunted into the phone. "If we make it that far." There was a slight pause on the line, then, "That's sixteen rounds in ten days."

Don hummed. "Some trip, huh?" He slapped shut the Scotland folder. "Bring your Tylenol!" Then he wrote a note to include a bottle for himself.

CHAPTER 18

January, 1998
Rudy Staedler

The letter sat like a beacon upon Rudy Staedler's office desk – a daily reminder of what was important in his life at this moment: getting organized for The Trip.

Not that his real estate development business wasn't important. Or his family. Of course they were. But this trip with his buddies to Scotland ... well, that just took precedence over anything else at this point. He got a silly grin just thinking about it.

He glanced at the letter for what was probably the twentieth time this day alone, then looked at the clock. Five-twenty-two. The meeting started at six.

He firmly shut the leather binder that contained all the "important" documents he had to approve, grabbed his jacket, and left the office. Behind him, the phone rang. Ignoring it, Rudy swept past the receptionist's desk.

"Mark me out, Stephanie," he called over his shoulder. "I'm not on my phone and I won't be back the rest of this evening."

"Yes, Mr. Staedler," Stephanie said, and returned to the busy phone on her desk.

Rudy skipped down the stairs, avoiding the elevator as it might contain someone he didn't want to see, then nearly ran to his car. Within minutes he was on the highway traveling east toward San Jose Country Club.

When he pulled through the heavy metal gates into the parking lot, Rudy noticed it was full. No, not full – jam-packed. There were cars parked everywhere, including two which had pulled forward onto the fifth fairway. Rudy silently cursed the drivers for their oversight.

As he maneuvered through the lot, he didn't see any of the cars that belonged to the guys. Trotting into the clubhouse foyer, he was met by loud music and the all-too-familiar sounds of a large party. With a frown, Rudy swung into the club office, relieved to see one of the assistants still at her desk.

"Good evening," Rudy said to catch her attention. When she looked up, he continued, "There's supposed to be a meeting with eight members, set up by Gary Vandeweghe. Any idea where they are?"

"I'm sorry," she said with a forlorn look, "but I don't think there are any members here right now. There's a wedding for an outside party, and I think it chased everyone away."

Rudy could feel the furrow between his eyes deepen. If Bev had been here, she would have teased him about it. He reached for the phone. "May I?" He didn't wait for an answer, but dialed Vandeweghe's number, by now all-too familiar to him. Thankfully, the call was answered.

"Hello?"

"Oh, hi, Barbara. This is Rudy. I'm here at the club, looking for Gary. Any idea where he might be?" Rudy glanced around the corner of the office as an elderly man stumbled into the hall.

"Loo?" the man asked with a distinct accent. Rudy waved toward the men's room down the hall as Barbara Vandeweghe said, "Oh, Rudy, they're at Charlie Quinn's place. I thought they would have called you when they moved the location of the meeting."

"No problem. I wasn't meant to be joining them. I was supposed to have a late meeting at the office, which ended up being rescheduled. So thanks, I'll head down to Charlie's."

"Sounds good," Barbara said. "Goodbye now."

Rudy handed the assistant the phone. "By the way, there are two cars parked on the fifth fairway," he said authoritatively. "Can you find someone to locate their drivers and get them moved? This isn't the Pebble Beach Concours d'Elegance."

The assistant rolled her eyes and reached for a walkie-talkie. "We've been chasing them off all evening. Thanks for letting me know. I'll take care of it."

Rudy nodded curtly, smiled, and trotted back to his car. Charlie Quinn's house was only a few blocks from the club entrance. If luck was on his side, he wouldn't miss anything important.

Dawn answered his knock, wearing a besmeared apron, a ladle in her hand. She was obviously playing chef this evening.

"Well, hello Rudy!" she said, opening wide the door. "Come on in. The fellas are at the table down by the putting green."

Rudy crossed through the kitchen. The smell of chocolate was overwhelming. He inhaled deeply. "Oh my gosh, Dawn. Are those your famous brownies?"

"For dessert," Dawn said. "But you have to finish all your meat!"

"Wasn't that a lyric from a song?" Rudy asked. "I didn't know anyone actually felt that way. Life's too short to wait until after dinner to enjoy dessert."

Dawn laughed, then shooed Rudy into the backyard. Below him, further into the expansive yard, was a small artificial turf putting green. Beside it, at a large patio table, were the guys. Plato was the first to notice Rudy's arrival. He smiled broadly and waved.

"Rudy! You made it!" Plato yelled. "Get yourself something to drink and come on down!"

Rudy waved and backtracked to the kitchen. Within moments he had a cold glass of chardonnay in his hands, and a strong admonition from Dawn to "not drop the stemware on that putting green, or I'll have you vacuuming that darn fake grass."

The moment Rudy pulled a chair up to the table, he sensed something was amiss. Al Braga looked downright depressed, Ridge's nose had turned the strong scarlet that denoted frustration, and Vandeweghe was grimly staring at a pad of paper.

"Well, dammit Al," Vandeweghe said, "it's already January. It's too late to pull out."

Rudy was confused. At all the previous meetings, Braga had been the most excited, most supportive. Rudy turned to the slumped Braga. "You want to pull out, Al? I thought you really wanted to go."

"I do, Rudy, I do," Braga said. "But things just aren't progressing at the range the way I had hoped, and I just can't see it getting better in a few months." He looked about to weep. "I can't justify leaving this year. Too much is riding on this golf range working out."

"But you've plenty of help, don't you?" Ridge asked. He leaned back in his chair and rubbed his growing beard. "I thought you'd be able to leave it with someone. Your assistant manager, or..."

Braga pinched his nose, then shook his head. "There are very few people I'd saddle with the responsibility of making sure my business doesn't fail." He glanced around at the group of men. "Any of you have a twin brother? A clone? Maybe that person I'd trust."

Chris frowned. "You'll only be gone for two weeks, Al. Surely it won't fail in that short of a time."

"I can't risk it," Braga said.

Vandeweghe tossed the pad on the table. "Well, okay... all right ... if you can't go, you can't go. We'll find someone else. But if we can't, you'll need to cover the deposits on the games and hotels. Most of them we can't get back at this point."

Rudy thought Braga really was going to cry. The guy looked so depressed.

Plato crossed to a line of putters resting against the yard shed. "I think I'll do some putting." He lined up a ball. "Anyone care to join me in a little friendly game?"

The tension was almost tangible, and Rudy nearly tipped over his chair in an effort to extricate himself from the table. Braga finished his wine and prepared to leave, shaking hands and saying his goodbyes to everyone.

"No problem," Vandeweghe said in response to Braga's request to be kept apprised of his replacement possibility. "I'll give you a call." They shook hands and Braga quickly crossed the yard, then disappeared into the house.

Rudy sunk a short putt on the fake green and glanced at Plato. The pro was leaning on his putter, surveying the sixteenth fairway, which ran behind Charlie's property. "What you thinking, Pro?" Rudy asked.

Plato sighed, and turned to the others. "Well, any suggestions? 'Cause I for one am not interested in a group of seven going to St Andrews. Looks bad and messes with the tee-times."

Rudy continued putting as a few names were tossed about. After nearly ten minutes of bandy, there was a lull in the discussion. Rudy sunk another putt from the edge of the green and smiled. He was glad none of the greens at the club were this flat. Made it too easy to control the ball. No challenge, no fun.

"What about Pat?" Charlie asked suddenly. He looked from beneath his eyebrows at each man. "He's a darn good golfer and I know he'd love to go. And I'd be really happy to have him along."

Vandeweghe pursed his lips then spoke. "He's so much younger than all of us, Charlie. Do you think he'd want to hang with a bunch of old farts?"

"Speak for yourself," Charlie said. "And yes, I know he'd like to hang with us. He does every Saturday morning, doesn't he?"

"Well, no." Rudy retrieved his ball from the cup. "Actually, he's way ahead of us, nearly driving the greens and making us all look bad." He grinned widely. "But I, for one, wouldn't mind seeing him taken down a peg or two. And what better place than at the Old Course?"

Vandeweghe laughed. "What better place, indeed! He'll meet his match at the Road Hole, I'll wager."

Chris waggled his wine glass. "Hey, if it's a vote, I'm all for it. I'd love to have P.Q. around. He's a hoot."

"And this time I'll allow you to bring the cigars," Plato said with a crooked smile. Chris gave him a thumbs-up and laughed.

Ridge snorted. "Patrick always has lots to say about your tee shots here at home, Chris. I'd sure like to hear what he'll have to say about your game at St Andrews." He glanced around at everyone. "Count me in."

Vandeweghe shrugged. "I like P.Q. He's the son I never had. So of course I don't mind. Especially if it makes Charlie happy."

Charlie squirmed in his chair. "Do you think Winterhalter would mind? I mean, he seemed to like Patrick, but he never said much."

Plato smiled. "Don was decidedly silent about most people beyond their game. I know he felt it just wasn't his place to judge. But I can assure you,

Charlie, Don couldn't care less how old Patrick is. He admires the way your son plays golf, and that's always been his number one criteria. But he also thinks Pat's a fine young man."

Charlie grunted. "You all make it sound like Patrick's a teenager. Heck, he's thirty-two years old and has a family!"

"Can you give him time away from the business?" Chris asked. "I mean, you're not in the same position as Braga, but it's still your business."

"And solid as a rock," Charlie said. "No pun intended. Don't you worry about my business."

Rudy lined up ten balls and began systematically putting them down the long side of the green. As he did so, the guys discussed the pros and cons to having Patrick along. Finally, Vandeweghe declared a vote.

"All in favor of P.Q. joining us, raise your hands," Vandeweghe said. Rudy joined as six hands went up in the air without hesitation.

"Okay then. Looks like our young Patrick Quinn is going along!" Vandeweghe said.

A small cheer went up. Rudy concluded his putting and followed the others as they moved to the upper deck, where Dawn was laying out an amazing dinner spread. Charlie disappeared, and Rudy had an idea what he was doing.

Sure enough, within five minutes Patrick arrived at the meeting. Amidst the joyful greetings and explanations of events, Patrick seemed surprisingly relaxed. Rudy wondered if he really did want to go, since he seemed so serene.

After dinner and dessert – the best brownies he'd ever tasted – Rudy went down to the fence at the back of the Quinn's property and watched a few golfers drive their way past Charlie's precious fruit trees. Motion to his right caught his eye. He turned and found Patrick sitting at a small tea-table hidden by large rhododendrons.

"What are you doing down here?" Rudy asked. "The activity's up there."

"I know," Patrick said, "which is why I'm down here. You old geezers are hard to keep up with."

There was a bright twinkle in Patrick's eye, and Rudy decided to ask his question outright. "Pat, do you want to go to Scotland, or are you doing this for your pop?"

Patrick looked like he'd been slapped. "You're kidding, right? No, no, no, no. I want to go, for sure. I've been bugging Pop about taking me along since you guys asked him."

Rudy clasped the younger man on his shoulder. "Don't take it personally. It was a function of who could go, who wanted to go, and who could afford to go. I guess we just assumed you'd have trouble with the latter."

"Thanks for your concern, Rudy." Patrick stood and stretched. "But I've been working at Pop's paver business since I was ten. I make enough."

"None of my business," Rudy said.

Patrick chuckled. "Okay, if I play so poorly that I get in the hole with you guys, then you can bail me out and say 'I told you so'."

"As long as you don't bet the clothes you're wearing, we should be okay," Rudy said. "I'm not giving up my good golf-wear for you."

"Like I could get one calf into your skinny slacks," Patrick said. "Jeez, Rudy, eat something once in a while, will ya?"

"Starting with some more of your mother's brownies? Come on," Rudy said, and headed back to the group, Patrick close behind.

As the second pan of brownies was being devoured, Vandeweghe got down to the business of the trip. "Okay, ladies. P.Q.'s inclusion to this great affair changes a few things."

Charlie frowned. "Such as?"

"Assignments!" Vandeweghe said. "Winterhalter and I have done our job."

"I'll say," Rudy said. "Sixteen rounds? If I didn't know better, I'd think you were trying to kill us."

"Leave that to the caddies," Plato said, grinning. "They all carry big whips."

"Well, you certainly won't need one, Pro," Vandeweghe said. "You scare us all with just a glare. Which I'm sure you'll be doing quite a bit in your new position as Caretaker of Pairings and Competitions."

Rudy thought Plato might crack a cheekbone with his smile.

Plato nodded repeatedly. "I'll come up with some interesting ones, too." He glanced around at the men at the table. "I assume none of you expected to play mild-mannered rounds of golf?"

Everyone chuckled. "Are you kidding?" Chris said. "We're all hoping the games kick Winterhalter's butt and we can win back some of what we lost over all these years."

"I'll just be happy not to come back broke," Charlie said.

Vandeweghe tapped the pad with his pen. "Okay, P.Q., since you always have that camera of yours in everyone's face, you're now our historian, in charge of taking the photos."

"But leave the video camera at home," Rudy said. "Nobody's interested in seeing how bad their swing is."

Vandeweghe pointed at Ridge. "And since the travel agency was able to easily arrange our ground transportation, you're now in charge of room assignments," he said. "I think we should rotate around, so everyone gets a chance to share a room with everyone else."

"Gee," Patrick mumbled, "You make it sound like a love fest. Should I start working on my pillow talk?"

Moans were mixed with chuckles, though Rudy noticed Ridge remained serious. "What is it, Ridge?" Rudy asked.

"Well, now," Ridge said, "I didn't realize we'd be sharing rooms."

"We don't have to share," Vandeweghe said. "We can all have separate rooms, if you want. I just thought it would keep the cost down. Significantly."

Chris nodded. "I agree with that. I don't suppose many of these places are cheap, and I, for one, don't really want to spend several hundred dollars a night, just to flop down on a bed."

"Conversely," added Rudy with a nod, "you don't want to stay in the cheap places. Over there, 'cheap' means roommates of a different kind."

"Not the two-legged types, I assume," Patrick said.

Rudy tipped his wine glass toward Patrick. "Exactly."

"Well, okay then," Ridge said. "As long as we all get the same kinds of rooms. None of this preferential treatment." He raised his bushy eyebrows and glared at Vandeweghe. "If you get what I mean."

Vandeweghe waved his hand dismissively. "No, no, of course not, Ridge. We'll all be staying at the same place."

"Do you expect me to make the reservations, too?" Ridge asked.

Vandeweghe shook his head. "I'll have the travel agents we use at the firm take care of that. If everyone's okay with it?"

A round of approval sealed the deal, and Rudy thought Ridge looked decidedly less anxious.

"Okay, then," Ridge said. "I'll flip a coin and sort y'all out. But don't any of you come complaining about so-n-so snoring."

Rudy glanced around. Charlie's face was gloomy and he was spinning his wine glass with gusto.

"What's up, Charlie?" Rudy asked. "You don't look happy with this arrangement."

Charlie shrugged. "Seems to me it'd be easier to just put us with someone we like, and leave it that way." He glanced at Patrick. "If it's all the same to the rest of you, I'd prefer to bunk down with my son."

Rudy nodded. That made sense to him, as well. He glanced at Plato, and his friend seemed to read his mind.

"Come to think of it, Gary," Plato said, "Rudy and I have traveled together before, and we settle into a routine very easily." He smiled. "I know I have to get to the shower first, or there'll be no hot water left."

Chris emptied a bottle of chardonnay into his glass. "And Winterhalter and I ended up together in Carmel during one of the Spyglass tournaments. I know I get along with his habits, and he with mine."

"That'd leave you with me," Vandeweghe said, nodding toward Ridge. "I'm fine with it, if you are."

"Sure, sure," Ridge said, nodding. "Long as you don't hog all the towels, I'd be happy to share a room with you."

Vandeweghe nodded. "So that's settled." He nodded toward Ridge. "I guess your job, then, is to simply dole out room numbers when we arrive at the hotels. That way there's no chance at 'preferential treatment'."

"Good by me," Ridge said with a curt nod.

Charlie pinged his glass with his index finger. "And while you're at it, put yourself in charge of wake-up calls. I may want to share a room with Patrick, but I sure don't want to be responsible for getting him up in the morning."

Patrick chuckled. "Especially if I've been out drinking all that Scottish beer, right Pop?"

"Beer?" Ridge's nose twitched. "Those hardy boys drink Scotch Whiskey. But either way, I have a brass horn laying around my work shop. I'll make sure it gets in the suitcase, just in case."

Rudy licked his fingers of the last brownie crumbs. He was very happy they'd managed to land Patrick as their eighth partner. He was a good kid – er, adult. He was a better-than-average golfer. And Winterhalter thought the world of him.

And that was what this was about, yes? Getting together with Don Winterhalter. Otherwise, why go? Rudy had already played most of the courses over there. Now it was his turn to share his school-of-hard-knocks knowledge of these places with someone who would actually benefit from it.

Charlie passed around yet another bottle of chardonnay. Then Vandeweghe stood, glass raised, and commanded attention. "Gentlemen," he said, "we're about to embark on a grand adventure. I'm not sure how we'll pull this off, other than all of us getting to Scotland. Heck, that's the easy part. But I know with this motley group, we'll manage to have one helluva time."

A round of "here-here!" and Ridge's "Amen to that!" endorsed Vandeweghe's words.

"So here's to Scotland and the games we'll find!" Vandeweghe said. "But most importantly, here's to the friends at this table!"

"And the one who's missing," Rudy added, "but only in body, not in spirit!"

"Here's to the eight balls!" Charlie said.

"Here-here!" and "Cheers!" and another "Aaaaa-men!" met the toast. Rudy took a large swallow of his wine.

"Eight Balls, Pop?" Patrick said, grinning. "We sound like a bunch of pool-players."

"You got a better idea?" Charlie asked. "Speak up."

"How about the Herd of Eight?" Ridge said. "That's about what we are, hoofing it around the course every Saturday, chewing up the turf."

"Yeah, a bunch of cowboys," Patrick said, then chuckled. "We're more like a gang of hoodlums, harassing the countryside and taking no prisoners."

"The Gangsters?" Chris said.

"No! I got it! The Gang of Eight!" Patrick said, leaning on the table with excitement. "We're the Gang of Eight, that's what we are."

Vandeweghe raised his glass for a third time. "To the Gang of Eight! May we rob the riches of each course and pay our pockets with grand delight!"

A collective moan met his statement. "What?" Vandeweghe said, "You don't like my poetry, go make some yourself. Jeez."

Rudy hoisted his glass. "To the Gang of Eight and their fearless leader, Gary Vandeweghe!"

To which all the other men responded with gusto.

Rudy watched Vandeweghe continue to organize the group. He certainly would need to be fearless, Rudy thought. The plan Vandeweghe had proposed was ambitious, and Rudy wondered how they'd manage to get it all to fall into place. He glanced around the table at the six men laughing and chatting and ribbing each other.

Well, there was his answer, by golly. These were accomplished men – intelligent, successful, used to getting things done. They may come from radically different backgrounds and work in vastly differing fields, but there wasn't a slacker among them.

With this group manning the ship, Rudy had no doubt they'd be in for the adventure of a lifetime.

And Scotland was just the place.

CHAPTER 19

March, 1998
Charlie Quinn

Charlie sat at the round table in his living room, a glass of cabernet and a bowl of almonds within reach. Methodically, he skimmed through the various magazines, travel brochures, and books he'd accumulated on Scotland.

"Find anything intriguing?"

Dawn stood beside him, her nightly cup of herbal tea steaming in her hand.

"Join me," he said, motioning to the chair on his right. "Scotland's a beautiful place. I wish you could see it."

Dawn settled into the chair and picked up the nearest brochure. *From Coasts to Castles! Experience Scotland!* Charlie watched her as she thumbed through the brochure. He adored the way she could focus so fully on something as mundane as a printed piece of publicity.

"Humph," she announced as she dropped the brochure on the table and retrieved another. "Looks beautiful, but then they're not likely to show the unsavory bits in a brochure, are they?"

Charlie grunted. "Notice they don't show many golf courses?" He shuffled pamphlets, then slid one across to Dawn. "In fact, this is the only one that has a photo."

Dawn looked surprised. "Really? I thought the courses were supposed to be the best in the world."

Charlie shrugged. "Oh they're damn good, though 'best' is a relative term. I'm sure there are lots of people who would argue the point." He tapped a photo in the brochure. "Notice how scruffy it looks? That's really tough, especially for us Americans, who are too damn used to groomed fairways and pristine greens." He took a swallow from his glass, shuffled through more of the brochures, and found the one he wanted.

"This course," he said, holding the cover up for Dawn to see, "Royal Aberdeen. Just thumb through this and look at those photos. You won't see a groomed patch of ground anywhere."

Dawn flipped a few pages, looking. Charlie went to refill his wine glass.

"Oh!" Dawn said. "This looks like a fax, Charlie. Did you see this?"

Charlie peered over the bar at the paper she held up. "Looks like the memo from Gucci." He gave his wife a crooked smile. "Just explaining the obvious."

Dawn read through it, then laughed. "Did you read this 'Rules' paragraph?" she asked. "This would keep me away from the place. And when are you going to grow your mustache?"

Charlie took the memo. On the second page were the paragraphs to which Dawn referred.

> *<u>Rules</u> - In Scotland, we will encounter some unique phenomena. There will be fences that are an integral part of the course, and rocks and pebbles that may be moved from a hazard. We will learn about rushes, bushes, whinns, heather, gorse, gnarleywood, and sea grass. Animals will have holes, casts, heaps, runways, droppings, skat, leavings, and dung. Sheep are outside agencies. There is no restriction on using a putter from off the green from any distance, and wedges are entirely optional and occasionally risky. At the Old Course, The Swilcan Burn is a creek, Granny Clark's Wynd (Chris, any kin?) is a road, and the Principal's Nose is a bunker to be avoided at all cost. So are the Beardies, the Benty, Kitchen, Hell, and Grave.*

Grooming - *Neatly trimmed facial hair will be barely tolerated. Mustaches are encouraged.*

Gary P - *How many days to departure!?*

Best regards,
GSV

"I'm pretty sure your son took that request for facial hair to heart," Charlie said. "Patrick's been growing a smudge on his face for the past few weeks now."

Dawn frowned. "He'll step out of this country clean shaven, or not at all," she said. Then she perked up. "How does he look?"

Charlie chuckled. "Like Patrick with a dirty face. How do you think he looks?" He picked up another large brochure and noticed a piece of paper sticking out toward the back page. He pulled it clear. *Scottish Update, May 19, 1998.*

"Another one?" Dawn said, reaching for it. "From Plato?"

Charlie nodded, sat back, and enjoyed his wine and the colors of the sunset as they played across his backyard.

"So do you know the answers to the riddles?" Dawn asked.

"What riddles?" Charlie took another swallow of wine.

"These..." Dawn said, pointed at the fax, then handed it to Charlie.

I have a riddle for the group. The first person to solve it will win a special prize. This is a two-part riddle.

* *Part #1* - *At St Andrews, what is the very unusual characteristic that relates to the double greens?*

* *Part #2* - *At St Andrews, what is the unusual characteristic that relates to the 16 greens adjacent to one another?*

He handed it back to Dawn, then flashed a smile. "I do know the answers, but I'm not telling."

"Not telling me? And why not? I'm not golfing with you guys."

Charlie began piling the brochures together. "Because you'll tell Pat, and he needs to figure it out on his own."

Dawn slapped the fax on the table. "Oh, don't be silly. I'm not going to tell Patrick. And what would it hurt if I did, anyway? I'm sure Vandeweghe or Winterhalter have figured it out already."

"Vandeweghe *better* know the answers, since he's a member of the R & A. Of the rest of the guys, more likely it will be Rudy who gets the answer in first. He's likes little bits and pieces of information like this."

Dawn looked over the fax again. "One hundred and one days to Scotland," she read. "Is it only that long before you leave?"

Charlie stood and stretched. "Yep. And I'm exhausted just thinking about it."

"Then let's get you to bed." Dawn retrieved her teacup, and glided from the room.

Charlie drained his glass as he watched her leave. She was a marvel, his wife. He glanced at the pile of brochures, and wished he could bring her along, show her Scotland. Having been there once, he was fairly sure there'd be days he'd prefer to spend with her – inside some museum or castle, out of the weather.

He sighed and stood. He'd go there with Dawn someday; this trip was for "the boys," and at least Patrick was joining them. That was something.

"Charlie! You coming?"

"Yes, dear!" he yelled. "Just putting the wine away."

Yep, someday he'd get her there. He'd just have to leave the golf clubs at home.

CHAPTER 20

May, 1998
Don Ridge

Ridge squirmed beneath the paper gown. A draft of cool air separated the opening in the back, causing him to shiver. He cursed under his breath and shifted his weight on the examination table. The paper under his butt-cheeks crumpled, becoming even more uncomfortable than it had been during the doctor's careful analysis.

The clock ticked. A quick glance around the tiny, antiseptic room told Ridge there were no magazines laying around to distract him. He tried whistling, but his lips and mouth were dry and all he could manage was a sad blowing sound.

Suddenly the door opened and a young nurse in brightly colored scrubs lit up the room. "You can get dressed now," she said officiously. "Doctor Whitaker will see you in his office, so come on out when you're ready." With a nod, she closed the door.

Ridge froze. He couldn't get off the table; didn't want to get dressed; certainly couldn't walk into the doctor's office. He knew Nellie would be there, waiting.

The clock clicked several more times. As if in a dream, he heard Plato's voice. *Pull the trigger, Don. Don't stand over the ball and freeze. You'll never hit a good shot that way.*

Ridge slid off the table and hurriedly dressed, leaving the offending paper gown spread-eagled on the floor.

Nellie was indeed waiting for him when he entered the office. She tried to smile, but her eyes belied her true emotion. So it was bad, after all, Ridge thought.

"Come on in, Don," Doctor Whitaker said, motioning to an overstuffed couch where Nellie perched. "Have a seat."

Ridge sat, resisting the urge to take Nellie's calming hand in his. He stiffened his spine. "So what's the prognosis, doc?"

Doctor Whitaker cocked his head and looked straight at Ridge. "It is cancer, after all," he said. "Prostate, though not far advanced, I'm glad to say."

Ridge exhaled. He hadn't even been aware he was holding his breath. Nellie sat ramrod straight beside him, not moving.

Panic welled up in Ridge's chest. Then, in his imagination he again heard the pro. "Assess the shot; where's the danger? Where's the best place to put the next shot?" Ridge focused on the doctor. "I play golf, doc," he said. "If I got a ball in a bad lie, I try to figure what's the best way to get that ball back into play." He leaned toward the doctor. "So what's the best way to get this ball in the hole?"

Nellie snorted, and stifled a chuckle. Doctor Whitaker shook his head and grinned. Ridge glared at Nellie. "Now you know what I mean, girl! I'm just trying to make sense of this thing the best way I know how."

Nellie waved a hand apologetically and tried to control her laughter. "I know, I know, dear," she mumbled. "It's just your choice of metaphor is, well, a bit explicit."

Ridge shook his head and turned to the doctor. "Well?"

Doctor Whitaker nodded. "I like your approach, Don. To continue the metaphor, you're on a par four with your drive lying buried beneath a bush, behind a tree. You're not out of bounds, nor have you lost your ball in a water hazard. While you've no direct shot to the green, you *do* have a chance of getting out on the fairway again. So –" He pulled a piece of paper from his desk drawer and drew a rudimentary diagram of a dog leg fairway, complete with a water hazard on one side and a bunch of trees on the other. He pointed his pen at the trees. "You're here. What we're going to do is try for three shots to the hole." He glanced at Nellie. "Sorry, Nellie, just – you know – keeping up with your husband here." Doctor Whitaker went back to the diagram. He drew a line from the trees directly across to the middle of the fairway. "First shot gets you out onto the fairway – that's hormones for about three, maybe four months. These are taken in pill form, and they should begin the process of shrinking the prostate."

"Okay, but I'm no closer to the hole," Ridge said. "So what's the point?"

Doctor Whitaker nodded. "The point is you're out from under the bush and behind the tree. Now you can see the green. From where you're at right now, with that prostate so enlarged, we can't really see the best line."

Ridge nodded. Made sense to him. "So what's the next shot?"

"Once the hormones have done what they can, we'll do a five week external radiation." Doctor Whitaker drew a line to the edge of the green. "That'll get you about here – closer to the hole, but just off the green. Once we've completed the radiation, we'll do a 'seed implant,' where we place a small number of 'hot' seeds into the prostate itself." He drew an arched line across the green, landing his metaphorical ball several feet from the tiny hole. "If we take a good line, and we're a little bit lucky, we'll get up and down in one –" He scribbled a wiggly line, which ended at the tiny dot of a hole. "And we'll get to the hole in par."

Ridge squirmed. This was all sounding particularly unpleasant. "And if we don't get lucky and we land short of the hole?"

Doctor Whitaker shrugged. "I'm certain we'll get close enough to make some minor adjustments and make bogey, at the worst." He smiled. "I'm pretty good with a putter."

"Glad to hear it," Ridge said. "But I'm supposed to go with a bunch of guys to Scotland in a few months. Is this whole process gonna keep me from going?"

"Don't worry too much, Don," Doctor Whitaker said and wadded the diagram into a tight ball. "This par four isn't going to end your game, either realistically or metaphorically. If you feel up to it, I'd suggest you continue with your plans to go to Scotland." He softly arched the paper ball into a small garbage can across the room. "And if you don't feel up to it, let me know and I'll take your place. I've always wanted to get over to Scotland to play."

Ridge frowned. "You're not going do something to make me feel all crummy, are you?"

Nellie nudged him and made a derisive noise, but the doctor laughed. "Well now," Doctor Whitaker said, "the thought hadn't crossed my mind, but if it'll guarantee me a spot at the Old Course, I might just have to make a mistake on your hormone dosage."

Ridge stood and held out a hand for Nellie. He winked at her then turned to Doctor Whitaker. "I trust you'll make enough out of my insurance to get there on your own dime, doc. Just get me those damn pills and I'll send you back a postcard or something."

Doctor Whitaker held out a hand for Ridge to shake. The grip was strong and firm. "I'll take you up on that, Don," the doctor said. "Now let's get you on the tee box, here." Ridge felt himself ushered out of the office and down the hall. "We'll need some blood drawn immediately to sort out the starting hormone level." The doctor motioned toward a door. "Step inside and we'll get you taken care of. Then you can go home and rest up for your big trip." With a smart salute, he was gone.

Ridge eased himself into the chair and grinned at Nellie. "Well, here we go."

Nellie shook her head, and smiled weakly back at him. "I expect you to make many a par on this trip of yours, Mr. Ridge." She cocked her head and Ridge noticed the little dimple on her chin that he liked so much. "Just watch that you don't make a hole-in-one until you're back on your home course."

Ridge threw back his head and laughed, and Nellie joined, relief filling the air. He had Nellie, and he had ... the laughter caught in his throat, his lungs clenched, and Ridge choked into great sobs. His chest heaved as memories of his daughter swelled in his heart.

Nellie folded him into her embrace. Ridge was vaguely aware that someone had stepped into the room, less aware that Nellie had shooed them away with a stern look and a dismissive wave of her hand. What he had become distinctly aware of was the warmth of Nellie's hand on the back of his neck, the sloppy feeling of tears in his beard, and – oddly – the sound of Plato's voice in his head.

Now don't dwell on the last shot, Don. The next shot is the only one worth thinking about. Move on. Don't bother reliving the past.

Ridge sucked in a lung-full of air, and the sobbing calmed. Nellie retrieved a tissue from somewhere in the room and Ridge mopped his face. After several more deep breaths he was able to manage a weak smile. Nellie smiled back, carefully dabbing at tears of her own.

"Well, now that that's over..." Ridge mumbled. "Let's get this done with so I can get out to the club and hit some balls."

Nellie crossed to the door and motioned to the nurse waiting outside. "You'll have time to play nine, if we hurry," she said.

Ridge nodded. The nurse prepared his arm, chatting amiably about the weather and the Giants' chances this season. Ridge imagined standing on the first tee on the Old Course and hitting the perfect drive – right down the middle of the fairway.

Next shot, Pro. *Don't look back...*

CHAPTER 21

June, 1998

Gary Plato

June 28, 1998

To: *Burger Deluxe*
Stone Hinge
Mission Prince
Shivas Irons
Old Tom Morris
Seamas McDuff
Tried & True
Silver Cloud

As of the date of this writing, we are exactly two months away from our arrival in the Kingdom of Golf, SCOTLAND.

The enthusiasm is evident, the anticipation is exciting, and the trip is at hand. In the following pages, please find:

1. *Your invitation to participate in a trip of a lifetime.*
2. *The introduction of the players.*

3. *The all-important Check List.*
4. *Ye Rules O' Play.*
5. *Summary page of Tee Times, Courses, Competitions, Accommodations, & Pairings.*
6. *Golf Course daily information.*
7. *Tournament Records & Pay Off.*
8. *Final Results Tally Sheet (to be completed).*

Lads 'tis the time to buff up the irons, refinish the wooden shafts & heads, apply the saddle soap to your leather grips, polish your shoes, practice your Scottish brogue, knit your wool cap, and wash your knickers. By the time you receive this package we will be less than 60 days from take off.

For those of you who didn't answer the 5/19/98 Scottish Riddle, here are the questions and answers.

QUESTIONS:

1. At St Andrews, what is the very unusual characteristic that relates to the double greens?

ANSWER: The holes that share double greens all total to the sum of eighteen.

2. At St Andrews, what is the unusual characteristic that relates to the sixteen greens adjacent to one another?

ANSWER: Other than Greens #1 and #18, the remaining greens on the golf course adjacent to one another all add up to a total of eighteen.

Gentlemen,'tis the time to prepare for a wonderful trip, so practice hard with your baffing spoons, mashies, and niblicks. We have but a wee bit o' time to prepare.

All my best to you lads,
"Shivas Irons"

CHAPTER 22
June, 1998
Chris Clark

Chris entered his home office and tore open his packet with gusto. The months of planning were coming to a close, and he was anxious to see what Plato had concocted for tournaments and pairings at each of the courses they'd play in Scotland.

The list of names at the top of the memo made him pause. He grinned. Plato was up to his tricks, creating personas for each member of the Gang, and Chris liked it. He quickly deduced "Burger Deluxe" was his – after all, his father had owned the Burger Pit restaurants – but he wondered who belonged to each of the other monikers.

He poured himself a glass of white wine, then sunk into his chair and skimmed the letter, pausing to enjoy the answers to the St Andrews quiz. He hadn't known them when Plato first asked, but a bit of research had secured the correct answers. He wondered who had not played along. Chris shrugged, then looked at the included document. He was met with Michael Murphy's opening lines from his novel *Golf in the Kingdom*: "In Scotland, between the Firth of Forth and the Firth of Tay, lies the Kingdom of Fife – known to certain lovers of that land simply as 'The Kingdom.'"

Chris chuckled. Leave it to the Pro to begin with a literary quote. The guy was better read than a librarian, at least where golf publications were concerned.

Beneath Murphy's words was a sentence in bold: "A Walk into the Past with Old Friends in the Kingdom of Golf." Pride swelled up in Chris. This truly was a trip with old friends – men he'd grown up with, who had seen him through some of his toughest times, and cheered his best accomplishments. What better way to explore the birthplace of golf than with men who were such a part of his personal past.

He read the checklist Plato had created.

- *Do not forget your PASSPORT.*
- *Do not forget your PLANE TICKETS.*
- *Old Tom, do you have your tickets?*

So Old Tom Morris must be Don Ridge. Ridge had a reputation of forgetting important things like tee times and plane tickets, though Chris had never personally witnessed any such loss of memory on Ridge's part.

- *Bring a Major Credit Card(s).*
- *Travelers Checks.*
- *Personal Checks do not work very well.*
- *US Cash works very well and often provides a slightly better exchange rate.*

Chris chuckled, thinking of tips to caddies. "A not-so-veiled hint, there, Pro."

- *Tried & True recommends $1,500 to $2,000 in walk-around money.*
- *Who do we entrust all of this cash to? Stone Hinge, bring the safe.*

Chris envisioned the idea of Charlie and Rudy as Charlie Chaplin and Marcel Marceau, the mime, dressed as if in a 1920s black and white silent movie, dragging around a metal safe.

- *Weather probably breezy, not cold – chilly in the morning then in the 60's or low 70's. Could get some Scottish mist (rain), so bring rain gear. Burger Deluxe is the Weather Chairman.*

Chris raised his eyebrows. "I am? And what am I supposed to do? Morning prayers for sunshine?" Best leave that to Ridge. He's probably got a direct line to the Big Man Upstairs and would be a helluva lot more effective.

- *You will need a sport jacket and tie for a couple of dinners and lunches.*
- *Seamus McDuff has arranged outstanding meals throughout the trip.*
- *Coach – bring the BBQ just in case. Burger Deluxe has volunteered.*

As with the safe, he enjoyed the image of them carrying a barbecue – an old, round, red one that used charcoal. He laughed outright at the picture of them trying to check it at the airport. Still, too bad they couldn't bring one – he could barbecue a darn good burger, if he did so say himself. He wondered what the food in Scotland would be like. What was that stuff everyone always commented on? Haggis? What, exactly, was haggis? He'd have to do some more research before getting on the plane.

- *Bring normal golf clothes, wind shirt, and full rain suit.*
- *Tried & True and his assistant Old Tom Morris are in charge of doing the laundry.*

At this, he burst into laughter. The idea of Ridge and whoever "Tried & True" was laundering this group's underwear struck him as delightfully ludicrous. He could just see Ridge tossing tighty-whities into a British washer ... and then cursing in that Southern drawl when they came out shrunken to child-size. No, he for one would bring enough clothing to last the trip, without laundering.

- *Bring a light bag, as golf carts are not the order of the day. Either caddies or trolleys.*
- *Golf Balls are expensive so bring enough. (14 Rounds – Old Tom bring a gross).*
- *Spikeless shoes are probably the safest bet. One or two pair of golf shoes.*
- *Chief Silver Cloud said he will have the ponies ready to get us from the airport to the courses in the countryside. He has also volunteered to herd the sheep off the courses.*
- *Burger Deluxe is our navigator. He promised to bring maps and a compass.*

Instinctively, Chris glanced at the manila folder that held pages of printed maps. He'd gathered them in every conceivable format before realizing he just didn't want the responsibility of steering the group around Scotland, on roads with names he couldn't pronounce and through towns which looked smaller than his high school campus. He'd tried to talk Rudy or Vandeweghe into that chore, since they'd been to Scotland before and probably had a better sense of direction, but to no avail. Finally, he'd done some research on tour buses, and discovered a small company that specialized in providing local drivers and vans for just such excursions as this. He'd booked it, then broke the news to the rest of the guys last Saturday after their round. Initially, there was resistance, but once Vandeweghe got on board, there was no going back.

Chris took a swallow of his wine. Either Plato had written this letter before Saturday and neglected to edit it, or he was still holding out hope that Chris would navigate. It didn't matter; the van was paid for, and the manila folder would remain here, in his study.

- *Mission Prince – bring the cameras and your diary.*

Gang of Eight: The First Tee

- *Stone Hinge – you are in charge of the alarm clocks. Don't forget the combination to the safe.*
- *Old Tom Morris is in charge of the room assignments and the score card audit. Bring your earplugs and your PC.*
- *If we have missed anything, please don't be bashful, send along your comments and suggestions so we can include them in the checklist.*

Nothing seemed to be missing, so he continued to read.

<u>YE RULES O' PLAY</u>:
- *Rules of Play: USGA and Royal & Ancient Rules of Golf shall apply.*
- *Tees to be used: Announced each day prior to tee-off.*
- *Play the ball as it lies unless otherwise specified.*
- *We are playing Golf lads; all balls must be holed out.*

Well, now, that was likely to raise a few eyebrows, if not annoy one or two. "Gimmes" were all too often employed, but Plato had a historical aversion to them, so his rule to hole out a ball wasn't much of a surprise. Still, Chris wondered how long it would last. "I give it four rounds," he mumbled. "Or maybe just three."

- *Turn your scorecards into Gary Plato's assistant (Don Ridge) at the conclusion of your rounds.*
- *The Rules Committee will make all rules decisions: Shivas Irons, Seamas McDuff, and Tried & True. When in doubt, proceed under USGA Rule 3-3 (Stroke Play Only).*
- *Play away without delay.*
- *In the Scottish Stroke Play you can only win in the division.*

The phone rang. Chris glanced at it, then heard Hally pick it up. When she didn't call his name, he turned his attention back to Plato's document.

"Introductions" were next. Now he'd find out who was who in this game of golf charade.

> *I would like to take this opportunity to formally introduce each of you to the distinguished group of gentleman golfers who will soon be venturing off to play this great game in the Kingdom of Golf.*
>
> <u>Burger Deluxe</u> *is the son of one of the "All Time Great Hamburger Tycoons." "Hamburger Bill" was years ahead of his time. It is only fitting that this young gentleman, Chris Clark, be appropriately named "Burger Deluxe." He is indeed deluxe in every sense of the word.*

His father's smiling face crossed Chris's thoughts. He'll like this nod to his business, one that had taken much of his time and kept him from many a game at the club. Chris still wished his dad had joined the Saturday group. Perhaps, like Patrick and Charlie, they'd be going on this trip together. A sigh escaped Chris and he forced his focus back to the list.

> <u>Stone Hinge</u> *has worked for a large portion of his adult life in concrete and building business in a variety of venues. Not only does he hinge the stones, he possesses one of the smoothest hinging actions in captivity. It is for these reasons we crown Charles Quinn – Stone Hinge.*
>
> <u>Mission Prince</u> *heads up that fabulous business venture and is truly a chip off the old block. Since Patrick Quinn is not yet the King of Mission Concrete, he must be the Mission Prince.*
>
> <u>Shivas Irons</u> *is the legendary Golf Professional in Michael Murphy's novel,* <u>Golf in the Kingdom</u>, *in the legendary Kingdom of Golf, at the legendary Links of Burningbush (St Andrews Golf Club). Since Gary Plato is the old pro journeying to the Kingdom of Golf, we must name him Shivas Irons.*

Chris shook his head. Plato enjoyed his game so much he forgot he was creating it. "Who's this 'we'?" Chris asked the paper in his hands.

> *Old Tom Morris was a famous old Scottish Professional with a full white beard. He won the British Open four times. His swing was recognized as one of the best. Who else could this be but America's own Carolina Sweet Swinger, Don Ridge?*
>
> *Seamas McDuff was a central character in Golf in the Kingdom, a novel by the eloquent Michael Murphy. It was said he was a "Wise Man" who was a special friend of Shivas Irons. A man of much wisdom, a deep thinker, and the conscience of the game. It is said that Seamas taught Shivas most o' what he knows about the game. May I introduce the one and only Rudy Staedler as the infamous Seamas McDuff.*
>
> *Tried & True is a gentleman who is just that, he has been Tried and we all know he is very True. However, this gentleman owns a horse that led the Kentucky Derby for part of this year's race. The horse's name was Old Trieste. Trieste is synonymous with dependable, faithful, secure, consistent, stable, unfailing, infallible, reliable, and trustworthy. Doesn't that say it all about our dear friend Gucci? We therefore bestow the name of Tried & True on none other than Gary Vandeweghe.*
>
> *Last but certainly not least is Silver Cloud. If you haven't had the pleasure of playing at Club Terravita, one of Arizona's premier courses, and stayed at his lovely home, then you haven't turned into one of Terravita's fabulous subdivisions, "Silver Cloud," adjacent this prestigious club. There are many names we could have bestowed upon this exceptional individual; however, Silver Cloud seemed to be so appropriate for none other than the last of the sweet singers, Don Winterhalter.*

Chris crossed to the family room and retrieved a bottle of chardonnay from the small refrigerator in his wet bar. He could hear Hally moving about the kitchen, preparing dinner. He sniffed the air. Hm. Spaghetti. He probably should have opened a cabernet. Oh well. With glass and document in hand, Chris sunk into the couch.

The remainder of the pages outlined the courses they'd play, along with tee-times, pairings, and the style of tournament. Chris whistled. There were now fifteen rounds scheduled over thirteen days of actual play. He wondered if Charlie's back would hold out.

Along with both the Old and New courses at St Andrews, the list included some of the best-known courses in the world: Turnberry, Carnoustie, Royal Troon. There were several lesser-known courses, and one marked simply "The Mystery Course." He sipped his wine. No doubt it would be worth the 'price of admission;' Vandeweghe would make certain of that.

"Chris?" Hally called. "Brooke! CJ! William! Dinner!"

"Coming!" Chris returned, and dropped the document on the coffee table. He could hear his children jostling for position and drinks from the refrigerator. They would all learn to play golf, though he wondered if any of them would really take to the game. He hoped so. This trip to Scotland was with the Gang of Eight, but he hoped it would also be a reconnaissance trip – a way to decide where to take Hally and the kids in the future.

"Chris!" Hally's voice cut into this thoughts, and he got to his feet. "Yeah, yeah, I'm coming!" He glanced at the document, and the feeling of pride washed over him once again.

Family. Friends. Golf. Yep, life was good.

CHAPTER 23

August, 1998

Don Ridge

"You be careful up there!"

Don Ridge waved acknowledgment of his wife Nellie's warning. "Did you hear me? I'm not just blowing smoke here!"

"Yeah, yeah, I heard ya!" Ridge yelled back, then exited the house through the back door. It was a warm morning and the sun was already high in the sky. Dang it, he should have managed to get up earlier.

In the barn, he paused to admire the five antique autos he stored there, all in various stages of restoration. Their dusty headlamps seemed to look at him with hope, and he hurriedly gathered the ladder and tools he'd need. Maybe tomorrow he'd work on the Model A.

Carefully he positioned the ladder against the fascia of the barn, hiked his way up, and positioned himself beside a loose sheet of jagged roofing metal. The sheet was almost too warm to the touch, and again he wished he'd gotten up earlier. Oh well, "suck it up" as Winterhalter often said.

The thought of Winterhalter made him smile. It was less than a month before they all converged on Scotland.

"Ow!" Ridge yelped. "Dag nabbit!" He sucked his throbbing thumb. How had he managed to smack it with the hammer? Stupid.

"Keep your mind on your business," he said aloud, then again set about the task of repairing the roof. Several minutes went by as he pulled, flattened, screwed, and hammered the metal back into place. He scrambled higher up on the roof, looking for the next loose piece. The back door slammed.

"Don!" Nellie yelled. "You up there?"

Ridge didn't look around. "Yeah, I'm up here. On the south end."

He pushed down a particularly twisted piece, nailed it into place, then prepared to screw it down more securely.

"How are you doing up there?" Nellie called.

Ridge glanced over his shoulder. She was now standing alongside the barn, looking up at him, her hand shading her face. Ridge pushed down on the screw and began twisting it into place. "I'm ... fine ... dear," he said between exerted twists. "Just ... finishing ... up."

"Why didn't you attach yourself to the safety hooks, Don?" Nellie asked, an edge to her voice. "If you slip there's nothing to catch you."

"Nellie, I'm just fine." He gathered his tools and stuffed them into his overall pockets. "I'm almost done, girl. I have one more small spot to screw down." He sat on his heels and looked down at her. "Why don't you go make some lemonade, hm? It's damn hot up here."

Nellie made a face. "I suppose you deserve lemonade," she said, implying maybe he didn't, really. "But I wish you'd tie yourself on up there."

"I'm just fine," Ridge said, gently, then clambered toward the last torn piece of sheet metal. He heard Nellie walk away, heard the screen door slam. He had just reached the trouble spot when his foot slipped and he went down hard on his knee. His other foot slid out from under him and wham! he was down on his belly, sliding. Panic gripped him. He clawed at the hot metal, and scrambled to get his boots back under him. The bucket of nails and screws overturned and the contents tumbled out, sliding and rolling down the metal with a terrible racket. He yelped, knowing the edge was near, and prepared to go over the edge. Then the rubber toe of his boot stuck to the metal. He stopped sliding. Quickly he scuttled up the roof, away from the edge.

He took a few deep breaths, willing his heart to stop pumping so hard in his ears, his hands to stop shaking. The screen door opened.

"Don, lemonade's done!" Nellie called.

"Fine, fine," Ridge yelled back, a bit louder than he'd intended. He drew in another deep breath. "I'm almost done here. Be just a minute."

The door closed. Lord, let me get off this roof, he prayed. In one piece.

He looked at the last spot of storm damage and decided it wasn't worth repairing at this point. He'd wait until some other day. Besides, all the screws and nails were on the ground, along with the bucket.

He slowly crawled to the ladder, feeling more secure with every step. He found two screws along the way and almost returned to the task, but decided to follow his initial instinct and get off the roof. He swung around, found the first rung with his left foot, grasped the edges of the ladder, and began to lower himself down.

Again, the screen slammed, and he heard Nellie say, "Don, you all done?" He half turned to answer her, and his weight fell against the side of the ladder. Before he could get a word out, the ladder wobbled, pitched, and began to fall away from the roof line.

Nellie screamed – not a high pitched, little girl scream from the movies, but more of a deep yell. Ridge realized, with a slow-motion sensibility caused by the adrenaline flashing through his veins, that he was falling backward from nearly thirty feet; that there was a power line to the house behind him; that the tree which might break his fall also had several dead branches which were sharp, and which he'd neglected to yet remove. All this ran through his mind in a flash, as Nellie screamed, or yelled, or whatever...

Ridge threw his body to the right. The ladder twisted and slid right, then forward. It smacked hard against the edge of the roof, then continued sliding. Nellie yelled Don's name as he rode the ladder until he was ten feet from the ground. He jumped. The ladder clattered to the hard ground. Ridge landed on his feet, hard. Unfortunately, he also landed on a section of jagged rock. The soles of his boots, though thick, could not withstand the impact, and split across the balls of his feet. Ridge let out a yell of pain, and crumpled.

"Don! Oh my God, Don!" Nellie yelled, then reached him. "Don, are you okay?!"

Don rolled over onto his back. Sharp objects jabbed at him. "Oh dammit!" he yelped, and pushed himself to his feet. "Blasted nails! They're stabbing me in the back!"

"Don, did you break anything? Can you walk?" Nellie fussed over him, touching, squeezing, prodding.

Ridge felt dizzy. He bent over, grabbing his calves to steady himself. "I don't think anything's broken, Nell," he said. "I just feel like I'm gonna throw up."

Nellie grasped his arm and tugged slightly. "Come on, let's get you inside," she said.

Ridge took a step and stabbing pain shot across his foot and up his leg. He yelped and nearly buckled.

"Don!" Nellie said. "What is it? Did you break a leg after all?"

Ridge gingerly bent over and reviewed the sole of his boot. Leaning on Nellie, he dug the long screw out from its imbedded place. "This probably has something to do with it," he said. He gingerly put weight on the foot. It was definitely sore, but the shooting pain was gone.

He allowed Nellie to steer him to the house. He leaned as much weight as he dared on his slender wife, and together they made the couch without incident. As Nellie went for cold towels and a bag of ice, Ridge removed his boots. Already his feet were beginning to swell, the balls turning an ominous shade of blue.

"Oh dag nabbit!" he yelled. "How am I gonna play golf on these!" He gestured toward his throbbing feet. "What am I gonna do?!"

Nellie entered the living room with her supplies – the large oval tub they used to wash the dogs, the bag of ice from the "party fridge," and a canister of epsom salts. "You're going to soak those feet in this," she said, and dropped it all beside him. She ripped open the ice, poured it into the tub, and pointed. "I'll go get some water, but stick your feet in there now," she said.

Ridge complied. The ice burned, and he gasped with renewed pain. Nellie returned with three large pitchers of water. She dumped them into the bucket, which brought initial relief, then an even sharper pain in his left foot. "Ow!" Ridge cried and jerked his foot from the tub. Pink fluid swirled around.

"You're cut," Nellie said. "Let me get some iodine."

"Bring me a shot of whiskey while you're at it," Ridge yelled as she disappeared down the hall.

"You need iodine, not whiskey on that!" Nellie called back.

"I'm not gonna use it on my foot, woman!" Ridge yelled. "I'm gonna drink it!"

Nellie came in, laughing. She poured a generous amount of iodine into the tub, turning the water a pale gold. Then she added the epsom salts. "That'll hurt like the dickens," she said, "but it'll help clean it out. Now stick your feet in there."

"It's gonna turn me yellow'" Ridge mumbled, but obediently followed directions. It wouldn't do him any good to argue. The salt and iodine burned fiercely in the wound, but he just gritted his teeth and kept silent. Nellie brought him a small tray with a tall lemonade, and two shots of whiskey. Ridge smiled wanly through the pain. "Can I have three?" he said, to which he received a playful push on his shoulder.

"You just sit there and soak," Nellie said, and turned on the television. "Call me if you want anything else."

A moment later, he heard the screen door slam. He looked out the window. Nellie crossed to the barn, and began picking up nails and screws and putting them in the bucket.

Ridge flopped back on the cushions. "How am I gonna play golf?" he moaned to the ceiling. "This here's a disaster." He downed the shots and sipped at the lemonade. The burning in his feet subsided. With his feet resting, numb, in the metal bucket, Don slipped into sleep.

"Well, you're lucky," the doctor said after examining the x-rays. "You've badly bruised both your feet, especially the balls, and you have that small puncture wound, but you don't have any substantial damage."

Ridge sighed with relief. At least he wouldn't have to endure a cast. That would have knocked him out of the trip completely. "But I can walk on 'em, right? I mean, I won't damage them more, right?"

The doctor made a funny face and shrugged. "You can do whatever doesn't cause you pain," he said. "I'd suggest you stay off of them for at least ten days, maybe two weeks, but if you can't do that, then take two pain relievers every four hours and do what you want. Obviously, the more you walk on them, the slower they'll heal."

Ridge carefully pulled on his slippers. "I assume ice is good for them?"

The doctor nodded. "The more the merrier. And keep them elevated as much as possible." He then left Ridge alone to suffer.

"Dog nabbit!" Ridge spat at his offending appendages. Scotland was two weeks away. "Not now!"

When he slid into the passenger seat of their car, he cursed again. Nellie bit her lip. "Well, there's no cast, so I guess that's a good sign," she said, then steered the car toward home. "What did he say?"

Ridge clenched his fist. "That I should stay off 'em for two weeks. I don't have two weeks!"

Nellie shook her head. "You have ten days. That'll have to do. I can pack most of your bag for you. Just tell me what you need. There's nothing pressing around the farm I can't handle on my own." She glanced at Ridge and smiled warmly. "You'll be fine, love. Just you wait and see."

Ridge sighed. He leaned back in the seat and closed his eyes, visions of Scotland assuaging his anger. "Thank you, Nells," he said softly. "At least the grass in Scotland is soft."

He hoped it was, anyway.

CHAPTER 24

August 27, 1998
Don Winterhalter

Don steered the car into the departure area at the Phoenix International Airport. He felt almost giddy. He unloaded his bag and golf clubs onto the curb, then turned to Penny. "Okay. Think I got everything. Let's see if the plane is still leaving."

Penny gave him a quick hug and an even quicker kiss. "You would have heard if it wasn't. Now go have a great time. Take lots of photos and I'll see you in gay Pari'."

Don gave her a kiss of his own. "Yes, you will." He collected his luggage, then marched through the sliding glass doors. He didn't look back.

The trip across "the pond" was uneventful, thank heavens, and Don even managed to get some sleep. When they arrived in Heathrow, he remained focused on the task at hand – getting to Scotland and, ultimately, Turnberry. He still had several hours of travel ahead of him.

The bag carousel came to an abrupt halt. He pursed his lips and frowned; his bag and clubs had not been delivered. He turned to look for the airline customer service desk, then turned back as, with a screech of gears, the carousel jolted to a start and the conveyor belt began to roll. Within seconds both his bag and his clubs slid down before him. With a sigh of relief, Don organized himself and followed the signs to his connecting flight to Glasgow.

It was midday in Great Britain. The plane slid gently through the air, and there was a clear view of the landscape below: a patchwork of greens and browns and the occasional blue of a lake or a river. There were no clouds, and he hoped the weather would be this bright and sunny for the next few weeks. Could they be so lucky?

Well, they had been so far.

"Turnb'rry 'Otel, sir."

The cab driver's Scottish brogue rolled through the name like rich syrup, but Don was too busy looking up at the expansive hotel to respond. A massive beauty, the white building stretched lengthwise along a ridge, its rust-red roof dotted by gabled windows and numerous chimneys. Its visage was both inviting and forewarning – enter all who respect the game and its history; woe to those who are ignorant.

Turnberry. Site of two famed Open Championships: the 1977, won by Tom Watson in a tight race to the finish against Jack Nicklaus, and the 1986, when Greg Norman galloped away from the field and into the record books. Turnberry. Considered one of the best courses in Great Britain, and, in Don's estimation, the world.

He grinned and a little hum of delight escaped his lips.

He had arrived.

For the first several hours, Don busied himself unpacking and getting the "lay of the land." He found the restaurants, discovered where the best Scotch, beer, and wine were served (everywhere in the hotel, it turned out), and what the schedules were for High Tea and other complimentary refreshments. Then he wandered outdoors, enjoying the warm sun and light breeze. Quite a few people were seated on the grassy hill that rolled gently down from the hotel toward the Clubhouse. They drank and nibbled on various foods, and watched the golfers below. Don had the feeling he'd just landed in a very genteel tournament.

He glanced at his watch. Six o'clock. No wonder his stomach was grumbling. Time for dinner.

The call of a Scottish bagpipe echoed across the grounds. A single strong note held for several seconds, then became a song powerful and bright. Don shielded his eyes from the sun and looked around. There, between the clubhouse and the hotel, moved a single bagpiper in full regalia. His pace was steady, but within moments he had crossed to the terrace.

Don trotted down the stairs. He paused thirty feet from the player, wanting to take in the whole experience but cautious not to get too close.

The piper was an older man who stood tall and proud. His jacket was as dark as his pipes, while his kilt was a plaid reminiscent of the surroundings – sky blue, carnation red, and limousine black. Behind him, the golf courses spread out, glistening in the sunset. He completed one song and seamlessly shifted into another.

Don's breath caught in his lungs, his eyes moistened with emotion. Don't be silly, he thought, and swallowed hard. But as the music played on, he decided there was nothing silly about the feeling of pride he felt. He also felt ... what?

Contentment, he decided. And a feeling of belonging. He was a golfer, had been his whole life. There was very little better than this.

If anything.

The next morning, Don was up before first light. Jet lag might have had something to do with it, but he was fairly sure it had more to do with excitement. Forgoing a large breakfast, he headed for the clubhouse. He stepped out the front door of the hotel and hummed. The sun was rising behind the large building, and before him lay both the verdant green of the Ailsa course and the shimmering ocean: the Firth of Clyde. Ailsa Craig, a dome shaped island, hung suspended just above the water in the distance, a lump of granite beckoning him to tee it up and drive a blazer from the beach. A breeze ruffled the tufts of tall grasses that dotted the hillside, and the occasional screech of a seagull danced on the air. Below him, the Dormy House sat quiet, resting before the bustle of the day to come.

He was soon to be joined by seven of his closest pals, and together they were heading out for a grand golfing adventure. But right now, in this moment, he was a lone golfer. In Scotland. At Turnberry.

For a brief second he felt as if he could look down and find knickers on his legs, a mashie at his side, a feather ball in his hand. The timelessness of the place was palpable.

A voice from the past, thick with an ancient Scottish brogue, echoed across the porch. "Excuse me, sir, but is there somethin' you'd be needin'?"

Don felt a chill run up his spine. If it was this magical here, he couldn't wait to get to St Andrews.

"Sir? You awl-right?"

With a start, Don realized the voice came from a young man standing beside him. Don hummed and grinned, then gestured toward the clubhouse. "I've never been better. Just taking in the view before heading out to play a round."

The young man, neatly dressed in the hotel's uniform, nodded vigorously. "It's the best, I'd 'ave t'agree. Ye've n'er bin here b'fore, no?"

Don shook his head. "Just seen it on TV when they televised The Open."

"Well, then," the young man said, "you're in for a grand day. Would y'be wantin' a cup o'coffee to take wit'ya, 'n maybe a bun? They're real fresh this time o'day."

"That sounds great. Can I get them down at the clubhouse?"

"Ay, but the freshest ones're right here. If'n ye'll wait just a few seconds, I'll fetch 'em for ya."

Don smiled. The young man's enthusiasm was infectious and, as much as Don wanted to get on the course, the rumbling in his stomach told him the coffee and pastry was probably worth the delay. "I'll wait right here. Room 137, for the tab."

The young man nodded briskly and trotted off. Don watched the sun's entrance place a glow on the dewey course and glint off the mild ripples in the ocean. He couldn't wait until the rest of the guys arrived to share all this beauty. Oh, they'd pretend to be too busy to notice, but he knew every one of them would be as struck as he.

Silver tray in hand, the young man returned. "I didn't know if y'required milk or sugar, so I brought 'em, just 'n case."

Don's mouth watered as he reached for the steaming coffee and the large, robust apple pastry. "No, just black," he said. "Okay if I leave the cup at the clubhouse? I'd like to head down there."

"Ye kin leave it anywhere ye'd like, sir," the young man said. "We'll find it, no doubt." He stepped back and nodded curtly toward the course below. "She's waitin' on ye, sir. 'Ave a good round, now."

And he was gone.

Don sipped the coffee and took a bite from the pastry. Damn it was good. He started down the path toward the clubhouse below. The sun warmed his back, and the view warmed his soul. All that was needed was a club to warm his hands.

CHAPTER 25

August 28, 1998
Rudy Staedler

Rudy stood at the end of Charlie Quinn's driveway and stared up the road. Nothing. He glanced at his watch. One-thirty-six. "You're late," he mumbled. "Blast it."

"Hey Seamas McDuff!" Patrick bellowed from the house.

"What?" Rudy called back, continuing to stare at the road. "I'm looking for the limo. It's late!"

"Well it won't come as long as you're standing out there," Patrick said. "You know the old adage: a watched pot never boils. Come on in and have some more champagne!"

Rudy wrinkled his forehead. "I'm not going anywhere until that damn limo shows up. Then I'm going to be the first one in."

"Suit yourself!"

Rudy looked at his watch again. One-thirty-eight. Where was the damn thing? Gary Vandeweghe joined him, standing at his side and looking up the street as well.

"You think he got lost?" Vandeweghe asked. "Did someone give him the wrong day?"

"No," Rudy said, "Charlie called the limo company himself. He certainly knew the date and the directions."

Vandeweghe stuffed his hands in his pockets and shrugged his shoulders. A big grin creased his face. "This is amazing, though, isn't it, Rudy? This is really going to happen!"

Rudy glared up the empty street. "Maybe."

"Oh heck, the limo will come," Vandeweghe said. "We've got more than three hours before the plane leaves."

"Takes two just to get to the airport," Rudy said. "More if there's traffic."

"I can't even remember all the work we've done to get this far," Vandeweghe said. "It just seems like yesterday I was in the club's parking lot talking to Plato about doing this. And here we are!" He swept his right hand in a wide arc. "About to get in a limo..."

"Finally!" Rudy exclaimed as a shiny black auto slid around the corner into sight. He turned toward the house and yelled. "Hey fellas! Limo's here! Let's get crackin'!"

"See, I told you it would come," Vandeweghe said, with a big smile. "Nothing's going to get in the way of our trip to Scotland. Not today!"

Rudy threw a cautious look toward his jubilant friend. "Don't jinx it, now, you big oaf. We don't arrive until tomorrow."

Vandeweghe raked the air with his paw. "Ack, you're being superstitious." The limo parked and the engine cut. With a flourish, Vandeweghe yanked open the back door and gestured to Rudy. "Get in before you trip on an acorn and break a leg. I'll get your bags."

Rudy snuffled and headed for the large stack of suitcases and golf bags piled high in the front courtyard. "I can get them myself. With my luck you'd forget my clubs and I'd have to rent a set."

"Nothing like a good niblet to make your round at the Old Course!" Vandeweghe said, and Rudy laughed as the tall man bounded to retrieve his own suitcase and clubs.

"Okay, here's my bag," Patrick said, dropping an extra large suitcase beside the limo.

Rudy laughed. The bag was bigger than he was. "Jeez, P.Q.," he said. "You bringing half of San Jose with you?"

Patrick grabbed his clubs. "Nope," he said. "But I'm planning on bringing all of Scotland back!"

Rudy relaxed as the limousine flew up Highway 280, making up for lost time. They arrived at San Francisco International Airport with more than two hours before takeoff. Joviality filled the air as the seven men checked their baggage. Lady Luck seemed to be working overtime as they learned there were seven seats available for upgrade in Business Class, and they all made arrangements to move forward from coach. They sauntered through the airport and found a sports bar in which to while-away the wait. The time slid by quickly, and soon enough Rudy followed his friends onto the plane.

He settled into his seat and breathed a sigh of relief. This was it. They were on their way. Beside him, Plato blew up a travel pillow.

A sedate male voice emanated from the speakers above. "Ladies and gentlemen, this is your captain." Rudy closed his eyes; this was going to be the usual rigmarole about welcome, thank you for flying, time in the air –

"...delay of about twenty minutes or so, depending on traffic control," the captain said. "So sit back and relax. We'll keep the air moving for your comfort."

Rudy gladly accepted a news magazine from the stewardess. They had an hour and a half to catch their connection in Heathrow; twenty minutes wouldn't be a problem. The stewardess returned with an offer of champagne, which he declined, then he quickly settled in to reading an article about Amsterdam, and the time slipped by.

"Well, ladies and gentlemen," the Captain delivered, "looks like we'll be a little longer. Air Traffic Control hasn't yet given us the go-ahead on leaving our berth, so we'll be at least another half hour before takeoff. I've given the cabin staff the okay to serve nonalcoholic, cold beverages. So sit back, enjoy a pop or some juice, and we'll get you on your way just as soon as they allow."

Rudy slapped his thighs with the magazine "Another half hour? We'll be cutting it close in London."

Plato nodded. "I know. But think of it as if we're standing on the tee, waiting for the group in front to find their drive. Nothing to do but enjoy the scenery."

Charlie and Patrick sat on Rudy's left, in the center aisle. They had initially purchased an extra seat in coach, for added comfort. "I'm not going to have Patrick elbowing me the whole trip, nor am I going to sit beside some snoring old fart for nine hours," Charlie had said with a grin. "I'm planning on being the snoring old fart, myself." Business class afforded more room, so the added seat wouldn't be necessary, after all.

Behind Rudy, Vandeweghe and Ridge were having a lighthearted conversation about the pros and cons of beer versus wine, while across the aisle Chris was deep into a work document he'd drug along, despite the unofficial position that this was a serious golfing trip – no work allowed.

Rudy realized no one seemed to be too concerned about the delay; they were all simply sipping libations and enjoying the moment. He settled into his seat. No sense in worrying, after all.

"Coke? Orange juice?" A stewardess from somewhere in the civilized South stood beside him. "Water?"

Rudy smiled. "I'll have an orange juice, thank you," he said, and flipped open the magazine. The metaphorical group in front of them, searching for their ball, could take all the time they needed.

Unfortunately, unlike the limousine driver, the pilot was unable to make up the lost hour. They arrived in London almost fifty minutes behind schedule. Then, to make matters worse, their plane was stuck on the tarmac at Heathrow, waiting for some other plane to exit their gate. It was more than ninety minutes from wheels-down to feet-on-the-ground in Heathrow, and Rudy knew they'd missed their connection to Scotland. He just hoped there was a later flight so they could get in that day. He wasn't keen on missing the first day of golf, simply due to travel glitches.

Huddled in a loose herd, the men moved as one toward the ticket counter for British Midland. A smartly dressed ticket agent, in what Rudy thought was one of the stiffest ties ever to grace a skinny neck, explained there was another flight leaving at five, and all their luggage would be transferred to that flight. He then proceeded to click his keyboard rapidly, arranging seating.

"I'll be continuing on in business, won't I?" Vandeweghe asked, towering over the counter.

"I shall look, sir," the ticket agent said, clicking more rapidly.

Rudy joined Chris, Plato, and Ridge, who had moved away from the counter and were waiting patiently for Vandeweghe to sort out his seating. The din from Heathrow was considerable, and Rudy felt himself lulled by the white noise. There were voices from every conceivable country, smells that rivaled a street fair, and a rather frenetic energy that seemed to emanate from the walls themselves.

"Did you get into business class again?" Ridge asked, nudging Rudy out of his stupor.

"Hm, what?" Rudy said, then quickly added, "Oh, no. No room in the inn."

"Me neither," Ridge said. "But it's only an hour flight, so what the heck. They won't have time to serve that bubbly champagne, let along give us time to enjoy it."

Rudy nodded in agreement. He just wanted to get going. Enough of this standing around. Charlie and Patrick joined them.

"Well we're all set," Charlie said, stashing tickets in his carryon bag. "Looks like we'll arrive in Glasgow in time for dinner, after all."

"Let's go find the gate," Ridge said. "And I need to find the men's room."

"Loo," said Patrick.

"What?" Ridge asked with a look of perplexed concern. "A who?"

"No. A loo," Patrick said. "They call it a loo over here."

Ridge grinned. "Well, whatever they call it, I need one real bad. It's been nearly half an hour and those hormones are working overtime again."

"We're still waiting for Vandeweghe," Plato said. "See if you can find one around here. Can't be too far."

Suddenly, Vandeweghe's voice carried above the din, booming through the hall.

"What do you mean there's no business or first class seats? There has to be at least one. For heaven's sake, I'm not used to batting eighth!"

Along with the rest of the Gang, Rudy turned in time to see the very confounded look on the ticket agent's face. He shook his head in confusion, and Rudy heard him ask, "Batting, sir?"

They all began to laugh. Turning to Plato, Rudy said, "Gary's forgotten he's not in America any longer. He just lost the poor agent to a baseball reference."

"Hey Van-de-waaay," Ridge called over the din, "ya might try a soccer reference. May get you more bang for your buck."

"Ah heck," Vandeweghe said as he crossed to them. "He works for an airline. He ought, at least, to understand baseball!"

Rudy began moving toward the gate. "What does one have to do with the other?"

"Well, they get free flights, after all," Vandeweghe said. "You'd think he'd traveled to New York, at least."

"And who on this planet doesn't know about the Yankees?" Patrick asked, eyebrows raised. "Even a goat-herder in the depths of Africa has heard about the Yankees!"

"Oh, okay, okay," Vandeweghe said, giving in to the ribbing. "I just didn't want to get squished between Charlie and Pat, sitting in coach."

"Don't worry, Gary," Patrick said, and slung an arm around his father's shoulders. "Nothing's coming between me and Pop. Not on this trip, anyway."

The gate loomed ahead, and Rudy noticed they had already boarded most of the passengers. He quickened his pace. "Come on. I'd like to make Turnberry for dinner, if it's all right with you guys. Airport food doesn't sit well with me."

"I'm with you on that one," Plato said.

At the gate, Rudy stepped aside and motioned for his friends to go first. Vandeweghe, Charlie and Patrick, Ridge, Chris, then Plato showed their tickets and entered the tunnel. Rudy looked around, taking in the scene. It was typical of an airport, yet different. "Folks is folks," his father used to say, and yes, they were. But there was something different – a variance in clothing, hair style, manner of walk and, of course, the lovely accents and diverse languages that sang through the airport. His attention lingered on the gate marquis. United 4816. Glasgow. 5:00.

Rudy shivered. This was actually happening, this trip to Scotland with all his buddies.

"Sir? Are you boarding?"

Rudy turned toward the charming young woman standing at the tunnel entrance. "You bet!" He handed her his ticket. "Let's go."

Ninety minutes later, he stood, arms crossed, before the luggage carousel. The others were spread out around the moving contraption, all anxiously looking at unrecognizable bags.

"There's one!" Patrick's voice rang out, and Rudy followed his pointing finger toward the luggage drop, where a generic black bag fell onto the carousel. Before anyone could get to it, a wiry elderly gentleman yanked it off the carousel, checked the baggage tag, and marched out the door.

"Okay, maybe not," Patrick said, his disappointment clear.

Chris nodded toward the drop and moved toward it. "That bag's not likely to be someone else's," he said. He grabbed the rectangular sack that held Charlie's clubs and yanked them off the carousel. "Charlie's playing!" he said. "He may be the only one, at this rate."

"Nope, I'm playing as well," Vandeweghe said, grabbing his clubs as they rolled past.

To his relief, Rudy's clubs arrived next, then Ridge's, quickly followed by the remaining sets of clubs. The seven men bundled the clubs together, set Charlie to keep watch, and returned to the carousel to retrieve their luggage.

They waited.

And waited.

After twenty minutes, the carousel stopped, the drop doors closed, and Rudy stood staring, blankly, at the few remaining pieces of luggage that clearly were not theirs.

"Oh, for Pete's sake," Vandeweghe said. "They've lost our luggage!"

"I told you not to jinx it," Rudy said with a wry smile. "You just couldn't help yourself, could you."

Vandeweghe waved a hand in frustration and searched the room for the customer service desk. Rudy pointed toward the back. "This way."

Rudy had to chuckle as the Gang, led by Vandeweghe, descended upon the small, young clerk, who instantly cowered behind his desk and reached for the phone, ostensibly to call for backup. After fifteen minutes, and much work both on the phone and computer, the clerk concluded their bags were held up either in San Francisco or New York, or perhaps in Frankfurt.

"Germany?!" Ridge hollered and threw his hands in the air. "What in the dickens are they doing there? We're in Scotland!"

"Yes, I know, sir," stammered the clerk. "It's just that often bags are routed –"

"We don't need explanations," Vandeweghe said in his best courtroom voice. "What we need are our bags. Clean clothes. Toothbrushes."

"Deodorant," Patrick added, sniffing.

"Golf shoes!" Rudy said. "I can't play in loafers, that's for sure."

Vandeweghe turned to him. "Didn't you put your golf shoes in your golf bag? I told you to put them in your bag."

Rudy snapped his fingers. "You're right, you did. And I did." He turned toward the clerk. "Skip the need for golf shoes. But socks would be nice."

"My razor," Plato said, rubbing his stubbly chin. "I feel like –" he pointed at Ridge, "that."

"Looks like you'll be growing a beard," Ridge said, tugging at his long tuff of gray. "Might be a good thing for all of ya."

Chris slumped. "I can't. Tried. Hally said I looked like I had a dirty face and told me to go shave."

"Smart woman," Plato said.

"Okay, okay!" Vandeweghe said and turned back to the clerk. "You get the point. Now when can we expect our bags, and what is this airline going to do about getting us necessities until they arrive?"

The clerk buried his face in his computer again, clicking madly on the keyboard. Suddenly his face brightened. "Sir, looks like we can get them to you tomorrow." He handed a clipboard to Vandeweghe. "If you'll fill out where you're staying, and a convenient number at which we can reach you, we'll shuttle them over just as soon as they arrive." He ducked beneath his desk, rummaged around a bit, then popped up with seven stuffed plastic bags. "And here – " He handed the bags to the men. "These should help hold you over until they arrive. At least in the toothbrush area."

Rudy tugged open the bag and looked at the contents. He started to chuckle. One toothbrush, a hair comb, a small tube of something (toothpaste, maybe?), a pair of socks, and, well, were those underwear? Hard to tell.

He shrugged. "Let's get to Turnberry," he said, motivating the Gang to move. "I'm hungry."

Vandeweghe threw up his hands and glared at the clerk. "That's another problem," he said. "Where we're staying they require jackets for dinner. We need our jackets!"

The clerk pursed his lips, and Rudy knew he'd had enough of the Americans. What did Vandeweghe expect the poor clerk to do? Produce spare dinner jackets? Rudy chuckled and corralled his friends, gently moving them back toward Charlie and their clubs.

"Thanks for your help," he said toward the clerk. "We'll look for those bags tomorrow."

"Hey, the clubs are here," Chris said. "That's the important part."

Plato chuckled. "Yeah, we'll look good playing in our boxers and undershirts and golf shoes."

Rudy thought of Charlie and Ridge in their boxers and golf shoes, and began to laugh. Suddenly he was laughing uncontrollably. Within seconds, the others joined. As they exited the airport, clubs in tow, all but Charlie were laughing uproariously.

"What's so funny? What?" Charlie asked. "I don't see how lost bags are so funny."

"Oh, they're not, Pop," Patrick managed to say through his laughter. "But Vandeweghe golfing in his boxers is!"

Rudy mopped the dampness from his eyes. "One good thing," he said, "Winterhalter will be mortified. The look on his face might be worth all this trouble."

Gang of Eight: The First Tee

They all agreed, and climbed into the bus marked with the Turnberry logo.

Despite his best efforts to do otherwise, Rudy fell asleep during the short ride from the airport to the hotel. An elbow to his ribs jolted him awake.

"We're here, Sleepy McDuff," Patrick said.

Rudy glanced out the window, and a chill went up his spine. The hotel was as magnificent as the photos suggested. And there, standing at the front door, was none other than Winterhalter! His friend's happy face and curt wave invigorated Rudy. Now the adventure could truly begin. The Gang of Eight was complete. Rudy sprung from the bus and retrieved his clubs. Quickly he crossed to Don and shook his hand.

"Good to see you, Don," he said. "You look rested –"

"Hey Winner-halter!" Ridge called as he lumbered from the bus. "You look like you're ready to play a round of golf!"

"Already done that, Ridge," Don said. "Played eighteen this morning. Fabulous. Absolutely fabulous. A tony seventy degrees, and not a cloud in the sky. Wore Bermudas!"

"Oh you dog!" Vandeweghe said, striding up and shaking Don's hand. "No fair getting the jump on us like that. Which course did you play?"

"Ailsa," Don answered. "Arran was booked solid. I couldn't even get a single walk-on."

Rudy grinned. "Well I hope you saved a few birdies for the rest of us."

Don nodded and hummed a bit as he shook the rest of the outstretched hands, then glanced around at their luggage. "Sooo... where's the rest of your luggage?" he said. "Or did you all decide to pack light for once?"

Patrick hefted his carryon backpack. "Yep. Really light," he said. "In fact, I'm wearing the magazine I brought to read. Plan to glue the pinup on my butt."

"She's too skinny to cover your butt," Charlie retorted.

Rudy chuckled. "Sad, but true, I'm afraid."

Patrick held the backpack out to Rudy. "Well she's not too skinny for yours, Rudy. Maybe you can make use of her."

"Whoa there!" Plato said, grinning. "Let's keep this clean." He turned to Don. "But yes, the airline lost our bags. All of them."

Don led them inside, and Rudy was struck by the opulence of the foyer. Not quite what he expected, he realized. While it was elegant, it was a bit too Americanized for what he had imagined. He felt like he'd stepped into a Hilton in New York. Still, nice not to have to worry about getting a hot shower. If this was any indication, the rooms would be comfy and functional. That was definitely a plus at this point.

They checked in and arranged to have their golf bags sent down to the clubhouse, chatting along with Don as they did so. Finally, as they squeezed into the elevator, Rudy broached the subject about which they'd all worried.

"So what about dinner, Don?" he said. "We obviously don't have our jackets."

Don pursed his lips for a moment, and his brow wrinkled. "Let me head back down to the front desk while you guys get organized in your rooms," he said.

Ridge held up his plastic bag. "Yeah, we have a lot of unpacking to do, as you can see."

Don chuckled. "That airline really took care of you, didn't they?"

Rudy retrieved a thin cotton tube from the bag. "Hey, they gave us socks. I think that counts."

"One size fits most," Patrick said.

"In Asia, maybe," Ridge said. "On a tiny woman. I won't get that thing over my big toe."

"Well you'll have the warmest big toe in Scotland," Rudy said, and stuffed the sock back into the bag. He stepped from the elevator and looked at his room key. "Plato, looks like we're down here."

"I'll go sort out dinner," Don said, and disappeared back into the elevator.

Rudy followed Plato into the room they'd share for the next three nights. It wasn't large, but it was very nicely appointed. And the shower was, indeed, ample and promising.

"Shower?" Rudy asked.

Plato motioned toward the bathroom. "You go ahead. I know you've been dying to take one since we landed at Heathrow." He shook his bag. "I'll just unpack."

"Watch you don't misplace those fabulous undies," Rudy said, and stepped into a stream of already steaming hot water.

"So here's the deal," Don said as Rudy and the Gang surrounded him in the hall. "They require jackets to eat in the dining room, so that's out for us." A round of groans caused him to raise his hand. "However, they understand our dilemma, so they've made arrangements for all eight of us to sit in a private room, just off the dining hall. It's more like a board room, but they'll serve us just the same as they would in the dining room. That okay with everyone?"

Rudy nodded vigorously. Food was okay with him, at this point. He'd eat on the front lawn if necessary.

The Director's Room, which was the name imprinted on the brass placard outside the door, was warm, comfortable, and perfect. Rudy agreed with Plato that it was actually a great way to start the trip, despite the fact they were wearing the same clothes they'd now worn for over twenty-four hours. The staff was congenial and very helpful, and the food was excellent. Vandeweghe ordered several bottles of wine, and Rudy judiciously tried both the white and the red before returning to sparkling mineral water.

At one point, two gentlemen in gray tails and stock-ties stuck their heads in and stared at the Gang.

"Come on in and join us!" Patrick said, waving a glass of red wine. "Gawker's welcome!"

The shorter man grinned and chuckled, but the taller man simply raised his chin a notch and said, "Our apologies. We were looking for a group of English gentlemen." They then stiffly exited.

The Gang laughed as one. "I'll have to work on that English accent," Patrick said. "Obviously I still sound too Irish."

As coffee and tea were served, Rudy felt his eyelids droop. It had been a very long day, and that single bed upstairs was calling his name. He roused himself a bit. "So what's the plan for tomorrow?" he asked.

"We have two tee-times on Ailsa in the morning," Don said. "First foursome goes off at 10:20; second goes off at 10:30. Pro, you've already got us paired off, I believe?"

Plato nodded. "Indeed I do. I'll bring the pairings with me to breakfast."

"Good," Rudy said. "Then I'm all for getting some sleep." He stood up. "Breakfast, I assume, does not require a jacket?"

"No, but golf will require proper clothing," Don said. "So why don't we convene for breakfast around eight, and we'll have some time to go into town and buy clothes. I'll check with the concierge about shopping."

They all agreed, drained their cups, and headed toward the elevator. Rudy lagged behind, breathing in the moment. They looked a ragtag group at the moment, with their rumpled travel clothes and tennis shoes, but that didn't diminish the fun.

"Coming?" Plato said, holding open the elevator.

"Yep!" Rudy responded, and trotted toward the Gang. He couldn't wait to jump into bed, not only because he was exhausted, but also because he really wanted the next morning to arrive. After months of planning and patience, it was a mere snooze away.

CHAPTER 26

August 30, 1998
Patrick Quinn

Patrick stood outside the Dormy House and looked at the score card for Ailsa. Eight of the holes were directly alongside the shoreline, with three more just inland. The ocean breeze was stiff here by the clubhouse; he couldn't imagine what it was going to be like out there, beside the water. He smiled. This was going to be a great test.

Plato called for attention and Patrick joined the other men huddled around the Pro.

"Okay, here's the info and pairings for the first game of our adventure," Plato said. "The game is the Turnberry Twosome, Low Gross. First tee time: Burger Deluxe and Old Tom Morris against Stone Hinge and Seamas McDuff. Second tee time is Mission Prince and Tried & True against Shivas Irons and Silver Cloud." He regarded the men, daring them to comment or disagree, but no one said a word. Patrick figured they were like him – just eager to get on the course.

Plato nodded, clearly pleased. "Now, go get your putters." He glared at Vandeweghe. "All of you."

Muttering and chuckling, the Gang retrieved their putters from their bags, which had been neatly lined up along the front of the clubhouse. When they returned to Plato, they found him holding a black marking pen.

"We are playing golf, lads," Plato said. "And it is our hope you will play the game and hole your putts out. However, for those of you who can't bring yourself to do this, an eighteen-inch mark will be put on all putters. Any ball touching any part of the mark is considered a gimme." He motioned with his hand. "Okay, hand 'em over."

Amidst general good-natured grumbling, all the putters were measured and marked. Someone mumbled something about the "circle of friendship," and Plato politely coughed. "You know, my feeling is this – if you run a hundred yard race, you don't stop at the ninety-nine yard line and say you've won the race. We've all missed putts that were a possible gimme. That's the fun of the game and might become the great story of the night. But –" he paused and looked each of his friends in the eye – "I realize we want to have some fun, so if you're feeling particularly generous, and the ball's inside the leather, hand over the gimme."

Patrick stood at the back of the Gang and inwardly grinned. The Pro had instilled a strong sense of putting-out in his juniors, of which Patrick was one, but had always struggled to get the older players to do the same. Patrick knew this was a last ditch effort to control his flock; he also knew it would be futile.

"We playing with caddies?" Ridge asked. "My feet are already killing me."

"Not this round," Don said. "We'll use the trolleys. We'll have caddies for the round at Aran this afternoon."

Ridge frowned. "Well, maybe they have some sort of foot pad in the club-house. I'm gonna go look."

Patrick loaded his bag on a pull cart and joined Don and Plato on their way to the "practice ground." He definitely needed to work out the kinks from travel before tackling the course.

Within minutes, all eight of the Gang were swinging away on the driving range, warming up. Then, one by one, they peeled off and headed back toward the first tee.

"Feet feel better?" Patrick asked Ridge as they walked toward the first tee.

"Ain't nothing's going to make these feet feel great right now," Ridge said. "But these pads certainly make them feel less like I'm walking on glass."

Gang of Eight: The First Tee

"Hang in there," Patrick said. "We can't carry you, and I doubt that rickety trolley will hold your weight."

Ridge snorted. "I'll crawl around the course if I have to. I didn't come all this way to sit up on the verandah and sip tea."

Patrick nodded in agreement.

Together, the Gang of Eight walked up to the first tee and looked down the fairway: gorse and tall grasses and potbelly bunkers, and a little snippet of stubby grass. Patrick swallowed, but he knew his eyes were shining with anticipation. He glanced around at the other seven men. They were all eyeballing the fairway with equal parts respect and pugnacity. Patrick felt his pride swell. These were golfers, good ones, and they wouldn't bow down to this course, or any other for that matter. He had a vision of all eight of them girdled for an ancient battle, and he began to chuckle.

"What are you laughing at, youngster?" Ridge asked, his eyes skewed like an old war captain surveying a new recruit.

Patrick gestured to the men. "I just had this silly image of all of us in fifth-century, Scottish battle gear, ready to wage war against an unknown foe."

Plato nodded and pointed his driver down the fairway. "That's unknown, all right. Links courses are nothing like what we play at home. You'll feel like you fought with a giant when we're done."

"Yeah, it's a lot of hit 'n hope in links golf," Rudy said. "You hit it and you hope it'll come down somewhere you can hit it again."

"Or at least where you can find it," Vandeweghe added. He looked at his watch. "Well, first group is up, and the lads ahead of us are far enough out. Saddle up ladies!"

Chris, Ridge, Charlie, and Rudy stepped forward as the other four gave way. Patrick was pleased to see his friend Chris had substituted a three-iron for his driver. There was an ominous line of bunkers approximately two hundred and fifty yards up on the left. With his driver, Chris was sure to find one.

All four drives landed safely, or so it appeared, and the first group was off and running. Patrick waited for one of the other men to step up to the tee. As anxious as he was, he wasn't about to step on the senior golfer's toes. He glanced around, and noticed they were all looking at him.

"What?" he said. "I'm not gonna hit first. Are you nuts?"

"Come on, Junior," Vandeweghe said. "Show us how to do it."

Plato stood with his feet spread, his arms resting on a fairway wood. He smiled and motioned toward the tee. "Youth before beauty."

Patrick shrugged and moved onto the tee. Far be it from him to argue. This was just too good. He focused beyond the scruffy grass and gorse that filled in the first hundred yards or so, found a spot to the right of the first bunker, and took aim. His long iron felt comfortable in his hands, and the air was light. The sun warmed his back and his ears – which he found funny, for some reason. He waggled the club, then focused on the ball. This was it; his first shot in Scotland. Make it memorable.

The ball left the tee with a resounding "whack" and screamed up the fairway, coming back to earth somewhere in the vicinity of his envisioned point. Patrick gave a little stomach pump with his fist. "Yes!" he said, just above a whisper. "Right where I wanted it."

Vandeweghe, Don, and Plato were all grinning.

"Got that out of your system, now?" Plato asked.

Patrick laughed. "Hopefully not!" he said. "This is just great!"

Don stepped up to the tee and placed a fairway wood right down the center. Then Vandeweghe and Plato followed, with only Plato flirting with danger as his ball bounced and rolled toward the lone bunker on the right.

"Oh siddown!" Plato grumbled at his ball. "Sit you bad boy!"

"It had ears for once," Don said, squinting toward the ball. "You're safe."

Vandeweghe elaborately motioned toward the fairway. "Shall we?"

Patrick leapt ahead, yanking his club trolley behind him with a jolt. "Last one to their ball is a piece of jerky," he tossed over his shoulder. He looked back just in time to see Vandeweghe turn to Don and ask, "What does that mean, anyway?"

Don shrugged. "Ask the author," he said, and led the other men off the tee.

Number one shot in the books, Patrick thought as he headed toward his ball. Two thousand more to come!

To Patrick's delight, Vandeweghe holed out his par-saving twenty-footer on the first green.

"What's this?" Vandeweghe asked, as he pulled a piece of paper from the cup, along with his ball. He began to grin as he read the two short sentences scribbled on a scrap of gum wrapper. "Looks like the four coconuts ahead of us all made par. Pressure's on!"

Don and Plato both easily two-putted for par, and Patrick rimmed-out his birdie putt, leaving himself an easy two inches for par.

"Gimme?" he said, and waggled his putter over his ball. "Anyone?"

The three more experienced golfers leaned on their putters and grinned.

"Go pound sand," Don said. "And sink your stinking par putt."

The second hole posed no more difficult for the foursome, who again all made par by playing smart off the tee. However, the longer, more problematic third hole caught Patrick by surprise, as the wind, howling in his face, caught his high second shot and slammed it back to earth thirty yards from the green.

"Oh rats," he muttered, watching the ball bounce in the fairway. "Jeez, that didn't go a hundred yards."

"Sorry, pal," Plato said. "Remember, you gotta hit 'em low, under the wind. You get up in those currents and you're dead."

The four men walked up the fairway toward the green, then stopped at Patrick's ball.

"Curtains," Vandeweghe said.

"Comatose," added Don.

"A corpse in front of the green," Vandeweghe declared with relish.

"The grim reaper with a club," Don said.

"Extinct."

"The Pale Horseman!"

"Terminated!"

"The Terminator."

Patrick rolled his eyes. "All right! All right! I get the point. Jeez, you don't have to beat –"

"A dead horse!" said both Don and Vandeweghe simultaneously.

Plato shook his head. "That was frightfully unimaginative." He surveyed first the lie of Patrick's ball then the three balls on the green ahead of them. "Rather like your shots to the green."

"Speak for yourself, Pro," Vandeweghe said. "I think that ball closest to the hole is mine."

"Read it and weep," Don said. "Read it and weep."

In the end, Patrick knocked his third shot into the deep right greenside bunker, managed to get out in one (for which he would be eternally grateful), and single-putted for a bogey. He felt relieved as they stepped up onto the tee of the short par-three fourth hole.

This was the first of the holes lying directly along the ocean, and the wind gusted across Turnberry Bay, bringing with it the distinct smell of seaweed and ocean salt. It wasn't unlike the smell at Spyglass Hill or Pebble Beach, but it still felt different. Less thick, he decided.

"Hey lover-boy, you hitting?" Vandeweghe said. "This week, at least?"

Patrick stepped up to the tee. The three other balls were resting in various locations on the green. Let's make it a nice, neat four, he thought, and lobbed his ball into the air, directly in line with the flag – only to watch a gust of wind knock it sideways.

"No, no!" he yelled. "Not there!"

"Good lungs, Little Prince," Don said as the ball landed just beyond the guarding right front bunker.

"Mission Prince," Patrick corrected. "And you've probably noticed, there's nothing little about me."

"I – uh – well, I think I'll leave that one alone," Vandeweghe stammered, and all four men laughed as they hoofed it toward the green.

The fifth hole was beautiful, but held one of the trickiest greens Patrick had ever played. He made par by sinking a delicate putt up and over several slopes. When the ball fell in the hole he allowed himself his second fist pump, but refrained from making any verbal comment. No need to get arrogant. Especially when all three of his playing partners were right there with him, making par.

The sixth hole, however, was dangerous and exhilarating. Patrick stood with Vandeweghe, Plato, and Don, and viewed the elevated par-three green with some trepidation.

"You sure there's a hole up there?" Don said. "I don't see a flag."

"Gotta be one somewhere," Vandeweghe answered.

Plato reviewed the official pamphlet, which held a drawing of the course. "Well, according to this there's at least, oh, maybe four bunkers on the left side and down front of the green. Looks like shooting a bit right and long would be the best option."

Don stepped up and teed his ball. He checked his line, and turned to the three men behind him. "Feels like I'm hitting up to Mount Everest."

"Stick a flag up there and I'd give it a try," Patrick said.

Plato smiled. "With your length you'd get there in three," he said. "Air's so thin the ball would probably go a mile before landing."

Don addressed his ball, then sent it howling up the hill.

Patrick watched the ball disappear up the hill, then back spin into view on the front edge of the green. "Uh oh," he said.

"Oh don't jinx –" Plato said, then groaned as the ball rolled into the front right bunker. He turned to Patrick, a mischievous look on his face. "All your fault, P.Q."

Patrick nodded. "I did it on purpose. Just for you, Don. I knew you wanted to be a hero on this hole."

Don shook his head, but smiled. "Gee, thanks. I should let you get it out of there and be the hero."

Vandeweghe and Plato both dropped their balls somewhere in the back, and Patrick flirted with danger to the left, but was pretty sure he was okay. He was vindicated when they arrived at the elevated green. His ball had miraculously landed in the rough between the left side bunkers. Don, however, was in jail. Or, more appropriately, a dungeon. Don lowered himself into the bunker and nearly disappeared.

"Scooter, you look like a dwarf down in that hole," Vandeweghe yelled. "When did you shrink?"

Don jumped up and down in the bunker a few times, then yelled up at them. "What do you think – fifteen feet?"

Vandeweghe looked from Don to the hole. "Fifteen feet? Are you kidding?" he hollered over the wind. "More like thirty-five."

Don shook his head. "Not the distance between me and the hole!" He waved his hand in the air. "The depth of this blasted bunker!"

Patrick laughed, as did the other two.

"You need oxygen?" Plato yelled.

Don addressed his ball, then stepped back to reassess the line. "No, but I could sure use a prayer."

"Where's Ridge when we need him?" Patrick said. "I think he has a direct line to the Golfing God."

Don waggled, wiggled, pursed his lips, cocked his head, and took a gigantic swing at the ball. Patrick cringed as a great cloud of sand flew everywhere. Thump. The ball landed ten feet onto the green, threatened to roll backwards again, and settled.

Patrick applauded, as did Vandeweghe and Plato. He couldn't believe Don had actually lobbed a ball out of that bunker.

"Well that makes my shot look miniscule, by comparison," Patrick said.

Vandeweghe grinned. "Don't blow it or you'll never hear the end of it. Ol' shorty there just landed the shot of the day."

Patrick managed to get his ball out of the rough and land three feet from the hole, then made his par putt. Both Vandeweghe and Plato made par from their various locations at the back of the green, but poor Don left his putt two feet short.

"Ah, Scooter," Vandeweghe groaned. "You had the line, my friend!"

"Leave him alone," Plato said, grinning. "He's exhausted from working his way out of the abyss. No wonder he left it short."

Don chuckled. "I could do those all day long if I had to." He knocked his ball into the hole. "But I'd rather not, thank you."

As they walked to the seventh tee, Patrick wondered if he could have managed to get out of that bunker. He'd never seen one so ... profound. It really had made Don look diminutive. Then that swing made him look like Superman. Patrick chuckled. He looked down the seventh fairway and located the bunkers left and right. He didn't know if he could follow in Don's footsteps, but he had no desire to find out. At least where fifteen foot deep bunkers were concerned.

The next two holes posed interesting challenges, all of which were met with success since no one accumulated another bogey. At the ninth tee, the view included the famous lighthouse and the deep blue of the Firth of Clyde. Seagulls flocked around the tower, encircling it like a living halo. The dark gorse and lighter green grass contrasted with the black rocks that lined the bay and the granite cliffs that upheld the south side of the lighthouse. He quickly took several photos – he'd been amiss in his photo-journaling assignment to this point – then watched with delight as a large bird swooped low over the bay, climbed back up the air stream, and dove into the water. It surfaced moments later, but was too far away to determine its success.

"Awfully pretty, isn't it." Don stepped beside Patrick. "Get some shots?"

Patrick nodded. "Looks like there should be a castle out there."

"There was," Plato said, dropping his driver into his bag. "Turnberry Castle was there, centuries ago. Supposedly Robert the Bruce was born there. You can still see the foundation of the castle around the lighthouse."

"So we're golfing on Robert the Bruce's playground?" Patrick mused. "Wonder if he ever played golf."

"I doubt it," Vandeweghe said. "He was too busy fighting the English to worry about shooting a round of golf."

"Do you think he likes what we modern-day-folk have done to his homeland?" Patrick asked.

Vandeweghe scratched his chin. "He might not mind us Americans on it, since we beat the red coats in the Revolutionary War," he said. "But I imagine he plays havoc with any ball hit by an Englishman."

Patrick grunted. "I'm a Quinn, so what's he planning for an Irishman?"

Plato pointed at the fairway. "Go find out."

Patrick took the strong winds into account, lined up his drive, and waggled his club. "This one's for you, Bobby," he said, and swung. The ball leaned into the wind, hooked a bit, and headed straight toward the tenth tee. Then some miracle happened and it slid right, landing safely on the fairway, parallel to the great lighthouse.

"Thank you, Mr. Bruce," Patrick said.

"That's King Bruce to you," Plato said. "Your new best friend."

Patrick chuckled. Robert the Bruce, the patron saint of the Gang of Eight. Somehow it seemed fitting.

They all made par on nine, and the tenth hole provided little drama for any of them, though Patrick eyeballed the famous island bunker in front of the green as he passed it. It fascinated him, and reminded him of why they were called "bunkers" in the first place. The trench of sand that surrounded the "island" hump of grass could easily have sheltered several men hiding from an enemy.

"Now that would require imagination to get out of," he said to Plato.

"Thank you, but I like the view of it from out here," Plato said. "I don't have that much imagination."

"Rather cool, though," Patrick said.

Plato grunted. "If you say so. Personally, it looks more like my version of hell."

To Patrick's surprise, the short par-three eleventh hole was the downfall for Vandeweghe, who started by landing in a deep bunker on the left of the green, took two strokes to get out, then three putted. He retrieved his ball from the elusive hole, and threatened to throw it into the ocean but obviously thought better of it. Patrick agreed with his restraint – golf balls were expensive on this side of the Atlantic. Instead, acting as if the ball was a badly trained puppy, Vandeweghe pretended to choke it, shaking it up and down.

Patrick laughed, along with Don and Plato.

"Go ahead and teach that ball a lesson!" Don said.

"I choked. Choked!" Vandeweghe said. "I couldn't breathe."

"So why take it out on the poor ball?" Plato said. "It was just following orders."

"Did you buy that ball here?" Patrick asked. "Maybe it doesn't speak English. Try a little Scottish on it."

"Okay," Vandeweghe said. "What's Scottish for 'get in the fucking hole'?"

"Get in the fucking hole," Don said. "I think it's a universal phrase, good in any language."

"Seems to me 'get in the bloody hole' would be more effective," Patrick said as they walked up to the twelfth tee.

Vandeweghe pointed back at the eleventh green. "It's 'bloody' all right. I left at least two pints there."

"Good thing you have more of the stuff than the rest of us," Plato said, grinning. He then hit his ball soundly into the far left fairway bunker. "Ah shucks," he moaned. He turned to Vandeweghe. "Got any I can borrow? Looks like I'm going to bleed my fair share on this hole."

Vandeweghe shook his head. "I'm running low myself, remember the eleventh?"

"'Remember the Eleventh.' Sounds like a bad bagpiper song," Patrick said, then groaned as his ball sliced into the right rough. "Which I'll be singing," he said amidst general laughter from the guys. Patrick knew the grass in that area was above his knees.

"Warm up that voice of yours," Plato said, and led the foursome off the tee. "I'll wager you'll sing that song a few times on these back holes."

Patrick decided it was time to have some fun. To the tune of *Old MacDonald Had a Farm*, he sang, "Young Pat Quinn he had a ball, ee ai ee ai oh. And then this ball it went awry, ee ai ee ai oh. With a slice slice here and a hook hook there, here a slice, there a hook, everywhere we had to look; Young Pat Quinn he lost a ball, ee a ee ai oh!"

He paused and turned to the three others. They stood, in the middle of the fairway, thirty feet behind him, hands over their ears, faces feigning agony in various renditions of *The Scream*. Patrick chuckled then slapped at the air in dismissal. He suspected he deserved it, though. He never could carry a tune.

Holes thirteen, fourteen, fifteen, and sixteen went by in a parring frenzy. That's not to say they were easy. It was just that all four of them seemed to be playing smart, and the inherent dangers on each hole – bunkers, grass traps, narrow fairways, hideous rough – were adeptly avoided. The wind wasn't as much of a factor as Patrick had expected it to be, and he began to feel a bit cocky. This links game wasn't as difficult as everyone said it was.

He stepped onto the tee at seventeen feeling sure he would easily make a birdie on this, the only par-five on the course. He looked out over the mounds of gorse and tall grasses and chuckled. "I feel like I'm hitting over a war zone."

"Fire in the hole," Plato said. "But take deadly aim; there's that bunker on the right side of the fairway, just about at your distance."

"No problem," Patrick said, feeling certain he'd sail the ball well beyond the bunker. He steadied himself, and swung. At the top of his backswing, the wind heaved mightily, almost knocking him off his feet. "Holy mackerel!" he roared. "Not now!"

His ball, which had been teed up for the marginal breeze, was sailing much too high for this gust, and Patrick watched in horror as the ball seemed to suspend in the air, then dropped like a stone, right into that blasted bunker.

"You've got to be kidding!" Patrick laughed at the absurdity of it all. He turned to Plato. "You hexed it! You called up that wind on purpose!"

Don and Vandeweghe were also laughing, but Plato looked deadly serious. "Remember what I told you after the Junior Championship? Well, it applies even more as you get older."

Patrick sighed. Yes, he remembered: *Your best hole would almost immediately be followed by your worst hole, and the probability of this happening grew exponentially with the arrogance with which you viewed your own feats. Golf is a game for the humble. It will knock pride from a man faster than the proverbial mother's backhand.*

Looking into the bunker, he groaned. His ball lay buried in the sand, a "fried egg" less than three inches from the wall of the bunker. He'd been backhanded all right. Probably by Robert the Bruce himself, who no doubt was doubled over in laughter.

Plato stood on the rim of the bunker, smiled, and nodded. "Time to be humble, Pat," he said, and headed toward his own ball, which lay safely in the middle of the fairway.

Patrick viewed his options and decided to lob the ball sideways into the fairway. He'd lose a bit of ground, and probably a shot, but he certainly had no chance of going forward. He grabbed his sand wedge and sighed. Humble pie wasn't exactly sweet.

In the end, he double-bogeyed seventeen, while both Don and Vandeweghe bogeyed with three-putts. It was a rather somber foursome that entered the tee-box at eighteen. Patrick hung back as the three elderly Gangsters teed it up and placed their balls in the sweet spot of the fairway, well back from the three yawning bunkers on the left. Then Patrick sighed and stepped up onto the tee. The ocean was at his back, and the great white Turnberry Hotel glared at him from atop the hill directly ahead. He could swear the bunkers had grown since the other three men hit. He looked up at the hotel. Wasn't his and Pop's room on the right? He squinted. Yep, the third window from the right was theirs. Right in line for his shot.

He eyeballed the window again, set his club, and swung. The ball headed straight in the direction of the window, and landed well into the fairway, smack in the middle. Patrick smiled but said nothing. Sometimes it was okay to be just a wee-bit self-assured.

Four hours and ten minutes after they'd teed off on one, the foursome walked off the eighteenth green. Patrick decided it was the best four hours of his life, thus far. He'd shot a solid seventy-three, while the other three had come in at seventy-four. They'd done themselves proud, even if pride wasn't encouraged.

Vandeweghe led them to the Dormy House, then upstairs to a casual, newer restaurant. There, sitting around a table meant for eight, sat Chris, Ridge, Rudy, and Charlie. Patrick saw his Pop's face light up like a Christmas tree.

"Hey there, Junior," Charlie said, standing and giving his son a firm handshake. "How was your first attempt at links golf? Wind beat you a bit?"

"Oh, he has a few bruises," Plato said, and sat down heavily. "But they're a long way from his heart."

Patrick smiled. "Shot a seventy-three, Pop. This links golf isn't as hard as I thought."

Plato coughed hard, then glared at Patrick with his best Teaching Pro look. His eyebrows rose.

Patrick threw his hands up in the air. "Okay, okay!" He tried to look as humble as possible. "I like it a lot, Pop. Can we play again this afternoon? I'd like to try to shoot a round under par."

Plato rolled his eyes. "You're incorrigible. Just like your dad."

Charlie grinned and slapped Patrick on the knee. "Wouldn't have him any other way! Now let's get some grub. I need fuel for the next round."

As the Gang recounted shots, Patrick sat back and counted his blessings. There were certainly many in his life, but right now … right now they added to eight – these seven men, and the waitress who was about to take their order.

He smiled. No humble pie on the menu.

CHAPTER 27

August 30, 1998
Chris Clark

"So what would you be having, gents?"

The slender young blonde hovered near the Gang, order pad at the ready. Chris thought she reminded him of someone from high school, but he couldn't put his finger on who. Regardless, that brogue was great fun to listen to, even if he did miss half of what she was saying.

"Hello darlin'," Ridge drawled, a big smile on his face. "What would you suggest?"

She smiled, a mischievous twinkle in her eye. "Well, if you're brave, I'd suggest the haggis. 'Tis the best this side o' Glasgow."

The Gang laughed. Chris didn't think anyone at the table was brave enough to try the famous meal of Scotland. If so, it would be Don Winterhalter, who had, over the years, proven himself the culinary brave heart. But when it came to haggis, even he backed down.

"What's your name, miss?" Don asked.

"Natalie, sir," she said "And only me mum calls me Nat, I'll thank ya'."

The men exchanged looks. Chris was pleased; this one was feisty and could certainly handle whatever banter the Gang could dish out.

"Well, Natalie, I thought about the haggis," Don said. "I really did. But the salmon steak looks just too good. So put me down for one of those."

"'Tis a good choice," Natalie said. She looked to Ridge. "Perhaps you'd like t'try the fish n' chips? 'Tis made with haddock, here. Very good, I'm told." She wrinkled her nose. "I dunna like fish, though, so I've n'er tried it, myself."

Ridge nodded. "Sounds good to me, darlin'." He slapped his menu shut. "And a beer, something stout."

Patrick's eyebrows rose. "Careful, Ridge," he said. "Stout around these parts means a beer you can chew on." He looked at the waitress. "I think he means something more along the lines of an IPA."

"I like a drink I can taste," Ridge said. "What's wrong with the stout?"

"We're talking sludge," Patrick said, and made a slicing motion with his hand. "Cut it with a knife."

Natalie laughed. "You be right there, sir." She looked at Ridge. "Perhaps you'd like a Red Cuillin. 'Tis an Isle of Skye brew. Won the Bronze Medal in the Champion Beer o' Scotland this year. Or a Caledonian, which was best beer last year."

Chris was impressed. "So you must drink beer, even if you don't eat fish."

Natalie grinned and flounced her long hair. "I'm Scottish, no?" She waggled her order pad at the men. "We're better at drinkin' ale than the Irish could ever wish t'be."

A round of "Watch out!" and "Whoa!" and "Them's fighting words!" went up from the Gang. Chris joined the others in pointedly addressing Patrick with raised eyebrows and knowing looks.

"Natalie, I'll take you up on the challenge," Patrick said. "Any night we're here, you just let me know." He winked. "And we'll start with the nineties, not the sixties."

It was Natalie's turn to raise an eyebrow. "So, y'know your Scottish beer, 'eh?" she said, and tapped her pad with her pencil. "I might take you up on it, but ye look a bit old for me, 'n I don't want'a hurt ya."

The Gang laughed as one, Chris included. It was the first time, he was sure, that Patrick had been tagged as "old," especially in this crowd, where he was still considered a kid.

"Hey, now!" Patrick exclaimed over the noise. "I'm only thirty!" He pointed around the table. "These guys are old! Pick on them."

Natalie flashed a sparkling smile at Vandeweghe. "Well, me Da's warned me 'bout you Americans, anyway. Trouble, you are. All of ya."

Vandeweghe threw up his hands in surrender. "Not me! Innocent as a lamb. Always!"

Chris waggled his fork at Vandeweghe. "Yeah, Barb would have you in shackles if you misbehaved. Tight ones."

"And rightfully so," Vandeweghe said. He smiled warmly at Natalie, "Now, I'm hungry. How about the lamb dish? Is that good here?"

Natalie returned to business. "Very good, sir." She turned to Charlie. "And for you, kind sir?"

Chris was now enamored with the girl. She pegged every one of them at first sight. "You got that one right, Natalie," he said. "He's got the biggest heart at the table."

"Why thank you, Chris," Charlie said with a little bow of his head. "And I'll have the lamb, too. With a soda of some sort. Coke? Pepsi?"

"Do you want ice?" Natalie asked, writing frantically on her pad. "I dinna think you'd like your Coke warm, no?"

Charlie gave her his best lopsided grin. "Only my heart's warm, dear. My soda I like cold."

Natalie turned to Rudy and raised her pencil, along with her eyebrows. Rudy straightened up in his chair. "My turn?" he asked. Natalie nodded. "I'll have the soup and salad, but could you tell me what is 'cullen skink'? Sounds like something dangerous."

Natalie smiled. "'Bout as dangerous as that one there," she said, pointing at Don, at which everyone laughed.

"And how do you know he's not dangerous?" Rudy asked. "He sure is a scoundrel on the golf course."

Natalie cocked her head, then pointed that particularly mischievous smile at Rudy. "I warrant you're th'rogue in this group. Trouble from the day y'was swaddled, no doubt." She tapped Don's shoulder with her pencil. "This'n? Wouldn't know trouble if it kicked him in the shin."

Chris joined the other men in another loud round of laughter, which became even more resonant as Don blushed a deep crimson.

"Off the course, you're probably right," Vandeweghe said. "It's on the course our Winterhalter sometimes gets kicked."

"And it's not on the shin," Patrick added, much to everyone's delight.

"You're a love, aren't ya?" Natalie said, smiling down at Don. "Bet all the girls liked ya, didn't they?" Before Don could answer, Natalie turned back to Rudy. "So," she crooned, "the soup's made with a lovely mix of cream 'n haddock 'n spices. Most everyone likes it, if you like fish. Hearty, 'tis."

Rudy nodded. "Then this rogue will have that, please. Sounds excellent."

Chris really just wanted a burger, but he didn't see anything on the menu that resembled one. Natalie stood with pencil poised, waiting.

"I'll try this Aberdeen Angus steak," he said. "Medium rare."

Natalie nodded. "We don't cook 'em any other way, sir. Waste of good beef. But you know that, don't ya?" She turned to Plato. "Y've been mighty quiet, sir. You must be the leader o'this motley crew."

More laughter. Chris was beginning to think the girl was psychic. "Did you figure that out by the big whip he has stuck in his back pocket?" he said.

"Or the big rule book?" Patrick added with a grin. "He flogs us with it around the course."

Natalie smiled. "No doubt you need floggin', the lot o'ya."

Plato grinned. "That they do, Natalie. That they do." He pointed at the menu. "I'll have this."

Natalie said something Scottish, which Chris couldn't even begin to understand, let alone pronounce. All but Plato stared at her with various looks of confusion and delight.

"Kidney Pie," Plato explained. "Though I hope it tastes just as interesting as the name spoken in Scottish."

"You'll not be disappointed, sir," Natalie said, and collected the menus. She jotted down a few more drink items, then with a curt and brilliant smile, departed.

"Isn't she a really nice, cute girl," Don said. "She can't be more than twenty, but she sure handled all of us." It was a polite, casual comment, but Chris could see puckish looks on many a face around the table. These guys weren't the kind to leave well-enough alone, and as the conversation at the table returned to the round just finished, and the round to come, Chris knew Don was probably in for a practical joke.

Sure enough, after lunch was consumed – the consensus being it was an excellent meal – Patrick jumped up, camera in hand.

"Natalie, let's get a photo of you for the scrapbook," he said. "Just stand over there behind Don and Vandeweghe."

Natalie paused, then shrugged, smiled, and acquiesced.

"Cheese!" Patrick said, and Chris wondered what would be the Scottish word for cheese, and did it make one smile? He also wondered where that photo would end up, in the end. Yes, Don should watch his back.

"Thank you, Natalie," Charlie said as he handed her the credit card slip, signed.

She glanced at the total and smiled broadly in return. "You've been m'best table today. Have a good round, gentlemen! 'N come back 'n see me, again." She pointed at Patrick. "But no beer drinking contest. I'd lose to that belly, I would."

The Gang laughed, waved farewell, and exited the Dormy House restaurant. They had exactly thirty minutes before their next round started at Turnberry's Arran course. Chris felt rejuvenated after the excellent steak, and ready to tackle the wind again. He'd not fared as well as he had hoped, shooting a seventy-seven on Ailsa that morning.

He walked a little faster and caught up with Plato. "Hey Pro, I had a realization on the third hole, back there on Ailsa."

"Yeah?" Plato asked, "What about?"

Chris squinted, remembering the play on the hole. "Well, the wind was blowing across the fairway, and I had a little over forty yards to get up and over. I had a sand wedge in my hand, and changed it for a pitching wedge, to keep it out of the wind."

Plato grinned. "You know what I'm getting at here," Chris said, and Plato nodded, then said, "But go on."

Chris adjusted his pace to Plato's. "So the ball goes up in the air, and the wind grabs it and sends it to the right. Okay, I miss the green. I started with a forty yard shot and now I'm lying sixty feet right of my line, thirty yards off the green. And I'm thinking, 'I have to rethink this hole.' Two more holes of this and I realized I'm rethinking the entire course, shot by shot." Chris tossed hands in the air. "And so this is what you guys meant by links golf?"

Plato patted Chris on the shoulder in a fatherly manner, and Chris had a flashback to when he was sixteen, walking down a fairway at a Junior Championship with Plato at his side, encouraging him with a calming hand on his shoulder.

"You got it," Plato said. "Welcome to links golf, where nearly everything needs rethinking, from your club choice to what shoes you wear."

Chris considered his score from this morning. He was only four back from the leaders. He'd figure out this links thing before they made it to St Andrews, he was sure of it.

CHAPTER 28

August 30, 1998
Charlie Quinn and Rudy Staedler

As the Gang stood in front of the Dormy House, Charlie leaned on his bag, relieving the ache in his back. He was glad they'd be using caddies on this round. Walking would be bad enough; he didn't relish pulling his clubs for another eighteen.

"Gather round, lads," Plato called, brandishing his marker. "Anyone need a refresher on their eighteen inch mark?"

"We're all good, Pro," Rudy said. "No one in our group wore theirs out." He turned to Vandeweghe. "What about your group?"

Vandeweghe shook his head emphatically. "Heck no. Not a gimme was needed."

"Or considered," Patrick mumbled.

Plato nodded curtly. "This game is Blind Best Ball Twosome. We'll split into two foursomes, but you won't know who your partner is until we all reconvene after the round. At that time, we'll pull names from the hat and blindly create the partnerships. Are you all ready for more gorse and wind?"

He was met with various comments, both sarcastic and affirmative. Charlie didn't mind the wind, or the gorse for that matter, since he rarely strayed into it. What he minded was the uneven land. Walking down the fairway could resemble rock-hopping in a stream, and it was deadly for his back.

He found himself in the first foursome with Don, Vandeweghe, and Ridge. They hovered in a loose group, waiting for their tee time. Finally, the starter at the clubhouse stepped out and asked if they were the Winterhalter group. Don approached the man and made arrangements for the caddies, and within minutes eight Scotsmen of various sizes and ages arrived. And apparent drinking ability, since the odor of liquor could be smelled from yards away.

The caddies seemed to size up the Gang, then each chose a player. Charlie was hardly surprised when both Patrick and Chris were chosen first. No doubt the caddies assumed the younger players would be the better. Little did the caddies know they'd simply chosen the two players who were more likely to have them running all over the course, chasing balls.

Names were exchanged – which took a few tries, as some of the brogues were very difficult to understand – and introductory chitchat conducted. They were just about to head for the tee when the starter again stepped out of the clubhouse.

"Gentlemen," he said, gathering the Gang with a terse wave of his hand, "You'll be delayed a few minutes. Mr. Norman has descended upon us." He pointed toward the hotel. A large black helicopter with Greg Norman printed in gold letters sat on the front lawn. "He has asked for the equivalent of two groups before and after him, in order to give himself room to do a little practicing. As always, we've agreed to accommodate him. Your first group will go off at three thirty-five. I trust you won't mind?"

"No, no" and "Not at all" and "He can join us if he'd like!" were said by the Gang. Most of the caddies dropped the bags and stepped aside to have a smoke. Charlie didn't see the one who smelled of scotch and wondered if he'd nicked back to the caddy shack for a few nips.

Patrick retrieved his camera from his bag and trotted toward the hotel.

"Where's he going?" Vandeweghe asked.

"To get a picture of Norman's helicopter, I suspect," Charlie said. Sure enough, Patrick stopped below the big black bird and snapped some photos. He returned, all smiles.

"Now there's the way to go, Pops," Patrick said. "You could play several different courses a day, flying around in that thing."

Gang of Eight: The First Tee

The Gang hovered around the first tee, expecting Greg Norman to arrive and give them a show. After several minutes, Charlie grew restless and approached the starter.

"Oh, he rarely begins at the first hole," the starter explained. "He doesn't want to draw a crowd when he's practicing."

Charlie shrugged and rejoined the huddled Gang. If you'd seen one golf star, you'd seen them all, and he was more interested in playing, anyway. Still, it might have been a hoot to send Patrick for an autograph.

At last the starter gave them the thumbs up, the caddies collected their bags, and the Gang headed to the first tee of Arran. Charlie walked as quickly as his back allowed. He was anxious to tackle this second links course and win back a little money.

Rudy walked a few paces behind his caddy, watching. He chuckled, then glanced over at Plato, who was also watching his caddy with a smile.

"I think my guy's at least seventy years old," Rudy said, quietly.

Plato nodded. "Probably closer to eighty," he said.

"And check out the suit." Rudy shook his head. "He even has on a tie. Looks like he's taking me to dinner. I didn't know I had a date tonight."

"Maybe you should tip him enough to go buy a nicer suit," Plato said. "That one's seen better days."

Rudy looked closer. The pant bottoms were frayed, as was the collar. The elbows were worn nearly through, and one of the back seams had come undone for a few inches. Rudy shook his head, "Air conditioning in the back's a nice touch. Man, I feel for the guy. He should be retired by now."

"Maybe this is his retirement," Plato said. "Who knows what he did before this."

Rudy watched the elderly caddy pack his bag as if it was a lady's shoulder bag. No, Rudy was fairly certain this guy had been caddying his whole life. He looked like he was part of the bag, part of the course. He just belonged.

When they arrived at the first tee, the two groups sorted themselves out and Charlie stepped up first. Rudy looked around. During World War II,

Turnberry had become an air force base, and there were still remnants of this "past life" scattered around the courses. Rudy knew the Arran course had a lengthy landing strip that sliced through it. As Ridge teed up his ball, Rudy located the end of the landing strip, off to his left, closer to the first green. He thought it intriguing they had left it there; a reminder of the tremendous sacrifice and difficulties Great Britain had endured during the war.

The first foursome completed their drives – all with irons as this was a par three, and only 179 yards at that. Rudy looked at the score card; again, only one par five on the course. Five par threes peppered the front and back, and the rest of the holes were par fours. Not many chances for birdies on these courses.

His turn to drive arrived and his caddy handed him a long iron. "Aim for the bunkers o'er th'right, there," the caddy slurred. "That wind'll carry ye back, laddie."

Rudy wasn't sure the wind was as strong as all that, and the double bunkers were well right of the pin, which was situated mid-left, but he decided to take the elderly gentleman's suggestion, if for no other reason than to show a little respect, and get off on the right foot with the old gent. He wiggled, waggled, wiggled again, and hit. The ball sliced out toward the ocean, well right of the bunkers, and Rudy knew all the wind in the world wasn't going to help that one get back to the pin. Sure enough, it landed out of sight in the thick rough, well off the green.

"Don't get confused," Patrick said, smiling. "The bunkers are the little pots of sand. That long strip is called a beach."

"And both should be avoided," Chris said.

Rudy chuckled. "You could have cleared that up before I swung."

The caddy, much to Rudy's relief, said nothing. He simply accepted the iron, stuffed it in the bag, and started down the fairway alongside the other caddies.

Rudy enjoyed the view as he walked to his ball. He knew that slice was an anomaly, not likely to happen again in this round, and he'd be damned if he was going to let the first hole ruin his round. Better to be delighted by the gorgeous panorama, if not by his drive.

In the end, his ball had landed in the one bare spot in the rough, and he managed to get up and down in two, for par. He felt as if he'd dodged a rock aimed at him by a Scottish slingshot.

When they arrived at the second tee, Rudy looked at his caddy. The man pulled the driver from the bag and handed it to Rudy.

"'Tis a par five, laddie," the caddy said. "Ye want to land just left o'that first bunker, 'n the same wind's slashin' across the fairway. So again, aim for the bunker o'the right." He hefted the bag and stepped back. "Oh. And make sure ye listen to your young friend's advice this time."

"That'll be a first," Patrick said, his dry wit cracking in the wind.

Rudy controlled his laughter and addressed his ball. Nice to know the old caddy had a sense of humor, after all. He swung, and placed the ball ahead and left of the front fairway bunker. Right where he wanted it.

"That'll do," the caddy said, and awarded Rudy with a very toothless smile.

Charlie squinted through the wind at his second shot on the long par-four ninth. He'd howled his drive down past the two right-side fairway bunkers, and had maybe one-fifty to the green. There were bunkers up there, everywhere. And this wind – straight into his face and hard as they come. He walked to his caddy, a hearty gent of about fifty who chewed on something incessantly. Charlie was pretty sure he didn't want to know what it was. He pulled a seven iron from the bag. The caddy grunted and shook his head.

"Ye'll no get there with that, laddie," he said.

Charlie sighed and yanked a five iron from the bag. He raised his eyebrows at the caddy, who just shook his head again.

Vandeweghe, who stood ten yards to the left of Charlie, motioned with his chin toward the green. "Do you think a three iron will get you there?"

The caddy inspected Vandeweghe with one eye squinted. "Ay, laddie," the caddy said. "Eventually."

Don and Ridge were clearly trying to keep their laughter in check. Then Charlie gave in to a chuckle, and Vandeweghe joined. Within seconds, all four men were rowdy with laughter. The caddies bunched together, as if to protect themselves from this nonsense, a mixture of incredulity and disgust on their worn faces.

Charlie took a deep breath in an effort to regain control, and crossed to his caddy, who pulled a fairway wood from his bag and held it out wordlessly. He stood over his ball, still grinning. Oh, yes, they'd all get to the green in this wind.

Eventually.

―――◆•◆•◆―――

Rudy stepped onto the fifteenth tee, a short par four at three-sixty-five, bunkered on the left with gorse on the right. At home he'd hit a fairway wood or a long iron and leave himself a nice short iron to the green. But the wind made this a totally different game than the one he normally played. The caddy handed him the driver, and Rudy wasn't going to argue. He teed it low, aimed a little right, and swung as clean as he could.

The shot landed dead center in the fairway, just ahead of the bunkers. Chris teed up, received hushed orders from his caddy, and swung. The ball flew about a hundred and thirty yards, then turned left as the wind shoved it off line.

"In the gorse!" Chris yelled at the ball. It landed precisely where he commanded. Chris shook his head in amazement. "Of course it's in the gorse."

Rudy knew how he felt. He tightened his visor and followed the other men into the wind tunnel, otherwise known as the fairway. He arrived at his ball and smiled. Couldn't be more than one-sixty to the pin, which was a little right and back, taking the left bunker out of play and leaving only a tall patch of gorse to worry him. Rudy looked at the caddy. "How far are we?"

The caddy looked left and right, noting landmarks and bushes. Rudy didn't see anything in particular that didn't look like a lot of other humps, bumps, gorse, and weeds.

"Ach," the caddy said. "You're 'bout one fifty-five."

Rudy assessed the wind, now blowing even stronger and straight into his face. He pulled a three iron from his bag.

"I don't think you'll get there w'that, laddie," the caddy said.

Rudy sighed. Okay. He replaced the three iron and pulled a two iron.

The caddy shrugged. "I dinna think you'll get there w'that, either."

Rudy wrinkled his forehead. The next club in his bag was a five wood. He normally hit it about two hundred and ten yards. Rudy's hand hovered over the club.

The caddy nodded. "Hit that."

"The five wood?" Rudy said. "If I catch this, it's gone. We'll be looking for it in the next county."

The caddy just blinked, then spat on the ground. Obviously he felt the five wood was the right choice. Rudy inwardly shrugged. Well, we'll see.

He took a stance over the ball and the wind pushed against his thighs. He wobbled a bit, widened his stance and hunkered down, and hit the ball right in the sweet spot. The ball took off screaming across the golf course. Oh, jeez, it's way over, Rudy thought, then held his breath as the wind got hold of it. It fluttered, seemed to bounce in midair, and dropped straight down, onto the green.

"Great shot!" Plato called from across the fairway. "What'd you hit?"

Rudy held up the five wood and motioned his disbelief with his other hand. "Go figure!" He handed the club back to the caddy, who looked smug, if not pleased. "Thank you," Rudy said, and headed toward the green.

Fifteen yards from its edge, Rudy paused. From this perspective Rudy could clearly see the first third of the green sloped sharply toward him, into a deep "burn" which cut across this end of the fairway. He looked back to where he'd stood three minutes ago. All of this was hidden; inconspicuous and indistinct from the otherwise flat lay of the fairway.

Rudy glared a bit at the caddy. "Hey, Liam. You didn't tell me about this burn."

"Aye, laddie," the caddy said. He adjusted the bag on his shoulders and scratched his ear. "There's why I had ye hit the five wood."

Rudy chuckled, then walked across the plank bridge that spanned the burn. Lesson number one to self, he thought. The caddies know their course. Lesson number two. Your "normal" game doesn't exist on their course.

Later, when he posted a seventy-six for his round on the short par sixty-eight Arran at Turnberry, Rudy remembered the shot with the five-wood, and the hidden burn.

Lesson learned.

———•◦•———

Charlie lumbered to the concierge desk at the Turnberry Hotel. They had all returned to their rooms, and found them bereft of their bags. Certainly there had to be a mistake; those bags were hidden somewhere in this hotel. They had to be.

"Good evening, sir," a young man said, smiling warmly at Charlie.

Charlie wished he felt as relaxed and comfy. Right now his quickly purchased shorts were feeling over-worn, his shirt was wrinkled, and his socks needed a soak, along with his feet.

"Evening," Charlie said. "I'm with the Gang of Eight – uh, the Vandeweghe group. We were expecting some bags to be delivered by United Airlines. Can you check to see where they might be?"

"Bags, sir?" The young man looked concerned. "I've been here all day and I've not had any bags delivered by an airline."

Charlie frowned. The young man quickly closed his ledger. "But I'll go check in the back and see if they managed to slip by without my noticing."

"Thank you," Charlie said, and sat down in the plump chair stationed in front of the gleaming mahogany desk. He looked around as he waited. The Turnberry really was elegant, with rich woods carved in intricate detail, thick brocade drapery, and large hoary-looking paintings gracing the papered walls. It was a nice way to start their trip. If only their damn luggage would arrive.

"Sir?" The young man reappeared behind his desk. "I'm sorry, but there's been no luggage delivered." He reached for a pad and pen. "Which airline were you expecting? I'd be glad to do a check for you, see if they can be located."

Charlie pushed himself from the chair. "United." He pulled a now crumpled piece of paper from his pocket. "Flight 954 from San Francisco to

Heathrow, then British Midlands from Heathrow to Glasgow. But I don't know that flight number because we missed our original connection. And the bags didn't make it to Heathrow."

"No problem, sir," the young man said, writing frantically. "I'll contact United and see if we can't rally those bags."

Charlie smiled. "If not, rally some clean clothes for us." He tugged at his shirt. "I don't want to wear this a third day in a row."

The young man dutifully wrinkled his nose. "No, we certainly don't want that. Which rooms shall I have them sent to, once they arrive?"

Charlie liked that the young concierge seemed so self-assured. Maybe there was hope, after all. He rattled off the room numbers for the Gang, thanked the young man with a ten-pound note, and returned to his room. Patrick lay face down on his bed, snoring softly. Charlie paused and gazed at his son. So grown up now. Thirty. When did he get so ... adult? It seemed like just yesterday he was teaching a five-year old how to hold a plastic driver.

The phone rang. The sound surprised Charlie, but before he could reach for it, Patrick started out of sleep and lunged.

"Hello? Hello?" Patrick said, rubbing his face. "Yes this is the Quinn room." He looked around, then focused on Charlie, who quickly moved to the adjoining bed and sat down. "Yeah, here he is," Patrick said, and handed the phone to Charlie. "Something about the bags," Patrick mumbled, and was again asleep before his head landed on the pillow.

Charlie chuckled. How he wished he could fall asleep that quickly. "This is Charles Quinn," he said, and listened as the young concierge explained. The bags had been located. They were being flown to Heathrow even as they spoke. With any luck, they would be in the gentlemen's rooms by morning. Should they arrive during the night, would the gentlemen like to be disturbed by their delivery, or wait for the morning?

"Please deliver them as soon as they arrive," Charlie said. "The hour doesn't matter." He wanted his own toothbrush and clean underwear. Enough of washing out this pair in the bathroom sink.

"Very good, sir," the young man said, as if acknowledging that Charlie had made the right decision. "If you'll simply instruct the others not to bolt the safety chain, we can slip your bags in while you're asleep, and hopefully not disturb you."

"Thank you." Charlie hung up. He gave another look of longing at the soundness with which Patrick slumbered, and headed for the shower. His clothes may be ripe, but he wouldn't go to dinner that way himself.

Seated on one of the opulent bench seats in the lobby, Rudy waited for the rest of the Gang. He had changed into his travel sweatshirt, leaving the now twice-worn golf shirt in a heap on the bathroom floor. He was warmer than he wanted to be, but at least he was a bit more decent.

The elevator doors opened and with a boom of laughter, the other seven men entered the lobby.

"Hey Rudy," Vandeweghe said. "You're our restaurant specialist – what have you in store for us tonight?"

Rudy stood and grinned. They were still a rumpled bunch, despite the obvious effort at cleaning up. "Well, since United has still not managed to get our bags to us, the dining room is out. I talked with the manager, and he suggested the Spa Restaurant, which is more of a cafe. The dress code is less stringent, and the food is good, if not heavy."

"I could do without heavy," Ridge said, patting his stomach. "A nice sandwich would do me just fine."

The rest of the Gang nodded in agreement.

"Good," Rudy said, "The Spa Restaurant it is. Follow me."

In anticipation of acceptance of what was, really, their only option short of crackers and bottled water, Rudy had checked out the location of the restaurant, then the adjoining spa. His aching back had called out for a quick massage, but one look at the price list had squelched that idea. That was definitely not on the budget he and Bev had discussed before he left San Jose.

"Here we are," he said, as he pulled open the door to the cafe. "Gentlemen, take your seats."

Dinner was indeed light, but very delicious. Don was dutifully needled about dinner without Natalie-the-Waitress, and they recounted the day's rounds. Rudy discovered that with the exceptions of himself and Vandeweghe, all of the Gang had bettered their first round. They drew the blind teams over dessert and coffee, and after all the scores were tallied, the team of Chris and Don took the pot. Rudy smiled. Despite the course, nothing was different from home; "Winner-halter" was still walking away with the money.

As the light faded outside, Rudy made his way to his bed. It had been a really long day, and his back ached fiercely. He couldn't imagine how Charlie must be feeling, with his chronic back issues. Rudy pulled a pad of paper from his travel bag. He plumped his pillows against the headboard and sat in bed. "Day 1" he wrote on the top of the first page. He then systematically jotted down the pertinent details of the past twenty-four hours. He knew he'd want to give Bev a clear picture of their time here in Scotland, and his memory wasn't what it used to be.

Dinner: Spa Restaurant (hotel), great, he wrote as the last entry. He shifted on the bed and a sharp pain shot up his back. He sighed. *Back aches,* he added to the journal.

He settled under the covers and listened to Plato complete his nightly obligations. Yes, it had been a fantastic first day, one he certainly would remember for the rest of his life. He slipped into slumber and slept soundly – except for the short nightmare he had about someone sticking a fork in his back...

CHAPTER 29

August 31, 1998
Gary Vandeweghe

Gary Vandeweghe opened his eyes. He must be dreaming; two suitcases sat beside the door.

"Hey, Old Tom," he said, springing from the bed. "We have clothes!"

A sound that resembled pebbles against a window made him turn. "And just in time, since it appears we're in for rain this morning."

Ridge just grunted and rolled over under the covers. Vandeweghe slung his suitcase onto a chair and popped it open. He rummaged for a few seconds, then pulled a plastic bag from the bottom. He smiled. Quickly he tossed on sweat pants and a t-shirt, then quietly left the room and trotted down to Rudy and Plato's door. He knocked softly; if they weren't up, he didn't want to wake them.

"Door's open!" Plato yelled from within.

Both Rudy and Plato were seated, reading a local newspaper. "Rudy!" Vandeweghe said, his excitement making him a bit louder than he wanted. "We got our suitcases. You know what that means!"

Plato chuckled and tugged at his clean golf shirt. "Yeah, it means I don't smell any longer."

Vandeweghe shook his head. "No, no, well, I mean yes, you aren't offensive any more, but this is something else."

Rudy grinned over his newspaper. "I know, I know. I'll bring them to breakfast. You bring yours."

"Perfect." Vandeweghe headed for the door.

Ninety minutes later the whole Gang was seated around a large table in the dining room. Vandeweghe waited until orders had been placed and the "how'd you sleep?" chitchat had been conducted before he caught Rudy's eye. Both men nodded.

"Hey fellas," Vandeweghe said firmly. "Rudy and I have something we'd like to share."

"Deodorant?" Patrick said. "Thanks but I finally got mine this morning."

Seated beside Patrick, Chris sniffed. "You need to change brands. You smell like a rose garden."

Rudy pointed at the rain-pelted window. "Given the weather, this will be even better than deodorant. Or roses."

Vandeweghe tossed a plastic bag onto the table, followed by one from Rudy. "Knowing how it can be over here," Vandeweghe said, "we both thought you could all use these." He then pulled eight rain jackets from his bag, as Rudy pulled eight pairs of rain pants from his.

"Hey hey!" Don said. "New rain gear!"

"But not just any rain gear," Vandeweghe said, and shook out one of the jackets. Embroidered on the left chest was *Gang of Eight, Scotland, 1998*. "These are special, just for you guys."

Exclamations of joy went up from the six men, and Vandeweghe joined Rudy in handing out the clothing. Don and Chris immediately stood and tried on their jackets, which fit perfectly. Vandeweghe gave a "thumbs up" to Rudy. They'd definitely scored on this one.

"This is really great, guys," Don said, looking most appreciatively from Rudy to Vandeweghe and back. "Really, thanks!"

"I'm hoping we don't have to use them much," Ridge said. "But they sure are fabulous!"

Plato fingered the lettering on the jacket. "Where'd you get the logos done? You should have let me know; I could have gotten them for you at wholesale."

Vandeweghe waved the air. "The guys over at Cypress took care of it for me." He poked a friendly finger toward Plato. "You're not the only pro with connections, you know."

"They're just great," Plato said. "And this is such a nice gesture, from both of you. I just wanted to make sure you didn't put out more than you should have."

Rudy shrugged. "You're all worth it."

"Well, I motion Rudy and Gary's breakfast is on the bank," Charlie said.

"I second that motion," Don said. "Lunch, too."

"Now don't get carried away!" Vandeweghe said. "But I'll take a beer with my fish 'n chips."

Joviality surrounded the table as breakfast was served and consumed. Vandeweghe felt particularly pleased, though he, too, had rather hoped they'd not need rain gear. He glanced out the window, which was getting lashed by the storm. He dabbed his face with his napkin and stood.

"First tee time's at nine-thirty?" he said, looking at Don.

"Nine-forty," Don said. "But you're in the second group, so you're off at nine-fifty."

"Good." Vandeweghe collected his rain gear. "Then I'll see you guys down at the starter's. I have something to do."

He strode through the dining hall, his mind ticking off the things that had to be done before they left Turnberry this afternoon.

In his room, he quickly changed into warmer clothing, and stuffed an extra pair of socks into his shoe bag. He then left the hotel and crossed down to the golf shop. The rain had lessened into an annoying spittle; he pulled the collar up on his rain jacket.

He entered the shop. "Rain gloves?" he asked.

"Aye, we've got 'em here," the young assistant pro said. He picked up a pair from the display.

"I'll need eight." Vandeweghe pulled his wallet from his pant's pocket. "Two extra-large, and the rest just large."

The young man frowned. "I dinna think you'll be needin' eight pairs. They last forever. I still have the pair I got as a wee bairn."

Vandeweghe smiled. "And I still have the pair I bought at Cypress ten years ago. But they're at home, and all these are for my friends." He waived his credit card. "Bag 'em up, please. We've got a game in half an hour."

Once the caddies arrived and were organized, Vandeweghe handed out the gloves to the Gang, though he noted with pleasure that the rain had ceased.

"What's this?" Don said as Vandeweghe handed him the glove envelope. "Tried and True, you're outdoing yourself!"

"And me," Rudy said, pulling on his gloves. "These are great, Gary. Did you bring them with you?"

Vandeweghe handed the last packet to Patrick. "Naw, I didn't even think about it until this morning at breakfast. They have them here."

"Now we will buy you lunch," Charlie said, and nodded heavily. "No arguments."

A sharp gust of wind cut across the Gang, causing Vandeweghe to shiver slightly. "You're on, Charlie," he said. "Let's hope the Dormy makes great soup."

"Nine-forty on the tee!" the starter called out, and the Gang huddled up and moved as one toward Ailsa's first tee. Vandeweghe was rather excited, despite the damp wind. This was traditional links weather, so what the heck. Let the guys feel what it's really all about. The clouds scudded across the sky, a lighter gray showing over the ocean.

It could be worse!

CHAPTER 30

August 31, 1998

Gary Plato

Plato breathed deep of the wet ocean wind from the Firth of Clyde as he walked down Ailsa's fourth fairway. This was great – sloppy, damp, windy, not really cold, but very challenging. Just what he came for.

He joined Rudy, Patrick, and Don on the green. The wind was now gusting, rather than continuous. Plato marked his ball and stepped aside as Rudy, who was on the back edge of the bowl-shaped green, assessed his line then stood over the ball. A gust of wind shoved him roughly and he backed off.

"Holy cow!" Rudy said. "It's like getting pounced on by a big dog."

Plato chuckled and wiped ocean mist off his face. A big sloppy dog, he thought. Rudy readdressed the ball and, again, a gust slashed across the green. Rudy's ball wobbled and shimmied and Rudy quickly stepped back, putter raised.

"Maybe I should tee it up," Rudy joked. "It might stay still, then."

The wind seemed to take a short rest, and Rudy reset over the ball, keeping his putter raised. As if in answer to his impertinence, the wind heaved and the ball actually rolled back an inch. Rudy quickly stepped away.

"You're all right," Plato said. "You hadn't placed your putter yet."

"Well," Rudy said, "if this darn wind's gonna move my ball, the least it could do it move it toward the hole."

"It might if you spoke nicely," Patrick said. "It's just getting back at you for all your whining."

Rudy grinned. "I haven't even begun to whine." The wind howled, and pushed the ball another inch back. "Oh come on!"

"Just hit it," Patrick said. "It's a downhill roll. You've been making those for the past two days, now."

Plato nodded. Rudy did seem to have a knack for making downhill putts. He willed the wind to relax as Rudy addressed the ball for the fourth time. The putt would be difficult enough from up there. Rudy didn't hesitate. He slapped the ball down the green toward the hole.

"Easy, easy," Plato said. There wasn't that much wind.

The ball curved toward the ocean at a much faster pace than expected, when suddenly another tremendous gust of wind pushed it back on line. It bounced on the back rim of the cup and dropped into the hole with a clatter.

Plato grinned widely. "There's my partner!" He retrieved the ball from the hole and tossed it to Rudy. "You slammed that thing right in there. Another great downhill putt."

"Slammed, hell," Patrick said. "He surgically sliced that thing into the hole. Just like a doctor." Patrick placed his ball at his marker. He looked up at Rudy. "Doctor Downhill, that's who you are."

"Hey, I like that," Rudy said. "Better than Doctor Dreadful, the guy who can't make a single putt."

Plato chuckled as the faces of several members back at home flashed through his mind – all of who would be better suited with that moniker.

"Laddies, play at proper speed, now," Plato's caddy said. "That wind ain't no reason to be fallin' behind. Ye' must keep up with the lads ahead 'o ya."

Plato laughed and placed his ball on the green. Figures it would be his caddy who'd say something like that.

They had less trouble for the next few holes, as the wind took a kinder attitude. Plato had managed to make par at all but the wicked number seven, where the undulating green caught him for a surprising three-putt. He stood on the eighth tee and glared down the punishing fairway. He'd have to fashion a slight hook on the ball to keep it in the short grass, as the fairway leaned away from the ocean, toward the deep bunker on the right. He wiggled, waggled, rechecked his line, then hit the ball. It sailed out toward the bunker, then hooked nicely toward the water, landed safely and bounced away from the bunker.

"Nice shot, Pro," Don said, and stepped up to the tee box.

"Lucky bounce," Patrick said. "You must have found the one spot on this course that has level grass."

"Hit and hope golf," Plato said. "Out here, you just hit and hope."

The wind picked up yet again as they walked to the twelfth tee. Plato removed his rain jacket and looked across the golf course at the lighthouse and the water. He felt so alive.

"Pro, you look like you're about to dance a jig," Patrick said and teed his ball.

"I just saved par with that putt," Plato said. "I should do a dance."

Patrick's drive sliced sharply to the right and disappeared into heavy gorse. "I'm not dancing about that one," he said, and handed his driver to his caddy.

The caddy spat then winked at Patrick. "Aye, that one's like gettin' your sister pregnant. You're not proud of it, but it's yours."

Plato burst into laughter, along with Don, Rudy, and Patrick. That was not likely to be a phrase he'd use at San Jose Country Club, but Plato was sure it was a comment he'd never forget.

By the time they'd made the par five seventeenth hole, Plato was desperately trying to remember all the funny comments the caddies had made. Their caddies yesterday, at Arran, had been supremely helpful, but few had the cutting sense of humor of these four. Plato found it relieved tension, especially when balls went errant.

All four Gang members dropped their drives into the fairway, then avoided the fairway bunkers on their second shots, and were well-placed to make the green in regulation. Plato watched as Rudy hit onto the putting surface, then Don wiggled over his ball. Plato furrowed his brow. Don was clearly off in his stance; did he have a bad lie? Don swung and, sure enough, the ball slipped right and landed in a greenside bunker. Plato pursed his lips; sometimes he wished he could stop a player before they made the mistake.

Both he and Patrick made the green with their second shots, then followed Don to the bunker.

"What a fried egg," Don said. His ball was buried into the wall of the bunker, the mere top third of the surface showing above the layers of condensed dirt, sand, and grass. "Anyone have a spatula?"

Plato pulled an old sixty-three degree wedge from his bag. He'd brought it for just such an occasion. "Here, use this." He handed it to Don. "Might be the closest thing to a spatula you'll find out here."

Don hefted it in his grip a few times, took several practice swings, then climbed down into the bunker. He twisted his shoes into the sand, took aim with the club, and swung high and hard. Dirt flew up over him in a blanket that was carried away by the wind. Plato winced. The ball was still buried in the bunker wall, perhaps even deeper than before.

Plato bit his lip to keep from making suggestions, and wished he had spoken up as Don again swung, and again left the ball in the bunker wall. Don stepped back, took a breath to calm his obvious frustration, then readdressed the ball. Plato glanced over at the group of caddies, all watching from the edge of the green. They, too, looked as if they were biting back recommendations. The third swing provided no better results, and Don climbed out of the bunker with the ball still buried deep in the dirt wall. He handed Plato his club.

"So much for a spatula," Don said. "Got a knife? I'll carve it out of there."

"How about a shotgun," Patrick said. "You could shoot the darn thing."

"Or myself," Don said, grimacing. He pulled a six iron from his bag and returned to the bunker. Holding the club like a baseball bat, he took aim and swung. The ball sprung from the wall, bounced off the left side of the bunker, ricocheted onto the putting surface and rolled to three inches from the hole.

"All right!" and "Hey hey!" and "Finally!" were said by the Gang, and the caddies applauded. Then, as Plato watched in amazement, three of them pulled a wad of bills from their pockets and passed money to Don's caddy.

"Were you betting on me?" Don asked, still standing in the bottom of the deep bunker.

"Oh, aye laddie," his caddy said, and winked. "These boys bet that ball would be sittin' there when we left the green. But I know y'be made of stronger stuff than that, oh aye. I just knew ye'd find a way t'get that bugger from the devil."

Plato nodded and laughed along with the others.

"That's our man," Patrick said. "Warrior Winterhalter, foe of the devil bunkers, defender of the bogey."

Plato made note of Patrick's comment. "Warrior Winterhalter" might stick. Maybe.

He watched as Don crossed to his ball and gently tapped it into the cup. He then retrieved the ball and carefully pocketed it. No, Plato decided, the moniker was unlikely to survive the moment, despite Don's heroic efforts in the bunker. The guy was just too darn nice. But all this would make a great story over dinner.

The eighteenth hole provided no major disasters, and all four men joined the rest of the Gang in the pro shop at the end of the round. Plato perused the wares – golf shirts and sweatshirts and club covers – and in the end purchased a cap. Ridge, Patrick, and Chris were huddled over a jar of ball markers, deciding which of the several designs they desired. Plato smiled in agreement. It was an easy souvenir to carry home.

He passed by the window. Their eight caddies were in the courtyard, gathered together, arguing in a brogue as thick as their dark beer. Plato burst into laughter. "Hey guys," he called to the other Gang members. "We're causing some consternation out there."

Vandeweghe peeked over Plato's shoulder. "What are they doing?" he asked. "Sharing tips?"

Ridge's face wrinkled into a grin. "They're sorting out their wagers."

"Wagers?" Charlie said. "On what? Us?"

"Exactly," Plato said. "They've been betting on shots all afternoon. I imagine they have a friendly wager on the two games, too."

Chris's caddy suddenly took a swing at Charlie's caddy, who ducked and danced backwards, glancing toward the caddy-shack.

"Or not so friendly," Don said. "What'd you shoot, Chris?"

"Sixty-eight," Chris said. "Almost had an eagle on seven."

"Charlie?" Don asked.

"Sixty-nine," Charlie said, grinning. He pointed at Chris. "I just followed this young'un around."

The argument in the courtyard calmed, and the Gang watched as the eight caddies settled up, passing notes between them. Clearly, though, Chris's caddy cleaned up. Plato wondered if this was common, then decided it probably was. If he spent his days carrying bags for golfers, most of which were not very good, he'd need a little distraction, too. Speaking of which...

"Showers, anyone?" he said. "I'm starved and we have to check out soon."

Affirmative comments followed, and the Gang followed Plato along the path to the Turnberry Hotel. The wind had calmed, the clouds were beginning to part, and the day was looking to be much brighter.

Not that he needed anything to brighten his mood, Plato decided.

After all, what could be better than this?

CHAPTER 31

August 31, 1998
Patrick Quinn

Patrick wandered away from the Gang. They had lunched in the Dormy House again, and he'd been disappointed that Natalie had not been available to waitress. Not that he cared to see her again; it just would have been fun to razz Don Winterhalter about her. Now they were waiting for their van to arrive. Bags and clubs were lined along the curb, and the men were comparing notes on the morning's game. Patrick had ended up with a sad seventy-four; he had nothing he wanted to share.

He pulled his camera from its bag and shot several pictures of the hotel and its surroundings. He was, after all, the chronologist for this venture. About time he did his job.

Fifteen minutes passed before he heard his name called. The van had arrived.

A balding, potbellied man who appeared to be in his forties loaded their bags into a small trailer hitched to the back of the van. The man glanced up at Patrick, paused, and stuck out his hand.

"Ken Clarke," he said. "Your driver for th'week." He squeezed Patrick's hand. "Nice t'meet you."

Patrick wiggled his fingers; hopefully this Ken hadn't broken any of his bones. He smiled. "Patrick Quinn," he said, then pointed at Charlie. "That one's whelp."

"Hey, now," Charlie said. "Don't disparage your dear mother."

Ken nodded and smiled. "All right now," he said. "We've the bags loaded. Shall we?"

The Gang quickly found seats. Vandeweghe was in the front, with Plato and Rudy behind him. Beyond that, Chris, Ridge, and Don sprawled upon individual seats. Charlie and Patrick chose seats further back. Patrick mentally noted where everyone sat; he figured it would not change for the duration of the trip. These guys were, if nothing else, predictable in their seating arrangements.

Ken jerked the doors closed and fired up the engine. It rumbled happily. "Where to, gentlemen?" he asked, looking at them in his large rearview mirror.

"The Marine Hotel at Troon," Vandeweghe said with authority.

Ridge glanced at his watch. "We don't have to be there until three, do we? Is there something around here to see?"

"We're not on a sightseeing tour," Vandeweghe said, rather gently.

"But we got the whole day before us," Ridge said. "I for one don't want to sit in a hotel room."

"Have ye seen Culzean Castle?" Ken asked. "'Tis a great sight, if you've not been."

"How far is it?" Charlie asked. "I wouldn't mind seeing something beside a golf course when we have the chance."

Patrick smiled. He doubted his Pop really cared about some old relic, but he knew Pop wanted his son to see as much as possible.

"Not far," Ken said, and put the van into gear. "I'll have ye there in no time a'tall."

Patrick shot photos from the window, while the sound of the engine lulled the Gang to thoughtful silence. They rounded a bend and Patrick sat up. They had been riding for less than fifteen minutes, and there, before them on a slight hill, against the crashing ocean, sat their destination: Culzean Castle. The entrance boasted a medieval wall surrounding a stone structure of varied levels and shapes. Round turrets anchored the gate building on both ends, while a tall structure took center stage, sporting a huge clock and several lovely windows. Beyond that stood the castle proper, graceful and imposing, and clearly built in a more elegant time.

Patrick whistled. "Wow, it really is a castle. I thought we'd be seeing the remnants of broken down walls."

Ken steered the van into the parking lot, which was surprisingly full of cars, buses, and motorcycles of every size and style. Several people were wandering around the grounds, drinking and eating.

"Ice cream!" Vandeweghe bolted from the van the moment Ken brought it to a stop. "Come on, fellas. We deserve a scoop or two."

"Or three," Chris said, close behind Vandeweghe.

Patrick fell in behind the Gang, who made a beeline for the front gate. Inside, in what might have been a kitchen, a small cafe had been assembled. Sure enough, ice cream was available, and all eight men chose generously. Ken, who had gone off to collect information, rejoined them, pamphlets in hand.

"So, the fee's twenty-pound a man to take th' tour," he said. "It takes about two hours."

Vandeweghe frowned. "Fellas?" he said, and the tone of his voice made clear his attitude on the matter.

"There's no point in taking the whole tour," Ridge said. "I'm good just seeing the outside."

Vandeweghe looked at Charlie and raised his eyebrows.

"I'm with Patrick, here," Charlie said. "I go with his decision."

Patrick grinned. All seven Gang members were waiting for him to decide. "Wow, I've never felt such power." He rubbed his hands together. "I've never experienced such control."

Rudy chuckled. "Get over yourself and tell us if we're taking a tour or not."

"Gosh, all this history just waiting to be discovered," Patrick said. "Just think what you might find inside —"

"Dusty furniture 'n rustin' armor, that's what ye'll find, no doubt," Ken said. "Oh, 'n your Eisenhower's apartments, given to him by the late owner in th' forties."

"Eisenhower?" Chris said. "As in President Eisenhower?"

Ken nodded. "For being Supreme Commander o'the Allied Forces during th' Second World War."

Patrick raised his hands, palms up. "See? You find the strangest things in old castles." He really would like to take the tour, but he could see the discomfort on several of the faces, and he knew the decision he had to make. "But I don't want to get to Troon really late, so let's just walk around outside and enjoy the view. We'll take the tour some other time."

Vandeweghe nodded vigorously. "Sure, sure, good idea. Let's go walk around some; stretch our legs." And he headed off toward the courtyard.

Charlie patted Patrick on the shoulder. "Wise decision," he said.

Patrick suddenly felt like hugging his dad and having a little cry on his shoulder. He took a big breath and laughed, but even to his ears it sounded forced. His head reeled. *What in the devil is this about?* "No problem, Pops," he said, forcing his voice to be level. "Like Ken said, it's probably just a bunch of dusty furniture and old junk."

In small clusters, the Gang wandered the grounds of Culzean Castle, eating their ice cream. The back of the castle was much more spectacular than the front. The noble estate looked down on graceful and lush gardens, its many windows and chimneys draped like jewelry upon the golden turrets and facades, and it was much, much larger than it appeared upon arrival. Patrick regretted his decision to decline the tour, as this side exhibited its magnitude. The view from the windows had to be spectacular. He imagined sitting there, looking out at the ocean and enjoying the sunset every evening. Yep, he could live here.

Patrick and Charlie read all the literature available, and learned it was the former home of the Marquess of Ailsa, for whom the golf course was named.

"I wonder if she liked to golf?" Patrick asked. "Or did she just own the property?"

Charlie shrugged. He turned the page on the pamphlet. "Says here it's been open to the public since 1987, so maybe she did play. The course has been there longer than that."

Patrick leaned over his Pop's shoulder and read as well.

"Not so old, really." Don Winterhalter had snuck up behind them as they were reading. "Built between 1777 and 1792. We'd already won the War of Independence."

Patrick nodded. It sounded old, and the castle looked older, really, with the way it was constructed. But 1792 was only two hundred years ago. Still, it was a really cool looking castle, and it was definitely nothing he'd find in the States.

"Hey fellas!"

Vandeweghe stood near the entrance, waving. He motioned for them to join him.

"Change of mind?" Don said.

"Or he found free ice cream," Charlie said with a lopsided grin.

The Gang converged at the entrance. Vandeweghe was standing beside an elderly Scottish woman, dressed in traditional garb. Vandeweghe gave her a beaming smile and said, "This wonderful woman has informed me that we can go in and wander without a tour. We just have to make a donation." He pulled out a five pound note and dropped it in a box marked National Trust for Scotland. "I'm up for it," Vandeweghe said. "Anyone else?"

Hearty agreement was voiced, and the men opened their wallets and dropped a donation in the bucket. Patrick noted that Rudy added a twenty-pound note. He caught Rudy's eye. Rudy shrugged and smiled.

"They gotta keep open long enough for us to take the tour next time we're here," he said, and followed the rest of the Gang into the castle.

Patrick held up the rear of the line as the woman led them up an enormous oval staircase, then smaller stairs to the top floor apartments. As best he could, Patrick peeked into the rooms they passed. He smiled. It wasn't dusty or particularly "old." It was beautiful. Shoot, wire the place for television and he could definitely live here.

Finally they reached the top and the woman explained that General Eisenhower first visited Culzean Castle in 1946 and stayed there several times during his life, including at least once while he was President of the United States. Patrick and the Gang looked into the office, which was richly appointed but surprisingly small. Another room held memorabilia of his life, much of it about his time as Supreme Commander. Patrick felt pride swell in his chest. He was in Scotland, and here was a tribute to his own President.

The world was pretty small, all things considered.

Half an hour later, the Gang was back on the outside. Patrick noticed a marked increase in activity since they'd gone up to the apartments. At least a dozen men were carrying cameras, lights, and sound booms. Suddenly the unique sound of bagpipes filled the air.

Chris pointed toward the back of the castle. "I think it's coming from there."

The Gang walked briskly around to the back of the castle.

"Oh, no way!" Chris said, and pointed again.

Lining the wall were twelve bagpipers, several drummers, and an official-looking leader, all in kilts or full regalia. The Gang watched, along with another thirty or so folks who had been visiting the castle. Several cameramen positioned themselves around the bagpipers and, at some unseen command, the music started.

Patrick stood behind the rest of the Gang. Rudy and Ridge were smiling broadly, while Chris and Plato appeared to be happily analyzing each musical note. Vandeweghe was shading his eyes and tapping his toe, and Pops had that great lopsided grin on his face. Don, however, had really shiny eyes and a small, tight smile. He looked like he was going to cry at any moment. Patrick felt a tightness in his own chest and realized he might join Don. He grunted quietly. That would be great; two grown men crying at Culzean Castle, listening to bagpipes. Americans, at that. How embarrassing.

The first song was completed and the cameramen repositioned themselves. Patrick smiled at Don, who finally hummed and smiled back, broadly. The Gang moved toward the parking lot.

"That was pretty special," Don said.

"Unbelievable," Plato said. "What a remarkable moment."

Rudy nodded. "I feel like I stepped back in time a few hundred years or so," he said. He looked around. "Where's Robert the Bruce?"

Charlie patted Patrick on the back. "There you go, son," he said. "A piece of living history."

As another song played, they walked back to the van. Ken sat in the driver's seat, reading a newspaper. Patrick almost asked if he was deaf, but then realized the Scotsman probably heard this stuff all the time and was immune to it.

"Are ya ready t'go?" Ken asked.

Vandeweghe took his seat in the front. "All ready, Ken. Let's get back to golf."

Patrick smiled, and realized this was probably his one and only cultural experience during this trip. He settled into his seat. He didn't mind. He'd rather bring the girls here, anyway. Make a long vacation out of it and really take in the sights. Leave the golf clubs at home.

Maybe.

The van rumbled comfortably down the highway, if that's what you could call this narrow, bumpy road, Patrick thought. The Gang was again lulled into silence, with each man whiling away the time in their own fashion. Twenty minutes into the trip, however, Ridge squirmed.

"Hey guys, I'm gonna have to make a pit stop," he said. "These hormones are working overtime again."

Vandeweghe turned in his seat and looked back at Ridge. His forehead was furrowed in concern. "Can you wait 'till we get to the hotel?" He turned to Ken. "How long before we can stop? Where's the next gas station?"

Ken shifted gears and slowed the van, steering it onto the edge of the road. "This here's your best shot, sir." He opened the van door. "Won't be a station 'till near Troon."

Ridge bounded from the van and relieved himself alongside the road. Patrick looked around for passing autos, then realized he hadn't seen one since they left the castle, anyway. Not a busy "highway," this one.

Ridge returned to the van, obviously much more comfortable. "Sorry, gents, but when I gotta go, I gots'ta go."

"No problem," "Totally understand," and "Hey, don't worry about it" filled the van. Ken recommenced the trip, but within fifteen minutes, poor Ridge was squirming again.

"Fellas..." he said, apology rich in his voice.

Patrick saw Ken glance in his rear view mirror. "We're close t'Prestwick Golf Club, gents," he said. "I suggest we make a stop there, no?"

"Excellent idea," Rudy said. "I could use a stop, myself."

"How long...?" Ridge asked, obviously uncomfortable.

Ken sped up the van. "Five minutes, sir," he said, and focused on driving as quickly as possible. True to his word, they were parked at Prestwick within five minutes.

Ridge trotted from the van and into the clubhouse. Patrick followed the Gang from the vehicle, and paused to take in the view. The clubhouse was a massive building – a brownstone with tall, slender windows and Edwardian sloped roof-lines. Several chimneys extended up from one wing, and Patrick assumed that might be the dining rooms. Golfers crisscrossed the immediate area, some pulling trolleys and others carrying their bags. The lawn surrounding the clubhouse was lush and manicured, but just beyond that was the rough and tumble landscape that comprised this part of Scotland, and therefore the golf course. Small rolling hillocks covered in scruffy grass were intermingled with thick patches of gorse and bush. Patrick grinned. It was a bunny's dream, but ominous to a golfer.

"Hey, Mission Prince," Rudy said, "you coming?"

Patrick caught up to the Gang as they entered the building. It was smart inside, but lacked the plush overstuffed feeling of Turnberry. Patrick liked this; less fussy.

"We never managed to get a tee-time here," Don said. "I'm going to run over to the pro shop and see if we can't sneak one in."

"Do you have the schedule?" Plato asked. "I'll go back to the van and get mine."

The two men went their separate ways, leaving the rest of the Gang to hang out in the clubhouse. A television was showing news, and Vandeweghe, Rudy, and Chris paused to watch. Patrick joined Charlie on a tightly upholstered leather couch that faced out toward the course. Ridge returned from the bathroom and shook his head.

"I'm gonna have to do something about this," he said to Charlie and Patrick. "I can't keep peeing alongside the road."

"You do what you gotta do," Charlie said. "We all understand, Ridge. Don't worry about it so much."

Ridge pursed his lips and flopped down on an adjoining chair. Several minutes later, Don and Plato arrived, smiling.

"We've got one tee time, at ten on Thursday," Don said.

"Just one?" Ridge asked.

"For the moment," Don said. "We'll keep trying for a second, or flip a coin to see who plays. We just can't have the second tee time too much later."

"We're playing Old Troon that afternoon," Plato explained, "but the courses are close enough to each other that we should be able to make both without trouble."

Patrick glanced at his Pops. Another thirty-six hole day. He was fine with it, himself, but he worried about his dad's back. Charlie would make every effort to keep up, often at the expense of his health and pain threshold.

"Good by me, long as they got buggies," Ridge said. "Or caddies at the very least. Now, if it's all right by you, I'd like to stop at this local store." He brandished a piece of paper with a name printed upon it. "The secretary here says Ken ought to know where it is, and they got a gas can I can buy."

"Gas can?" Vandeweghe said. The Gang members had regrouped and were walking slowly back toward the van.

Ridge nodded. "I can't keep stopping us every time I need to pee, so I'm gonna buy a gas can to use." He looked around at the blank faces of his friends. "In the back of the bus! Don't you see? I can just pee in the gas can and we won't have to stop every five minutes."

"It's been more like fifteen," Rudy said, smiling. "But who's counting. Sounds like an excellent solution to me. Heck, I might use it myself once in a while."

Ridge's beard wiggled. "I'm not sharing my gas can with anybody. You want your own porta-potty, get your own can."

"All right, all right," Rudy said. "Don't get your knickers in a twist."

Gang of Eight: The First Tee

The Gang loaded into the van, explanations were given as to the added stop, and Ken fired up the vehicle. Within minutes they were at the store. Ridge went in by himself – a smart move, Patrick though, since most likely if the entire Gang went in, they'd be there for an hour, browsing the local fare. In five minutes they were on their way again, and over the next twenty minute drive, Ridge sat comfortably, gas can at the ready.

Patrick dropped his bag in the room at the Marine Hotel, overlooking Troon Golf Course. He sighed. Jet lag was catching up to him and he needed sleep.

"You want to shower first?" Charlie asked.

Patrick flopped onto his bed. "No, you go first. Wake me when you're out."

"Won't be five minutes," Charlie said. "No point in sleeping."

"There's always a point in sleeping, Pops," Patrick mumbled. "Even if it's only for..." And he was out.

He woke when Charlie closed the door. It wasn't loud, but it was followed by complete silence, which wasn't right. Patrick sat up.

"Pops?"

No answer. Patrick scrambled from the mattress and hurriedly pulled on his shoes. He jerked off his golf shirt and grabbed a clean one from his bag. Then he ran from the room, pulling on the shirt as he bounded down the hall toward the lobby. He found the Gang assembled around Rudy.

"So we have several options," Rudy said, a pad of paper in hand. "But the folks here suggest this place, The Scotch Broom."

Vandeweghe shook his head. "I've been there. Not much atmosphere. What else you got?"

Rudy consulted the pad. "Two other places. Liam's Pub and The Lion. The pub sounded rather interesting."

"Just pub food," Vandeweghe said and wrinkled his nose. "Nix that one. The Lion? Isn't that an Italian joint? I think we've been to that one, Barb and I. Weren't impressed."

Patrick glanced around. There were mixed emotions on the faces of the other Gang members. A few were clearly uncomfortable that Vandeweghe was taking charge of what had been designated as Rudy's "job." Others were mildly amused by the whole affair. Patrick rather felt sorry for Rudy. He obviously had done some homework prior to arrival.

Rudy dropped the pad to his side. "So where would you like to go, Gary?"

"Let's go to the Piersland," Vandeweghe said, and zipped up his wind jacket. "I think it's only a block or two, and the food is excellent. But of course this is your area, and if you think we should go to one of these others" – he pointed at Rudy's pad – "then by all means, let's go."

They all looked at Rudy. No one was going to okay any suggestion unless he did. Rudy nodded curtly, then smiled. "Piersland it is. And we'll hold you responsible for the food, Vandeweghe."

"Of course, of course," Vandeweghe said. And they all followed him out into the early evening air of Scotland. Patrick hoped, for Rudy's sake, that the food would indeed be good.

It was. In fact, the Gang agreed it was the best meal they'd had thus far. Vandeweghe ordered several bottles of wine, and each man chose from the limited but interesting menu. The service was excellent, though it lacked a Natalie, Patrick noted with a small smile.

As if some impish pixie had heard his thoughts, Don rose and excused himself for the bathroom, and Vandeweghe leaned in to the group.

"Fellas, I have an idea," he said, and Patrick instantly knew this was going to be trouble.

He was right. By the time poor Don returned from the bathroom, the plan had been set in motion.

As a loose group, the Gang stood outside the Marine Hotel, satisfied and jocular. The hotel overlooked the eighteenth fairway at Troon, and had a spectacular view.

"When are we playing the Old here, at Troon?" Chris asked. "It looks fabulous."

"It is," Plato said. "One of the regulars on the Open Championship tour."

"We play it Thursday," Don said. "But only the Old, since we canceled Portland to play Prestwick."

"Let's hope we get that second tee-time," Vandeweghe said. "Otherwise we should have stayed with Portland."

The sun set, slipping into the ocean like a lady into a bath, and the golf course glowed golden. Patrick took a deep breath. It was a perfect evening. Reluctantly, he followed the Gang into the hotel lobby.

"Barassie tomorrow morning, gents!" Plato said. "Be downstairs at six-thirty sharp for breakfast. Bus leaves at seven-fifteen."

"Excuse me!" A woman waved at them from behind the check-in counter. Patrick turned away to hide his smile. "Are one of you a Mr. Win – uh, Wintrap...hater?"

Don grunted. "Winterhalter?" he said, and approached the counter. "Yes, that's me."

She beamed. "I have a message for you." She handed a small note to Don.

"Everything okay?" Charlie asked, as sincere as Patrick had ever heard him. Way to go, Pops, Patrick thought.

Don frowned, pursed his lips in a thin line, and turned a discernible shade of red. "It's a note from a Natalie. It says she called and asked for me...?"

Patrick felt guilty. The guy was obviously disturbed by the possibility that some young Scottish girl was pursuing him.

Don looked at the woman behind the counter. "Are you sure she asked for me? Don Winterhalter?"

The woman didn't blink. "I dinna take the message, sir. It came in before me shift."

Patrick about gagged. Vandeweghe, who, on their return from dinner, had hurried ahead of the Gang under the guise of getting his camera from his hotel room, had obviously schooled the woman very well. They might just pull this off.

Don frowned and read the note again. "Natalie?" he asked the woman. "You sure the caller said her name was Natalie? Not Penny?"

The woman froze her face and shrugged. Don looked at the Gang, and Patrick noted a sincere concern, and perhaps a small bit of panic. "Why would she be calling me? How would she know we were here?" Then Don looked around at the Gang, and started to laugh. "Ah, come on, guys." He pointed at the woman behind the counter. "You put her up to this, didn't you?"

"Who? Natalie?" Ridge said. "None of us have spoken with her since we saw her at the restaurant. At least I haven't." He looked from one man to another. "You?"

"Nope." "Not I." "Wouldn't know her again if I ran into her..."

Patrick said nothing. He'd flunked drama in high school, and he was pretty darn sure he couldn't keep a straight face in this little play. He quickly found a snag in his golf shirt and focused upon it with enthusiasm.

"Naw, I don't believe you," Don said, and wadded up the little paper then dropped it into an ashtray on the closest table. "She's not calling me. If anything, she'd be calling Gary, here." He pointed at Vandeweghe. "She thought you were the cat's meow."

"Me?!" Vandeweghe feigned perfect surprise and indignation. Patrick decided he should be up for an Oscar.

Don slapped at the air with his hand and walked toward the rooms. "You guys are pulling my leg. Natalie didn't call."

The rest of the Gang smiled at one another. Rudy gave a slight thumbs-up. Patrick returned to his room. Maybe Don hadn't bought it completely, but they had him going for a minute there. It had been fun to see the usually unflappable Don Winterhalter get a little ... flapped. The Gang hadn't been able to get his goat for a while now. Maybe, Patrick thought, just maybe this would be useful on the course tomorrow.

That is, if they weren't teamed up together. If the truth be known, the prospect of playing with Don as his partner was far more pleasing than the possibility of watching him squirm.

CHAPTER 32

September 1, 1998

Don Winterhalter and Rudy Staedler

Don stood in the lobby and watched the rain pelt the van as Ken pulled it up beside the front door of the Marine Hotel. Don snugged his turtleneck collar up around his chin. It better stop raining this hard, or they were going to be miserable out there.

Chris joined him and glared at the slashing weather. "Think we should can it?"

Don made a little face of aversion. "Cancel? Naw. We came all this way to play. What's a little rain?"

Chris's eyebrows rose. "A little rain." He chuckled "I would call this a deluge."

Don nudged Chris with his elbow. "You flat bellies. You're all wimps. You won't melt."

The remaining members of the Gang entered the lobby, all carrying or wearing their rain gear. Ridge was obviously agitated.

"They're just gone!" he said to Plato. "Stolen. I certainly did not leave them at Turnberry."

Don wrinkled his brow. "What's up, Ridge?"

"One of his pairs of golf shoes went missing last night," Plato said.

"From the room? During dinner?" Don found that disconcerting. He had an expensive camera in his room. Maybe he should always carry it with him.

"Naw," Ridge said, and his beard wiggled fiercely. "I put them in the window to dry. Both pairs, because they were wet from playing at Turnberry. Now I have one pair. Someone nicked the other."

"Go tell the hotel management," Chris suggested. "Maybe they can track them down."

"What? Off some fellow's feet?" Ridge nearly yelled. "Naw, they're gone. At least the guy had the decency to leave me one pair."

Don agreed. It would have been a dreadful – and expensive – situation had Ridge been forced to buy a new pair of golf shoes here in Scotland.

Ken stepped into the lobby and shook the rain off his slicker. "Ready, gents? I got th'van all warmed up for ye."

Almost reluctantly, the Gang loaded into the van. The rain beat the roof of the vehicle like a drum, rendering conversation impossible. Don hunkered down in his seat and watched the water-drenched scenery as they drove to Kilmarnock's Barassie course.

It wasn't long before they pulled up in front of the squat clubhouse. The rain hadn't abated at all. If anything, it was worse. Here, along the coastline, the wind drove the storm and the rain slashed sideways at times. Well, they didn't come thousands of miles to whine.

Ken hunkered down in his slicker and smiled from the front of the van. "Aye, you're in for it today, gents," he said. "It be dumpin' dole, for sure."

Don wrinkled his brow. "Dumping dole? Did I hear you right?"

Ken nodded. "Aye, that be Scottish for 'it's rainin' so hard that you'd be stupid to go out'." Then he smiled, pushed open the door of the van, and jumped into a puddle.

"Suck it up, ladies," Vandeweghe said as he tightened the neck and waist lines on his rain jacket. "We're in for a squall."

To Don's slight disgust, the Barassie pro informed them there would be no caddies. They'd have to pull trolleys or carry their bags.

Rudy grunted and smirked. "Maybe they're smart."

"You're up, gentlemen," the Barassie pro said. "'N ye can all play t'gether, if you like. I've no other players today."

Don chuckled. He didn't doubt it.

"First tee?" Plato said. "Where is it?"

The pro gave them directions, and the Gang walked out into the hammering storm. Don popped open his umbrella and held it over himself, Chris, and his bag as Chris attached the bag to the pull-cart. Chris then repaid the favor. A strong gust of wind tore across from the ocean, and they all struggled to keep their umbrellas open and intact.

"This is nuts," Rudy said. He was huddled under his umbrella, clearly shivering. "Sorry to wimp out on you guys, but I'm not doing this. I'll sit this one out in the clubhouse."

"I'm joining you," Ridge said. His umbrella had popped inside out in the gust, and now he was fighting to return it to useable form. "This isn't any fun."

Patrick turned to Charlie. "You want to sit out, too, Pops?"

Don knew Charlie well enough to know he'd play, just to make Patrick happy, so it was no surprise when Charlie said, "You playing? Then I'm playing with you."

"Okay, let's go," Vandeweghe said. "Rain gloves on?" He led the already soggy group across the yard, through a small metal gate, across what appeared to be a cow path, then through yet another small gate.

Don wondered if they'd left the course and landed in a pasture. Ahead, he saw the tee markers and realized they'd found the first hole, after all. He was a bit disappointed. It was a short par three, flat and boring. Ahead, through the sheets of rain, he could see the flag flapping wildly in the wind.

"Uh, remind us why we're doing this?" Chris said as he teed up his ball.

"We've no place to go but back to the hotel," Don said. "At least this will make a good story."

Chris chuckled and drove his ball into the water-logged rough on the right.

"More like a bad hallucination," Patrick said, and stepped up to the tee box.

Don drove last, and managed to place his ball on the green. He felt some small battle had been won. He hunkered under his umbrella and started down the fairway. The wind ripped at the large red and white stripes, and

Don found it increasingly difficult to hold the umbrella with one hand and pull the trolley with the other.

"Oh, to hell with it," Vandeweghe said, and folded his umbrella.

Apparently he'd been having the same problem, Don realized, and folded his umbrella as well. It made for easier walking, but by the time he'd putted out on the first hole, he was soaked clean through. Rain ran off his ball cap, down the back of his neck, and across his shoulders. By the third hole, his shoes were soggy. By the sixth tee, he didn't think he had a single item of clothing on his body that was dry. Heck, even his underwear felt wet.

"Remind me why we're doing this again?" Chris asked with a smirk. "My brain's so water-logged, I can't remember."

Don chuckled. It really was miserable, and yet there was something ridiculously fun about it. So far, the course was dull and uninteresting, with little visual interest. The storm provided a challenge.

The sixth hole spread before them, lined with trees and gorse. Don squinted, trying to determine the distance to the burn he knew was out there. He pointed. "Is there water out there?"

The men all chuckled. "There's water everywhere!" Vandeweghe said.

"I mean, is there a creek, a burn, that cuts the fairway?" Don said.

Plato, who had wisely placed his score card in a plastic baggy, scanned it for details. "Looks like it. Maybe two, two-fifty."

Don pulled his driver from the bag. The wind was still gusting irregularly, so he clubbed for it, rather than be short. He wiggled once, set his jaw, and swung. The ball leapt off the club face, then hovered in the air before dropping – and disappearing.

"I think we can now safely say there is a burn out there," Patrick said. "You've shown us the way, Winterhalter."

Don pursed his lips and pulled a new ball from his bag. He changed to a five wood and cleanly hit the ball again. It had no more left the club when the wind died completely, and the now unencumbered ball sailed – right into the burn.

"Oh, no!" Vandeweghe yelled. "You couldn't do that again if you tried!"

Don shook his head in disbelief and disgust. "So what do I use this time? My wedge?"

"That certainly would leave you short of the burn," Plato said. "And you'd get to the green–"

"Eventually!" Vandeweghe, Chris, and Patrick all completed the sentence simultaneously. Everyone laughed, including Don. It was funny – the whole situation.

He yanked a two iron from his bag. He certainly wasn't going to drive this into a creek some two hundred plus yards away. He teed up another new ball – this was becoming an expensive hole, he thought – wiggled, waggled, then swung. The club hit the ball directly in the sweet spot, and sent it sailing. It landed around one-ninety, hit something hard and bounced high, sailed another thirty yards, bounced again – and disappeared into the burn.

Don stood in amazement as the other men hooted and hollered. This just wasn't possible; he couldn't lose *three* balls on one hole.

"I can't even believe you just had such rotten luck!" Vandeweghe said. "What a crummy bounce!"

Don stepped off the tee and waved back at it. "Please, someone else get up there and hit. I can't even think right now."

Charlie and Patrick both drove safely down the fairway before Don retrieved yet another ball from his bag and stood over it on the tee box. In his hand he held a six iron. He was already lying six before he even hit, so what the heck. Lob this darn ball down there and chip his way to the green, if necessary.

He swung. The ball landed as neatly as possible, right in the middle, approximately sixty yards from the burn. Don "harrumphed," slapped the club in his bag, and headed down the fairway. The rain had become a steady downpour, which didn't help his current mood. Oh well; this round didn't count for anything in Plato's Scotland Tournament, anyway. Laugh it off.

His mood lifted considerably when Patrick found two of his three balls in the burn. "Got 'em!" Patrick said as he stood down near the creek, waving his fists in the air. "Sure you want them back?"

Don held out his hand. "No doubt they'll have another chance to land in a burn somewhere."

Patrick grinned. "It's not likely there will be another Winterhalter Burn on this trip. You only get to name one."

"I hadn't planned on putting my name on anything," Don said. "Certainly not a burn."

He watched from under his umbrella as Patrick, Chris, Plato, and Vandeweghe putted out. Then Charlie walked to his ball marker, on the far edge of the green, and paused. He simply stood there for a moment, then reached down and picked up his marker.

"I'm done, fellas," he said. "I'm wet to the bone and this is just no fun for me." He grabbed his trolley. "I'll see you back at the clubhouse."

We should all join him, Don thought.

Vandeweghe waved them on. "I'm not quitting." He glared at the four remaining men. "You quittin'?"

They all murmured a response and headed for the seventh tee. For the first time in a long while, Don was glad there were only eighteen holes in a round.

Rudy and Ridge sat stiffly in the clubhouse, flipping through golf magazines and sipping coffee and tea. It was quiet – no radio or television; only the tick-tock of a large clock to break the silence. Rudy felt somewhat uncomfortable every time the Barassie pro would enter the room. He'd walk over, ask if they "were needin' anything?", then disappear again.

During one of these "check-ins" Ridge nodded and said, "Yep, do you have a ball marker with the course name on it?"

"Aye, we do," the pro said.

"Good." Ridge stood and looked down at Rudy. "Chris'll want one, and I'm pretty sure they won't wanna shop when they get in."

Rudy nodded. It was just like Ridge to be thinking of the other guys.

When he returned, Rudy stood and stretched. "Let's make a bank run while the guys play. I'm short on funny money."

Ridge nodded. "I saw Ken in the bar," he said. "I'll go get him."

Minutes later they were in the van, driving through the rain into town. Ken found a parking lot large enough for the van and the trailer, then pointed in the direction of a bank.

"I'd check there, gents," he said. "They'll 'ave no problem changin' your money."

Rudy and Ridge trotted to the bank under their umbrellas, exchanged money, and exited the bank. Rudy looked left and right, checking for traffic.

"Ridge, check that out," he said. "That store sign has a golf club hanging from it. Let's go see if they have anything interesting."

They moved quickly through the rain to the small, aged door beneath the sign. *DT Antique Shop.* They stepped in. It smelled of old dust, well-oiled furniture, and buffed leather. Rudy breathed in deeply. "That's grand. The smell of Scottish golf."

An elderly gentleman in slacks and a tweed jacket entered from a back room. "Can I 'elp you?" he asked, his brogue so thick Rudy had to guess what he might have said.

"I don't think so," Rudy said. "We're just getting in out of the rain, waiting for some friends to get off the course."

The gentleman wrinkled his brow and glanced outside. The rain still fell in prodigious amounts. "There's some out playing in th'rain?" he asked. "Are they daft?"

Ridge rumbled into a full-chested laugh. "Today they are. But we're here, to enjoy your shop."

The gentleman gave them a wide smile, and Rudy was pleased to see he had all his teeth. He'd become accustomed to caddies with few teeth.

"Pleased to have ya," the gentleman said. "You're golfers then, are ya?" Rudy and Ridge nodded. "Ach, take your time. I'll be in th'back if ye have need o'me." He bopped his head once and exited through the door from which he'd come.

They began unsystematically browsing the shop. It held many an old, wooden club, but Rudy was delighted to see a well-preserved niblick and an even better "spoon." In a glass case, he found antique golf balls, including a few feather and gutta-percha balls. There was furniture and some clothing, as well, but they held less interest for him, and apparently for Ridge, as well, who stood in front of another glass case, looking at maps of the area and aged score cards.

Rudy pointed to one. "Look. A score card from Turnberry."

The elderly gentleman appeared out of seemingly nowhere. "Aye, that's the score card for th' 1924 Scottish Ladies Amateur," he said with pride. "Miss Montgomery won that year. This 'ere's her card for th'second round. She shot a respectable eighty-two."

Rudy grinned at Ridge. "An eighty-two, and she was probably playing with some of those clubs." He motioned toward the old niblicks and mashies. "What's our excuse?"

They wandered through the store for a few more minutes, then decided they'd better get back before Ken came looking for them. Sure enough, Ken was pacing outside the van, looking up the street with an anxious look.

"I thought ye'd been kidnapped," Ken joked after Rudy explained their detour. "I should'a known you'd find th'one golf store in town."

They drove the short distance back to Barassie. Rudy and Ridge decided to wait in the clubhouse, just in case the guys came in early, and they left Ken settling in to the driver's seat for a nap.

The clubhouse was, if possible, even more quiet than before. The tick-tock of the clock seemed heavier, louder, and baleful against the sound of the rain on the windows. After only moments, Rudy gave up. "I think I'll go sit out at the caddy shack and watch the rain. Better than watching my feet grow roots."

Ridge dropped a magazine on the table. "I'll join you," he said, and both men readied themselves for the weather.

The wind had abated a bit, and Rudy had no trouble holding his umbrella. It wasn't cold, really, and the sound of the rain was actually pleasant.

"Over there," Ridge said, pointing at a small shack that faced what Rudy assumed was the eighteenth green. "I think there's a bench on that far side."

Sure enough, a long wooden bench had been set under the eaves, which extended quite a ways out on this side of the small building. It was protected from the wind, as well. They sat down and folded their umbrellas.

For quite some time they both sat quietly, enjoying the storm. Then Ridge asked a question about the possible changes to the men's locker room at San

Jose Country Club, and that led to a conversation about the current board's position on the trees along the first fairway, which then segued into trees in general and how they were lacking on links courses. The conversation wandered from subject to subject, slow and easy. Rudy was surprisingly comfortable on the bench, with the rain providing a wonderful backdrop.

The crunch of boots on gravel interrupted their conversation. Was the Barassie pro coming out to see if now they "were needin' anything?" Rudy hunkered down into his rain jacket.

A tall, big boned man came around the corner of the shack, and stopped suddenly. Probably surprised to see us here, Rudy thought.

"Nice day, no?"

A small shock ran through Rudy. He knew that voice. He looked up, and yep, he'd been right. Colin Montgomerie stood over them, bundled in rain gear and looking ready to play.

"Liquid sunshine, we call it at home," Ridge said, his accent thick.

Colin chuckled. "Just another day, we call it here. You chaps playing?"

Rudy laughed. "In our heads. I'm currently on hole nine, sitting three under par." He looked at Ridge. "You?"

"I'm in already," Ridge said. "Five under for the round."

Colin nodded and smiled. "Aye, that's about right," he said. Rudy noted his accent was lighter, more cultured than most of the Scotsmen they'd met thus far. Colin continued, "I think I'll have the same sort of game myself. Keep from catchin' pneumonia." He nodded in farewell and disappeared around the corner.

Rudy smiled broadly. He looked at Ridge and found he was smiling as well. "That was Colin Montgomerie," Rudy mouthed silently. "Wow!"

"The guys are never gonna believe us," Ridge said. "We should'a asked for a picture or something."

Rudy shook his head. He'd never have had the courage to ask Colin Montgomerie to take a picture with them. Though it would have been awfully nice to put in the scrapbook.

The rain picked up and became a steady downpour, and they sat quietly with their thoughts for several minutes. Rudy glanced at his watch, then turned to Ridge. "Hey, you haven't gone to the john since we left the hotel. That's over two hours ago."

Ridge rolled his eyes and grinned. "What, are you keeping a log now?"
Rudy nodded. "A daily diary."
Ridge just grunted. They settled back into contemplative quiet and the minutes ticked by. Then something moved through the sheet of rain.
"That Charlie?" Ridge asked. "Looks like Charlie."
He was heading toward the clubhouse, so Rudy stood and waved. "Hey, Quinn! Over here!"
Charlie paused, then changed direction and came toward them. He stepped under the eaves and sighed.
"Jeez, Charlie," Rudy said, "you're soaked! Have a seat."
Charlie shook his head. "I'm going in to the clubhouse and try to dry off. Do they have coffee or something in there? I need to warm my insides."
"They have coffee," Ridge said. "It's strong, though. I had to cut it with some water."
Charlie nodded once and headed toward the clubhouse.
"I can't imagine what the rest of them will look like when they get back," Rudy said.
"Drowned rats," Ridge said, and settled back onto the bench to wait.

Don pulled his ball from the water-filled cup on the seventeenth green. The rain had not lessened for one moment, and his tolerance was just about to run out. He just wanted to get through the next hole and get back to the hotel. A hot shower and dry clothes were exactly what he needed right now.

All five Gang members drove safely down the eighteenth fairway, then found the green with their second shots. The rain and wind were now blowing directly toward them, and Don felt like he was wading through an ocean as he leaned into the storm and trudged up the fairway. The others appeared to be feeling the same way.

He managed a small smile and a quiet chuckle.

They were all nuts.

Rudy looked at his watch. Three hours had gone by since the playing Gang members had crossed the cow path for the first tee. He and Ridge probably had another hour to wait. Of course, in this rain it could be a six-hour round. He sighed. This bench was starting to get hard.

Ridge dozed lightly beside him, his beard resting on his chest, his hands lightly in his lap. Rudy slowly unzipped his jacket, trying to be quiet. His rain gear was no longer wet, but under them he felt like he was sitting in a sauna.

The rain was literally falling in sheets, and it was difficult to see the eighteenth flag, a mere forty yards away. But was that a ball on the green? To his left another ball rolled to a soggy stop, five feet from the hole. Quickly, three others followed, dropping onto the putting surface like random hailstones in the storm. The wall of water obscured the fairway; he couldn't see any of the Gang. They were out there, though, he knew. They were still playing. Well, too, if the placement of those balls was any indication.

Amazing.

He softly nudged Ridge.

"Huh? What?" Ridge grunted, and heaved himself into a more upright sitting position. "Time to go back?"

"Almost," Rudy said, and pointed down the fairway. "Here they come."

Slowly, like a camera coming into focus, the five men emerged. Lumps in the rain at first, indistinguishable. Five ghosts from the past. Rudy stood. The five ghosts became Vandeweghe, Don, Patrick, Chris, and his best friend Plato. He grinned and waved. No one waved back, but he thought he saw Plato nod his head in acknowledgment.

The men marked and putted in a very businesslike fashion. No conversation, no nonsense. Within minutes, all five balls had dropped into the cup, and Patrick replaced the soggy flag.

Rudy and Ridge opened their umbrellas and joined them as they walked back to the clubhouse.

"Well, well," Rudy said. "You made it!"

Vandeweghe grinned, and Rudy could swear there was moss on his teeth. "You ol' dog!" Vandeweghe said. "Put that umbrella away. You're killing us!"

"We're just a lot smarter than you crazy coots," Ridge said. "We know when to get outta the rain."

"Now sounds like a good time to me," Chris said. "I hope Ken's close by."

"Like in the van, with the engine running," Plato said.

Charlie and Ken emerged from the clubhouse and helped remove the bags from the trolleys. There was a short discussion about bailing on Western Gailes and heading back to the hotel, but Ken informed them the weather report called for afternoon sun.

"Let's grab lunch here, then," Rudy said. He'd already scoped out the restaurant and the menu looked fine. Might not be the best food they'd have in Scotland, but he was sure it would be edible.

After a bit more discussion, a consensus was reached to stay and eat. They crowded into the men's bathroom and Rudy leaned against a wall as the others mopped up as best they could with paper towels. Then they stripped their rain gear, opened up shirt collars, loosened shoelaces, and converged on the restaurant, which was surprisingly full of customers and bustling with energy.

Lunch was simple, but tasty, and the conversation threaded between the round, the course in general, and the weather.

"Two under," Chris said, and pumped a thumb toward Patrick. "In this mess, he has the audacity to shoot two under."

"Maybe you should pray for rain every day," Charlie said. "'Course, you'd be playing by yourself an awful lot."

"Make it easy to win the overall championship," Plato said. "The uncontested winner."

Patrick wrinkled his nose. "No fun in that. And I don't need rain to beat all of you, anyway."

A general ruckus of comments, all meant to tease, followed. Patrick, in an obvious effort to deflect the harassment, said, "Now you all need to hear the story of Winterhalter's Burn."

"Winner-halter's burn?" Ridge asked. "Is there really one named that?"

"No, no," Plato said. "But it should be. Our dear fellow here put three – count them, *three* – balls from the tee into the burn on six. All with very different clubs."

Don was cajoled into providing the details, and Rudy was sorry he'd missed the event. It was a rare day when Don made such a dynamic mistake. When the conversation calmed down, Rudy nodded toward Plato, seated across from him. "How'd you play?"

"Even par," Plato said. "And I'm darn happy for that, due to the rain. Not much of a course, unfortunately. They could use a lot of upgrading. There's potential, but you didn't miss anything today."

"Hm. That's too bad," Rudy said, and meant it. There were too many good courses in Scotland to waste their time on mediocre ones.

They remained in the restaurant for nearly an hour, drying out. By the time they left, the rain had stopped, though the clouds were still hanging, ominous. The van pulled around, the little trailer bumping along behind. Ken loaded their clubs quickly. Then they all jumped in and Ken pulled away from Barassie. The Gang settled down, and soon conversation stopped altogether. A comfortable silence permeated the vehicle.

Fifteen minutes into the ride, Ridge made a "gas can stop" in the back of the van. On his way back to his seat, he stopped by Chris and pulled the Barassie ball marker from his pocket.

"Gotcha this," Ridge said. "Figured you'd want one to continue your collection."

Chris took the marker and turned it over in his fingers. "Wow. Great! Thanks, Ridge. I'd forgotten to pick one up after lunch. That's awfully nice of you. What do I owe you?"

Ridge made a face. "Aw, nothing. Just leave it in the hotel room next time we play, will you? I'm afraid it might bring more rain."

A warm glow filled the van.

"Hey! Sunshine!" Rudy said. The clouds were breaking up overhead.

"Perfect timing!" Don said. "Maybe now my shoes will finish drying."

"Eventually," Patrick said, and winked.

Rudy felt his spirits rise. They might all be able to play this afternoon. He shifted to allow the sun to hit his upper back, and closed his eyes. He'd get in a nap before they all hit the links. The whole Gang, back on the course together.

CHAPTER 33

September 1, 1998
Chris Clark

When they drove up to the clubhouse at Western Gailes, Chris shivered. It wasn't due to cold; it was a response to the simple, elegant, effortless course that spread out before him. He clambered from the van and walked to the back of the clubhouse, which was really designed to appear more like the front. This was what he came for. This was what it was all about for him.

A rough and tumble expanse of grass, gorse, sand dunes, and shrubbery lay stretched before the building. Beyond that lay the Firth of Clyde, with the hump of Ailsa Craig shimmering in the sunshine.

"Awesome view," Don said, joining him.

Chris just nodded.

The rest of the Gang arrived. "So un-American," Plato said. "If this was in California, or Florida, there'd be houses all around this place. You'd hardly see the ocean."

"Thank heavens we're not in America," Chris said. He knew there'd be more damage than just houses. Most Americans would try to "fix" the course, perk it up with fancy greens, define the fairways by bulldozing the undulations flat. No, this was perfect. Clearly no one had "improved" the land. They just routed the course through the dunes, and around the gorse and tall grasses. It was so not manufactured that Chris felt like he was standing on the edge of an ancient, untouched field.

He breathed deep and sighed. "Let's go play."

They entered the clubhouse and checked in with the man behind the counter. It took a moment before Chris realized he was having no problem understanding the guy.

"You're American," Chris said, and was instantly embarrassed by the obvious skepticism in his tone. "I mean, you *sound* American."

The man nodded and smiled. "I keep trying to hide that fact, but try as I might, I can't get the brogue."

Charlie stepped up and thrust out his hand. "Charles Quinn," he said, smiling his wonderful lopsided grin. "We met at the Olympic Club some years back. Nice to see you again."

"Oh, yeah!" The man vigorously shook Charlie's hand. "Mark Elsington. I remember! You're a member over at San Jose, aren't you?"

"We all are," Charlie said, then jerked a thumb toward Don, "except that dope. He migrated south to Arizona."

The two men chatted for a moment longer, then Mark directed the Gang to the locker room to change their shoes. Chris was surprised by the distinct odor that filled his nostrils when he entered the room.

"Smells like the San Francisco Golf Club," Plato said, scratching his nose. "Staid and old, but wonderful."

Charlie put his golf shoes on, walked around the locker room for a moment, then sat back down and proceeded to change back to his walking shoes.

"What's up, Pops?" Patrick asked, concern all over his face.

Charlie shook his head. "My shoes are still soaking wet. I don't want to walk eighteen holes in soggy socks and shoes."

"What size are you?" Plato asked. "Ten and a half? I'll trade you, if you want."

"No, no," Charlie said. "I'm tired anyway. I think jet lag has caught up with me. I'll just sit this one out."

Chris felt a pang of disappointment. Something told him this was going to be a great round of golf, and he didn't want Charlie missing out on it. "Do you want me to see if they have a set of shoes you can borrow?" he asked.

"Thanks, Chris, but I'd rather just sit in the clubhouse and watch the ocean," Charlie said. "They probably have a glass of wine I can enjoy."

"If not, I'm sure Ken can hop into town and get you a bottle," Rudy said. "He'd probably like the distraction."

"From what?" Patrick said. "The movie that plays on the back of his eyelids?"

The Gang laughed. Yes, Chris thought, Ken did do a lot of sleeping in the van, but what else was the guy going to do?

Plato coughed to draw attention, then explained the afternoon game. "Highland Blind Fling," he said. "First nine holes are the first and third Best Ball foursome. Second nine holes are the second and fourth Best Ball foursome. At the end of the round, we'll draw for the teams." He looked at Charlie. "We'll just average in your handicap, Charlie."

They returned to the pro shop, and were assigned their caddies.

"They're on their second round for the day," Mark said, "so don't be surprised if they're a bit knackered."

Vandeweghe frowned. "I'm not paying for a guy who can't keep up. Don't you have fresh caddies?"

Mark grunted. "In the rain we had this morning, I was surprised we even got this many guys to show up for work. I'll check with the leader of the bunch, but I doubt there's anyone fresh who's available. This is Scotland."

After a few minutes, they were told that no, these were the only caddies available. Take 'em or leave 'em. Vandeweghe grumbled, but obviously wasn't distressed enough to pull a cart on his own. When the caddies arrived, Chris had to bite his lip to keep from bursting into laughter.

They were certainly the most ragtag group they'd encountered thus far. All eight – for they hadn't received the message Charlie was not going to play – were in rumpled, tattered, highly worn clothing. Their shoes were taped together, missing laces, or obviously thin in the sole. Their hats were soggy and sun bleached. To Chris, all of this was disturbing; what made it laughable was the fact they all were plastered. Stone cold, stumbling drunk.

Patrick rolled his eyes in amazement and sidled up to Chris.

"I think they have more fingers than teeth," Patrick whispered.

Chris chuckled. Then several of the caddies asked questions, and he leaned toward Patrick. "Did you understand a single word?"

Patrick shot him a definitively negative look. "Marbles. That's what it sounded like to me. A mouth full of marbles."

Chris nodded. This was going to be an interesting round.

The wind was gentle, coming in off the ocean and bringing the scent of salt and seaweed. The sun was warm and steady. The few clouds that dotted the sky were far to the west. Chris couldn't have dreamt of a better situation. He teed up on one and sent the ball sailing straight and true.

His foursome included Patrick, Ridge, and Rudy, and Chris was sure they'd all play great.

It was, unfortunately, not to come true. Right off the first tee, Ridge started having trouble, dropping his ball into a particularly deep patch of long grass. It took him and his caddy the better part of five minutes to find the ball. Chris could see the rest of the Gang members on the tee, waiting. He knew they'd be wondering if this was an omen.

It was. Poor Ridge took two swings to get the ball out of the rough and into the fairway. Then he went for the green – a short iron shot, to be sure – and shanked it into a dune. His caddy made the unfortunate error of obviously swearing in Gaelic, and received an earful from Ridge about holding his tongue. Chris joined Rudy and Patrick in biting back laughter, but Chris could see they all found the incident sadly funny.

Finally the first hole was behind them. Chris went to the second tee sure the round would improve for his friend. Patrick and Rudy were holding their own, and had joined Chris in making par.

Again, Rudy, Patrick, and Chris drove their balls onto the fairway, and then watched as Ridge sliced his wildly.

"Oh, oh!" Patrick cried, as the ball sailed toward the old railroad tracks that ran the length of the course. "I think it's trying to make the four-fifteen to Edinburgh!"

Ridge glared at his caddy, daring him to make another comment, then turned to Patrick with a crooked smile. "If it makes the first class car, I'll get on with it and see y'all at the end of the two weeks."

Patrick waggled a finger at Ridge. "Don't even think about it. I'll hold that darn porta-potty gas can ransom if I have to."

Chris nodded in agreement. The trip wouldn't be the same without the bearded codger.

Luckily, the rest of the hole gave Ridge no problem, and he joined the others for a nice, neat par. The third hole moved them closer to the ocean, and the breeze picked up a bit. Chris recalled Plato's advice and teed the ball low. It screamed across the top of the grass, then hit a mound and bounded left, into the rough. When Chris found it, he realized he had little chance of making the green in regulation. There was no doubt in his mind that this course would punish anyone who was not careful – and accurate.

His caddy, who seemed to have sobered up considerably during the past two holes, handed him a six iron and winked.

Chris wiggled into a stance, pulled the club back a few times to ensure a channel through the tall grass, gritted his teeth, and swung.

"Look at the salad coming off that club!" Rudy yelled from the fairway. "Holy cow! It's gonna make the green!"

To Chris's amazement, the ball landed twenty yards from the front edge of the green and rolled to a stop a mere two feet from the flag. He gave a little whoop and trotted out of the rough. Here he'd thought he wouldn't make par; now he was looking at a very doable birdie.

He watched the others putt out before dropping his ball for the bird. He looked out over the course, toward the ocean, and felt a tremendous amount of joy. God he loved this game.

"Nice save," Patrick said. They walked to the fourth hole, a particularly humpy, bumpy slight dogleg left, still going away from the clubhouse. "I don't know what it is, but this course suits you, Chris." He scratched his ear. "Maybe you just need a good shower in the morning before you play."

Chris smirked a bit. "An eighteen hole shower?" He grunted. "No thanks. If that's really what it takes, I'll skip it and just play my usual crummy round."

Once they reached the fifth hole, the course turned back toward the clubhouse, and ran directly alongside the ocean. The wind gusts made for some tricky decisions in clubbing, and the undulating fairways made for interesting lies and stances. Much to his amazement, Chris had, so far, managed to avoid the bunkers, which looked like rough holes dug into the dunes by sheep.

Ridge, to everyone's dismay, had not managed to avoid them. Hole after hole was played, and Ridge seemed to find every bunker, pothole, or thicket of rough available. On six, Ridge drove it long off the tee, missed the fairway and landed heavy into the thick of the rough.

"You're in th' love grass, sir," Ridge's caddy said.

"Love grass?" Ridge said. "There's nothing to love about that rough."

"Oh, aye," the caddy said, and reset his cap upon his head. "But if ya get into it, you're foo'cked."

The four Gang members burst into laughter. It was, Chris decided, the perfect adage.

"Well, get on up there 'n get a little love, then," Ridge said, and sent his caddy scurrying ahead to look for the ball.

From then on, the poor Scot intelligently became a fore caddy – running ahead and watching where the ball landed, then standing over the errant item until Ridge arrived, mumbling, beard bouncing.

The eighth tee sat directly across from the clubhouse, and when they arrived at it Patrick trotted off to check on his Pops. Chris joined him, hoping to find a soda. Inside, Charlie was sitting on the couch, happily chatting with Mark.

"Hey, Pat," Charlie said. "We might be able to procure another tee-time at Prestwick on Thursday." He nodded toward Mark, who smiled and nodded.

"I know the director over there," Mark said. "We play together every week. So I just gave him a call and asked for a favor. He's going to see if he can rearrange a few players, get you another tee time."

"That's great, thanks!" Patrick said.

Mark held up a hand. "Don't thank me until it happens. I've got the number for your hotel, so I'll call if it gets managed."

Patrick nodded, then turned to his father. "So, Pops, you're okay? Wanna come out and play the back nine with us? It's a great course."

"No, I think I'll just finish my wine and enjoy the scenery," Charlie said, and brandished a half-full glass of white wine. "I can enjoy the course from here."

Chris could see Patrick was clearly disappointed, but understood Charlie's decision. Chris turned to Mark. "Sodas? Are there any we can take on the course? We're all parched."

"Absolutely," Mark said, and headed off toward the kitchen. Moments later he was back with four diet cokes in hand. "No ice, of course," he said, and handed them to Chris and Patrick. He winked and added, "Scotland."

Chris and Patrick jogged back to the eighth tee and found the rest of the Gang, waiting.

"Hey, Gooch," Chris said, and tossed a can at Vandeweghe.

"What's this?" Vandeweghe asked. "Room service?"

"Almost. You can tip me when we're done."

Vandeweghe instantly proffered it back. "I'm not gonna take your soda. Here. Take it, take it."

Chris waved dismissively. He yanked his driver from his bag and stepped up on the tee. "I don't like diet. And you're gonna need all of whatever's in that can to keep up with me."

His ball landed twenty yards ahead of the other three, then rolled for another fifteen yards. Vandeweghe popped the top on the soda. "Guess you're right," he said, and everyone chuckled.

Chris's foursome moved on down the fairway, leaving Don, Plato, and Vandeweghe sitting on the bench at the tee. Chris looked back and waved. The three waved back. Too bad they couldn't continue on together, it would have been even more fun.

The back nine caught everyone by surprise. Ridge continued to have difficulties avoiding the hazards – and there were many – while Patrick simply wore out around the thirteenth hole. Rudy, having not played that morning, was fresh enough, but his swing was more stiff than usual.

Chris was a bit tired, too. He could feel it in his swing, and his concentration was easily swayed by the amazing scenery. There had been one short rain shower as they played fourteen, the only par five on the back, but it dissipated into a sun-riddled drizzle by the time they made the green, and disappeared altogether by the fifteenth tee. As they walked toward the eighteenth green, the sun was low over the water, the breeze light and playful, and the clouds high.

Chris wanted to stay here the rest of the two weeks. This was a course he could play every day and never become bored. He picked his ball out of the cup on eighteen. "Bogey for me." He calculated quickly. "Eighty." Nine over. He sighed. Normally that would have upset him. But who could be upset here?

Charlie was waiting for them on the porch. "Well, how'd you all do?"

"Not bad, Charlie," Rudy said.

Ridge chuckled and tugged on his beard. "Speak for yourself, Rudy. I shot, what? Ninety-four, maybe?"

"Ninety-two, Ridge," Rudy said. "Don't go exaggerating. There's a lot of trouble to be found out there."

Charlie frowned. "Unfair course?"

"No, no, not at all," Chris said promptly. "You'd have liked it, Charlie. You stand on the fairway and you can clearly see where to go, and where you shouldn't go. If you hit a bad shot, you were penalized, that's all." He demonstrated with his hands. "I mean, here's the fairway. This crap here, the 'love grass' as one of the caddy's called it –"

"I'll explain that one later," Patrick interjected.

Chris nodded. "Good idea. So here's the garbage you don't want to get into. This way or that way, you're into the same stuff. Short left, you're in this bunker. Bomb it, and you're in that bunker. But you can see all this stuff. You just have to hit it straight."

He paused. The other three Gang members had arrived as he was talking, and now all seven men were standing around him, grinning. He looked from face to face. "Well? Am I right?"

"They should hire you as a spokesman," Don said.

"Heck, let me play for free and I'll take the job," Chris said. "Just point me in the direction of the cameras."

"Okay, Arnie," Charlie said, "let's get you out of here before you start powdering your nose."

Amidst more ribbing, Chris joined the others in loading their clubs and settling into the van. He felt his bones sigh as he sat. It had been a long day, and with the variations in weather and locale, it felt more like two separate days. He closed his eyes and began to replay from memory the afternoon round. But before the second tee, he was dreaming.

"So what've you got for us tonight?" Vandeweghe asked Rudy. "Anything exciting?"

Chris stood behind the huddled Gang and waited for the dinner decision. He was in such a good mood that he could eat tofu and be happy. Okay, maybe not tofu, but something unusual. But not haggis. He wasn't that happy. He doubted he'd ever be that happy.

Rudy produced his pad of paper and began to read from the researched selections. "Okay, here's what I found: Black Beard's Steak House; Top Shelf, which sounds more like a cafe than a restaurant; Macgowans, which is in Kilmarnock, so we'll need Ken to drive, but it comes highly recommended by the staff here –"

"We don't want to drive," Vandeweghe said. "Walking distance, and not far either. I don't know about the rest of you, but I'm knackered."

Rudy checked his list. "Well, then, it looks like the best option might be Chung Pao's Chinese. Just up the street."

"Chinese?" Vandeweghe said. "We're in Scotland. I can't imagine the Chinese food would be any good."

Rudy shrugged. "Got great reviews –"

"By the two Chinese who immigrated during the war," Vandeweghe said. "Let's just eat here at Rizzio's. Solid Italian food."

Rudy gestured resignation, and smiled wanly. "I supposed more Italians immigrated, so the food's gotta be better."

"I like the idea of not having to walk anywhere," Ridge said quickly. "And heck, what can they do to pasta?"

"Overcook it to sop," Patrick whispered to Chris. "Kind of like they do vegetables. But who's gonna argue at this point?"

"We a go?" Vandeweghe said. "Or do you want to try one of these?" He pointed at the pad. "'Cause I'll go wherever you suggest. It's –"

"I know, I know," Rudy interjected. "It's *my* job." He chuckled. "Rizzio's it is. Gentlemen?"

Chris joined Patrick in the rear of the Gang as they headed toward the restaurant. "Does this feel like it's becoming a nightly ritual?"

Patrick nodded. "Like flossing teeth. The dentist told you to do it, so you do, but it sure isn't fun."

Chris agreed. He just wondered at what point Rudy would rebel. And would it take the form of an inter-clan skirmish, or resemble the Battle of Culloden?

Time would tell.

CHAPTER 34

September 2, 1998
Don Ridge

The alarm in his room went off with a vengeance. Five a.m. Ridge smacked it a few times to make it stop, then rolled over and promptly fell back asleep.

He woke to Vandeweghe's happy voice.

"Hey, Don, get your snorin' ass outta bed, my friend. You have half an hour to find some suitably clean clothes and straighten out that scruffy beard of yours."

Ridge sleepily tried to prepare a suitable retort, then his eyes popped open. That's right – this was the early morning. They were heading to some mystery course Vandeweghe had arranged. Hush, hush. Secret, secret.

Ridge always loved a surprise. He scrambled from bed, quickly showered and dressed, and was waiting at the door before Vandeweghe had his shoes tied.

"Ready?" Vandeweghe said.

Ridge brandished his gas can. "You bet."

"Great, let's go," Vandeweghe said, and slapped Ridge on the back. "You are gonna love this, my friend."

Ridge hoped so. He hated early mornings.

Ken drove the van around and opened the door. He looked like he'd been drug from his bed. His shirt was mis-buttoned, his belt on too loosely, and he wore two different colors of socks. Apparently he disliked the early hour as well.

To everyone's dismay, rain fell heavily, and the sky was a dark, dull gray in all directions. In a rather subdued manner, the Gang loaded their clubs, collected cups of coffee-to-go, and shuffled into the van.

Ken yawned. He looked at Vandeweghe through the rearview mirror. "Where to, sir?"

"The airport," Vandeweghe said. He looked at his watch. "Our flight leaves in an hour."

Ken glanced at his own watch, then rammed the van into gear. "Right, then." He stepped on the gas pedal and the van lurched into action.

"The airport?" Chris said, voicing Ridge's question.

Vandeweghe turned in his seat to address them. He was glowing, Ridge noted. "Gentlemen," Vandeweghe said. "You are about to embark on a most glorious adventure."

"I thought we were already on one," Patrick said. Ridge joined everyone in a chuckle.

"This is going to be the second most fabulous round of the trip," Vandeweghe said. "Second only to playing the Old Course next week."

"Okay, we're hooked," Don said. "Where are we headed?"

Vandeweghe seemed to grow a foot taller. "Machrihanish Golf Club. On the Kintyre Peninsula, west coast."

"Oh, aye, 'tis a good thing you're flyin'," Ken said. "The Kintyre Peninsula is near seven hours by car. Ye'd no be playing today if I was taking ya."

"I know, Ken," Vandeweghe said. "That's why I've chartered a flight to get us there this morning, and bring us back this evening."

Charlie, the banker, appeared to be calculating the cost in his head. Did "the bank" have enough to cover such an expense? Not that it was a huge worry; someone would just put it on his credit card and they'd all pay him back later. But it was an unplanned expense.

"We're flying?" Rudy said. "How wonderful is that? We'll get a great view of Scotland from a charter plane."

"Yes you will Rudy," Vandeweghe said. "Yes you will."

"And how much is this going to set us back?" Charlie finally asked.

Vandeweghe smiled rather sheepishly. "Nothing, fellas. This one's on me."

"Oh no, Gary," Don said. "Let us help. It's gotta be expensive."

"Wouldn't think of it, my friend," Vandeweghe said, and Ridge knew he was speaking from his heart. There was a different tone Vandeweghe used when he was being "deadly earnest." Ridge had come to know it from the years they'd spent at the card table. Vandeweghe didn't play often, but when he did, he tried to bluff. His voice always gave him away.

Chris and Rudy tried to talk Vandeweghe into accepting payment, but they didn't get anywhere and, in the end, hearty thanks were voiced by all seven Gang recipients.

"This is awfully special," Ridge said. "Though I am surprised you've been able to keep this under wraps all this time. Hard to keep a secret from this group."

They arrived at the airport and Vandeweghe instructed Ken to drive to the private hanger. There they found a small plane, her twin engines turning slowly, warming up. The rain had stopped falling, though the gray clouds were still thick. Vandeweghe said a few words to the pilot, nodded several times, then returned to the Gang waiting beside the van.

"Okay! All set," Vandeweghe said. "Grab your clubs and make sure you have your rain gear. Did you all bring the extra set of socks, and the sweater and extra shirt I told you to bring?" Ridge nodded, as did the others. "Then let's go!" Vandeweghe turned to Ken. "We'll be flying back at six tonight, and I've arranged for the commuter van from the Marine Hotel to pick us up, so you're off for the day. See you tomorrow morning."

Ken yawned, nodded, and lumbered back into the van. Ridge grinned. No doubt the Scotsman would just sleep the day away.

The clubs were loaded into the small cargo space, and the Gang boarded the plane. To Ridge's surprise, there was a stewardess – a young, plump brunette who introduced herself as Annabelle.

"That's a Southern name, darlin'," Ridge said, and gave her his best smile. "Your mama come from the Southern states?"

Annabelle giggled. "Oh, no, sir," she said in a brogue that definitely was not Southern. "Born and raised in Glasgow, was I. Near never been out o' Scotland, if th' truth be known."

"I believe you," Ridge said, and stepped into the cabin. Annabelle quickly put out an arm to stop him.

"I'm sorry sir," she said, then pointed at his gas can. "But ya can no bring flammables on to th'plane. 'Tis against regulations."

The guys chuckled.

"He's flammable, all right," Rudy said. "Downright toxic with that thing every now and then."

"Now, now," Ridge said. He brandished the empty gas can – for he had emptied and cleaned it last night in the hotel room, and hadn't used it yet that day. "This here's my porta-potty. It's got nothing in it at all right now, and if we're lucky, it won't have anything in it when we land."

Annabelle looked very confused. "Porta potty?"

This caused even more laughter from the members of the Gang, and Ridge suddenly felt very silly. "Aw, come on fellas, give the girl a break." He turned to Annabelle. "I'm taking some medication that makes me have to – uh – use the bathroom all the time. We can't always stop when I need to go, so I carry this with me, just in case."

Annabelle turned a slight shade of pink, but nodded curtly. "Very good, sir. My da's got th'same problem. 'Tis a good solution y've made for yourself. I'll no be taking it away."

"Thank ya, darlin'," Ridge said, and took a seat on the right side of the plane.

Chris and Patrick followed, and Annabelle directed Patrick to sit opposite of Ridge. Don and Rudy then entered, and she arranged them to sit opposite of each other. Charlie, Plato, and Vandeweghe were then arranged in what appeared to be no logical fashion. Ridge shrugged; probably the dear girl just liked having control of her environment.

The plane's engine revved, and within minutes they were taxiing down the runway. Then the engines began to scream, and the little plane bounced into the air. Ridge felt as if he was sitting on the back of a cat, leaping after a butterfly. He had a moment of panic as he thought the plane wouldn't get off the ground, then it lifted and surged upward, pushing him back into his seat.

"Woohoo!" Patrick yelled. "Mister Toad's Wild Ride!"

They finally leveled out, and the little engines settled into a loud but steady rumble. Ridge looked out his window, then across the aisle through Patrick's window. The bright blue of a lake or river could be seen far below. Ridge unbuckled and started to stand up, hoping to catch a better view. Annabelle reacted immediately.

"Sir, sir! Ye must sit down, immediately." She frantically waved for him to be seated. "We must keep th'plane balanced, 'n if ya move t'the other side, we'll tip. Gareth, the pilot, would be most unhappy."

The guys chuckled, and Ridge sat back down in the seat. He grinned. Now he knew why Annabelle had been so particular about where they sat. Ridge looked over at Rudy, seated across from Don. Rudy was the smallest guy on the plane, and Don – though not big by any stretch – was still probably half again his size.

Ridge grunted and pointed at Rudy. "We should've handicapped you, tied some weight on you before you got on the plane."

Rudy playfully gave him a hand gesture that explained what he thought of Ridge's idea.

Patrick turned and looked back at Rudy. "Ah, heck, Ridge, Rudy's just my carry-on luggage."

Even Annabelle laughed at that one.

The next half hour was spent in quiet, as the engine noise made conversation difficult. The countryside passed beneath the plane in a vivid patchwork of colors and textures. They didn't fly very high, so buildings, roads, vehicles, even people on bicycles were clearly visible. Soon there was water as they flew over the Firth of Clyde. They sailed over the Isle of Arran, then more water, then the tip of the Kintyre Peninsula. They passed over a small cluster of buildings.

"'Tis Campbeltown, below," Annabelle yelled above the engines. "A lovely town. If'n ya have the time, do go'n visit."

The plane tipped, and began a circling descent to a thin ribbon of runway.

"Hey, P.Q.," Rudy hollered, "we're going in a circle. I think you might want to change sides. Balance us out a little."

Patrick grinned. "You want me to come sit on your lap?"

"He's your luggage," Ridge said. "He should sit on yours."

The plane leveled out and dropped onto the runway. The engines cut as the pilot applied the brakes. Suddenly, the sound of a siren split the air. Ridge plastered his face against the window, trying to see behind the plane. An older model fire engine was racing along, lights flashing.

"Are we on fire or something?" Vandeweghe said, concern heavy in his voice.

"Ach, no," Annabelle said, completely indifferent. "Regulations require there be immediate emergency support at any airport. Since Campbeltown is so far from 'ere, we canna provide that. So the local fire department just follows the planes when they land. 'Tis no problem, really."

Ridge chuckled. He couldn't imagine an American airport coming up with such a solution.

The plane came to an easy stop.

"Here we are gentlemen," Annabelle said. She smiled mischievously. "Ye' kin now move about without tippin' the plane."

Ridge verified they would be using the same plane for return, tucked his "porta-potty" under his seat, then stepped onto the plane's stairs. The sun shone warmly. Not a cloud in the sky. He patted his belly and breathed deeply. It was going to be a good day.

Two taxis arrived and he frowned. They'd need both of those, and probably a third, just to get their clubs into town, let alone the Gang themselves.

The taxi drivers made some comments, none of which Ridge understood through the brogue, then stuffed their clubs in to "the boot." He winced as the drivers shoved and pushed and crammed the bags.

"I hope I have straight clubs when we get to the course," Charlie said.

"I just hope they're in one piece," Don said.

Rudy chuckled. "Might help my game if they're bent a little."

At last the drivers were satisfied. Neither could close the trunk lids, but obviously this was not unusual, for both instantly produced short ropes and simply tied the lids down. They opened the taxi doors and motioned for the men to seat themselves.

Vandeweghe clucked. "Are you kidding? They're going to try to stuff us in there, too?"

"First one in gets the window seat," Patrick said, folded himself into nearly two, and climbed into the taxi.

Ridge sighed. He squeezed in between Patrick and Rudy. Vandeweghe waved a hand in the air and opened the front door on the passenger side. The driver complained, though again Ridge had no idea exactly what he'd said. Vandeweghe simply ignored him and closed the door behind him.

Don, Charlie, and Chris squeezed into the back of the other cab, with Plato taking the honors of the front. Soon they were motoring across farmland. Ridge tried not to squeeze either of his car-mates as they careened around corners. His shoulder muscles were cramped, and his knees rammed into the seat at every bump in the road, and there were many. Obviously pavement was at a premium in this part of Scotland.

Ridge was relieved when they pulled to a stop amidst a small cluster of buildings. Another ten minutes would have rendered him incapable of playing golf. The Gang unraveled themselves, stretching out like a line of paper dolls cut from the same piece of paper.

Ahead of them, several stout buildings staked a claim against the ocean winds and storms, which undoubtedly blew in from the North Channel. Ridge shouldered his golf bag and followed Vandeweghe toward the largest of the buildings.

"Welcome to Machrihanish!" Vandeweghe said. "Probably the least known gem of the Scottish golf courses. This course is *fantastic*."

The Gang lined their bags along the clubhouse wall. Inside, the smell of bacon and eggs was strong, and Ridge realized he'd not had breakfast. His stomach growled.

A short, round, balding man nearly danced around the corner. "Welcome, gentlemen! You must be th'group from America, no?"

Vandeweghe nodded. "That's us. I don't imagine you have two groups in one day."

The man shook his head exuberantly. "No, no, that we don't, t'be sure." He waved for them to follow. "This way, now. It'll be getting cold, and that makes th'cook grumpy."

"And we don't want a grumpy cook," Patrick said under his breath.

In a small dining room piles of sizzling bacon, mounds of rolls, and pitchers of orange juice crowded the center of a long table. It was a spread for kings.

"What's this?" Don said, obviously pleased. "Gary, did you order breakfast, too?"

Vandeweghe stood at the head of the table and surveyed the provisions with delight. "Not me! I didn't even think about food."

A very round woman entered, carrying a large oval of scrambled eggs. "Good mornin' to ya! Sit, sit! Ye' can't be playing the best course in all th'land with an empty belly." She slid the platter onto the table, and wiped her hands on her apron before resting them on her ample hips. "Now eat, eat, all'ya. I want none o'that food left a'fore ya leave th'table."

Ridge rubbed his hands together and joined the Gang in passing the steaming food. The plump cook continued to bring plates and bowls with various tidbits: sliced tomatoes; wedges of a light, white cheese; and a pile of cold cuts. Ridge was tempted to squirrel away a small sandwich to enjoy during the round, but decided he'd just eat heartily now.

"So where are we, exactly?" Don asked.

"A little southwest of Glasgow, as the crow flies," Vandeweghe said. "On a peninsula directly across from Northern Ireland. You'll be able to see it when we get out on the course. They can take a ferry across the Channel, then around the tip of the peninsula to Campbeltown, that little town we flew over."

"Is this the course Old Tom said was 'specifically designed by the Almighty for golf'?" Plato asked.

Vandeweghe nodded. "He was talking about the lay of the land. The designers didn't do much to it to make the original course. Just mowed down some greens, cut some holes, and stuck a few flags in the ground. It looks pretty much the same today, though they've actually done a lot of redesign. If I'm not mistaken, Old Tom Morris added holes to make it eighteen. Oh, and I know he was the designer of the first hole, which – when you see it – is a beauty."

Ridge patted his full stomach. He felt ready to take on the world. "When was the course built?"

Vandeweghe wrinkled his brow. "Late eighteen-seventy-something. The R.A.F. confiscated some of the land for a base during the war, and I'm sure that runway we landed on was theirs."

"The fire truck might have been, as well," Patrick said with a grin.

After breakfast was consumed, and the plump cook thanked and generously tipped, the Gang focused on the matter at hand – golf. They found their bags neatly tied to trolleys, ready to go. Ridge was marginally disappointed. His feet were still store, and he'd seen several carts parked along the clubhouse. It would have been nice to ride during this round.

He followed the others to the tiny pro shop. It looked more like a shack or a small trailer, and he smiled. Anything bigger or more grand would have been wasted on this place.

They checked in, and discovered Vandeweghe had already paid for the rounds, as well.

"I wanted to do this," Vandeweghe said, in answer to his friends' concerned comments that it was too much. "Let me do this, will ya? This is my treat."

"We'll make it up to you, somewhere along the way," Plato said.

"Yeah, yeah, of course you will," Vandeweghe said. "Buy me an ice cream when we get back."

"Seven scoops," Rudy said.

They arrived at the first tee, and Ridge was completely taken aback. He'd played the courses along 17 Mile Drive in Carmel several times, and many of the holes there were spectacular, but this was clearly a special first hole. The tee box was placed facing a small inlet of the ocean, around which lay a long, wide fairway. You could obviously play it safe and aim to the right of the bay, but the score card labeled it a par four, and playing it safe meant playing for bogey, at best. The savvy golfer would have to aim over the inlet – and pack a wallop of a drive.

"Now that's what I call an opening hole," Charlie said. "What a sight."

"What a challenge," Chris said.

Ridge waggled his driver at Plato. "So do we have a game here? Or are we all just playing for fun?"

"Oh, we have a game," Plato said. "Vandeweghe told me to get something prepared. So gather round, lads."

The Gang huddled in a loose circle.

"The game is 'Golf the Old Way'," Plato said. "Individual net. Tee it high and let it fly!"

The eight men sorted themselves into two foursomes. Ridge stepped back to let the first foursome of Chris, Rudy, Vandeweghe, and Plato drive. He tugged at his beard. Individual net meant he and Charlie were out before they even hit the first ball. They couldn't compete with the length of the youngsters, nor with the consistency of Don, Rudy, and Vandeweghe. And heck, Plato was – after all – the professional.

"You okay?" Plato asked.

Ridge twisted his mouth this way and that. How much did he want to say?

"Out with it, my friend," Plato said. "I can always tell when you're not happy. What's up?"

"Well, all right, since you asked," Ridge said. "I know we're not playing for much money here. But heck, I'd like to be competitive, and individual net just means I can't be."

Plato frowned. "You're a darn good golfer, Don. You're just as competitive as the rest of us." He paused as Rudy wiggled, waggled, and hit the ball. It sailed into a beautiful hook, and landed smartly on the beach. The white ball gleamed like a shiny seashell, taunting. Plato gave Ridge a knowing look. "See what I mean?"

Plato stepped up to the tee and Ridge sighed. He knew Plato was wrong, but he certainly wasn't going to argue the point. Heck, he'd just have fun; let the scores talk for themselves.

Plato's ball followed Rudy's onto the sand, while Chris's and Vandeweghe's mocked them from safe perches on the fairway.

"Check it out," Vandeweghe teased. "The hacking amateurs are in the fairway. But where's the pro? Oh, there he is – on the beach! Who's that guy down there asking 'where's the green'?"

Plato laughed at the ribbing. "Good thing the tide's not in. I'd be swimming."

"Did you bring your trunks?" Patrick asked. "Watch out for sharks!"

Once on the beach, Plato and Rudy sorted themselves out of trouble. Rudy simply whacked the ball sideways, back up onto the fairway.

"Smart move," Don said.

Ridge nodded in agreement. Plato stood beside his ball, then jumped up and down, waving.

"What's he doing?" Chris asked. "Calisthenics? We're not giving him enough exercise?"

Vandeweghe trotted along the edge of the fairway, then pointed in an exaggerated manner, back toward the green.

"Holy cow, Plato can't see the green from where he is on the beach," Chris said.

"He's not going for the green, is he?" Don said. "Is he really going for it?"

Vandeweghe walked back toward his own ball, but Plato yelled something, and Vandeweghe returned to some determined spot on the edge of the fairway. He looked at Plato, looked back at the flag, then moved a few yards to his left, and stood tall and straight.

"He's giving our pro a line," Ridge said with a grin. "Lucky if the darn blue-blood doesn't get his head knocked off."

Plato squiggled his feet into a solid stance, glanced up at Vandeweghe again, then swung. The ball leapt off the sand, sailed right over Vandeweghe, and landed well onto the fairway, maybe thirty yards from the green.

Ridge joined his three friends in a loud, vocal appreciation of the feat.

"Guess that's why he's the professional," Patrick said.

Ridge nodded. And why individual net wasn't fair.

To his pleasant surprise, Ridge made par on the first hole. He'd cleared the beach, had a great bounce and roll on his second shot, and neatly two-putted.

The second hole was dissected by a wide, deep burn, and Ridge decided to play it safe and lay up. Both Chris and Patrick aimed at shooting over it, missed, and said some choice words as both balls went in the water.

Patrick turned to Don. "Didn't I give you back those water-seeking missiles of yours? Did you get into my bag last night and exchange them?"

Don hummed and smiled brightly. "You'll never know, will you."

Pars on two and three had Ridge thinking maybe he could be competitive after all, as both Patrick and Chris continued to find trouble with their long, reckless drives. Don, of course, kept abreast of Ridge, making pars like a machine.

On the fourth tee they caught up with the guys in front, who were waiting for the group ahead of them. The Gang stood on the tee, surrounded by scruffy bushes, tall grass, and gorse. Suddenly, from beneath the bushes a large rabbit bolted. It dashed across the tee, dodging the men's legs, then headed toward the green. A weasel shot out from beneath the bush in hot pursuit. After about ten yards, the rabbit ducked into another patch of bush.

"Run you stupid rabbit, run!" Vandeweghe yelled. "Don't stop!"

The weasel ducked into the brush. A high-pitched scream slashed the air, followed by snarls. One last scream, and silence.

"Oh my God, that was gnarly," Patrick said, and Ridge thought the guy was about to puke.

Vandeweghe looked away. "What a stupid rabbit."

Ridge swallowed hard. It may be the way of nature, but it sure wasn't pleasant to watch. Or hear.

"We're up," Don said, breaking the silence. "They're off the green."

The foursomes separated, and continued play. Both Ridge and Don made par on holes four and five. It wasn't until the sixth hole that Don faltered and shot bogey, but the guy was so unflappable that he just bounced right back, barely missing a four foot birdie putt on the seventh.

They turned their back to the ocean at the ninth hole, and the wind blew straight up the fairway from behind them. Ridge glanced at the score card. A 354 yard, straight par four. No problem. He pulled out his driver, set up, and swung. The ball jumped off the top of the club face and sailed high into the air.

"What're doing up there!" he yelled. "Go! Go!"

The ball dropped onto a tall diagonal mound that sliced the fairway about halfway to the green. To Ridge's disgust, it bounced backward, toward the tee, and rolled for at least thirty yards.

"Heck, I could have thrown it further," he said.

When he reached the ball, he discovered it lay in a deep divot. Insult to injury.

"Good thing it found that," Chris said, nodding at the divot. "It might have gone another ten yards back."

Ridge glared at Chris, who shrugged, palms pointing up at the bright sun. "I'm just saying," he said. "Could be worse."

"Like yours," Patrick said as he passed by.

"Yeah, like mine," Chris said lightheartedly. He joined Patrick and moved away from Ridge. "Like all of mine, today."

Ridge tried not to focus on the fact that his ball was sunken an inch below the grass. He pulled out a seven iron and took aim. And rolled his eyes in dismay as the ball landed in the middle pot bunker on the left edge of the green. So much for par.

In the end, he managed to get up and down for a bogey, so he wasn't too disappointed. Holes ten, eleven, and twelve were the only par fives, and decent par three, on the course. Ridge joined Don and Patrick in shooting par, despite fairways that resembled roller coasters, which produced uncomfortably uneven stances. Poor Chris ping ponged along, shooting bogey, bogey, bogey.

A wild drive on thirteen started the demise of that hole into double bogey, and Ridge stood on the fourteenth tee a bit rattled, but determined. This was turning into a good round. It wasn't time to blow it by getting upset.

He made par on the remaining holes, and picked up his ball on eighteen with a seventy-three on the score card. Patrick was closest with a seventy-seven, Don next with a seventy-nine, while Chris had struggled for an uncharacteristic eighty-one. Ridge looked back to the course, laid out along the ocean and protected by large sand and grass dunes. It was, indeed, a special place.

The first foursome had hovered around the eighteenth green, waiting for their friends. "So what'd you think?" Vandeweghe said, patting Ridge on the back.

Ridge nodded and grinned. "Horrible place. Dreadful course. Can we come back tomorrow?"

Vandeweghe laughed heartily. "And every day after that. But then we'd miss St Andrews, and that would be a sin, now wouldn't it?"

The eight men headed for the clubhouse. A single golfer walked toward them, bag on his shoulder. He nodded as he passed Vandeweghe and Plato, then stopped abruptly.

"Excuse me," he said. As one, the Gang paused and turned. "Pardon me, but where y'from?"

"California, most of us," Vandeweghe said. He thumped Don lightly on the shoulder. "This goof's from Arizona."

"From America, then?" the golfer said, his face registering true surprise. "How'd you find this golf course? We don't ever get Americans here."

"You'll be getting a lot more of them, if we have anything to say about it," Plato said. "I'm sure all of us are going to talk it up when we get home."

"Heck, no!" Rudy joked. "I don't want it spoiled by a bunch of hackers. I'm keepin' this gem all to myself."

"Well, I'm glad t'hear you liked it so," the golfer said. "Come back again!" He waved and continued to the first tee.

The Gang walked on in silent reflection. Don finally voiced what Ridge suspected was all their thoughts.

"That is some course," Don said. "Can't thank you enough, Gary. What a find."

Plato's face lit up. "I think this is even better than yesterday."

"Less rain," Charlie said. "My feet aren't wet."

"I told you not to play in the puddles near the clubhouse," Patrick said. "You never listen to me."

Plato shook his head. "Not Barassie, you goofs. Of course I'm speaking about Western Gailes."

Chris pounced. "Well, now, I'd argue that one. Western Gailes is awfully perfect, for my money."

"And for Vandeweghe's money?" Rudy teased. "Machrihanish any better for that?"

"The best ever," Chris said. "No contest."

They arrived at the clubhouse and parked their bags along the wall. The same balding man met them at the door, his smile even broader, if possible.

"Are ya ready for lunch, lads?" He motioned for them to enter. "Cook's got it all laid out for ya."

Ridge's eyebrows rose. "Lunch, too?" He looked to Vandeweghe, and realized he was just as surprised by the announcement.

"We're getting spoiled," Chris said.

Vandeweghe shook his head. "I have no idea what we did to warrant this one. But I'm not arguing. I'm starved!"

Again, the spread was significant, and Ridge dug in with relish. He'd had a large enough breakfast to hold him through the day, but a renewed appetite arrived with the first bowl of steaming baked chicken.

The conversation focused on the round for the first few minutes, then lapsed into contented silence. After the last crumb of bread disappeared, Charlie pushed back his chair.

"Hey Plato," he said. "Any word on the Santa Clara County?"

Ridge's hairs prickled on the back of his neck. Why was Charlie broaching this subject now?

"The Senior Championship?" Plato asked, his voice very level. "What about it?"

"Have they decided what to do about the age brackets this year?" Charlie asked.

Ridge glanced across at Rudy. The color was creeping up on his neck, and he was heavily focused on reorganizing the placement of his silverware on his plate.

"You know they aren't going to change that, Charlie," Plato said, and Ridge was surprised by the definite edge in the pro's voice.

"Well, why the hell not?" Charlie said. "Hank should have won that thing that year they changed the brackets, and you know it."

Ridge sighed. Ah heck, here we go.

"Look, Charlie," Rudy said. "Hank knew what the age brackets were. For Pete's sake, he chose to play. You can't keep blaming Plato."

Charlie's eyes flashed. "I can blame the person responsible. And sorry, Gary, but you were the guy who had the final say that day."

Ridge decided he was not going to let an old argument ruin a fabulous day. He leaned on the table and glared at his friend. "Why are you bringing this up now, Charlie? It's old news."

"Because the Championship comes up when we get home," Charlie said. "I'd like to know what's being done to fix it."

"Nothing's being done, Charlie," Rudy snapped. "Because nothing needs to be done. It's been fine for the past twenty years. Let it go."

"Don't tell me what to do," Charlie flared. "And it's not fixed, damn it."

Don's lips were pursed tightly and he leaned heavily on one hand. Chris was intently fiddling with a fork, and Patrick – who was sitting between his father and Rudy – was intently staring straight ahead at the wall.

Vandeweghe threw his napkin on the table. "Plato made the decision that had to be made, Charlie. What do you want him to do now? He's not even on the board any longer."

"He still has a lot of friends," Charlie said. "You can get them to change it back."

Rudy shook his head. "He's not getting involved, Charlie. You want it changed? Send a letter and ask for a petition. It's done."

"I'm not gonna send a letter!" Charlie said. "Plato's sittin' right here!"

Plato stood up. "I'm done with it, Charlie, like Rudy said. I'm going to the men's room."

Charlie's jowls were bright red, and his eyes were on fire. If he kept this up he might give himself a stroke. How far away was that fire truck? An ambulance? A hospital?

"I think we're all done with the conversation," Vandeweghe said. "Let it go, Charlie."

"It was what it was," Rudy said, his tone softening. "It was years ago, for crying-out-loud."

Charlie seemed to deflate. Carefully, Patrick stretched and rested his arm on the back of Charlie's chair. It was a loving gesture, protective.

The plump cook entered, a laden tray in her hands. "Coffee? Tea?"

A resounding "Yes!" relieved the tension in the room. But Plato did not return until the pot had been drained.

Don looked at his watch. "What time is the taxi coming, Gary?"

"Five-fifteen," Vandeweghe said. "We almost have time for another nine. Anyone in?"

Ridge pursed his lips. The offer was tantalizing, but he'd played so well this morning, and he might not repeat. He didn't want to spoil the memories.

"We really only have about ninety minutes," Don said. "Not enough time to get around a whole nine."

"Let's hop down to the pro shop," Patrick said. "I want to find a shirt or something."

Charlie smiled at his son. "You haven't filled up that suitcase yet, have you."

"Not even close," Patrick said, and stood.

The Gang profusely thanked and tipped the plump cook and her balding messenger, then walked to the pro shop, near the first tee. They entered the tiny building, and Ridge noticed Patrick's eyes blaze with delight. The shop was stuffed with goods; every wall, nook, and shelf was brimming with items sporting the Machrihanish logo. Ridge headed straight for a rack of shirts while the rest of the Gang pawed through the sweaters, jackets, and vests. The shirts weren't very interesting, though, and Ridge sighed. On the far wall, a stack of ball caps sat precariously on a thin shelf. Well, he owned a bunch of caps, but at least these looked more interesting than the shirts.

"Watch out!" Charlie said. "Don't step on the vest."

Ridge looked down, and laughed. Clothes were everywhere across the shop: on the floor, draped over racks, hanging from lamps. Both Chris and Patrick were pulling sweaters over their heads, and Plato was zipping up a jacket. Vandeweghe had a Machrihanish shirt on over his own shirt, and Don was comparing three different ball caps. The Machrihanish pro stood behind his counter, arms crossed but smiling broadly.

Ridge waved vaguely at his friends. "Have you ever see such a bunch of nuts before?"

The pro shrugged in delight. "I've nothing t'do but clean up later. Have at it!"

In the end, Chris bought a heavyweight, lined sweater vest; Rudy, Charlie, and Vandeweghe bought shirts; and Don chose a beige cap with the logo blazoned on the front. Plato decided upon a lightweight wind jacket. Not surprisingly, Patrick left with the heaviest bag.

"I can't make up my mind," Patrick said with a chuckle. "So I'm just gonna buy it all."

Ridge settled on a simple but elegant metal-stamped ball marker. He had "more shirts than God," as Nellie was always saying, and he rarely had need of a sweater as his body was prone to running warm. Might as well add to his growing collection of ball markers.

They left the Machrihanish pro very satisfied, and strolled back toward their clubs.

"Well that was fun," Rudy said. "Now what?"

"Let's go into town," Chris said. "There's a cab parked in the lot. He can probably call for another one."

"That sounds good," Vandeweghe said. "There's gotta be some place that has ice cream."

Everyone laughed. They walked to the single cab, chatting about items they'd seen in the shop and the Machrihanish pro's delightful attitude.

Vandeweghe waived at the cabby. "Can you call for another cab? Take us all into Campbeltown?"

The cabby wriggled his face, then scratched the patchy growth on his chin. "Aye, but it'll take 'em least thirty minutes t'get here," he said. "We've only two in town, 'n I know Angus is busy with a bunch of ladies over at the chapel." He opened the back door of the cab and motioned with his hand. "Get in 'n I'll come back fer th'rest."

Ridge crawled into the cab beside Chris and Patrick, and Vandeweghe again sat in the front passenger seat.

"I think I'll stay behind," Don said. "Go putt and chip or something."

Plato nodded. "Good idea," he said. "I'll stay too."

Both Rudy and Charlie agreed to stay behind as well, and Ridge was mildly surprised, then pleased. Given the argument over lunch, he had expected Rudy and Plato to give Charlie a bit of distance for the rest of the afternoon. As the cab pulled away from the curb, the four men were walking back toward the clubhouse, shoulder to shoulder, chatting. Ridge sighed contentedly.

Campbeltown was almost as small as the pro shop, and just as charming. A few tiny boutiques, a general store, a book store, and a brightly lit cafe lined the short main street, anchored by a gas station and a small church. Within minutes, Vandeweghe found the ice cream parlor, which apparently doubled as the hardware store, much to Ridge's amusement. Chris and Patrick joined Vandeweghe in buying a double-decker cone, but Ridge indulged himself with a chocolate float – along with a miniature screwdriver with the Scottish flag imprinted on the handle, for Nellie. She'd like that better than a ball cap.

From the bookstore owner, Ridge learned there were approximately four thousand residents in Campbeltown, a much larger number than he expected.

"If ya walk up th'hill at th'end o'town, ya kin see th' coast of Northern Ireland," she said, pointing toward the ocean. "'Tis only ten miles across." The charming woman waved up the street. "Ye kin also visit our lighthouse, if ya like."

"Lighthouse?" Patrick asked. "How far is it?"

The woman thought for a moment, then shrugged. "'Tis a walk, to be sure. But good for th'heart, no?"

Vandeweghe thanked her and they left the store.

When they reached the gas station, Patrick asked about the lighthouse, and it was determined, after mathematically calculating meters into miles, that the Mull of Kintyre, as it was called, was at least ten miles out of town.

"She was right," Chris said as they left the gas station. "Too far to walk."

"At least in fifteen minutes," Ridge said, consulting his watch. "Maybe we should get back."

They found the driver – who they'd paid to wait – having coffee in the little cafe. He waved in acknowledgment, gulped down the last of his cup, and trotted out to the vehicle. Another cab pulled up behind them as Ridge was folding himself into the back seat.

"'Tis time for your plane," the cabby said. "So I told Angus t'come along."

As they pulled up to Machrihanish Golf Club, Don and Rudy were on the practice putting green, while Charlie and Plato sat on a nearby bench, talking, glasses of beer in hand. Ridge rubbed his beard. Obviously, the lunchtime argument had been forgiven and forgotten.

The bags were quickly stuffed back into "the boots," lids tied, and last minute pictures taken by Patrick. Then they were off, madly driving back to the airport. In an identical rendition of that morning, they loaded their bags and entered the plane. Ridge found his gas can stashed under the seat. He buckled in, and the plane took off.

He looked out the window and smiled. Yep. The fire truck was chasing them down the runway, lights flashing. What a captivating sight.

The flight to Glasgow was quiet as the Gang was too tired for banter, and the commuter bus ride to the Marine Hotel was just as uneventful and subdued. When he stepped out of the bus, Ridge was surprised by the numerous deep puddles that dotted the wet pavement.

"Gee, looks like it's been raining here," Plato said. As if on cue, a light drizzle began.

"And still is," Charlie said.

Patrick waved him into the hotel. "Come on, Pops. I'm not giving you a chance to jump in any puddles. Don't want your feet wet."

Charlie chuckled and scooted into the hotel lobby ahead of the rest of the Gang. They agreed to meet in an hour for dinner, and Ridge shuffled down the hall to his room, gas can in hand. His feet hurt and he desperately wanted a hot shower.

Inside, Vandeweghe waved toward the bathroom. "I'm going to make a call to Barb," he said. "You shower first."

"Give her my best," Ridge said. "And thank her for today, as well. I imagine she knew about the surprise."

Vandeweghe grinned. "It was her idea. Machrihanish is one of her favorite courses."

An hour later, freshly scrubbed and comfortably clothed, the Gang convened in the lobby. Ridge crossed his arms and waited for the ritual to begin.

"So where we going tonight, Rudy?" Vandeweghe asked.

Rudy zipped up his jacket and Ridge realized he wasn't carrying his official note pad.

"The Anchorage Pub," Rudy said. "Downtown Troon. Ken's waiting outside with the van."

Ridge could feel the rest of the guys hold their breath.

Vandeweghe nodded and grinned. "Excellent, excellent. Fabulous steaks. Great choice."

Ridge glanced around at the rest of the Gang. They were all smiling in relief. "Let's go," he said, and headed for the door. "I could eat a whole cow."

"That would be really messy," Patrick said. "But let me try to help you."

It was still raining, and the wind had picked up. They piled into the van, and Plato asked Ken if it had been like this all day.

"Oh, aye," he said. "Rain all th'day long. Been miserable, it has."

"What a contradiction," Don said. "We had sunshine all day."

"Lucky, that," Ken said.

Yes, lucky that. And lucky, us, too, Ridge realized. Very, very lucky indeed. And not just about the weather.

CHAPTER 35

September 3, 1998

Patrick Quinn and Gary Vandeweghe

"So did we ever get another tee-time over at Prestwick?" Vandeweghe asked. The Gang hovered in the lobby, organizing bags and clubs, and checking out of the Marine Hotel.

Charlie shook his head. "I wasn't able to get a-hold of Mark again, to see if his friend had been able to secure a second time. I'm guessing not."

Vandeweghe frowned. One tee-time didn't do them any good since they wouldn't be allowed to stuff eight guys on the tee. At home, no problem, but not at Prestwick.

"I'm willing to bow out, anyway," Charlie said. "My back's killing me. I'd like to rest before we play this afternoon."

"You played Prestwick last time you were over here, didn't you?" Vandeweghe asked. Charlie nodded. "Well, then, okay." Vandeweghe looked at the other guys. "But that still doesn't solve the problem. Three other guys won't be able to play."

"I can't play thirty-six either," Ridge said. "My feet won't take it. So I'll hang with Charlie."

"Count me into that foursome, as well," Rudy said.

"Which?" Vandeweghe asked. "The one playing, or the one sitting?"

"Sitting," Rudy said. "I don't want to play thirty-six either, and I've also played Prestwick, though it was a long time ago. I don't imagine it's changed much. Let someone who hasn't played go."

"That's not the point," Vandeweghe said. "We should all play, or none of us."

"And do what?" Ridge said. "Watch you eat ice cream? Give at least four of us a reason to avoid that torture."

Everyone except Vandeweghe chuckled. He wasn't finding the humor in the situation. It was setting a bad precedent. This was the Gang of Eight, not of Four.

"I think we're counting our chickens before they hatch," Plato said. "Or something to that effect. Let's see what we have when we get to Prestwick. Maybe there's a cancellation."

"Now you're talking," Vandeweghe said. "Are we all checked out? Everyone have their bags?"

Affirmative comments were made by all, so Vandeweghe waved toward the van waiting outside. "Then let's get out of here."

When Ken pulled the van beside the Prestwick clubhouse, Vandeweghe had a premonition they wouldn't all be playing. The place was busy – the parking lot was nearly full, golfers were crossing the grounds, and there were at least eight men standing around the first tee, waiting.

Sure enough, the assistants at the counter looked at him like he was crazy when Vandeweghe asked if there was a second tee-time available.

"Maybe next month," one of them said. "At midnight on a Sunday."

Vandeweghe pursed his lips. Well, then, that was that. Someone else had to drop out. He joined the rest of the Gang, waiting beside the van.

"No luck, fellas," he said. He glanced at the faces. Patrick, Plato, Chris, and Don all looked sincerely disappointed. He made a quick decision. "So you four are playing. I'm gonna head over to Troon, check out the situation over there, make sure we're all copacetic. We can meet back here later this afternoon."

"You should play," Don said.

"Absolutely," Plato said. "You've done a lot for us this trip. You're the one who takes the fourth. The kids should play, too." He nodded at Chris and Patrick. "Don and I will flip a coin."

"Don't be a couple of coconuts," Vandeweghe said. "I get over here more than you do, and I have a small headache, anyway. I don't want it to get worse. You four go. I have things to do."

To Vandeweghe's relief, there were no more arguments. Patrick, Chris, Don, and Plato collected their bags.

"So, meet you at the clubhouse around one-thirty?" Don said.

"Yeah, yeah," Vandeweghe said. "We'll catch you for lunch." The four headed toward the clubhouse. "Have fun!" he called after them. And he meant it.

"I could use a cup of tea," Charlie said. "I think I'll go find the restaurant in that big building."

"I'll go watch them take off," Rudy said. "then I'll join you, Charlie. I could use some tea, as well."

"Well, heck," Vandeweghe said. "What are we thinking? We can all watch them tee off, then get our stuff done. Come on."

Charlie, Rudy, and Ridge followed him over to the first tee. They watched several other golfers drive down the idiosyncratic first fairway, then their four friends arrived. Chris, Patrick, and Don were pulling trolleys. A young caddy walked beside Plato, easily carrying his bag.

"You guys lose your caddies?" Vandeweghe said. "What's with the trolleys?"

"There weren't any caddies," Plato said. "But when I mentioned we'd never played here before, this nice young man offered to carry for me. He's going to give us the lay of the land."

Vandeweghe assessed the young man. He didn't want some goon giving his friends bad advice. "You've played this course, I assume?"

The caddy smiled and nodded. "Aye, sir, I've played it many a'time."

Vandeweghe noted that his brogue was light. He also noted the young man was dressed like a golfer, not like the Scottish caddies they'd encountered thus far. "You're not a caddy, normally, are you?"

The young man shook his head. "No sir. The only man I usually carry a bag for is my da'. And then only if I'm not playing myself."

"What's your handicap?" Vandeweghe asked. He was intrigued. The kid was clearly educated. What was he doing here? Why wasn't he at school somewhere?

The young man looked sheepish. "Oh, now, last week I slipped to a seven, on account I've been at school and not playing much."

Vandeweghe chuckled. A seven would know how to play this course.

"Okay, Gary, you satisfied?" Plato asked, grinning. "Or do you want the kid's resume?"

"I might," Vandeweghe said, "so we can hire him as your replacement when you retire."

"Ten o'clock on the tee!" the starter yelled. He waved at the Gang. "Which o' ya's playing, lads?"

The four players separated themselves from the others, and Vandeweghe stood, grinning, as they began their round. He bit his lip when Chris sent not one, not two, but three balls slicing over the six-foot rock wall that separated the course from the railway line which ran the length of the fairway. Finally the fourth ball hit the wall and bounced back into play.

"Clark's Wall," Patrick said. "I'll have a plaque made and we'll post it."

Chris pulled his ball cap over his eyes and moaned, and the four hoofed it up the fairway. Vandeweghe wished he could walk with them, at least. Blast it, he should have offered to carry Don's bag. Or at least pull the cart.

Oh well. He gave a short wave. They'd be the Gang of Eight again this afternoon.

"Let's go check out the clubhouse," he said, and led the way back to the massive stone building.

Patrick stood on the third tee, slapping a fairway wood on the ground. The caddy carrying Plato's bag – "the kid" as the Gang had quickly tagged him – had insisted he substitute it for the driver, and Patrick was none too pleased.

The kid pointed up the fairway. "Ye have the Cardinal's bunker before you," he said. "Ye don't want to land anywhere near them. Lay up."

"Cardinal's bunker?" Don said. "The bird or the guy?"

"A monk from an abbey down near Turnberry," the kid explained. "'Tis gone now, the abbey is – well, the monk, too, to be sure – but this bunker was named after the gent. He played a match against one o'the Lords o'Culzean, and bet his nose as the wager."

"Who won?" Patrick asked, his frustration replaced by fascination. Who would bet their own nose on a game of golf?

The kid shrugged. "I don't really know. But since the bunker's named after him, I assume the Cardinal did."

"Or maybe his nose is buried in the bunker," Chris said. He made a funny, ghostly "Ooooooh!" sound and opened his eyes wide. "Watch out for those nostrils!"

The kid appeared very perplexed. "Don't worry about him," Patrick said, jerking a thumb toward Chris. "We'll lock him back up in the asylum when the round is done."

Moments later, Patrick stood looking at the deep, wide bunkers that comprised the Cardinal, and was thankful he had listened. The kid knew the course. On the other side of the fairway, Chris stood over his ball. Always the brave one, he slammed a three-wood, trying to cut the corner and make the green in two. Patrick winced as the ball – which seemed to favor a slice today – took a hard right turn, bounced in the rough, and landed in the Pow Burn, a substantial creek that ran the length of the hole. For the fourth time today, Chris buried his face in his cap and swore in private.

Patrick grinned. "You're gonna turn that beige cap blue, if you keep that up."

"Or burn a hole in it," Plato added. "Your ball crossed into the water way up there. You'll be able to drop close to the green."

"Small consolation," Chris said.

Patrick, learning his lesson, pulled a seven iron and lobbed his ball over the Cardinal's bunker.

"Oh that was magic!" the kid said. "You'll no need a hankie or a prayer today."

Don started to laugh and stepped away from his ball.

"Compose yourself, Winner-halter!" Patrick hollered. "It's not as big as Lucente's schnoz!" He could see Don's shoulder's shaking in laughter. "Okay, so maybe it is bigger than Hank's nose, but you've avoided that all your life. You can avoid this one too."

Don took two practice swings, and hit. The ball carried the bunkers and took an advantageous bounce around the fairway corner.

"Did you say a little prayer before you swung?" Chris asked.

"For our souls?" Patrick said.

"I don't have that much skin on my knees," Don retorted. "You're on your own for that."

Patrick nearly holed out from his position in the middle of the fairway, and snagged his first birdie of the day. When they arrived at the fourth tee, they discovered a foursome sitting on the grass, waiting for yet another foursome to drive.

"Uh oh," Chris said. "Where's the ranger?"

"That we don't have," the kid said. "Usually we don't need one."

Patrick stood beside his bag and gazed across the course to the ocean beyond. The Isle of Arran rested in the haze of the morning. He wondered what it would be like to be on the island, looking back at the golf courses that dotted the shoreline of Scotland. He glanced at the tee. The foursome ahead of them was finally driving. He walked over to the kid. "Any suggestions?"

The kid pointed across the course. "See that big egg-shaped rock over there?" Patrick nodded. "Aim for that and let it rip."

The wait seemed to help Chris, who made his first par of the day, and certainly didn't hurt the others, either. Still, more waiting on the par-three fifth tee was annoying, as both foursomes ahead of them struggled to safely get over either the Pow Burn or The Himalayans, the severe fairway humps that filled the two hundred plus yards between the tee and the green. The Himalayans rendered the green blind, and Patrick was pleased the kid was along to tell them which direction to line up, otherwise he'd have no idea where to aim.

Don peeked at his watch.

"We're not going to make it, are we?" Patrick said.

Don shook his head. "Not at this rate."

Patrick felt a small pang of disappointment. This was a short course, to be sure, but quirky and fun. A great challenge. Heck, they'd played something like twenty-four Open Championships on it over the years. He wanted to play all of it, not just a few holes.

Finally, after the eighth hole, the first slow foursome gave up and hiked back toward the clubhouse along the railway fence line. Patrick became hopeful they'd finish the round after all, as they clocked along, no longer waiting on any given tee or fairway.

He walked beside Chris on the thirteenth fairway. They had both utilized the kid's knowledge of the course to get off the tee in the right direction.

"So did you also think that other flag was the one we were shooting at?" he asked.

Chris nodded. "I would have had no idea the green for this hole is around to the right, back toward the ocean."

They crested one of the many tall hillocks that comprised the fairway. The kid joined them.

"Jeez, kid," Patrick said. "Ever hear of a bulldozer?"

The kid chuckled. "These are the Hartz Mountains."

"Well, I wouldn't quite call them mountains," Chris said. "Hart's Hills, maybe."

"For the Secretary, Harry Hartz, these were mountains," the kid said. "He was so short you couldn't see him when he walked down the fairway. He'd just disappear."

Patrick and Chris simultaneously turned and walked backwards, looking up the fairway to where Plato and Don walked. Both men were clearly visible. Chris and Patrick laughed and looked at each other knowingly.

"Shorter than Winterhalter?" Chris said. "Is that possible?"

As the foursome stepped onto the sixteenth tee, Don glanced at his watch again.

"It's twenty past one," he said. "We need to get off the course around one-thirty if we want to have lunch before we play Old Troon."

"Let's play out this hole," Plato said. "We can walk in after that."

The kid stood with the four men and pointed to the left. "Ye cannot see it, but o'er that hill lies Willie Campbell's Grave." He pointed to the right. "Ye want to aim for that big scruffy bush on the right. And I'd suggest you club down one, as well. It's only two-eighty-eight to the green."

Chris grunted. "I hit my driver around two-eighty-five. Why not go for the green?"

The kid tilted his head a bit to the left and stared at Chris. "Aye, you've hit it long enough t'make the green. But you've a nasty slice, and if you want to get home before midnight, I'd suggest you lay up."

The four Gang members laughed.

"He's got a point," Don said.

They all pulled mid-irons and laid up, safely avoiding trouble.

Patrick sidled up to the kid. "So what's this bunker called? Somebody's grave?"

The kid said, "Willie Campbell's Grave. He was leadin' the Open in 1887 and buried his ball in this bunker. Took him four strokes t'get out. He ended up losing the Championship because of it."

Patrick grinned. "I'm surprised he didn't come out here in the dead of night and fill in the damn bunker."

"I'm sure the thought crossed his mind," the kid said.

When the last ball fell into the cup on sixteen, Patrick's stomach rumbled.

"There's our alarm clock," Plato said. "Time to bag it in and head for grub."

Shoulder to shoulder, they walked down the seventeenth fairway, following the foursome in front of them. As they approached the green, Patrick could see one of the golfers was struggling to get out of a bunker. Patrick stood with the other Gang members in the fairway and wondered what could possibly be so difficult that it took seven strokes to get out.

When they finally passed the bunker, Patrick rolled his eyes.

"No wonder the guy was in trouble," he said, pointing at the humongous hole that stood sentry in front of the green. "Jeez, guys, there's thirteen steps down to it! Must be ten feet deep."

Both Plato and Don walked over and looked into the bunker.

"Fill it with water and you could float the Queen Mary in there," Don said.

Plato shrugged. "Looks worse than it is, really. Just get the ball in the air."

Patrick chuckled. "Easy for you to say."

"And do," Don added.

Patrick knew it was past their appointed meeting time with the other Gang members, but he was disappointed they'd not been able to play out. He mentioned it to the kid as they dropped their bags and entered the clubhouse.

"Ach, you've seen the best of her," the kid said. "You've not missed anything to write home about."

Patrick nodded. That was good. His penmanship never had been very legible.

Vandeweghe drug his bag out of the trailer and proceeded to clean his clubs, shoes, and anything else he could find. Charlie and Rudy had settled in for breakfast and tea in the restaurant, and Ridge had crawled back into the van for a nap. How he slept on those small, hard seats was beyond Vandeweghe to imagine, but then Ridge had a little padding of his own, so that probably helped.

He was finishing the last club when Rudy rounded the corner.

"Did you still want to hop back to Troon?" Rudy said. "If so, I'll join you."

Vandeweghe placed his bag in the trailer. "I saw Ken go into the clubhouse. I'll go rustle him up." He flipped a wrist toward the van. "Go wake up Ridge and see if he wants to go. If not, throw him off the van."

Rudy grinned. "I think it would be more fun to just drive the van someplace and park it. Let Ridge wonder where he's at when he wakes."

"He would sleep through a drive, too," Vandeweghe said, then headed toward the clubhouse. He found Ken in the bar, sipping a dark soda of some sort. Hopefully it was not spiked. Vandeweghe chided himself. They guy had been an ace this whole week; no point in thinking there'd be trouble.

Ken eagerly agreed to drive them back to Troon, poured his drink into a plastic cup, and followed Vandeweghe to the van. Ridge stood beside Rudy, stretching and yawning.

"Wake you?" Vandeweghe asked. "You coming with us?"

Ridge pulled his beard. "Naw. I think I'll join Charlie in the clubhouse. They got a tele in there? I'll watch the news or something."

"Okay," Vandeweghe said. He motioned to Rudy and Ken. "Let's go."

The drive to Troon was fifteen minutes. It was amazing how close all these places were to each other. This part of Scotland just seemed to breed classy golf courses.

Troon was big and lively, its many windows brightly lit. Vandeweghe and Rudy entered a door, and were met by a stalwart Scotsman in a tweed jacket. He looked them up and down disdainfully. "Sorry gentlemen. You'll need to use the visitor's entrance. This here's for members only."

Vandeweghe looked around. "I didn't see a sign. Is there a sign?"

The man ignored the question and opened the door, showing them the way. "The visitor's entrance is 'round the left. 'Ave a nice day."

Vandeweghe followed Rudy through the door.

"Well, wasn't that special," Rudy said. "I suddenly feel like I landed in Georgia, circa 1800." He shifted his voice down an octave and attempted a Southern twang. "There's the door, blackie. Don't come back."

Vandeweghe laughed, but it had been an uncomfortable moment. "They could put up a sign. Make it easier on everyone."

They found the visitor's entrance, and entered what felt like a lobby. There were golfers, no doubt, but there were also the "regular" folk on "holiday." Vandeweghe led Rudy to the pro shop, then waited in line while Rudy browsed, casually looking at clothing. When his turn came, Vandeweghe verified their tee-times on the Old Course.

"Three-fifty and four," the assistant said. "But are ya sure you don't want to play our Lincoln course? 'Tis a lovely round, 'n a bit easier on th' nerves, if you know what I mean."

Vandeweghe wrinkled his brow. "Ah, no. That thing's flat as a pancake. My wife played it and shot a twelve under par or something. We'll stick with the Old."

The assistant tightened his jaw and smiled tersely. "Very good, sir. You're all set, then."

Vandeweghe sighed. They'd be The Gang again. He turned to find Rudy standing at the counter, wallet in hand.

"I found a nice sweater for Bev," Rudy said. "Thought I'd buy it now, while I had the time."

"Sure, sure," Vandeweghe said. "We have time." He turned to another assistant, one who looked less like he had a stick up his rear. "Where's the best place to have lunch around here?"

"I'd suggest th' grill, sir," the assistant said. "Very good lunch special."

Rudy and Vandeweghe decided to check it out, and found the "special" meant a buffet. Vandeweghe wasn't keen on buffets, but the number of items was extensive, and it was very reasonably priced.

"Looks good to me," Rudy said. "And I'm not hungry right now, so that's saying something."

Vandeweghe glanced up at the clock on the wall. "We have a few hours. Let's go walk along the beach."

"Without a club in my hand," Rudy said, grinning. "What a novel idea."

They stashed Rudy's purchase in the van, informed Ken he was free for an hour, and located the access to the beach. It was sunny, if not particularly warm, and the ocean breeze was gentle. They couldn't see much of the course, which ran the length of the beach above them, and Vandeweghe was rather pleased by that.

They strolled along the sand, chatting about San Jose Country Club, friends and foes, and membership issues. It was relaxed and casual, and Vandeweghe was feeling very content when they returned to the van.

Ken was waiting.

"Head the ponies to Prestwick," Vandeweghe said. "Let's go collect the rest of our posse." They were back at the aged clubhouse within minutes. Vandeweghe verified the four players weren't off the course, then settled on an overstuffed chair, shut his eyes, and began reminiscing of the day thus far, waiting.

Don's voice broke into his thoughts. "Well, look at these bums." Scooter stood over him, grinning.

"'Bout time you got your sorry butts back here," Vandeweghe said. "We were about to leave you here for good."

"No thanks," Chris said. "It's a nice course, but I don't want to play it every day."

"Get awfully expensive," Plato said. "All those balls over Clark's Wall."

"What you got there?" Vandeweghe said, and motioned for Chris to hand over the club he held.

"We stopped in the pro shop," Chris said.

Ridge swiveled in his chair. "Of course. Get a ball marker?"

Chris tossed one to him. "Just for you. Even if you didn't get your Confederate tush onto the course."

Vandeweghe weighed the putter he held. It was a little heavy on the backside, but he liked the balance. He stood up and let it rest in his hand. It hung straight and true.

"Pretty nice putter," Plato said, then looked at Chris. "Though I don't know how you're going to get it home. It won't fit in your suitcase."

"I think they'll ship it for me," Chris said. "I was told to check at the main desk, here."

Vandeweghe handed the putter back to Chris. "Well, get to it, then. I'm starved."

Chris sauntered off in the direction of the main desk, and the conversation turned to lunch. All agreed to eat at Troon, and once Chris returned – sans putter – they hustled to the van, loaded, and set out for their next destination.

The pros and cons of Prestwick were discussed over lunch, and then Plato stood and pinged his glass with his fork.

"Laddies, we are about to head out to the Old Course at Royal Troon," he said. "Home of the Open Championship seven times, the most recent being last year when Justin Leonard –"

"Possibly my future son-in-law!" Vandeweghe interjected with a laugh.

"– carried off the Claret Jug," Plato continued. "You are about to walk the fairways Bobby Locke walked, putt the greens Arnold Palmer played, and drive in the shadows of Tom Weiskopf, Tom Watson, and Mark Calcavecchia. The motto of the club is 'As much by skill as by strength.' Are you ready?"

Vandeweghe grinned and joined in the soft applause made by the Gang. He knew others in the room were listening, and perhaps they weren't appreciative, but Vandeweghe loved it when Plato got on his soapbox about the game. The man was a walking golf encyclopedia, after all.

Plato held up his palm and resumed. "The game today is Sterling Cha Cha. Foursome one against foursome two. Odd holes, best ball twosome. Even holes, gross twosome. Any questions?"

Vandeweghe raised his hand. "Yes. What the heck is a cha cha?"

Plato grinned. "I have no idea. I just needed a name and it came to me late one night."

"Go to bed earlier," Patrick said. "You'll save yourself some embarrassment."

And everyone in the room laughed, including the waitresses.

Lunch over, the Gang collected clubs, changed shoes, and generally organized themselves into playing mode. Vandeweghe watched the process, and realized they'd become a well-oiled machine. Everyone knew where everyone else was going to be, who sat where, and who had a shoehorn. Plato handed a collection of tees to Rudy without being asked, and Chris tossed Don his hat. The banter never slowed; it all just happened.

Vandeweghe shook his head. What a coup. What a grand coup.

Patrick dropped his bag on the rack outside the clubhouse.

"They got buggies," Ridge said, nodding toward several quietly buzzing toward the first tee. "I'm gonna go get one." He pointed at Patrick. "Tell your dad he's riding with me." Ridge trotted off toward the pro shop.

Don, Vandeweghe, Plato, and Rudy arrived and dropped their bags alongside Patrick's.

"Where's he off to in such a rush?" Don asked. "He just used the potty."

"Carts," Patrick said. "He discovered they have 'buggies.' He's going to get one for him and Pops."

Plato frowned. "They're not playing together," he said.

Patrick looked at Plato. "They are if Ridge gets a buggy. I'll swap places with Pops."

Chris and Charlie joined them, and the Gang waited for what seemed an eternity. Ridge never returned. "Where'd he have to go to get it?" Rudy said to no one in particular. "Siberia?"

"I'll go find out what's happening," Vandeweghe said.

Charlie waved at Patrick. "Junior, go with him and pay for my side."

Ridge stood at the pro shop counter, legs spread, arms crossed over his barrel chest. One assistant was behind the counter, his back to Ridge, his focus buried in paperwork.

"Ridge!" Vandeweghe said. "What's the hang-up? We're on, man!"

Ridge turned and Patrick knew something was wrong. Ridge's face was brilliant red above his snow-white beard. He looked like a sun burnt Santa gone mad. "They say they can't rent me a buggy 'cause I didn't make arrangements before we arrived," Ridge spat. "I've sent for the pro, but it seems they can't find him."

Vandeweghe leaned over the counter. "Excuse me young man. I just saw the pro outside on the putting green. Would you like me to go get him?"

The young assistant turned, and in a voice dripping with condescension, said, "I've explained to the gent 'ere that ya must call for buggies in advance. He dinna do so."

Patrick glanced at Vandeweghe and scrubbed his mouth to hide a smile. Oh, this poor kid just picked a fight with the wrong tiger.

Vandeweghe seemed to grow a foot in height. In his courtroom voice he said, "Do you *have* buggies available? Are they *all* on the course?"

The young man thrust his chin out but stayed well behind the counter. "That's not th'point, sir. He dinna 'ave a reservation."

Vandeweghe glared at the young man. "I'll ask you again. Do – you – have – buggies – available? Yes or no?"

Patrick really felt for the kid; he certainly wouldn't want to be in the young man's shoes.

The young man sniffed. "I'll go fetch the manager." And he nearly ran from the pro shop. A rowdy foursome entered and began perusing the wares. Within seconds, an older man arrived, bearded and wearing a full suit. He was closely followed by the young assistant. Patrick thought of an old Disney cartoon – baby cub hiding behind papa bear.

"There seems to be a problem, sir?" the older man said gently, smiling between Vandeweghe and Ridge.

"No problem at all," Vandeweghe said. "We have two players who find it difficult, for physical reasons, to walk eighteen. They need to rent a buggy. We'd simply like to rent one now."

There was a discernible delay while the older man seemed to size up Vandeweghe. Suddenly he turned to the assistant and said, "I believe we 'ave one available for their use, don't we Timmy? Fetch one, will ya,"

Patrick about choked. The kids name was Timmy. Of course it was.

Timmy nodded curtly and bolted from the shop.

"Thank you," Vandeweghe said. "We all greatly appreciate your help."

Patrick watched Vandeweghe's whole body relax. What a difference.

The older man moved to the register and rang in a number. Ridge withdrew his wallet. "There'll be two of us riding. What do I owe you?"

The older man pulled the register paper, wadded it up, and tossed it in an unseen garbage can beneath the counter. He smiled at Ridge warmly. "Ye no owe me anything. 'Tis on th' house. Just remember to make a reservation next time ya play."

Ridge nodded and thrust his hand out. "I thank you kindly," he said, and shook the older man's hand.

"Timmy'll 'ave it outside, near your clubs," the older man said. "'Ave a nice round, gentlemen." He then turned his attention to the other shoppers, and Patrick felt they had been dismissed.

Vandeweghe glanced at his watch and Patrick followed him from the shop. "Damn, we're late," Vandeweghe said. "Let's hope they haven't given our tee-times away."

"My apologies, Gary," Ridge said. "I didn't think this was gonna be such an ordeal."

"No, no, of course you didn't," Vandeweghe said. "I just don't want to lose our chance to play over it."

That'd be an even bigger battle, Patrick thought. And one less likely to be won.

They rounded the corner and found Plato directing the loading of the golf cart with Ridge's and Charlie's clubs. The rest of the clubs were shouldered by caddies, all properly dressed in what appeared to be a uniform of brown pants, blue shirts, and darker blue golf sweaters. Patrick was pleased to note there wasn't a hole or stain to be seen.

"They've called us twice now," Charlie said, and motioned to the tee. "We're late."

Charlie and Ridge clambered into the buggy and made for the first tee. The rest of the Gang hustled behind, and arrived to find Ridge on the tee, wiggling and waggling over the ball. The starter, a mountain of a man in knickers and a tweed jacket, was watching with a rather sour look on his face. Ridge drove the ball straight down the center of the fairway, then Charlie followed suit. By the time Plato teed up, the starter was smiling. Plato's ball sailed nearly 300 yards, landing perfectly center. Patrick noted, out of the corner of his eye, that the caddies were passing appreciative looks amongst themselves.

He exchanged a look and a grin with Chris. Plato's drive was at least twenty yards further than usual; clearly their pro was taking some anger issues out on the ball.

Vandeweghe followed the rest down the middle, though his drive was considerably shorter than any of the others. Patrick wondered if he'd spent all his energy on that display in the pro shop. Patrick hoped not.

The starter nodded. "Good show, gents. Continue on!"

Patrick sighed with relief. They were off and running. As the first Gang members made their way down the fairway, Patrick allowed himself the indulgence of enjoying the view. The ocean shimmered in the sunshine and the fairway mimicked the waves with its own undulations. As he'd come to expect, gorse, high grass, and shrubbery lined both left and right. Patrick closed his eyes and turned his face toward the warmth of the sun. He felt himself relax.

"You're on laddies," the starter said. "No practice swings. Tee it up 'n hit, if ya please."

Rudy waved a hand toward the tee. "Scooter? Give us a show." Don stepped up and did, indeed, with a drive that was – Patrick was sure – the longest and straightest he'd had since their arrival in Scotland.

After Rudy and Chris had placed their balls safely on the fairway, Patrick teed up and stuck his ball nearly where Plato's had landed. He dropped his driver in his bag and looked at the starter. The portly man gave a short, curt nod, and said nothing, but his eyes were shining with delight. Patrick felt like he'd just passed some sort of exam.

"Coming, P.Q.?" Rudy said.

Patrick turned. Chris and Don were already half way to their ball. "Yeah, yeah," he said, and pushed his trolley ahead of him. "Wouldn't miss it for the world."

Vandeweghe followed Plato onto the eighteenth green. They'd had fairly similar rounds, with Vandeweghe playing lights out, and the pro only a few shots behind. Here, on the last green, they'd mirrored each other. Their golf balls were both lying three feet from the hole, on opposite sides.

Vandeweghe marked his ball and stepped back. As he waited for the others to putt, he looked around. It had been a good round on a good course. He was glad they'd played it, but he was anxious to get to St Andrews. He wanted to feel comfortable – and appreciated. St Andrews was home. When his turn came, he putted for par, and realized he was one under for the round.

"Hey," he said. "I think I matched Hale Irwin's round."

"The one he played when he was ten years old?" Charlie said.

"Go on," Vandeweghe said. He and Plato started toward the clubhouse, and Ridge drove the buggy slowly beside them. "No, I think Irwin hit a one under during one of the rounds at the Open."

"Then there's the other three rounds at, what?" Charlie said, "Seven under? You gotta match those to be bragging."

Vandeweghe shrugged. "All right, all right. Gee you know how to deflate a guy."

"It was a nice round," Plato said. "That birdie on the Postage Stamp was a joy to watch."

Vandeweghe smiled. "So was yours! It was good, wasn't it? Sure felt good."

Plato chuckled. "Always does."

They loaded their clubs in the trailer, and Ken opened the van door.

"You set to go?" he said. "Or are ya havin' dinner here?"

Vandeweghe checked his watch. It was seven-thirty, and they had at least a three-hour drive to St Andrews and the hotel. He wanted to get going. "Let's go. We can eat on the way or when we get to St Andrews. The other guys should be coming in any minute now."

Plato and Charlie hopped on the van without comment, and Ridge started for the clubhouse. "I'm gonna use the bathroom before we get going," he said. "Be right back."

Vandeweghe grinned. "Hopefully you didn't have to make an advanced reservation for *that*."

Ridge chuckled and jogged off. Within a few minutes he returned, followed by Don, Rudy, Chris, and Patrick, all looking a bit confused.

"You're loaded in the van?" Rudy said. "We were waiting for you over at the clubhouse."

"There's a really beautiful lounge," Patrick said. "And the pro shop has a lot of cool stuff with the Troon logo."

"It also has a bunch of really neat memorabilia," Chris said. "And I could use a beer. It's been a long round for me."

Don hummed and smiled. "You did get your money's worth on this one, didn't you?"

"I think I played twenty holes to your eighteen," Chris said.

Vandeweghe squirmed. They didn't have time for all this. "We can have a beer when we get to St Andrews. Let's get going. I don't want to be driving all night."

Patrick's lips pursed. "What's the rush, Gary? It's a three-hour drive whether we do it now or an hour from now. You can sleep on the van."

Vandeweghe felt his temper flare. He didn't want to sleep on the van. He wanted to get to St Andrews. "I don't think Ken wants to drive in the dark." He turned to the driver, who was leaning against the van, picking his teeth. "Do you?"

Ken shrugged. "I'm no getting in the middle o'this one. But truly, I dunna care when we drive over."

Vandeweghe glared at Ken. Damn the man. "Well the roads aren't safe in the dark. I'd rather get to St Andrews in one piece."

"Ah, come on, Gary," Patrick said. "One hour won't kill us. Let's go sit down, soak up some atmosphere, enjoy the place for once. We don't have a round until tomorrow afternoon."

"You can sleep in," Chris said.

By now the other Gang members had exited the van and were standing in small clumps, listening. Vandeweghe felt besieged. This wasn't a vacation tour, for Pete's sake! They were playing golf. "You can get atmosphere on the course." He realized the tone of his voice had become hard. He tried to soften it when he added, "It's just a bar, after all."

"It's Troon!" Patrick nearly yelled. "You don't get Troon in San Jose!"

Vandeweghe threw his hands in the air. "Fine, great, go get your beer. I'll wait here in the van." He stepped up onto the van's stairs.

"Oh come on, Gary!" Patrick said. "Don't be a sore loser."

Vandeweghe paused. He looked at Patrick. "Loser?" His voice was again hard in his own ears. "I rarely lose, Mr. Quinn. And when I do, I'm never sore about it." He looked at the rest of the men. Charlie was clearly upset, his cheeks blazing red and puffed, but the others appeared amused. Why, Rudy was actually grinning. Vandeweghe felt his anger snap like a twig. His shoulders slumped.

"Okay, okay." He stepped off the van. "Let's go check out the pro shop. But we don't have time for a beer. Just buy your stuff and let's get out of here."

Charlie nodded curtly at Patrick, then said, "Good compromise. Let's go fellas." He turned to Ken. "We'll see you in fifteen minutes or so."

"Fifteen minutes?" Patrick asked, frustration clear in his tone. Charlie steered him toward the pro shop before he could say anything else.

Vandeweghe waited until Ridge, Rudy, Chris, and Plato had followed, then joined Don. The shorter man walked quietly beside him, cleaning his nails with a broken tee.

Vandeweghe smiled. "You know you do that when you're tense about something?"

Don paused in his cleaning and looked up. "Do I? I thought I just did it when my nails were dirty." He shrugged. "Besides, what would I have to be tense about?"

Vandeweghe grunted. "I didn't mean to get nasty with P.Q., but this isn't a pleasure cruise."

Don hummed. "It's his first time over here. Cut the kid some slack and we'll all get what we want."

Vandeweghe slung an arm over Don's shoulders. "You're right, of course. We'll give them half an hour."

Don nodded and put the tee in his pocket. "Sounds sensible to me."

Vandeweghe stuffed his hands into the pockets of his trousers. Yep, sensible was what he was being. And sensible he would remain, because, if the truth were told, he could use a beer, too.

He'd just have one at St Andrews.

CHAPTER 36

September 3, 1998
Charlie Quinn

Charlie stood in the lobby of the Rusacks Hotel, St Andrews, and scratched his newly shaved chin. It was nearly ten in the evening, but the sky was still a little dusky. He wriggled his nose in thought. At home it would be pitch dark by now.

Patrick arrived. Charlie pursed his lips slightly. The sleeves of his son's clean golf shirt were peeking out from beneath a new sweater vest, which sported the logo from Troon. Charlie didn't need any more arguments. He sighed. "You had to wear it, didn't you? Couldn't leave well enough alone."

Patrick made no comment; he just stared out the window at the course.

Charlie gave up. "It looks good on you, though. Nice color."

Patrick smiled a little. "Thanks, Pops."

The other Gang members arrived in a boisterous group. Charlie wondered from where they got the energy. He was bushed.

Rudy brandished his notepad. "Okay, fellas. I have it on the best of authority –" he waved the notepad and bowed in the direction of Vandeweghe – "that the only place to eat is at Je T'Aime."

"French?" Ridge asked.

"Known for their veal," Rudy said. "Am I right, Gooch?"

Vandeweghe nodded. "And, the only place open this time of the night."

Charlie checked Vandeweghe's face for any traces of anger. Ken had made up quite a bit of time on the drive over, but Vandeweghe had been the only one unable to sleep on the drive. Charlie saw only relaxed delight on his tall friend's face. Good. Maybe the tiff was forgotten.

"...directions from the concierge," Rudy was saying. "You fellas want jackets or something? We'll be walking."

Moments later, they exited the hotel, en mass. Charlie breathed deeply. The ocean air was damp and cool, and there was a slight bite to the breeze. Autumn was coming.

"We go left here," Rudy said, and checked his notepad. "Yep, left at first corner."

"You sure?" Vandeweghe said. "I remember taking a right here."

Rudy showed him the pad, and Charlie could see it had someone else's handwriting.

"Okay," Vandeweghe said. "Left it is."

The walked the length of two blocks, and followed the directions to the right. This put them in a residential area, and Vandeweghe again questioned the notepad. More turns, left and right, got them back to the business district, but by then they'd walked at least half a mile, maybe more. Charlie was beginning to feel sharp pains in his back, and one glance at Ridge clarified he was suffering, as well.

"Okay, I think we're lost," Vandeweghe said. "This guy obviously didn't know where we were going."

"Or he sent us purposefully on a wild goose chase," Plato said.

"Gosh, I hope not," Rudy said. "He seemed really nice and helpful. Hate to think he was really a schmuck."

They walked another two blocks before making a left turn and seeing the sign for the restaurant.

"Voila!" Rudy said. "Dinner."

But when they got to the sign, there wasn't a door – just a brick wall.

"I guess you have to know the magic word," Patrick said. He touched the brick. "Abracadabra."

"Nice try," Don said. "Now try something in French."

The men spread out, searching for a way into the building. Charlie and Patrick walked toward the end of the building. Around the corner, they discovered an ornate porch. The sign over the door said *Bell Green Hotel*.

Charlie shrugged. "I'll go in and ask."

The lady at the counter explained the French restaurant was indeed in this building, but in the basement. They needed to come through her lobby to get to it.

Charlie sent Patrick back for the others. He checked his watch. Ten-thirty. He hoped the kitchen was still open.

They were the only customers in the place, but yes, thankfully the kitchen was open. They ordered quickly and Charlie was pleased when Vandeweghe asked for two bottles of French chardonnay. He was in desperate need of a numbing agent.

The Gang settled in, and it wasn't long before the conversation turned to that afternoon's round at Royal Troon.

"Did you notice how much of Prestwick you could see from the tenth tee?" Rudy said. "I didn't realize they were adjacent."

Chris chuckled. "Yeah, but you'd have to jump up and down on one of those fairway humps to see Royal Troon from Prestwick."

"From one of the Himalayans," Patrick added. "Gooch might be able to see Troon from one of those."

The Gang laughed and Charlie joined. Yep, everything was back to normal.

"So what's with that big white house in the middle of the golf course?" Chris asked.

"Some American, no doubt," Patrick said. "Like Plato said, there'd be houses all over if we ever got our hands on these places."

They all turned to Plato for an answer.

"Don't look at me!" he said. "I have no idea who put that thing there. For all I know, it was there before the course. Maybe they just built the Old around it."

"I think Calcavecchia lives in one of those stately homes along seventeen," Don said. "At least I read he had a house on a fairway here. Those were the only ones I noticed."

The wine arrived and was poured. Plato held his glass high and the table grew quiet.

"Here's a toast," he said. "To great friends and to great golf. May the two forever be entwined."

"Here, here!" "Cheers!" "Amen!"

After they all drank from their glasses, Charlie stood and raised his glass to eye level. He looked at Patrick. The men at the table waited.

"And here's to fathers and sons." He could feel the mood shift toward the somber. He looked between Plato and Vandeweghe. "And to birdies on the Postage Stamp!"

Laughter, congratulations, and cheers followed.

"Did you see the expression on the caddies' faces when we all made the green?" Ridge said.

"Oh yeah," Vandeweghe said. "Big surprise for them."

Ridge nodded vigorously. "They said most the time they play a foursome, not one of 'em hits it. But there we were – me, Plato, Vandeweghe, and Quinn. We all hit it. Sure made their day."

Charlie chuckled at the memory. "Our caddies were in disbelief, as well, that's for sure."

Dinner was served, and the mood continued to be light and joyful. The food was plentiful and delicious, and Charlie felt the pains in his back lessen. Hole by hole the course was replayed during the meal. Charlie realized he'd matched Vandeweghe's score at one under, and another toast was made in his honor. He finished his veal and pushed back from the table.

"Jeez, Charlie," Chris said, "you ate that whole thing!"

Charlie wrinkled his brow. "Why wouldn't I? It was really delicious."

"I wasn't sure you'd have room for more after that Whopper you had at Burger King," Chris said. "You scarfed that down like it was your last meal."

Charlie chuckled.

"It might have been, the way Ken was driving," Vandeweghe said, smiling.

"What a hoot," Rudy said. "Imagine finding a Burger King in Scotland! Who would have thought."

"My dad," Chris said. "He'd have a burger joint on every corner in the world if he thought he could get away with it."

"I'm glad we stopped and got a photo," Ridge said. "No one would believe us."

"Tasted different, didn't it?" Plato said. "Not bad, just different."

"Scottish cow," Patrick said. "They only eat gorse."

"Turn them loose on the golf courses, then, will ya?" Ridge said. "They need to reduce that gorse to a reasonable level."

Patrick raised his beer glass. "Good thing you didn't put me in charge of food, Gary. 'Cause we'd be eating cheese burgers every meal."

"Aye!" Ridge said, and raised his wine glass in a toast.

The Gang enjoyed a moment of humor, and Charlie finished his wine. He looked at the bottle, hoping to memorize the maker. Good wine; he might be able to find it when he got back home.

"Hey, Pops."

Charlie opened his eyes. Patrick was leaning over him, shaking his shoulder.

"You might want to walk back to the hotel with us," Patrick said, a twinkle in his eye. "The chef wants to go home."

Charlie realized he'd fallen asleep. He pushed himself out of the chair. The room was empty. "They all leave us here?"

"That would be funny, wouldn't it," Patrick said. "No, they're waiting outside. I think they needed some fresh air to clear the wine from their heads."

Charlie followed Patrick up the stairs from the cellar. The rest of the Gang stood on the sidewalk, chatting and laughing.

"Hey, Charlie!" Rudy said. "Are we keeping you up now? You want a cab back?"

Charlie wriggled his face a bit. "Actually, a cab might be nice. I don't relish that long walk back."

"Turns out it's not a long walk," Vandeweghe said, wryly. "The waitress gave us better directions back to the hotel. I was right, we should have gone the other way at that first corner."

The Gang began walking slowly down the lane.

Rudy rolled his eyes. "Guess the guy is a schmuck. Disappointing."

Charlie chuckled. "Maybe we looked like we needed to walk off some burgers." He gave Chris a friendly elbow in the ribs.

Chris feigned wounded ribs, and friendly banter continued until they reached the Rusacks Hotel. The Gang paused to watch the moon rise over the Old Course. Charlie sighed. The moonlight made the course look tame, benevolent, and beautiful. He knew otherwise. Oh, it was always beautiful, but rarely subdued, and never benign. Charlie smiled a bit to himself. *Golfer Beware* should be the motto of this place.

One by one, the Gang said their good nights and entered the hotel. Charlie paused at the door.

Patrick still stood on the sidewalk. "I'm gonna stay down here for a few minutes." He grinned and raised an eyebrow. "Soak up the ambiance."

Charlie grunted. "You do that. See you upstairs."

All in all, a good day, he decided. A good day, indeed. And made better by Patrick's presence. For Charlie, that made the trip worth every penny, every pain, and certainly every point of principle won and lost in an argument with his pals. Watching Patrick was, for him, the most memorable part of this trip.

CHAPTER 37

September 3, 1998
Patrick Quinn

Patrick watched his Pops enter the Rusacks Hotel. When he was sure Charlie had truly gone up to their room, Patrick crossed the road to the short wooden fence that separated the town of St Andrews from the eighteenth fairway of the Old Course. He leaned on the fence and immersed himself in the view. It was a melancholy but glorious sight, and Patrick was surprised by the emotions it stirred within him.

This is where it all began for every golfer out there. Here, on this little patch of Mother Earth. This wispy, scruffy, wind and rain-swept scrap of dirt. It was perfect in its imperfections, glorious in its simplicity. The birthplace of golf.

Patrick pulled a bulky cell phone from his pocket and dialed. He was glad he'd brought it with him, though the European service cost him a fortune. He hadn't actually used it much, but it had been handy to call home.

He calculated the hour. Midnight here; one in the afternoon there. Sue would be home, doing what she did while she waited for the girls to return from school.

"Hello?" Sue's voice was clear across the line and Patrick envisioned her standing before him, in the middle of the fairway, holding the handset against her beautiful face and looking at him with that particularly beguiling look she often had.

"Hello?" she said again.

"Hey, it's me," Patrick said.

"Well hello there!" Sue said. "What are you doing calling me? Isn't it late there? Shouldn't you be in bed? Don't you have an early tee time tomorrow, or something?"

Patrick smiled. Always the caretaker, mother, wife. "It's midnight, and I'm standing on the eighteenth fairway of the Old Course. The moon is up, the tower is lit up with this amazing glow, it's just–" Tears welled up in his eyes. "I wish you were here."

There was a slight pause, then in a voice filled with warm humor, Sue said, "Would you please…"

Patrick chuckled through the tears. She wasn't buying any of it, of course. Sue was always the pragmatic one.

"Don't get all emotional on me over there," she said. "Go have fun on your little golf trip. I'll see you in another week."

Patrick laughed, and relief washed over him in waves. "Yeah, you will. But someday I'm gonna bring you and the girls here. It's really fascinating."

"Only if the golf clubs stay in the garage," Sue said. "I won't be a golf widow on my vacation."

"It's a deal," Patrick said. But of course he could always rent a set.

They chatted a few more minutes about the girls, school, the pump in the pool, which was starting to fail. Then with no more sentiment than she would have expressed had he been calling from the country club, Sue said goodnight and hung up.

Patrick put the phone back in his pocket and sighed. He felt particularly blessed. He'd just spoken with the love of his life, and his mistress lay before him in the moonlight, beckoning.

With one last look, he crossed the street and entered the hotel. He'd need sleep if he was to successfully entertain this mistress tomorrow. She was bound to be demanding.

Patrick smiled a little.

He was the luckiest guy alive.

CHAPTER 38

September 4, 1998

Chris Clark and Rudy Staedler

Rudy woke with a start. Where was he? He could hear movement in the room, but it was still dark. He sat up.

"Did I wake you?" Plato asked. "Sorry, I didn't mean to wake you."

Rudy slowly remembered. Scotland. Gang of Eight. St Andrews.

"No, you didn't wake me," he mumbled.

Plato harrumphed in disbelief. "Then why are you sitting up talking? Go back to sleep."

"What time is it?" Rudy asked. It felt like some ridiculously early hour.

"Four in the morning," Plato said.

So it was a ridiculous hour. "What are you doing up?" Rudy asked. "Go back to sleep yourself." He flipped on a small bedside lamp. The warm glow filled the room with shadows.

Plato sat in his bed, the blanket rumpled. "I can't sleep."

Rudy wrestled his pillow into a comfortable position behind his back and leaned against the headboard. "Bad food last night? I thought it tasted pretty good, but it was awfully late."

Plato smiled ruefully. "I doubt this has anything to do with the food."

"You okay?" Rudy asked. It wasn't like his friend to be troubled.

Plato chuckled a bit. "Never better." He settled back against his headboard as well, then paused. Finally, he smiled ruefully. "You're looking at me like Lynea does when she thinks I have the flu or something. Stop being a mother hen."

Rudy stuffed his pillow back down onto the mattress and flopped into a lying position. "Fine. Keep your thoughts to yourself. I'm going back to sleep."

There was quiet for some moments. Plato did not turn off the light, and Rudy lay with his back to his friend, eyes closed. He was beginning to doze back to sleep when Plato said, "Okay, I'm worried."

Rudy opened his eyes. "About what?" he muttered.

"The game today," Plato said. "I know that sounds utterly ridiculous."

Rudy chuckled sleepily, and rolled over to look at Plato. "Yes, yes it does sound ridiculous. Why in the devil are you worried about a game?"

Plato shook his head, then said nothing, and Rudy could tell he was searching for words. This is silly, he thought, then recollected something Bev said to their grandchildren all the time. He emulated his wife's tone and said, "Indoor voice. Use your words."

Plato laughed. "Yeah, really. Okay, this is the thing. We've brought all these guys over here, at great expense. And the whole focus of the trip has been on preparing for the Old Course." He took a deep breath, exhaled, then quietly said, "But what if it's a flop? What if they don't like it, or they play lousy, or something happens with the tee times and we can't all play? I mean, Gooch just got confirmation this evening that we had the second time. Jeez, a myriad of things can go wrong."

Rudy leaned up on an elbow. "How could they possibly not like it? And what difference is it if they play lousy? Not any of them have played badly since we arrived. Hell, I've played the worst of all, I think, and you don't see me complaining." Plato shot a look that clearly stated he thought the last comment was bogus. Rudy grinned. "Okay, so maybe Chris has played worse."

"That chip on sixteen on the Arran," Plato said, fondness warming his voice. "And how many balls has he lost to the gorse?" He shook his head. "That poor kid..."

"There's nothing poor about that guy," Rudy said. "So you can stop worrying about him. I don't see him crying in his soup at night, do you?"

Plato sighed, but Rudy could tell his friend was lightening up. He flopped back down on his bed and punched his pillow into a comfortable shape. "I'll bet you dinner they all play lights out this afternoon. And Gooch is not going to let anything happen to the tee times, so stop worrying about that." He snuggled into the blanket and closed his eyes. "Now go back to sleep, or you'll be the one whining about your lousy game."

He heard Plato turn off the light and relax back into his blankets. Soon, his friend's breathing became steady and shallow, and Rudy knew he'd fallen asleep. My turn, he thought. With memories of the first time he'd played the Old Course, he slowly drifted back to sleep.

Chris trotted down the hall to the small "lift." He'd awoken early, all excited for the day, then drifted back to sleep and slept through his alarm, as well as Don's movements through the room. Now Chris was late for breakfast, and since they only had one tee time confirmed, he really wanted to be there in case they arm-wrestled for a place.

"Come on, come on," he mumbled at the closed elevator doors. "It's only two floors."

Finally it showed up. Chris jumped in and punched the first floor button a dozen times. The doors slowly slid closed.

"I was beginning to think you'd chickened out," Patrick said when Chris slid into the chair beside him.

Chris signaled a passing waitress. "Can I have a full Scottish breakfast, please?" The waitress nodded and trotted off.

"Can't believe Don didn't wake me," Chris said.

"He was gonna send me up in five minutes if you hadn't arrived," Patrick said. "He wouldn't have let you miss it."

Chris felt mollified, but he didn't feel his body relax until the coffee arrived and he'd gulped down a steaming cup. He glanced around the table.

The rest of the guys were almost done with their breakfast. Chris's plate arrived as Plato stood and commanded attention.

"Laddies, we've arrived," he said. "The Kingdom of Fife, on the Firth of Forth. You are about to stand on the same tee upon which every great golfer has stood." He paused for effect, looking directly at every man at the table. "Count yourselves lucky."

Chris nodded in agreement. He did, indeed, feel lucky. Plato continued.

"Today we begin the Scottish Stroke Play Championship," he said. "Golf the old way! Individual gross. Tee it high and let it fly. And hole all the putts!"

Plato sat and Vandeweghe waved his hand. "Before you all run off helter-skelter, I should tell you when you play."

"We did get a second tee time, then?" Charlie asked.

"For ten this morning," Vandeweghe said. "Which is why we called you to breakfast at the ungodly hour of eight." He gave Chris a funny look. "Some of us managed to get here on time."

Chris waved his fork in the air as he swallowed. "Hey, I was up at five this morning. It's the rest of you who are slackers."

Vandeweghe ruffled the air with the fingers of his left hand. "Yeah, yeah, whatever," he said. "So Plato and I flipped a coin, and here are the foursomes. Ten o'clock: Chris, Charlie, Ridge, and Plato. One-thirty: P.Q., Rudy, Scooter, and me. I'd suggest hiring at least one caddy for each foursome, especially the morning group, where I won't be there to help you find your way through Miss Grainger's bosoms, over the Coffins, and around Hell Bunker." He wadded up the scrap of paper upon which he'd written the foursomes, and tossed it onto his plate. "Oh, and happy birthday to Mr. Don Ridge!"

A slew of "happy birthday!" congratulations were offered by the Gang, and Ridge graciously accepted them.

Vandeweghe stood, authoritatively. "And now, anyone here to play golf?"

Chris took a last swallow of coffee and stood along with the rest of the Gang. He was glad he was going out with the morning group. He didn't know if he could wait until one-thirty to play. Vandeweghe, Patrick, Rudy, and Don squeezed into the lift to return to their rooms, and Plato led Chris and the others toward the clubhouse. As Plato had been there before, albeit quite a while ago, he was still the one with the local knowledge, and Chris followed him willingly. They made arrangements for one caddy and three trolleys, then went to the parking lot and retrieved their clubs from the trailer.

"Where's Ken?" Chris asked, wondering where their unobtrusive driver disappeared to at times like these.

Plato shrugged. "Too early for the pub," he said good-naturedly. "Maybe having a big breakfast in town."

They shouldered their bags and walked back to the course. Chris felt like he needed to pinch himself. It was as if he'd landed inside the post card of St Andrews he'd had, as a young man, thumb nailed to the cork board in his bedroom.

Their caddy was waiting when they arrived. As Chris expected, the caddy was older, but tidy in both appearance and behavior. Not a drop of liquor had passed his lips before he arrived; though, Chris reminded himself, it was only nine-forty-five in the morning. Names were exchanged, and they learned the caddy's was Albert. He'd been a caddy for forty-two years now. All four of the Gang had agreed the caddy would carry Charlie's bag, but yes, Albert said he'd be happy to help all of them with their direction on the course.

"Oh, aye, for sure you'll all be needin' to know which way to hit," he said. "The Ol' Course is a tricky lass. She'll punish ya hard if you're not knowing where to go."

As Albert led them to the first tee, Ridge sidled up to Chris. "Did you get any of that?" He motioned his beard toward Albert. "I have no idea what he said."

Chris chuckled. "Basically, aim where he tells you or you're screwed."

"Ah. Far be it from me to argue with the man," Ridge said. "He looks like he'd take my five iron to my backside if I did."

After what felt like an eternity, the starter called their time. In silent agreement, Chris, Charlie, and Ridge all looked to Plato to start. The pro looked back, and seemed about to argue the point, then nodded decisively, grabbed his driver from his bag, and stepped up onto the tee.

Chris took a deep breath and looked around. The history of the place seemed to permeate the very air. The clubhouse for The Royal and Ancient Golf Club of St Andrews stood sentry over him. People lounged everywhere, watching. In fact ... Chris smiled and waved, for there stood Vandeweghe, Patrick, Rudy, and Don. They trotted down and joined Chris alongside the tee.

"Nice shot, pro," Rudy said to Plato, who had sailed his first drive down the fairway, just left of center as Albert had suggested.

Ridge next stepped up to the tee.

"Hey Ridge, what could be better than playing the Old Course on your birthday?" Don said.

Ridge turned and wiggled his beard. "Well, it could be my thirty-third or forty-fourth birthday, rather than my sixty-sixth!"

"Ah, go shoot your age," Vandeweghe said. "Challenge the course record."

"And mine," Ridge said, then hit a slight hook which landed in the mounds on the left. Albert quickly assured him he had a good shot to the green from there, and not to worry.

Then Charlie got up, placed his ball, and turned to the small gallery of his friends. "You know, I've driven this hole before. But never with all of you sandbaggers standing around, watching." He graced them with his best lopsided smile. "I'm awfully glad you're all here to see this." He promptly addressed the ball and with his stiff but highly effective swing, sent the ball shooting over Granny Clark's Wynd toward the Swilcan Burn, which dissected the fairway, just in front of the green.

"That's my Pops," Patrick said with obvious pride.

Chris stepped up and teed his ball. He was dying to take a practice swing, but Vandeweghe had explained they were particularly frowned upon at the Old Course. "Pace of play," Vandeweghe had explained. "And the attitude that you should just get up and hit the ball. Besides, it doesn't help – the blasted ball's gonna go where it's gonna go, regardless. That's just the nature of the links game."

Chris looked down the broad fairway and felt his muscles relax. It was like driving onto a bunch of football fields; it was huge! Essentially he had two fairways, so he couldn't miss. What's the worry? He waggled once, checked his line, and exhaled. Rip it, he thought, and swung.

The ball screamed up the fairway, flirted with a slice, then straightened out and dropped to earth, rolling to a stop just short of the burn.

Feeling like Superman, Chris turned to his friends. Thumbs up, fist pumps, and low hoots were his reward.

"Monster crush!" Patrick said. "You're lucky if you have fifty yards to the green."

Chris stuffed his driver in his bag. "I'm playing the Old Course. What are you turkeys doing?"

"Watching you start the round of your life," Vandeweghe said "Have fun!"

Chris followed the others down the fairway.

"I'll bring a rope in case I have to rescue you from Hell Bunker!" Patrick called after him.

Chris waved in response but focused on the hole ahead.

Rudy rubbed his palms together and watched his four friends march away from the tee. "Well?"

Vandeweghe looked back at the clubhouse. "Would you like a tour of the R & A?"

Rudy was surprised by the uncertainty in Vandeweghe's voice. Was he kidding?

Don hummed and Patrick's face turned pink. Rudy's mouth opened to say something, but nothing came out. Vandeweghe looked crestfallen.

"Well, okay, sorry I asked," he said. "I just thought maybe you'd like to see the inside –"

The three men pounced on him. "Yes!!" "Of course!" "Are you nuts!"

"Jeez, Gooch," Rudy said. "I'd give my eye teeth to see the R & A. I'll even race you there." He jogged off in an exaggerated manner, circled, and returned to his friends.

Vandeweghe was shaking his head and laughing. "You're a beauty. If you weren't one of my best pals, I'd be embarrassed to be seen with you." He strode toward the Rusacks Hotel, passing the clubhouse.

Rudy exchanged a look of surprise with Don and Patrick.

"Hey, Gooch," Patrick said. "The, uh, clubhouse is…" He jerked his thumb, pointing over his shoulder.

"Yeah, yeah," Vandeweghe said. "Of course it is. Oh! Yeah. Sorry, forgot to explain. We'll need coats and ties. That is, if you want to see the whole place. Otherwise, you're only allowed in the library, the men's locker room in the basement, and the club storage room." He paused at the door to the hotel. "Well?"

Don pulled open the door to the hotel and held it. "Coat and tie sounds really good to me. I'll even play in it, if I have to."

Patrick passed him and entered the hotel. "You'll be mistaken for a caddy. You're almost as short."

"But he has better teeth," Rudy said, and followed them in.

Fifteen minutes later they were at the Royal and Ancient Clubhouse, dressed appropriately. Rudy noticed Vandeweghe was sporting the official dark blue R & A Member's tie. Well, why not. Where else was he going to wear it without getting razzed mercilessly?

Rudy followed Vandeweghe into a small, glass enclosed porch. Patrick leaned close to him and said, "I feel like I just got the proverbial shoulder tap." Rudy agreed.

"This way, fellas," Vandeweghe said and led them into the clubhouse proper.

Rudy immediately noticed a simple but gleaming cabinet and its contents. "Is that...?"

Vandeweghe stood beside the ceiling high cabinet and gave it the Vanna White, double handed unveiling. "Here you are, gents. The Claret Jug."

Rudy studied the renowned trophy. How many famous hands had held that cup over their heads in victory? He read the names that appeared on the side facing the glass. He distinctly remembered, and could picture in his mind, at least twenty of them.

"It's a lot bigger than it looks on television," Don said. "I'll bet it's a lot heavier, too."

"I understand it has some weight to it," Vandeweghe said.

"Young bucks," Don said. "They can lift anything at that age."

Patrick chuckled. "Young, my foot. I don't care what age I am. If I win the Open Championship, I'd be able to life a tank over my head. Adrenaline would take over."

"Humph," Rudy grunted. "Who cares about the heart attack after that."

Motion to his right caught his eye. Sitting behind a large round desk was a tall, young man wearing what could only be described as a spiffy uniform. He was silently observing them with a warm and welcome smile, his hands folded on a leather-bound notebook.

"Hello," Rudy said. "Sorry, I didn't see you there."

"I often take a back seat to the Jug," the man said, then stood and nodded at Vandeweghe. "Good morning, Mr. Vandeweghe. Nice to see you t'day. Are ya playing?"

"Absolutely," Vandeweghe said. "Fellas, this is one of our fine hall porters, Ford Horsfield." Vandeweghe introduced each of the Gang, who promptly shook Ford's hand with a warm "hello." Rudy noticed it was a strong, firm grip.

Mr. Horsfield crossed his arms on his broad chest after he shook Patrick's hand. "A Quinn, are ya?" he said. "Irish, then?"

Patrick chuckled. "As Irish as a pint of Guinness. I just have American labeling."

"Beefed up, and watered-down," Don said. "I'm sorry to say this American version can hold far more liquor than his ancestors."

Mr. Horsfield rocked back on his heels. "Oh, aye. I've heard ya boys from across th' pond will drink a man under the table, for sure they will."

"I know we have a few Scottish caddies who could give him a run for his money," Vandeweghe said, half in jest. He moved to a door on the left of the entrance hall. "So here's the library."

Rudy and the others stepped into the small room. It held a bar, as well as floor-to-ceiling shelves of leather-bound books. A strange shiny object in a trophy case caught Rudy's attention, as well as that of the others.

"What is that?" Don asked, moving toward the case. Rudy and Patrick joined him. Inside the case were two old putters laden with silver golf balls. They were bunched together, resembling a fat bunch of shiny metal grapes.

Vandeweghe took a deep breath and exhaled slowly. "I was afraid you'd ask about that. Okay. This, gentlemen, is the Captains' Balls."

"The Captains' Balls," Don repeated, dumbfounded.

"No wonder there's so few Captains," Patrick said. "They castrate the poor bastards."

The men laughed, then Vandeweghe explained. "It's part of the initiation for the new Captains. The new guy tees up a ball on the first tee and hits the ball out onto the first fairway. Then all the caddies race out to get it. The one who returns it to the Captain gets a doubloon, a five pound gold coin. The ball is then painted silver and attached to one of these putters."

Rudy shrugged. "Sounds harmless. But I'm sure there's a wicked story attached to it, somewhere."

"Well," Vandeweghe said, and squirmed a little. "At the Annual Dinner, they do make the new members kiss the Captains' Balls. Everyone gets a kick out of it. By the way, with all the silver golf balls, those putters are really heavy."

Rudy winced, then joined Don and Patrick in laughing.

"Okay, enough of this," Vandeweghe said. "Let me show you the rest of the place." They crossed the entrance hall, and he pointed out the club storage room. Then, with a nod to Mr. Horsfield, Vandeweghe led them up the stairs.

"Hey Gooch," Rudy said. "Do you leave a set of sticks here?"

"Naw," Vandeweghe said. "They'd grow mold. I'm not here enough."

"How often are you here?" Don said. "It feels like you never leave San Jose."

"I didn't," Vandeweghe said. "Especially when we were taking Cobra public. I couldn't get twenty feet from my office. Now I can get away, but I'm too busy with other stuff to travel all the time. I guess I get over here about twice a year, if I'm lucky."

They toured the offices, board rooms, and private sanctuaries that made up the top two floors, and Rudy was relieved it was Saturday and no one was at work. He would have felt uncomfortable admiring the rooms if they'd been occupied by employees and members, especially the Secretary's office, which sported elegant, dark wood furniture, tall, graceful windows, and French doors that opened onto a porch overlooking the first tee. However, empty as the offices were, they simply invited Rudy to selfishly enjoy this moment of golf history voyeurism.

They returned to the first floor and Vandeweghe led them into the large, classically appointed and appropriately named Big Room. At the large windows that lined one wall, Rudy found himself looking out onto a spectacular view. He was joined by the others, and Vandeweghe defined what they were seeing.

"First and eighteenth holes, of course." He pointed off to the side. "Then those are the Himalayas, otherwise known as the Ladies Putting Course, which is not for the twitchy or faint of heart."

"Appropriately named, then," Patrick said.

Vandeweghe pointed to the other side. "On this side, almost straight over the first green, is the Old Course Hotel."

There were several members lounging in the room, individually and in small groups, their voices hushed and reverent. The Gang drifted away from the window, and began looking at the many pictures that graced the walls. Rudy felt a bit like he'd walked into the inner sanctum of a church. He wove toward Don, who stood beside a large, ornate desk. "What'd you find?"

Don pointed at a stack of paper. "Letterhead. You want to write a letter to someone? You can use the official R & A letterhead." He opened a drawer. "There's envelopes, too."

Rudy chuckled. "Would it be kosher to write a letter to myself?"

Don hummed and his eyes sparkled. "No, but I'll write one to you if you'll write one to me."

Vandeweghe joined them. "You two want something to drink? There's coffee and tea, and you can order cocktails, or whatever you want. Help yourself and get comfortable. I'm gonna hit the head. Be back in a moment."

Vandeweghe sauntered out of the Big Room, pausing once to greet a fellow member. Rudy and Don each poured a cup of tea, and Rudy was pleasantly surprised to find it was quality, loose tea. Oh heaven, he thought as he streamed hot water through the strainer; real tea. They joined Patrick in a corner arrangement that faced the large windows.

"Slap me," Patrick said. "I gotta be dreaming."

"I'm not going to slap you," Rudy said. "I'm in this dream with you. I don't want you to wake up!"

They grew quiet, sipped their tea, and gazed out the tall windows onto the green course beyond. At least twenty minutes passed, and Rudy began to wonder where Vandeweghe had gone. As if reading his mind, Don said, "Where'd Gooch go?"

"Said he was going to the head," Patrick said. "Must have had to go to Machrihanish to find one."

"What, they don't have bathrooms at the R & A?" Don said.

Rudy leaned toward his friends and, in a low voice, said, "Too tawdry. Only the common man pees." Patrick and Don chortled. "It's true!" Rudy nodded in an exaggerated manner. "I read it in Golf Weekly. No potties necessary for the Golf Gods."

"No wonder Gooch only comes here twice a year," Patrick said. "Hard on an ass –"

"Hey, hey!" Rudy cut in quickly, as Don simultaneously added, "Watch yourself."

"What?" Patrick said, and looked genuinely contrite. "I'm talking anatomy, not personality. Jeez, guys. You really think I'm that hypocritical?" He swung his arm in an arc. "Notice where I'm sitting?"

"Okay, my apologies," Rudy said, and meant it. Patrick was the most appreciative kid he'd ever met. He chided himself for thinking Patrick might have been disrespectful. Heck, the kid probably didn't even know what the word meant.

Don pointed out the window. "Check out this guy."

A small, thin man in black pants and a brown, tightly buttoned tweed jacket was walking briskly up the eighteenth fairway. He had a cap precariously perched upon his head, and only one club in his hand. By the look of its length, Rudy assumed it might be a three or four iron. There wasn't a caddy to be seen within his vicinity, though a foursome appeared to have paused behind him in the fairway, waiting.

The man reached a ball and, without breaking stride or taking a stance, smacked it with the iron. The ball skidded along the fairway, hopping and hurdling from one grassy patch to another for about a hundred yards. Without a break in tempo, the man continued to where the ball came to a rest and repeated his drive-by smack. In this manner, he reached the Valley of Sin in three strokes, whacked it out of the Valley and onto the green, and then proceeded to putt it into the hole in two strokes – while using only the iron in his grasp.

A muffled smattering of applause came from the bystanders near the eighteenth green. The man, who Rudy could now see must be in his eighties or nineties, tipped his cap in acknowledgment and quickly moved beyond Rudy's view, toward town.

Don hummed happily and Patrick joined Rudy in an amazed grin.

"Do you believe that?" Rudy said. "What a kick!"

"Out for his morning constitutional," Don said.

Patrick sat back in his chair. "That's one way to ensure you never make it into one of these bunkers. Maybe Chris should give it a try."

Just then, Vandeweghe returned, blowing into the room like a gust of summer wind. He paused again at another table of members and chatted before joining Rudy, Don, and Patrick.

"So you guys hungry?" he asked, and clapped his hands together. "Let's get a proper lunch."

Rudy set his teacup on a nearby table. "Where we going? I hear there's some good restaurants in town."

"Well, yes, we can go into town, if you want to," Vandeweghe said. "But I thought maybe you'd like to eat here. Food's pretty good."

Rudy turned to Patrick. "Okay, now it's your turn to slap me. That dream just got better."

"Where's the dining room?" Patrick asked. "Did we miss it?"

Vandeweghe nodded and led them from the room. "I didn't want to ruin the surprise." They went back up to the second floor, and crossed to a set of doors they'd passed earlier. Vandeweghe opened one and ushered them in.

Rudy sighed. If the Big Room was beautiful, this was heavenly. The windows faced the same direction, but at this height, the view was even more complete. The tables were set with china, crystal, and silver. Rudy felt as if he'd walked into a five-star London restaurant. He knew he had a ridiculously cheesy grin on his face, but he didn't care.

Lunch was more than "pretty good;" it was fabulous. The four men chatted about the trip thus far, and all at the table agreed that, with the exception of Barassie, it had been everything for which they'd hoped. Vandeweghe gave them a member's perspective on the Old Course, filling in with humorous anecdotes from his own rounds.

Two men entered the dining room. Vandeweghe paused in mid-sentence, and stared at them.

"See a ghost?" Rudy asked, turning to see what had caught his friend's attention.

Vandeweghe had a bewildered look on his face. Not a look with which Rudy was familiar, he realized.

"That guy has on a Cypress Point member's tie," Vandeweghe said. "But I don't recognize him."

"Maybe he's a new member," Don said. "When was the last time you were there?"

Vandeweghe thought, then said, "About a month ago. But, yeah, certainly there are members I don't know, and there are a few who don't go often." Their meal was done, so Vandeweghe pushed back from the table. "You guys don't mind if I go over and introduce myself, do you? Order dessert. It's great. I'll be right back."

Rudy watched as he crossed to the two gentlemen. Vandeweghe introduced himself and the man with the tie gave his name and shook Vandeweghe's hand. Vandeweghe pointed at the tie and innocently said, "I'm a member at Cypress Point, and I noticed you are as well. Obviously we've never met, so I thought I'd just introduce myself. Nice that we meet here at St Andrews."

To Rudy's – and clearly Vandeweghe's surprise – the man began sputtering.

"Oh, well, er, um – I'm not actually a member..." He stroked the tie as if hoping the insignia could be rubbed off. "You see, a good friend of mine is a member at Cypress Point, and, well, I obviously needed a tie to have lunch, so he lent me this one..."

Rudy began grinning widely. He glanced at Don and Patrick; both were eavesdropping as well, and were clearly having as much fun as he, listening to this guy back-track. The man's lunch partner excused himself and almost ran from the room.

Vandeweghe became very stiff, and Rudy knew his friend was controlling some bubbling anger. "So you're not a member of Cypress Point?" Vandeweghe said. "Who's your friend? At Cypress –"

"Oh, I'm sure you don't know him," the man said. "He's a very new member."

"Who obviously needs to be informed you don't lend out the member tie," Vandeweghe said. "It's to be worn only by members. I'd be happy to drop him a kindly note, if you'll give me his name."

Rudy watched the man turn three shades of red in two seconds. He really felt for the guy. What a horrible predicament! The entire dining room had become quiet; all were listening to the saga unfold. Some were blatantly staring at the man in amazement, others were still eating, but clearly paying close attention, still others were obviously making an effort to control their laughter. This was this guy's worst nightmare.

The man stood with as much dignity as he could muster under the circumstances. "Er, Mr. uh, Vande–-?"

"Van-de-way," Gucci said, over exaggerating the pronunciation. "Gary Vandeweghe."

"Well, yes, Mr. Vandeweghe…" He looked past Gucci, and Rudy noticed the man's friend was standing at the door to the Dining Room, beckoning. "Oh!" the man cried, and began walking toward the door. "My friend here is calling. I'll just, uh, yes…" He paused at the door. "Nice to have met you!"

And he was gone.

The room broke into nervous laughter, then became a buzz with excited conversation. Vandeweghe stood for a moment longer, hands on his hips, then returned to the table. Rudy couldn't believe what he'd just witnessed.

"What a jerk!" Vandeweghe said. "I actually feel embarrassed for him."

"What a place to get busted!" Rudy said. "St Andrews. Jeez."

"I'll bet he's burning that tie, right now," Don said.

Patrick chuckled. "I wonder where he got it? They're not just lying around on the ground."

"Or even in the Cypress Point pro shop," Vandeweghe said. "You couldn't walk in and buy one. And wearing a member's tie when you're not – wow, what a huge no, no, never."

"He won't set foot in here again," Patrick said.

"There isn't a hole small enough for him to crawl into," Don said.

Rudy motioned toward the door. "Don't look now, but you're being proved wrong."

The entire room seemed to turn as one and watch as the man and his companion returned to their table. Rudy noted that the man was now wearing a conservative blue and red striped tie. They were very focused on each other, laughing and talking loudly about nothing in particular, and Rudy felt a twinge of admiration. You had to give the guy credit for having balls.

The Gang ordered dessert, coffee, and tea. Rudy surveyed the view through the window as Patrick answered some vague question about his father's business, which had been asked to focus attention away from the incident. Dessert arrived, and the diversion shifted.

"Still can't believe that guy," Vandeweghe said, and swallowed a huge spoonful of ice cream.

Don hummed and tore his overly large chocolate chip cookie in half. "Pretty gutsy."

"Uh oh," Patrick said, interrupting them. "Might want to change the subject."

To Rudy's utmost astonishment, the man was heading their way.

"You're kidding?" Vandeweghe said, and turned in time to meet the man face to face.

"Excuse me, Mr. Vandeweghe," the man said, and stroked his new tie as if to draw attention to it.

Vandeweghe just stared at him, and Rudy bit his lip to keep from bursting out in hysterics. Vandeweghe looked completely confounded.

"Yes?" Vandeweghe finally managed to say.

"I just wanted to apologize for what was evidently a large faux pas," the man said.

Vandeweghe nearly choked. "Evidently?"

"Let me buy you all a drink, to make up for the misunderstanding," the man said. He motioned toward a waitress. "What are you all having? Whatever you'd like."

The waitress arrived, only to be waived away by Vandeweghe. "Thank you, but it's not necessary. We're heading out for a game in a few minutes."

"Oh, of course, of course," the man said. "Then let me get you a bottle of wine for when you return. Would you prefer red or white?" He waved his hand nervously, and continued without waiting for an answer. "Silly of me. Let me just buy you one of each. That's the least I can do."

"Yes, silly of you," Vandeweghe said. "But again, not necessary." He checked his watch. "Gentlemen, it's twelve-forty. Should we don our golf togs and hit the links?"

They all stood, and the man stepped back, but did not leave. Rudy wondered if he was ever going to get the hint, or if he planned on following them around the course, bowing and scraping apologies.

The Gang moved toward the door, and the man inserted himself beside Vandeweghe. "I just wanted to make it clear that I didn't know about the tie," he said, quietly. "I thought it was just a nice looking one … didn't have any idea it was a *member's* tie."

Vandeweghe stopped outside the dining room and, pulling himself up to his full height, stared at the man with a mix of amazement and disgust. Rudy, again, caught himself biting his lip.

"I'd greatly appreciate it if we could keep this little incident quiet," the man continued. "I don't want to get my, um, friend – you know, who's the Cypress member – don't want to get him in any trouble."

"I'd still like to know his name," Vandeweghe said.

The man fumbled in a pocket for a moment, then pulled out a small business card. "Here's my card." He handed it to Vandeweghe, who surprisingly took it. "Again, I'd like to buy you a few bottles of wine, so just check with the porter tomorrow. And maybe we can have a drink sometime, or a game – yes, that would be great, wouldn't it? If ever you're in Glasgow, just give me a call. I can get us on any course you'd like. On me, of course."

Vandeweghe glanced at the door, clearly trying to escape. "Yes, well, thanks anyway. Now, if you'll excuse me, we have a game." He turned to his friends. "Come on fellas."

Reluctantly, the man stood aside, and Vandeweghe launched himself down the stairs, with Rudy, Don, and Patrick closely behind. They'd gone only a few steps when Rudy heard the man call after them.

"Thank you, Mr. Vandeweghe, for being so nice about all this! Very understanding of you!"

Rudy knew Vandeweghe well enough to know he was not being understanding, at least not on the inside. Rudy half expected Gooch to turn and light into the guy, but they continued down the stairs.

They reached the porter and Vandeweghe tossed the man's card on the table. "Ford, can you find out who this –" he looked at the card, "Professor Lickrish is? I'd like to know if he's an R & A member, or someone's guest."

The porter nodded and pocketed the card. "As you wish, Mr. Vandeweghe. I'll do me best."

"Thanks," Vandeweghe said with sincerity, and strode from the entrance hall into the glass-enclosed porch. He paused, and Rudy got the distinct impression he was collecting himself.

Patrick stretched. "I hope I make a swing after all that food." He patted his stomach. "But it tasted so good I couldn't stop eating."

Don nodded. "Watch out. This is Gooch's way of leveling the field."

Vandeweghe laughed. "If I wanted to do that, I'd have let that guy buy us drinks, or maybe that bottle of wine. There is a cellar here that would knock your socks off."

Rudy didn't doubt it. He paused and looked around at the entrance hall. It may be a very long time before he was here again – if ever.

Vandeweghe held open the door. "Come on pal. It isn't going anywhere, and you'll be back. Don't worry."

Rudy suddenly felt foolish. He followed the others to the hotel, changed back into his golf clothing, then closed the room door behind him and sighed.

The Old Course waited.

Chris stood at the edge of the tiny pot bunker and looked down at his ball. How'd he hit it *there*? He shook his head and looked around. The fairway on this part of the third hole was fairly wide, and undulated quite a bit. His drive had landed at least twenty-five yards back, and had proceeded to scoot into the bunker as if drawn by a magnet.

Plato and Charlie joined him. "How'd you find that thing, Chris?" Plato said. "Can't be ten feet across."

And nearly as deep, Chris noted.

"I think this is why they make golf balls tiny," Charlie said. "They gotta fit inside these teacup bunkers."

Chris pulled his camera from his bag. "Aw, I just threw the ball in there to get a picture." He handed Plato the camera. "Here, take one so the effort won't be wasted." He grabbed his wedge and trotted down the steep wooden stairs that gave access to the bunker's floor. He carefully swung the club to ensure he had room. Once he was convinced he wouldn't break his wrist by hitting the walls of the bunker, he wiggled his stance into the sand, set his focus, and swung.

Sand flew everywhere, and he closed his eyes and spun away.

"Holy cow!" Plato said. "That thing came straight up out of there like a rocket." He handed Chris the rake. "Here, cover your mistake."

"Chris, you made the green," Ridge said.

"Aye, that ya did," Albert said. "Too bad 'tis the fifteenth green, not th' third."

"Hey, I'll take any green I can get from down in that bucket," Chris said.

The caddy nodded curtly. "Aye, 'n ya missed th' mighty Cartgate bunker." He led them toward the green. "There's somethin' t'be said for that."

"No doubt, something unpronounceable in mixed company," Ridge said, which made Chris smile.

He was lying two on the wrong side of the big double green, but heck, it was only an eighty foot putt. What was there to whine about? He waved to hold off the foursome about to hit on to the fifteenth, trotted over and marked his ball, then waved them up and got out of the way. With his back to the moon-shaped, abysmal Cartgate Bunker, he stood in a perfect spot from which to observe all seven golfers putting. In an intricate negotiation, they noted who could be a possible disturbance to the other, and gave way accordingly. Chris loved this. It was like playing with the Saturday morning group at San Jose Country Club. Golfers everywhere, and all of them knowing their place in the dance.

Finally it was his turn. He'd seen enough to know he'd need to aim at least fifteen feet to the left of the third hole. He lined up, and gave the ball a hard whack. It leapt off the putter and Chris bit his lip. That actually might be too much.

"Look at it turn!" Plato said.

"Come on, baby," Charlie said, tilting his head toward the hole. "Come on home."

As the ball rolled off the fifteenth side of the double green and onto the property of the third, Chris followed it. The ball hit a ridge, slowed, then crossed over and picked up speed as it rolled down a slight slope. The hole loomed in its path.

"Come on, come on!" Ridge yelled. "Get in the hole!"

The ball aimed for the hole – and ran out of steam, coming to a rest eighteen inches from the cup.

Charlie, Ridge, and Plato expressed their disappointment in a collective, "Aaww!" Two of the golfers on fifteen politely applauded and Albert gave Chris a thumbs-up.

"Shucks," Plato said. "I thought I was witnessing a miracle."

Chris knocked his ball into the hole. "The miracle is making par from that little punctuation mark in the fairway."

They traversed to the fourth tee.

Ridge chuckled. "I find it a miracle just to make par from anywhere on this course."

"I resemble that remark," Charlie said, and stepped up to hit his ball.

Chris looked down the fourth fairway. Undulations and indentations created a moonscape terrain. Massive clumps of gorse reached out from the right, and Albert had warned him the elongated Cottage bunker was waiting on the left, just within his reach. His hand hovered over the three-iron; should he play it safe, or go for it? Clint Eastwood's voice popped into his mind. "Do I feel lucky?" Chris pulled the driver.

The ball, unfortunately, had obviously never seen *Dirty Harry*. Chris moaned as it sailed toward the gorse on the right.

"We'll find it, laddie," Albert said, and shouldered Charlie's bag. "No need for a provisional."

Chris wasn't so sure, but he followed the others down the fairway. Albert did, indeed, find the ball – tucked under a patch of gorse, a hundred and ten yards from the green. Plato and Charlie concurred with the wise caddie that the only shot was a low skipper back out into the fairway. Chris had no chance of making the green. At least not the one for the hole he was playing.

The other three guys made their second shots, with varying degrees of success. Chris chose a line, and smacked the ball out from under the foliage. To his amazement, it stopped short of the left bunkers.

"You found th'ridge," Albert said. "Ye'll need your wedge in, but know this green won't hold a ball."

Chris walked to his ball and gawked. A tall hump covered in grass hid his view of the green. Charlie and Albert crossed to him.

"That's unusual," Charlie said.

"Unique, all right," Chris said.

"Welcome t'the Ol' Course," Albert said. "She's got all sorts o' surprises."

Chris set up, aiming in the direction of the center of the green.

"Ay, laddie, ye don't want t'hit it there," Albert said. "Aim for th'steeple, there." He pointed. "No?" He and Charlie moved away.

Chris was certain the steeple was too far right of the hole, and thought about ignoring the caddy, then shifted his line. The ball sailed high in a beautiful arc, and came down in what Chris hoped was in the vicinity of the fourth green.

"Nice shot!" Ridge said.

To his amazement, Chris found the ball ten feet from the hole. He had a chance for par, after all. As he stood on the edge of the green, waiting for Ridge to putt, Chris looked back toward "the hump." From this vantage point, it was hidden. Chris rubbed a smudge of grass from the dimples on his ball. It was a unique course, for sure. He caught Albert's eye and nodded to him in thanks. The ruddy caddy grinned. With Albert to help them, the Old Course was unique. Without him, it would be downright wicked.

Chris two putted to mark a bogey on four, and proceeded to five feeling pretty good about the round, so far. He'd heard from some of the guys at San Jose that the Old Course was just a patch of weeds, a "cow pasture." Chris had expected to come here and shoot under par, especially since most of the holes weren't very long. Heck, he should have been able to drive the green on some of them. But you couldn't, safely anyway, and that's what made the course so darn fabulous for him. He was being challenged in a way he hadn't been anywhere – except maybe Western Gailes – and, well, this was the Old Course.

He turned to Albert. "So what's hiding on this hole?"

"The green, for starters," Albert said wryly. "Ye kin no tell this'n from the one for thirteen. 'Tis one big green, really. Hundred yards deep, this'n."

Chris raised his eyebrows. A green as big as a football field? "A hundred yards? Not feet?"

"Aye, laddie," Albert said. "But th' trick is t'get there."

He lined Chris up with the gorse to the left of the greens, and told him, "Take it to her, laddie." The ball sliced a bit off line, but landed safely on the fairway, just right of The Elysian Fields. His second shot sailed safely over The Spectacles bunkers, and was captured by a natural indentation that guarded the front of the green. Chris walked to the ball thinking he might make up that bogey on this hole; a birdie was possible, if the pin placement wasn't random. And he couldn't wait to see a hundred-yard deep green.

It was still a surprise, though, when Chris walked to the front edge and looked across the green. Or greens – plural – he reminded himself. The other double greens they'd played thus far still had some definition between them. You could tell which was which, really. But this was quite literally one big green with two flags stuck in polarized positions. It was ... odd. Just not something you were supposed to see on a golf course.

Chris loved it.

"You gonna play, or stand and gawk?" Charlie said. He, too, had placed his ball in the indentation. "I need a read, so have at it, will ya?"

Chris grinned. "Much obliged to be of service, my friend." He then chili-dipped his ball onto the green. It ran, and ran, and ran, finally coming to a stop some forty feet from the pin.

"I need a read to the pin on five," Charlie said, his grin lopsided, "not thirteen."

"Just helping you out for when we play the back," Chris said.

It was three more strokes with the putter before Chris heard the ball land in the cup. A bogey, again.

Ridge had not fared any better, with a double-bogey. He re-covered his putter and said with reverence, "The lesson for this hole: a big green sure doesn't mean an easy one."

Chris nodded, but the lesson for him was one he'd heard from Plato his entire life, and never really faced until now. Accept adversity in the game; no whining.

He had a feeling the next thirteen holes were going to give him many a chance to really own that lesson.

Rudy stood with Vandeweghe, Don, and Patrick, and watched the foursome ahead of them drive off on the first tee. Rudy had been twitchy on the practice green, but now he felt relaxed, calm. He glanced up at Patrick. The young Quinn was resting, both hands on his driver, looking like this was just another round at San Jose.

"What are you thinking?" Rudy asked Patrick.

Patrick looked down and smiled. "This is it."

Rudy turned to Don. The man stood as Rudy had seen him stand a hundred thousand times: propped up by his club, weight on one leg, the other crossed, one hand on his hip. The Winterhalter Stance. "Don?"

Don hummed, and gave his tightlipped grin. "What am I thinking? Don't knock it out of bounds on the right or into the burn!" Then he showed Rudy his right arm, and a serious tone came into his voice. "Look, bumps. I'm about to tee it up where the greatest golfers have teed it up. Not everybody gets to do this. I'm getting goose bumps." He shook his arm and stuffed his hand deep into his pocket. "Silly, huh?"

"Not at all," Vandeweghe said. "I'll bet more than half those guys out there felt the same way."

"What about you, Gooch?" Rudy asked. "You play here all the time. Is it still special?"

Vandeweghe glanced back at the R & A Clubhouse. He tapped the ground with his driver as he spoke. "There's always a gallery of people watching from those windows. Some of them I know; most I don't. But I always want to make a decent swing." He stopped fidgeting with his driver and focused on Rudy. "It's the most difficult shot in golf – to tee it up on the first at the Old Course. Hell, I just want to get the ball in the air!"

"And you?" Don asked Rudy. "What are you thinking?"

Rudy laughed. "I'm nervous! This is just so special, being here with you guys." He waved his gloved hand in the air. "I know, I know, that sounds mushy and all, but it's just so much darn fun. Heck, it's the Old Course we're at, not San Jose Muni!"

The starter halted conversation as he loudly stated, "One thirrr-ty tee-time, on the course!"

Patrick nodded curtly. "This is it, for real."

"Have at it, Junior," Vandeweghe said. "Show us the way."

Rudy felt a chill go up his spine when Patrick connected with the ball in a swing that sent it screaming low and straight.

Robert, their caddy, whistled low and appreciatively. "That's no in th' burn, laddie, but 'tis darn close."

Rudy stepped up next. He took a deep breath, wiggled, waggled, checked his line. Focus, he thought, then swung. The ball leapt off the sweet spot and sailed a solid two hundred and forty yards, dead straight. Rudy felt light headed. What a rush!

Don and Vandeweghe followed with drives nearly as perfect. Rudy grabbed his trolley and stepped from the tee.

They were off and running.

But after the first five holes, Rudy adjusted his assessment to "stumbling." He'd bogeyed all but the first. For reasons he couldn't discern, he was having a lot of trouble with the uneven lies he kept finding in the fairways. Once he got to the green, he was fine. It was the getting there that was causing trouble.

He felt his frustration mount on six, when he found his perfect drive sitting in a deep divot left by some lazy golfer before him. Here he'd managed to avoid all those bunkers, left and right, and he lands in a divot.

Patrick came up beside him and looked at his ball. He turned to Robert, who rested a few yards away with Vandeweghe's bag.

"Hey Your Highness," Patrick said, joking – for they'd immediately razzed Robert about his likeness to pictures of Prince Charles – "Rudy's ball has discovered a bunker not on our course maps."

Robert walked over and surveyed the lie. "Oh, aye, that ya 'ave, sir." He squinted at Rudy. "What would ya like we call it?"

Rudy shook his head as he took a stance over the ball. "You could not print for the public what I have in mind."

He swung. The ball jumped up, slicing hard.

"Not in the gorse!" he yelled. "Get out of there!" The ball disappeared, somewhere to the right of the hole. He glared at Patrick. "Don't say a word."

Patrick, eyes gleaming mischief, buttoned his lips with his fingers. Then he walked away, humming *Highway to Hell*.

Rudy chuckled and felt his frustration dissipate. It just wasn't possible to stay heated when Patrick was around.

Robert found Rudy's ball sitting pretty on the seventh tee, well clear of divots. Rudy stood over it, and looked up at the flag. Way on the other side of the double green, at least one hundred feet away, Patrick was marking his ball. Rudy paused, then, when Patrick was out of his line of sight, he chipped the ball neatly onto the green. Both Don and Vandeweghe putted in for par. As there was still a foursome on the adjacent twelfth green, and Patrick had to wait, Rudy putted, lipped out, and putted back for a bogey. He pursed his lips to keep from delivering the expressions running through his head.

The four men waited a few more moments before the twelfth was clear and Patrick could finish the sixth.

"Okay," Patrick said, pulling his ball from his pocket. "I'll go whack it back into my own zip code."

Rudy grinned. Yep, hard to stay aggravated around a Quinn. Were they ever lucky he'd come along.

By the time they'd come to the celebrated par-three eleventh hole, Rudy had felt every emotion possible on a golf course. He'd made par on seven and eight, then landed in the End Hole on nine and sculled the ball for a double bogey, then drove the green on ten, left the eagle putt short, but birdied. He was seeing more of the course than he wanted to, but things were leveling out, if not looking up.

Don had driven the tenth green as well, and shared Rudy's birdie score. Rudy realized Don was only one over for the round so far. He smiled; it was always fun to watch Don play well.

"You're up, Rudy," Don said. "You had the near eagle."

Rudy looked out at the yawning Shell Bunker and stepped back off the ball. He looked at his friends and sighed. "Man that thing's big."

"It's just a mind game," Vandeweghe said. "Played on the seven inches between your ears."

"Or in his case, four inches," Patrick whispered.

Rudy chuckled. "I heard that." He readdressed his ball.

"Nothing wrong with being a pin head," Patrick said. "You just have a compact brain."

Rudy swung. The ball sliced off line and neatly sailed over the huge bunker and landed midway between the eleventh and neighboring seventh flags. Rudy twirled his five iron. On, and safe, though he'd left himself a sassy seventy-foot putt, at the least.

Don teed his ball and swung. It soared high, and Rudy squinted as the wind caught it and pushed it right.

"Hold the line," Don said, coaxing the ball to stay between the Hill and Strath bunkers.

It landed to the right of the Strath, bounced fiercely, and shot neatly into the Shell.

"Aw, damn!" Vandeweghe said. "What an unlucky bounce!"

Don slapped the ground with his iron and shook his head, but when he looked back at the others, he was smiling.

"In the beach!" he said. "I have a fabulous chance to be a hero and hole it out from there."

After Patrick and Vandeweghe made the greens – plural, for Patrick again found the shared green rather than the intended one – Rudy tugged his trolley into obedience and walked beside Don.

"Wild bounce," he said.

Don shrugged. "That's links golf. I'm getting used to it, learning to hit different shots. You get a bad bounce – go hit it again!"

Patrick caught up with them. "And, in my case, again and again. And maybe again, again!"

Don did, indeed, nearly hole out from the Shell, airmailing a shot from the bottom of the bunker that Rudy felt should make the evening news. Even Robert clapped. They all walked away from the famous hole with par.

"Ye're lucky there, laddies," Robert said to them. "This here's one o'the toughest greens on th' course. More than not I watch 'em three or four putt. Ye tamed her today, y'did."

Robert then gathered them into a group at the twelfth tee, and – with course book in hand – gave them a rather dire description of what to expect.

"Ye'll need a bit of a longer iron 'cause th' wind'll knock it back in your face," he said, "but make sure you're left o'them far bunkers. Or ya can go t'the right, but it's more narrow, n' ya run the risk o' landin' on th' road. 'N who knows where you'll end up if that happens."

Patrick and Vandeweghe both followed directions perfectly, and watched their balls bounce happily down the left side of the fairway, cleanly avoiding trouble. Rudy chose to play it safe and lay it up a bit short of all the bunkers. His ball bounced along, as well, before skidding to a stop just short of the Stroke bunker. Don teed it up and tagged the drive better than Rudy had seen him do all day. Rudy squinted, waiting for the bounce. This was going to be good ...

"Did you see it bounce?" Don said.

"No, I didn't see it bounce," Vandeweghe said. "Anyone?"

"I missed it," Patrick said, "Did you see it bounce, Rudy?"

Rudy frowned. "I didn't see it bounce, either, and I was looking."

"Aye, laddies," Robert interrupted with a deep sigh. "Sand don't bounce."

Rudy joined the rest in laughter. Sure enough, once they reached their balls, they found Don's planted in the small pot bunker, seventy yards from the green.

"Well, there's a new lesson for you," Rudy said. "Sand don't bounce."

Don chuckled and trotted down the wooden stairs to the floor of the bunker. "Aye, laddie," he said, mimicking Robert. "That it doesn't."

Chris walked down the fairway of the fourteenth hole and hoped to high heaven Albert was wrong.

"I do believe y've landed in Hell," Albert had said after Chris duffed his second shot, which had been resting in a horrible lie. "You're about t'see what th' Ol' girl can dish out."

"Well?" Plato said, coming up behind Chris. "What's it look like?"

Chris chuckled. "Hell."

The bunker was shaped like a deformed cashew, and was dug into a mound of earth at least six feet high on the side facing the green. Chris's ball was deep into the narrow left channel.

"Hit it back onto the fairway," Plato said.

"Backwards?" Chris said. He pointed. "The green's over there."

"And so is that wall of peat," Plato said. "Remember the Open in '95. Nicklaus took four shots to get out of this very bunker. I think he ended up with a ten on this hole, if I'm not mistaken. Ordinarily I'd suggest being in his company on a round, but not in this instance." He walked away.

Chris grabbed his sand wedge and stomped across the sand to his ball. The wall of peat before him was almost over his head. He took a stance and visualized the shot he'd need to get over the bunker face.

"Impossible," he muttered. He walked around to the other side of his ball and carefully swung his wedge to ensure he had a full swing. To his dismay, the club bounced into the peat not halfway into his backswing. He moved around the ball, trying to find a stance that allowed him a swing, and still gave the ball a chance. The only direction he could go was sideways out of the bunker, which put him in the deep rough between the ends of the "cashew." He took a deep breath, and swung.

The ball popped up, ricocheted off the peat, bounced toward the tee, and landed back in the bunker. Chris swore to himself and stomped to the ball. Out of the corner of his eye he could see Albert watching. Chris realized he should swallow his pride and pitch it back out onto the fairway in the direction of the tee, but he had a swing here, and the hole was over there. He dug his feet into the sand, aimed, and swung. The ball moved out of the bunker sluggishly, barely cleared the peat wall, and dropped softly into the deep rough.

Well, he was out of the bunker.

Albert picked up the rake and silently began erasing the evidence of Chris's mistake.

"Thank you, Albert," Chris said, and hiked around the big bunker to his ball. Albert made no comment, and continued to rake the vast expanse that Chris had marred.

Chris glanced over at his pals. They were in a small clump, looking out at some vague point, and ignoring him. Chris almost found it funny. Almost.

His ball was now buried in the deep grass, a mere foot from the edge of the bunker's front face. From this vantage point, Hell Bunker looked even deeper than it had standing on its floor. Chris stepped around cautiously, careful not to fall into the bunker. That would just make the trip – to break an arm in Hell.

He aimed, and whacked the ball. His limited stance on the edge and the deep grass conspired to defeat him, and the ball barely left the club face, hopping a mere four feet and landing in more rough.

Chris threw his head back and groaned loudly. Thank heavens none of the guys responded; they were still obviously ignoring him. Albert was nearly done raking the bunker. Chris realized there was another foursome of golfers standing in the middle of the fairway, waiting. And watching.

Okay, enough. He grabbed a five iron and took aim. His body responded to the adrenaline running through his veins, and the ball came screaming out of the rough, airmailed the entire fourteenth green, and landed somewhere on the down slope beyond.

"Had enough?" Plato said. Chris had a flashback to his youth, when the pro would reprimand him for taking too long, or being too demonstrative, or any of the myriad of lessons Chris had had to learn during a tournament. It was the same tone of voice.

Chris waved his club in the air. "Just getting my money's worth," he said with an amiable, wry smile. He followed the other three Gang members to the green.

When Chris marked his score card with an asterisked eight – having actually shot an unbelievable ten – he was awfully glad Plato had instigated the triple-bogey rule for the tournaments. He hadn't thought he'd need to use the rule, after all. Probably jinxed himself.

As it was, he managed to avoid any more negative experiences, playing the last holes with much more grace. When he stood on the eighteenth tee, he fully felt the enormity of where he was. The Swilcan Bridge, the R & A Clubhouse, the monument – it was all right there, staring him in the face. In a surreal moment, he felt himself in a kilt and a tweed jacket, a cap askance upon his head. He knew this exact spot on the course, knew where to aim the ball, knew it would land to the right of High Point if he hit it just right. He looked at his club, expecting it to have a wooden shaft.

"Chris, you okay?" Ridge asked. "You look like you've seen a ghost."

Chris shivered. "I wouldn't put it that way." He aimed and swung his very real, graphite shafted Titleist driver. The ball glided through the wind and landed.

"Aye, laddie," Albert said. "You're safe, just to th'right o'the bumps we call High Point."

Chris stepped back and closed his eyes. Weird. This was just weird. Fortunately – or unfortunately, depending on how you viewed it – he didn't have a repeat of the incident, and the rest of the hole was played out in real time, if not played real well. With a two putt, he only made par, but looking back at the rest of the round – especially that disaster at fourteen – par seemed pretty darn good.

"What do you feel like doing?" Charlie asked, as they stood on the edge of the eighteenth green, reticent to leave. "We have a few hours before the rest of the guys get off the course."

Ridge wiggled his beard. "I don't know about the rest of you, but I could use a nap. My doggies are killing me."

Charlie nodded. "I could go for that, too."

Chris didn't feel like a nap, but he wasn't about to impose his will on the elder statesmen. "I'll head back to the hotel with you. Then maybe I'll go putt the Himalayas, or get a beer, or something."

Plato began walking toward the parking lot and the van. "I'll start with a shower, then see what happens. Maybe I'll join you, Chris."

Chris decided he liked the idea of a shower, as well. They passed the R & A Clubhouse, and he looked back at the first fairway. Again, he had the distinct impression he knew how to play the hole, where to put the drive, how the wind at his back would divert the ball. He took a deep breath and fought the urge to slap himself.

He was a Clark, after all.

Rudy stretched his shoulders and wobbled his head, relaxing the muscles in his neck. The Gang in his foursome had played well these last holes. They all successfully avoided Hell Bunker on fourteen, made pars on fifteen and sixteen, and arrived at seventeen feeling comfortable. The sun was shining, the wind was stronger, but still being kind, and they hadn't once had to wait for the foursome ahead of them. Rudy hoped Plato was having the same kind of day.

He stood on the tee of the seventeenth, the infamous Road Hole. He looked at the windows in the building almost directly in front of the tee, and the old railroad sheds over which he was being directed to shoot. He wondered how many "bullets" hit the building every year, and then decided it must not be much, since it was still there, unprotected.

Luckily, they all managed to finagle the corner with success, though Patrick flirted with danger by cutting it close.

"Whoa!" Vandeweghe said as the ball slid past the shed. "I think you creased it, P.Q. We're gonna see a streak across the paint."

Rudy landed his second shot in the hideously tiny Round bunker, and it took him two shots to get out, then two more putts to get the ball in the cup. He rolled his eyes when he retrieved his ball, and groaned.

"Is that a whine I hear?" Vandeweghe said. "Oh no, say it isn't so!"

Rudy displayed an indiscriminate finger in jest. "At my age, I'm allowed one whine per round. Especially when I'm eleven over, with one hole to go."

"So how much whining does that leave me?" Patrick asked. "More, or less?"

"None," Don said. "Not until you reach sixty are you ever allowed to whine."

Patrick chipped his second shot, and watched it skid over the green and bounce across the road. "I may not make it to sixty years old, at this rate. You can just bury me on this hole."

They crossed to the eighteenth tee, and Rudy felt a wave of nostalgia sweep over him. As of now, they only had one tee-time tomorrow. The prospects didn't look good for another round anytime soon. Rudy took a long look at the eighteenth fairway and all that surrounded it, absorbing as much of the specifics as possible. The fairway hugged the road, and the shops that lined it seemed ridiculously close.

Don and Patrick stepped up beside him. "If you had a slice, it would be intimidating," Rudy said.

Don nodded. "You wouldn't have to hit a bad shot at all to tag something. Cars, the hotel, people. Take your pick."

"This wind would take it toward the clothing store if you flirted with it," Patrick said.

"Probably happens all the time," Rudy said. "I just want to make sure I don't do it."

"Stick to the green," Don said.

"You're to aim at th' clock, laddies," Robert said. "The road there – that one that crosses th' fairway – is in play. Oh, and just so you know, that road's called Granny Clark's Wynd. Today ye need all ye got t'get close, so loosen your girdle 'n let it fly."

Patrick chuckled. "I thought Plato owned that phrase. Isn't there a patent on it?"

Vandeweghe grinned. "That phrase is so old the patent went out centuries ago."

The wind was now blowing hard, and straight into their face. Rudy waited until all three of his friends had hit their drives before he stepped up onto the tee himself. Don and Patrick hit clean shots, just left of center, and Vandeweghe had played it closer to the dissecting road, and right. Rudy aimed for the clock and swung. He smiled broadly. His final drive on the Old

Course was straight and true, bouncing favorably and stopping just short of ol' Granny Clark's Wynd.

"Nicely done," Vandeweghe said, and followed Robert off the tee.

Ahead lay the Swilcan Bridge, the celebrated stone arch that crossed the burn, and upon which every player who walked this course stepped, professional and amateur alike. Robert bounded across it without regard, but Rudy crossed it slowly, savoring the moment. He noticed the others did the same, including Vandeweghe.

Don hummed when he stepped onto the grass on the far side. "That's just something special," he said.

"We need a photo," Rudy said.

Vandeweghe glanced behind them. "Let's come back with the whole Gang, later. We have a group on our tail."

Rudy was disappointed, but Gooch was right – they could come back that evening, and it would be better with everyone.

A note played on the wind. Rudy frowned and looked around. Someone must be playing a radio loudly. Another note cut through the wind, then suddenly a song filled the air. The four men paused.

"Holy mackerel, it's a bagpiper," Don said.

Vandeweghe smiled broadly. "It must be four o'clock. They have a bagpiper play every afternoon at four around the Martyr's Monument." He pointed. "There. You can't see the piper from here, but the wind carries the music."

Rudy felt his face flush, and his guts tightened a bit. He was afraid to look at the other men, especially Don, who he knew would be emotionally affected as well. Rudy took a deep breath and they continued up the fairway.

"That's just ... amazing," Patrick said. "I wish the other guys were here."

The song continued, the notes riding the wind down the fairway. Rudy found his ball and began to laugh. It had bounced up onto a lovely patch of divot that had not been replaced. The ball sat, neat and tidy, as if on a tee. "Fellas," he said, "I have been redeemed."

"Take a photo," Don said. "You'll never see that again."

Patrick yanked his camera from his bag. He focused, then moaned. "Oh rats. I'm out of film."

Rudy shrugged. "Just something to remember, I guess."

"I don't have t' remind you about th' Valley o' Sin, now do I?" Robert said. "Stay t' your right a bit, laddie."

Rudy took his wedge and stroked the ball easily. The first seventeen holes, and all the difficulties, became a happy memory as Rudy watched the ball arc beautifully over the deepening shadows of the nearby shops and land softly on the green. Rudy remained in the middle of the fairway and watched as his friends played their second shots.

Vandeweghe placed his ball into the Valley of Sin. He leaned on his club, head tilted, and stared at the ball as if willing it to roll up hill, out of the Valley. Rudy chuckled quietly. That would be his friend Gooch – expecting the laws of physics to not apply to him.

"If I could only play my regular game just once," Vandeweghe said mournfully, and Rudy gave in to laughter.

"It's not funny!" Vandeweghe said, but his voice resonated with humor.

Don stepped behind his ball to find his line. He shook his head.

"What?" Rudy asked.

"There must be fifty people lining the fence behind the green," Don said. "I feel like I'm in a park, not on a golf course."

"Well, it becomes a park on Sundays," Vandeweghe said, then refrained from explanation as Don addressed his ball.

Don's ball floated on the notes of the bagpipe song, landed on the front edge of the green, and rolled straight for the pin. For a moment, Rudy thought it might go in, but it stopped short.

"Woof," Vandeweghe said. "You almost eagled, my friend!"

Patrick pulled an eight iron from his bag, then smiled at Rudy. "The people, the R & A…" He shook his head in disbelief. "I think I've seen this shot a thousand times on television."

Rudy nodded. "I know how you feel."

Patrick hit the shot thin, and the ball came up short, joining Vandeweghe in the Valley of Sin.

"And you've probably seen your next shot a million times," Rudy said.

"Obviously seeing them doesn't help me," Patrick said.

The bagpipe music faded, the last note carried on the wind like a Scottish hero on the shoulders of his admirers. Rudy and Don marked their balls, then stepped aside and leaned on their putters, waiting for Vandeweghe and Patrick to exit the Valley of Sin. Not surprisingly, Vandeweghe managed it with more success than Patrick, who left himself a tricky twenty-five foot putt for par. He whittled it down to four feet on the next putt, but Rudy knew that was still no gimme on these greens. He hoped his young friend didn't double-bogey here. Not in front of the gallery. Vandeweghe made his ten-footer for par, and Rudy placed his ball beside his marker. One last time, he glanced around, taking in the feeling of standing on the eighteenth green, then smacked his ball. It slipped past the hole by three inches, which didn't surprise Rudy, and he finished out for par. He pulled the ball from the cup with a solid sense of accomplishment. He'd post an eleven over for the round, but by God, he'd made par on eighteen.

Much to Rudy's relief, Patrick sunk his bogey putt. Don was the last to finish, and Rudy watched with anticipation. Don's level stroke sent the ball pouring toward the hole, and Rudy bit his lip. If it missed the cup, he'd be ten feet past.

It didn't miss. With a clatter, it landed in the cup. Applause broke out amongst the gallery, and someone yelled, "Nice birdie!"

"Hey, hey!" Vandeweghe said. "Great putt!"

Don hummed, smiled, and waved in acknowledgment, then smacked Patrick's raised palm for the congratulatory "high-five."

"I don't see many of those," Robert said. "Well done, Mr. Winterhalter."

Vandeweghe's eyebrows went up. "You just scored a touchdown with the caddy," he said to Don. "If you haven't noticed, no one gets called by anything other than 'laddie' until they earn the right to have their name remembered."

Rudy patted Don on the back as they left the green. "Terrific way to end at the Old Course. What did you end up with? Five over?"

Don beamed. "Seventy-five. Three over."

"Three!" Rudy exclaimed. He hadn't realized Don was playing that well. "Gosh that's great! If you're not leading this tournament Plato's got going, I'll be surprised."

Don briefly wrinkled his nose. "Ack, I imagine Plato's done better than me. But I gave him a run for his money!"

Rudy hoped his best friend had done as well, but either way, a great guy would lead after the first round.

"Anybody else hungry?" Vandeweghe said. "Should we collect the other guys and find some food?"

They found Ken fussing around the van and loaded their clubs.

"The others are waitin' for ya in th' hotel," Ken said. "They looked bushwhacked, they did."

Rudy laughed along with Vandeweghe, Don, and Patrick. "Sounds like they might have seen more of the course than we did." He motioned for his friends to follow. "Come on, I could use a shower before we head for dinner."

When he walked into the hotel room, Rudy discovered Plato sound asleep in one of the overstuffed chairs. Rudy tiptoed around, showered, and got dressed before Plato opened his eyes.

"Oh, you're back," Plato said. He glanced around the room as if disoriented. "What time is it?"

"Five-ten," Rudy said. "We're meeting the Gang in the lobby in twenty minutes. Do you need to freshen up some more before we go?"

Plato scuffled his hair and shook his head vigorously before saying, "I just need to wake up. Gosh I was out." He suddenly seemed to focus. "How'd you play?"

Rudy frowned. "Not good. Eleven over, but I had some good shots, and I made par on eighteen. No double bogeys, so that's nice. Don's only three over, with a birdie on eighteen. The gallery applauded him. It was a nice touch."

"Three over," Plato said. "That's great. No one in my foursome did that well. Chris and I are both seven over, Ridge matched you, and poor Charlie found every pot bunker out there. He came in with an eighty-six."

Rudy's eyebrows shot up. "Fourteen over? Wow. That's not like Charlie."

Plato stood and stretched. "No, it's not. We're going to treat him to a really good bottle of wine tonight."

"Two or three," Rudy said, and grabbed a sweater, just in case.

They met up with the others in the lobby.

"Rudy, you don't have your pad of paper tonight," Chris said "Have you memorized the town's restaurants?"

Rudy shook his head. "I've given up. In this town, there isn't an eating establishment worth its salt that Gooch doesn't know. I'm just reinventing the wheel."

"And yours has four corners," Patrick said. "Might as well give up."

"Okay, okay," Vandeweghe said. "Are you done razzing me?" He looked at Rudy. "So where are we going tonight? There's a great fish 'n chips place on South Street, an Italian place I think is on Market ..."

Rudy turned his palms upward and shrugged. "What did I say?" he jested.

"Well, I'm just trying to be helpful here!" Vandeweghe said, sounding injured.

Rudy sighed. He wanted to tease Vandeweghe, not hurt his feelings. "Honestly, Gooch, I hadn't thought about it much. This is your town. I figured you'd have a favorite you'd like to share."

Vandeweghe's mood instantly lightened. "I have a few favorites, places Barb and I frequent when we're in town. But I've never eaten here, at the Rusacks. Should we give that a try?"

They all agreed that having dinner in the hotel was favorable to walking all over town, small as St Andrews was. They were seated immediately, and Rudy felt exhaustion sneak up on him. No wonder Plato had passed out after his round. Rudy wished he'd had time to take a nap.

He poured more wine into his glass and focused on the conversation, which was a comparison between everyone's round.

Sleep would just have to wait until later. There was golf at hand.

Chris joined Patrick on the doorstep of the Rusacks Hotel.

"Find anyone?" Chris asked.

Patrick shook his head negatively. "Maybe we could ask one of the desk clerks at the hotel."

A couple in their thirties stepped out of a nearby shop and came toward them.

"I'm not sure who to ask," the man said. "The place is rather intimidating."

The woman tucked her arm around the man's and pulled herself close to him. "They don't bite, honey," she said. "At least they speak English. It's not like what you went through in France."

Chris and Patrick looked at each other. Americans. Hallelujah.

"Excuse me," Patrick said, stepping onto the sidewalk and blocking their way. "But could you help us?"

The couple stopped and stared, surprise written all over their face.

"Yeah, Americans," Patrick said and pointed to himself. "California, to be exact."

The couple laughed. "Sorry!" the woman said. "We've been in Scotland for three weeks now, and we haven't heard an American accent the whole time. Rather strange, actually."

"So what can we do to help you," the man asked. "We don't know the town at all as we just got in tonight."

"Actually, we need someone who can take a photo for us," Chris said. "There's eight of us here, playing golf, and we'd like a group photo on the Swilcan Bridge."

"Yeah, sure!" the man said. "But isn't it out on the course somewhere? Can we walk out there now?"

Chris and Patrick pointed across the street.

"About three hundred yards down that fairway," Chris said.

"Or a short drive and a wedge," Patrick said. "Unless the wind blows you into town."

"Wow, I'd be glad to help," the man said. "Can you take a photo of us, then?"

"You bet!" Patrick said. "Let me go get the others." He trotted into the hotel.

"So will you be able to play the Old Course, do you think?" the man asked Chris.

Chris was slightly taken aback by the question. Then he remembered Vandeweghe telling him the tee-times were determined by a daily lottery. People requested times months in advance, and unless you were willing to play in the middle of winter, there was only a small chance you'd get the time you wanted.

"We played this morning," Chris said. "It was great."

"How'd you get on?" the woman asked, and was granted a severe look from the man. "What? We need to know so you can play."

"It's okay," Chris said. "One of our Gang, um, I mean group, is a member of the R & A. That helps." They both looked crestfallen. Chris quickly added, "But the starter's shack is right there." He pointed. "Stop by really early and put your name on the walk-on list as a single. They often have cancellations or, amazingly enough, no-shows."

A burst of laughter made Chris turn toward the hotel door. The Gang was exiting, en masse, talking and laughing and generally being rowdy.

"Gosh that was a horrible meal," Charlie said. "Did you like yours, Gooch?"

"No, no!" Vandeweghe said loudly. "It was terrible! Dry and boring and overcooked."

"I think they forgot the salmon in my salmon pasta," Rudy said. "I couldn't find a single piece."

"Welcome to the Gang of Eight," Chris said apologetically. "They're typical Americans, too."

Introductions and hearty thanks were made, and the couple was shepherded down the street toward the eighteenth tee. When they were across from the Swilcan Bridge, they hopped the low white fence and trotted across the fairway. It was close to eight o'clock, and the course was now closed and free of golfers. The sun was low on the horizon, but there was certainly enough daylight to take a good photo. Chris was pleased to note the sun was setting behind the eighteenth tee, which meant they had perfect light aiming toward the R & A Clubhouse and the Rusacks Hotel.

The Gang organized themselves on the bridge, and Chris stood between Charlie and Ridge. The man took a few shots, and Chris hoped at least one of them would come out with everyone smiling. Then they exchanged places with the couple, and Patrick took two photos of them standing on the bridge.

The couple left, and the Gang hung around the bridge. They'd become quiet.

"It's an old bridge," Charlie said, as if to break the ice. Don hummed in response.

"This is really unique," Ridge said. He motioned toward the couple, now hopping the fence back onto the road. "I mean, that poor sod can't get a single tee-time, and here all eight of us were able to play together."

"We had some help," Rudy said.

"I know, I know," Ridge said. "But I think it's still darn special."

Chris agreed. Their camaraderie had felt special all day, but it seemed to coalesce as they stood on the bridge.

"Men walk on the moon all the time," Don said, "but what do you do to get up there? All those people, working together. That's what makes it remarkable. Just like this."

"I don't know about walking on the moon," Vandeweghe said, "but I can't think of much that matches this for me – the eight of us on this bridge. I'll always think of this now. Walking on hallowed ground with my best pals. Taking that picture. Pretty great."

They drifted away from the bridge, but instead of returning to the road, they strolled casually up the fairway. Chris made his way to Plato. "Thank you," he said.

Plato looked surprised. "For what?"

"For helping me to become a decent golfer, and for getting me involved in all this."

Plato looked bashful. "Heck, your dad had more to do with it than I ever did. He's the one who kicked your butt onto the driving range every weekend."

"And twice on Sunday," Chris said, then added in a more serious tone, "You were the one who got me playing with the Saturday morning group."

Plato chuckled. "Ah, yes, the herd. Man did I get harassed by the rest of the membership about you guys."

Now it was Chris's turn to be surprised. "You did? Then why didn't you shut it down?"

Plato looked around at the Gang. "And miss the chance to be a part of this kind of friendship? Not on your life."

They'd reached the hotel. In silent agreement, Chris hung back with Patrick, saying goodnight from the lobby to the other six.

"Beer?" Patrick said.

"Breakfast is at seven, right?" Chris checked his watch. "We have ten hours to drink the town dry. Come on."

They trotted down the entrance stairs, and Chris felt like a school-kid again. He glanced back toward the Swilcan Bridge, now resting somewhere in the dark. He smiled. His school-kid dream of playing the Old Course had come true.

CHAPTER 39

September 5, 1998

Don Winterhalter

Much to Don's pleasure, breakfast at the Rusacks Hotel turned out to be much better than dinner the evening before. The Gang took over a small section of the lounge, with windows overlooking the eighteenth fairway of the Old Course, and enjoyed a leisurely morning meal.

Vandeweghe tapped his glass with a knife to draw attention. "Gents, I have unfortunate news. I was unable to get a second tee-time on the Old Course for today."

Don raised his eyebrows. It was surprising Gooch had not waged a successful battle to secure the second tee-time. The man was used to getting his way.

"So here's the result," Vandeweghe continued. "We have one foursome playing at one-ten on the Old Course. And we have a foursome playing on the New Course at twelve-forty. The question is who plays where. Suggestions?"

Don made a quick decision. "I'm up for playing something different," he said. "I'll volunteer to play the New."

"Me too," Charlie said. "I've been here three times now. Let the young bucks play the Old."

Rudy nodded. "I'm with Charlie," he said.

"Well, then, I'll play with you, too," Ridge said. "We'll just make it the Senior Tour Side Trip."

The men laughed.

"Sounds good," Vandeweghe said. "So we're settled? Plato, Chris, and P.Q. join me at the Old, and you four seniors play the New?"

A round of approvals announced the acceptance by all in the Gang, and Don was struck by the ease with which that decision had been made.

"We have a few hours before we play," he said. "Anyone want to join me at the British Golf Museum? It's just down the street."

"A sight-seeing trip?" Patrick said. "Are we allowed?"

Simultaneously, several of the Gang reacted with "Whoa there!" "Watch out!" "Careful…"

Don looked at Vandeweghe for his reaction. The tall man was grinning with joy.

"It's the golf museum," Vandeweghe said. "Allowed." He stood and stretched. "I'll even lead the way."

"Now there's a novel idea," Chris said in jest.

Don hummed as Vandeweghe chuckled in obvious delight at the ribbing.

They walked the two blocks to the museum, paid the fee, and drifted into small groups as they wandered the many galleries that split up the information. Don particularly enjoyed the Inter-War gallery, though the Unusual Clubs were also fascinating.

After an hour, they congregated in the entrance. "Now what?" Rudy said.

"There's some great old ruins just up the road," Patrick said. "I wouldn't mind seeing them in the daylight."

Don grinned. "Been sleep walking, P.Q.?"

Patrick thrust his chest out with pride. "Chris and I escaped last night and did the town. We found some great pubs."

"And didn't get in until two this morning," Charlie said. "Must have closed the joints."

"Almost," Patrick said. "Come on. Let's go up to the ruins." He turned to Vandeweghe. "There is a connection to golf there, you know."

Vandeweghe smiled. "Oh, I know, I know. Lead on, Macduff."

Their first stop was the Martyrs Monument, and Chris and Patrick instantly ran up and clambered onto the base.

"Photo op," Patrick said. "Americans desecrating a monument, again!"

"Great opportunity," Rudy said, "but you have the camera."

Patrick tossed it down to Charlie, who promptly passed it to Don. "Here, you're the other photographer in the bunch. Get a photo of my progeny before they haul him off to jail. Then I can explain to his mother why she'll never see her son again."

They walked down The Scores, the road that lay alongside St Andrews Bay, considered, then opted out of touring the Castle ruins, and found the majestic crumbling remains of the Cathedral.

Patrick led them deep into the graveyard, alongside a wall, and paused beside a large, flat monument with a golfer carved in relief. "Gentlemen, I provide you with a little history of golf."

Don nodded. He'd been here before, years ago with Penny, and knew he was standing beside the graves of Old Tom Morris and Young Tom Morris.

Plato surveyed the view from the graves. "What an amazing place to spend eternity."

"Yeah," Rudy said, "just a hop, skip, and a jump from the course."

Don wandered around, looking at the dates on the gravestones, and snapped a few photos of the towering cathedral remains. He found Charlie and Rudy appraising the noble stone walls.

"What a shame this was destroyed," Charlie said. "I'll bet it was beautiful in its day."

"It was a symbol of everything they hated," Don said. "They didn't see the beauty; they saw oppression."

Rudy sighed. "It's sad. People don't think of the future. Especially in the height of emotions."

After a few more snapshots, the Gang silently reassembled and moved along North Street, back toward the course.

"Ice cream!" Vandeweghe said. He motioned toward a small shop sporting a sign shaped like a big pink cone.

"How can you have any pudding if you don't eat your meat?" Patrick chanted in a bad British accent, mimicking a line from a song which Don vaguely remembered hearing years before. "If you don't eat your meat, you can't have any pudding!" Patrick sang.

Vandeweghe looked very confused, and both Chris and Patrick laughed.

"*Another Brick in the Wall* from Pink Floyd," Patrick said. Vandeweghe just shrugged, and Patrick playfully slugged him. "Oh, you're hopeless."

"Generational differences," Charlie said. "Patrick has no idea who The Platters are, either."

"Ice cream, pudding, and platters of meat," Ridge said. "I'm getting hungry."

Don glanced at his watch. Five past eleven. "There's probably a place to grab a sandwich before we all go play. Gooch, do you know of any place close by?"

Vandeweghe thought for a moment, then lit up. "Yeah, over by the course, there's a pub owned by a couple of Americans. They do some pretty good sandwiches, our style."

Their pace quickened and within a few minutes they were entering the Dunvegan Hotel. Don had walked past it a dozen times with Penny, but had never paid it any particular attention. He was surprised it was owned by Americans.

They huddled around the bar and ordered sandwiches to go, and Don learned it was only the husband who was American, from Texas in fact; his wife was as Scottish as they come. Don read the motto over the bar and smiled. *Only a 9-iron from the Old Course (depending on the wind!)*

Plato sidled up to Don and read the motto. He chuckled. "Could be a driver on a bad day. And sometimes that wouldn't even get you to the eighteenth green."

They collected their sandwiches, cans of soda, and bags of potato chips and walked the short block to the corner fence surrounding the eighteenth green. Don liked being a member of the gallery while he ate his lunch. It was a different perspective on the course, and the three foursomes that played through while he was standing there all demonstrated just how difficult the course could be. Not one of the players made a birdie, and most three-putted the green for a bogey.

"Well that was a nice snack," Patrick said. "Shall we go find lunch now?"

Don turned and half sat on the fence. Across the street was a store he'd seen before, but never entered. He pointed. "Let's wander into there for a few minutes. It intrigues me."

"Yeah, sure," Vandeweghe said. "Auchterlonie's is a nice establishment. And we have a half hour or so to kill."

The Gang trotted across the street and entered the corner golf store. Don felt instantly at home. The printing on the door said it was started in 1895, and it looked it, but in a warm, overstuffed, comfortably maintained sort of way. There was a vast array of modern wares, but Don was more interested in the old clubs that graced the walls.

"The founder was the pro at the R & A until '63," Vandeweghe said. "They still make custom clubs here."

Don stopped before a club that resembled a claw. He chuckled. "Can you imagine playing with something like that?"

Vandeweghe grinned. "Yeah, to fish my ball out of the Road Hole."

"Or the pond at San Jose," Don added.

The "bing" of a cash register made them both turn toward the front counter. Patrick was placing his credit card back in his wallet while a young woman tried to stuff several bulky items into a plastic bag.

Vandeweghe shook his head. "That kid's going to bankrupt the family here. Sue's gonna divorce him."

"Not likely," Don said. "But she might provide an addition to the Captains' Balls."

Forty minutes later, Don was standing at the starter's shack for the New Course. He'd left Vandeweghe, Plato, Chris, and Patrick putting on the Himalayas, and walked briskly ahead of Rudy, Charlie, and Ridge.

"Checking in for the twelve-forty for Vandeweghe," Don said to the starter. "Foursome."

The starter stared at his clipboard, flipped the page back and forth a few times, checked another clipboard, then made a funny face. "I'm sorry sir, but ye no have a tee time on my sheet," he said. "Could it be under another name?"

Don frowned. "Well, I suppose Gary might have put it under one of our other names, but it's unlikely. Try Winterhalter."

The starter went through his flipping and checking routine. "No, sir," he said and raised his eyebrows as if to say, "Another?"

"Okay," Don said, feeling exasperated. "Um, Plato?"

"No, sir."

"Staedler."

"No, sir."

"Quinn?" Don shook his head. This was futile.

Rudy walked up. "What's up?" he said, obviously reacting to the look of frustration Don knew he must have on his face.

"They don't have us playing today," Don said. "We've tried every name in the Gang. No go."

Rudy looked at the starter. "The time was made by an R & A member. Last night around nine."

The starter looked genuinely disconcerted and apologetic. "I'm very sorry sir, but there's none o'the names this gent has given me on th' list provided this mornin' by th' Secretary."

Don looked at his watch and turned to Rudy. "Where's Ken? Can we get to him quickly?"

Rudy nodded. "Should be at the van, still. He was cleaning out the trailer."

Don smiled grimly at the starter. "Thanks for your help. We'll sort this out some other time." Don motioned for Rudy to follow. "Let's go. We can get to Drumoig in time and get around, but we'll have to hustle."

Rudy kept pace with Don. "Drumoig? Can we walk on?"

"Don't have to," Don said. "I arranged a tee-time months ago and never canceled it. Must have been a premonition." He met Charlie and Ridge, who were walking back from the New Course Clubhouse.

"Grab your sticks," Don said. "We're heading to Drumoig and we have fifty minutes to get there and make our tee-time."

"Drumoig?" Ridge said. "I just paid for a caddy here!"

"Vandeweghe can get you reimbursed later," Don said. "Come on. I'll explain while we walk."

The four men nearly ran to the van. To his credit, Ken had them loaded and driving in less than ten minutes. Don sat in his seat, pleased. Ken seemed relaxed, even lethargic, most of the time, but he could find another gear when necessary.

It was seven-fifteen, and the sun was still high in the sky, when Don entered the Rusacks bar. Seated in several of the wing-backed, overstuffed leather chairs were Rudy and Plato, drinks in hand. Rudy waived.

"What are you having?" Don said, pointing at their nearly empty glasses.

Plato waved his hand. "I'm good. One's my limit."

"The usual," Rudy said. "Gin and tonic, minus the gin." He grinned "And I think I can handle a second. Thanks, Don."

At the bar, Don ordered, collected their drinks, and rejoined the others.

"I hear you had a little drama today," Plato said. "Ended up at Drumoig?"

Don chuckled. "I've never seen Ken drive so fast. That van has the engine of a sports car."

"He was on a mission," Rudy said.

Commotion in the lobby attracted their attention. The remainder of the Gang had arrived.

"Hey, hey!" Vandeweghe said as he entered the bar. "If it isn't Captain Prepared!" He shook Don's hand. "So you were a hero today with your surprise tee-time."

Don hummed. "Glad I never bothered to cancel the thing. Saved our bacon."

"You can tell me all about it over dinner," Vandeweghe said. "I'm starved. Where we going tonight, Rudy?"

Behind Vandeweghe, Chris, Ridge, and Patrick stood in a small clump. The three men exchanged knowing looks, and grinned. Here we go, Don thought.

Rudy produced a small scrap of paper and read, "Ciao Roma's Italian. No discussion."

"We passed that place last night," Chris said. "Looked like a nice restaurant."

"It is," Rudy said. "I have it on the highest authority."

"Oh?" Vandeweghe said. "And who's that."

"Your wife," Rudy said.

To Don's delight, Vandeweghe was genuinely surprised. "Barbara?!" He looked around. "Is she here?"

"No, no, of course not," Rudy said. "I called her when we got off the course. Asked her what your favorites were in town. She recommended this place. End of discussion."

Vandeweghe laughed. "And she's right, as always. Well, let's go!"

They walked the few blocks to Ciao Roma's and were seated at a large table in the back. Don perused the menu and realized he was famished. It had been a long time since he'd eaten that sandwich.

Vandeweghe immediately ordered several bottles of wine, both white and red, and the waitress produced them almost immediately. Don wondered if she was afraid they'd change their mind. They ordered, and settled in to recount the day.

"So how'd you all play?" Don said, looking between the four who replayed the Old Course that afternoon.

"Much better," Plato said. "It started out a little overcast and windy, but the clouds broke around the fourth hole, and we had great weather until seventeen, when the clouds rolled in again. But no rain."

"I managed to avoid Hell Bunker today," Chris said with a grin. "And the Road Hole, though only because I overshot the green and landed in the middle of the road itself."

"Yeah, he's over there with his putter," Patrick said, "trying to bang it off the pavement without destroying the club face."

"Where were you?" Chris said. "I don't remember where you were standing."

Patrick chuckled. "I was whacking away at the weeds on the other side of the green. I had a good vantage point of your predicament."

"The Road Hole..." Charlie said. "That's seventeen, right? I was in that bunker yesterday."

"And you're still trying to get out, aren't you," Don said.

Charlie slowly shook his head and gave a heavy-lidded grin, "I have no recollection of getting out of it. I just remember being in it, looking up."

"The human brain tries to forget our worst nightmares," Plato said.

"Well, I probably have forgotten how many strokes it took me to get out of that damn thing," Charlie said. "I mean, I ended up with, what, an eighty-five?"

"Eighty-six," Plato said, "but who's counting."

"You are!" Chris, Patrick, and Rudy said simultaneously.

"P.Q. said you guys got the bagpipers on eighteen yesterday," Chris asked, looking from Don to Vandeweghe.

Don felt a lump develop in his throat. He nodded, afraid to say anything.

"Gets a man, right in the gut," Vandeweghe said. "At least it always does to me."

Chris nodded vigorously. "I know what you mean. That happened to me today. It was overcast when I drove off the eighteenth tee. Start walking down the fairway, the sun comes out, I swear, just as the bagpiper starts to play. Shafts of sunshine beaming down, bagpipe music, no wind." He took a deep breath and shook his head, then continued. "I could hardly hit the ball."

"I remember thinking, it just doesn't get any better than this," Patrick said.

The lump in Don's throat grew hard. He reached for his wine and then redirected his grasp to the water glass. Thankfully, the waitress arrived carrying several plates of hors d'oeuvres, and Don joined the others in devouring them. Within minutes, the plates were empty.

"Gee, we weren't hungry or anything, were we?" Patrick said.

"That was just the pre-hors d'oeuvres," Chris said. "The real ones are coming."

"Did you notice the corner markers they have around the course?" Plato said, glancing around the table.

"The ones with the inscriptions," Vandeweghe said. "Yeah, they're fascinating."

Plato nodded. "I asked the caddy today what they were, and he explained they marked the corners of the property. Instead of a fence, they put up those."

"Too bad they've faded over time," Vandeweghe said. "Some of the adages are very applicable."

"Is one of them 'Please avoid slow play'?" Ridge joked. "'Cause I think the caddy's have that one inscribed on their forehead."

The Gang laughed.

"Oh, so true," Vandeweghe said. "They like to get a few rounds in every day, so they crack that whip pretty hard sometimes. I feel for the high handicapper who comes out here and expects to take their time. The caddies are brutal."

"They can be," Plato said, "but they're awfully useful."

Ridge nodded and pushed his glasses higher onto his nose. "Without them, I wouldn't have had any idea where to hit half the time."

"I know I wouldn't have done as well as I did yesterday without Robert," Don said. "He saved me from suicide a few times."

"So did the guy we had today–" Plato said.

"Muddy," Vandeweghe interjected.

Plato nodded. "Yes, that was his name, Muddy–"

"Wait, wait," Rudy said. "The guy's name was *Muddy*?"

"Well, his real name is Dairmud," Vandeweghe said, "but since no one can pronounce it correctly, everyone just calls him Muddy."

"Poor guy," Charlie said.

"A boy named Sue," Don said. Patrick and Chris clearly didn't understand the reference, and Don chuckled. "Another generational thing."

"I had this one hole today," Plato said. "I don't remember exactly which hole it was –"

"That's a generational thing, too," Patrick said, to which Plato shot a look of humorous outrage. Don joined in the ensuing laughter.

"Somewhere on the back, I think," Plato continued. "It was a dogleg around the corner, with a little hill on the right, and the green was sitting on the back. There was a stairway back there, behind the green. And I'm a hundred and twenty yards from the green, and the caddy, Muddy, says, 'I want you to hit a shot to that stairway. Hit it about fifty feet to the right.' And I'm thinking, why would I want to do that? But I figure they know the course so what the heck."

Plato paused to take a swallow of his wine. Don glanced around the table. As usual when Plato was telling a tale, he had his listeners mesmerized. They all waited for him to continue.

"So I hit the shot the way he wants me to, and I get up there and darned if the ball isn't about eight fee from the pin! Of course, soon as I get round the corner, I see this hill behind the green. My shot had hit the hill, ran off, and came all the way down to the pin." Plato sat back in his chair and gestured with his hands. "It was the only way you could get close to that pin placement, but if I hadn't had the caddy, I would have never known that, and I never would have gotten close to that hole. Nowhere near."

"I hope you tipped him well," Charlie said.

Plato chuckled and shrugged. "Oh, I did, but more in the hope he'd get a new pair of shoes. I still double putted for par, so he definitely helped, but it didn't make me any money."

Charlie leaned on his elbows and twirled his wine. "This guy I played with last time I was here, with the guys from Palm Springs, well, the caddy tells him to aim for this one bush, and the guy's not paying attention, and the caddy kinda gets on him a bit and tells him in no uncertain terms, aim for that bush. So the guy complains, but he aims for the bush and he hits the ball, up to this green you couldn't see, and it goes up over these mounds. So we went up to the green and we all found our balls except for him. We looked all over the place and there was someone else playing on the other half of the double green, and they hadn't seen it, and finally someone crossed to the hole and there it was, in the hole. He'd had a double eagle and didn't even know it, all because he did what the caddy told him to do!"

Dinner finally arrived, and the Gang grew quiet while they ate. Don looked around, absorbing the scene. It was eight guys, eating dinner; nothing unique. And yet everything about it was special. If it wasn't for golf, our paths would have never crossed, he thought. This dumb game had changed all their lives.

"So how was Drumoig?" Patrick asked.

"Fantastic!" Ridge said. "We had buggies!"

"Thank heavens," Charlie said, "because my leg was killing me."

"Do you need me to find you a doctor?" Patrick asked, his forehead wrinkled. "It's been bothering you an awful lot the past few days."

"Why didn't you say something?" Vandeweghe asked Charlie.

Charlie glared from beneath his bushy eyebrows. "What're *you* going to do about it, that a battalion of surgeons and specialists haven't been able to do?"

"I don't know," Vandeweghe spat, "but *something*. Find someone to give you an adjustment, give you some pain killers that work –"

"Cut off your leg altogether," Patrick said with a grin. "That might help."

"The pain, maybe," Charlie said, "but won't do much for my golf game." He pointed at Don with his fork. "But you got us buggies, so that made the day. Thank you."

Don shrugged. "Totally selfish on my part, Charlie. I was tired of walking."

"So how was the course?" Vandeweghe asked.

"A little flat," Don said, "but the placement of the bunkers –"

"And the water," Ridge said. "There's just enough water to get you into trouble."

Charlie chuckled. "Yeah, I lost two balls. Brand new ones, too."

"Well," Ridge said, "y'know new balls have a magnetic attraction to water. You should never use a new ball on a hole with water. You gotta whack it around a few holes first."

The Gang laughed.

Don nodded. "There's a pond that can come into play on a few holes on the back nine. But what really came into play were the sheep."

"Sheep?" Plato said.

"As in baa, baa, black sheep?" Patrick said.

"More like Mary had a little lamb," Charlie said. "These were skinny little things, running all over the fairways."

"I think they'd just been sheared," Ridge added. "Made 'em all look naked."

"They had sheep on the course?" Plato asked. "Could you have clocked one with a drive?"

The men chuckled. "They weren't on *every* fairway," Don said. "Just a few, and yes, you had to take them into account in your club selection." He nodded toward Rudy and grinned. "Seamus McDuff, here, tried a few times to bring home dinner. Unsuccessfully, I might add."

"Nothing like playing for your dinner," Rudy said. "But don't worry, I left all the poor critters happily mowing the grass at Drumoig."

Ridge chuckled, and his beard bounced jauntily. "Though, just for the fun of it, I tried to herd a few around with the buggy."

"Okay," Vandeweghe said, "but besides the four-legged hazards, the course was okay?"

Don nodded. "It's a Nicklaus course, so how bad could it be?"

"Nicklaus designed it?" Chris asked. "I didn't know that."

"It's not common knowledge," Plato said. "The owner's didn't want to pay his full fee, so Jack allowed them to use the design, but they can't advertise his name."

"Well then it couldn't have been half bad," Vandeweghe said.

"It has a few holes that are rather interesting," Don said. "On one of the holes, the green is set up against a quarry wall, so there's a high rock backdrop. It's rather pretty."

"Until you fly a ball against it," Ridge said. "Then it's not so pretty."

The Gang laughed. "I take it you know this from personal experience?" Chris asked.

"Nope," Charlie said. "He was just a spectator."

"But you'd go back?" Vandeweghe asked. "It was worth it?"

Don furrowed his brow. "Yes, I think I'd play it again. Why the interest? Do we have to?"

"Did we get a cancellation?" Rudy asked. "'Cause I'd probably be happy to play it again, if we had to."

Vandeweghe wiggled his near-empty wine glass. "No, no, we're fine. You know, just once again looking for new places to take Barbara when we're over here, that's all."

Don smiled. That was Gooch – always thinking ahead.

The meal was one of the best Don had experienced on the trip, and he left the restaurant overstuffed, and very happy. By mutual, unspoken consent, the Gang turned away from the hotel and shuffled aimlessly through the old town of St Andrews. Occasionally, some window display would catch their attention, and twice they paused to peek into a bar, only to decide it was too smoky or too loud to frequent, and they moved on. Don listened to the jovial banter provided by Chris and Patrick, to the erudite information dispensed by Plato and Vandeweghe, and to the dry wit doled out by Charlie. Don laughed at Ridge's jokes, and wished he'd remember them in order to tell Penny when he returned home. But he knew he wouldn't – they were part of the moment, and while Don knew he'd remember nearly every drive, stroke, and putt he'd play this entire trip, he also knew moments like this would endure in his soul, rather than be stored in his memory. Special occasions with friends were to be savored like a fine wine, recollected in the senses, cherished for their translucence.

As they strolled along The Scores, the ocean sounds lulled them into a contented silence. This was their last evening in St Andrews, and Don felt nostalgia settling upon him. He assumed the others felt it, as well, since no words were spoken as they passed the Martyr's Monument, skirted the eighteenth green, and entered their hotel lobby.

Waiting for the lift, Don looked around the small lobby and at the faces of his friends. They looked – satisfied.

"New Course tomorrow?" Charlie whispered.

Vandeweghe nodded.

"Breakfast at eight?" Chris asked, also in hushed tones.

Again, Vandeweghe nodded but said nothing. The lift arrived and, silently, Vandeweghe, Charlie, and Ridge tucked themselves into it and pulled the cage door across. Vandeweghe waved, and they disappeared as the solid door closed.

"Did someone die?" Patrick asked with a lopsided grin. "We're all so damn somber."

Don smiled and hummed. He wasn't sure how to communicate how he felt. It would probably come out all sentimental and mushy. Ridiculous, at the very least.

Rudy shrugged. "I think we're all tired. I know I could sleep a week."

"At least," Plato said.

The lift returned to their floor. Don waved Rudy, Plato, and Chris into the small compartment. "You guys go ahead," Don said. "We'll wait."

"No argument from me," Chris said. "I'm also bushwhacked."

The lift disappeared, and Don stood beside Patrick, waiting. He was suddenly very conscious of Patrick's height – at least six inches above himself. How did this kid get to be so tall? As if in answer, Patrick slung his arm over Don's shoulder.

"Thanks, Winner-halter," Patrick said. "For everything, but mostly for letting me come along on this little shindig."

Don nodded and fiddled with a tee he'd found in his trouser pocket. "It wouldn't have been the same without you," he said. The lift arrived and Don stepped in and held the gate open for Patrick. "Coming?"

Patrick tilted his head and smiled. "Naw," he said, finally. "It's our last night here. I think I'll go down a few beers."

Don smiled. "Leave a little for the locals," he said, and waved as the door closed. He sighed and dropped the tee back into his pocket. They had three more days in Scotland, but Don knew he could leave tomorrow and be happy.

Very happy.

CHAPTER 40

September 6, 1998
Gary Plato

Plato rolled over in his bed, sleep backing away from him like a satisfied lover. He sighed and opened his eyes. A weak sunshine filled the room. He sat up and scrubbed his face with his hands, then yawned widely. Rudy stood by the window, staring out, a cup of coffee in his hand.

"What are you looking at?" Plato asked.

Rudy turned, smiled, and said, "Good morning." Then he returned to looking out the window. "There's a guy out on the course. He has a rope and he's driving these stakes around the green. Now he's tying the rope to the stakes, surrounding the green." He paused and sipped his coffee. "Awfully hard to get to the green with a rope around it."

Plato smiled. "That's the point." Rudy turned and gave him a quizzical look. Plato continued, "The Old Course is closed on Sundays. It becomes a public park, so they rope off the greens to keep the public from romping all over them."

Rudy's eyebrows shot upward. "It becomes a public park? Are you kidding? As in dogs and baby buggies and kids with rubber balls?"

Plato headed to the bathroom. "Yep. All that and more. Just not golf."

"Jeez!" Rudy said. "They must lose a fortune in revenue. Why do it?"

"Spoken like a true businessman," Plato called from the bathroom. "I think it was part of the original land deal – they had to provide access to the beach for the locals on Sundays. The other courses are open, though. It's just the Old Course that's closed." He crossed to stand beside Rudy at the window. Thick fog blanketed the area, making it difficult to see the course beyond the eighteenth fairway and green. But sure enough, several people were already meandering around the course. A man threw a frisbee for his dog on the fairway, and a couple with four small children were crossing the Swilcan Bridge, most likely on their way to the waterfront.

"That's wild," Rudy said.

Plato chuckled and rummaged through his suitcase for the day's clothing. He'd need something warmer if the fog continued. "If you think about it, makes sense. No one can hurt those fairways, that's for sure."

Rudy grunted in agreement. "Yeah, they're not exactly groomed, are they. But it is rather odd..."

Plato gave a little wave. "You keep an eye on things, I'm heading to the shower." With that, he left his friend standing at the window, drinking his coffee and pondering the apparent absurdity of the golfer's hallowed ground desecrated by mere mortals.

Plato stood outside the Walden House Hotel, where the Gang had gone for breakfast. He frowned. He had hoped this pea-soup fog would have lifted while they were eating. Alas, it seemed thicker than before. He couldn't even see across the street to the Old Course any more. He sighed and wiped the mist from his glasses. Nothing to be done about it; golf must be played. Today they were to tackle the New Course, and whining would not be tolerated.

Vandeweghe lurched through the hotel door. "Scottish sunshine! Great weather for high handicappers."

Plato replaced his glasses. "Meaning?"

Vandeweghe chuckled. "They're the only ones who can see where their ball lands."

Plato smiled and nodded. "Yeah, this stuff won't be easy on Chris. We should hire a fore caddy just for him."

"Don't we wish they had such a thing," Vandeweghe said. "Sure would come in handy, for many a golfer out here." He turned as Ridge led the rest of the Gang from the hotel.

"...so the guy hits the ball right into the tree," Ridge said, demonstrating the trajectory of the ball with his right arm. "And it lands right back down at his feet. 'Well,' says the old geezer, 'of course when I was your age that tree was only four feet tall.'"

Chris and Patrick laughed heartily, while the others chuckled and, in Don's case, hummed.

"Ah, heck," Ridge said as he glared into the fog. "We still got this blanket laying on us." He turned to Vandeweghe. "Can't you do anything about this? Doesn't the R & A control the weather around here?"

Vandeweghe nodded vigorously. "Sure, sure. I'll just trot over to the clubhouse and place an order. Sunshine around ten work for you?"

"Well, that's the first tee time, isn't it?" Ridge asked. "Maybe make it nine, so we can warm up a bit."

"Gotcha," Vandeweghe said and, chuckling, led the way.

At the New Course, they rented pull carts and checked in with the starter, just to make sure nothing had gone wrong with their tee-times this time. Moments later they stood on the driving range. The fog swirled and clumped, creating a thick barrier through which their balls disappeared.

Plato turned to Rudy. "It's like being in a Star Trek episode. I feel like I'm hitting into another dimension."

Rudy chuckled. "Beam me up, Scotty. Or beam down some sunshine."

"At least there's no wind," Plato said, then quickly added, "Though that might make this stuff go away faster."

Charlie appeared out of the fog, mopping the mist from his face with a large, bright white handkerchief. "Somehow I missed the announcement at breakfast. So what's the game today, Pro? Hide and go seek?"

Plato smiled. "Not a bad idea, but we'll finish the Stroke Play Championship today."

"Ah, too bad," Charlie said, and his eyes twinkled behind his heavy eyelids. "I was kinda hoping you'd forget that whole thing."

Plato patted his friend gently on the shoulder and said, "You're not that far behind the rest of us, Charlie. You can make it up today and win the whole pot."

Charlie grunted. "Only if this fog swallows every one of your balls," he said, and disappeared back into the fog.

Rudy checked his watch. "Nine-forty-five. We should get going." He dropped his driver back into his bag. "Torpedoes ready, sir," he said gruffly, and saluted Plato.

Plato frowned and gave Rudy a look that clearly conveyed his confusion.

Rudy grinned. "Just keeping with the Star Trek theme. That's a famous line of Chekov's."

Patrick appeared, bag on his shoulder. "Don't call me tiny," he said in a strange voice.

Plato shook his head and sighed. He yanked his golf trolley into motion and walked along the driving range, beckoning to the other Gang members to follow.

"That's from Sulu," Patrick said. "Don't you remember that movie? *Star Trek III: The Search for Spock?*"

Plato raised his eyebrows. "They made more than one movie? I thought it was over after the second series left television."

"Star Trek? It'll never leave television," Ridge said. "I'm pretty sure it's still on, somewhere in the world."

Chris fell in beside Plato. "You? What planet is this?"

Plato perked up. "Hey! That one I remember," he said. "Wasn't that the doctor? In the episode about Chicago?" They rounded the corner of the Links Clubhouse, Plato in the lead. "Mac, Mac – something?"

Simultaneously, Chris and Patrick cried, "McCoy!"

To Plato's joy, at least three golfers in the vicinity looked up, expectantly. He laughed. "I think we have a few of his family members here."

"Could be, since the name comes from the Scottish Highlander Clan MacKay," Rudy said. He shook his head. "And don't ask me how I know that. Just one of the many useless pieces of information rolling around in my head."

Vandeweghe jerked his thumb toward Chris and Patrick. "I think they just looked up 'cause these goons sounded like fog horns."

"More like sick Klingons," Patrick said. "Still, McCoy was the kind of character who would play golf."

"In space," Rudy said. "It probably looked a little like today, really, with all this swirling fog."

The Gang chuckled. At the starter's, they were given the familiar course book and reminded to remain in two foursome's, which made Plato smile. *If the guy only knew from whence we came,* he thought. *No one at St Andrews – except Vandeweghe, of course – would ever condone the San Jose Country Club herd mentality.*

After Rudy drove his ball somewhere to the left of nowhere, Plato stepped up to the tee, swung, and watched his ball disappear into the gray sky. He shrugged and smiled at Patrick as the young man stepped past him onto the tee box.

"Just like magic," Plato said. "Watch the little white ball disappear before your eyes."

Patrick wiggled, waggled, and swung. A dull thud forewarned of the result: The ball scudded barely off the ground and went limping into the mist.

In a bad Scottish brogue, Patrick said, "I'm giving her all she's got, Captain!" He then immediately responded to himself. "All she's got isn't good enough, Scotty!" He chuckled and shrugged. "Where's Kirk when you need him?"

Plato rolled his eyes and then grimaced at Don. "I think we're in for a long round, Don."

Don hummed as he teed his ball. With a smooth swing he sent the ball screaming into the fog. He pursed his lips and nodded curtly. "Space, the final frontier."

Plato moaned, but Patrick and Rudy burst into laughter.

"Winner-halter!" Patrick exclaimed. "You're a Trekkie! A closet Trekkie!"

Don shook his head, but his eyes sparkled with delight. "The girls watched it on television. I was just brainwashed."

The four men walked down the first fairway and were swallowed by the fog. Plato noticed Don was studying the course book as they walked.

"Looking for something in particular, Don?" he asked.

Don grunted. "Landmarks, so we don't get lost out here in space."

Plato laughed. Ahead, three balls lay neatly in the middle of the fairway, though Patrick's was at least thirty yards short of the other two. He pointed. "There's your landmark. Just like stars."

"Only mine landed in a black hole," Rudy said, and headed off in the direction of the gorse on the left.

Patrick stared into the fog. "Can any of you see the flag?" Without waiting for an answer, he yanked an eight iron from his bag, addressed the ball, and swung. The ball sailed into the clouds, straight and true.

"I may not be able to see the flag," Plato said, "but I'm sure that ball will find it. Nice shot."

The three men moved to the next ball and determined it was Don's. All three peered intently into the thickening gray air, searching for the flag.

Don opened his course book again, studied it, and looked around. He began to chuckle, then shook his head in amazement. "Where's the yellow line?"

Plato's forehead furrowed. "What? The yellow line?"

Don brandished the small booklet. "Yeah, see? This shows a dotted yellow line. I don't see it on the fairway."

Plato and Patrick exchanged looks of amazement, and burst into laughter.

"I want my damn yellow line," Don joked. "Patrick, run back and complain, will ya?"

Plato wiped the tears of laughter from his cheeks, while Patrick remained doubled-over, laughing silently.

Rudy trotted up to them. "I found my ball. But I can't see the green. Anyone got one of those little books? I think I dropped mine." He observed the three men laughing. "What's so funny?"

Don waved his course book and Plato, still barely able to speak for his laughter, choked, "Go find the yellow line!"

Rudy's face scrunched with perplexity. "The yellow what?" He took the book from Don's hand and examined the diagram of the first hole.

Meanwhile, Don and Patrick were motioning toward up the fairway, laughter still rendering them uncommunicative.

Rudy shook his head and chuckled. He pointed away from them. "I don't know what's wrong with you goof-balls, but there's the line, right there, straight up the fairway." He handed the booklet back to Don. "Now pull yourselves together and follow the yellow dotted line." Chuckling, he turned and walked toward his ball, back into the fog.

Patrick took a deep breath and regained control. He waved toward Rudy. "Who was that pointy-eared bastard?" he said, mimicking Captain Kirk. He then switched to a different voice and said, "I don't know, but I like him!"

Plato blinked and, leaning on his nine iron, stared at Patrick.

"What?" Patrick said. "Too much?"

Don yanked a nine iron from his bag and stood behind his ball. "You're usually too much, Patrick. But please don't stop." He moved to address the ball, and checked his direction. "Now, where's that blasted yellow line?" he muttered.

Plato turned away and tried to control the rush of laughter. Hopefully, the shaking of his shoulders wouldn't disturb his friend's concentration.

For the next seven holes, the fog covered the peninsula and the wind remained asleep. Plato played conservatively, knowing how quickly a ball could be lost in the mirk. Rudy, in particular, was struggling with the loss of visibility; he'd lost two balls to the gorse and the fog, and had yet to make a birdie. Plato was pleased to note that his best friend was still in good spirits, joking and poking fun at himself as he struggled along.

Of course, having Patrick in your foursome was bound to contribute to the round. The kid was shooting lights out and, as they stood around the tee on nine, Patrick was one under.

"Okay, birdie man," Don said, and motioned with his driver for Patrick to go ahead and hit. "Show us the way."

Patrick teed his ball then stood behind it for a moment, desperately trying to see the flag, over two hundred and twenty yards in the distance. He shook his head. "The book says it's straight to the green."

Rudy waved Plato's book, which he had confiscated on the third hole. "It also says to aim slightly right." He pointed. "So maybe that direction."

Patrick sighed, set up, and swung. The ball flew off and developed a nice, easy slice before disappearing into the fog. He grunted. "That could be on the tenth fairway, somewhere."

Plato walked onto the tee box. "I didn't hear anyone scream with pain, so at least it didn't hit the foursome in front of us."

"Maybe," Rudy said. "In this fog, they could lose a guy and it would take two holes before they noticed."

Plato swung and knew he'd come up short of the green, but it was probably in the middle of the fairway, at least. Don and Rudy followed, with Don's probably a little to the left. In a loose huddle, they trundled down the fairway. The ocean was to the left, though they could only hear it through the fog.

Sure enough, Plato found his ball twenty yards from the front edge of the green. Rudy walked ahead and did a little jig when he found his resting fifteen feet from the flag. Patrick headed right, Don to the left, both men disappearing into the "other dimension," as they had all come to refer to it. Plato waited and, sure enough, within a minute two balls came sailing out of the haze and landed with dull thumps on the green. Plato neatly chipped his up, nearly holing out.

Suddenly a gust of wind cut across the green. Don's cap flew off his head, and in a nice feat of acrobatics, Patrick jumped up and caught it neatly in his left hand. The flag began to whip loudly.

"Jeez, where'd this come from?" Rudy said, pulling his rain jacket from his bag.

They finished the hole with four pars, and moved to the tenth tee. There was now a steady breeze, with occasional strong gusts. Plato didn't mind the breeze – it would dissipate the fog, which had become very boring – but he didn't like the random gusts. They would play havoc with the Gang's shots.

The foursome in front of them must have run into some trouble on ten, as one of their players was standing in the middle of the fairway, waving his club. Plato waved back in acknowledgment.

"Oh, look P.Q.," Rudy said. "They have a guy down. Are you sure that was your drive you played out of that bush?"

Patrick and Don chuckled, then turned as a ball landed behind them, no more than ten feet from the tenth tee.

"Chris finally found his groove," Patrick said. "That has to be his drive."

"Right over the green," Plato said. "Wonder how they're doing."

The four men waited patiently, as the stranger remained in the fairway, eagerly looking between the tenth tee and somewhere down the fairway. The wind was clearing the fog quickly, but the tenth green still lay shrouded in mystery.

Soft thumps announced the landing of three other balls onto the ninth green behind them. Within minutes, the other Gang members arrived. Plato waved and walked over to them.

"What's the hang up?" Vandeweghe asked. "Someone get lost in the fog?"

Rudy joined them. "We think P.Q. leveled a guy with his drive off nine," he said with a smirk.

"Really?" Vandeweghe said, his brow furrowing. "Has someone gone ahead to call for a medic?"

Plato waved his hand in the air. "No, no, not really." He shot Rudy a stern look. "Rude's just kidding. We found Patrick's ball in the gorse just right of the green. I'm guessing these guys found a fairway bunker and can't get out."

Vandeweghe harrumphed. "More likely they found gorse. There's only one bunker, and it's nearly three hundred yards out."

Ridge joined them, and Plato noticed he was all smiles and red cheeks. "What's up, Old Tom? You look mighty cheery."

Ridge grinned from ear to ear. "I eagled the first hole!" He demonstrated with his hands as he said, "Knocked my drive at least two-sixty, then made a nice little chip that landed and rolled right into the hole! An eagle! On the New Course!"

Rudy yelped for joy. Plato thrust out his hand and Ridge grabbed it tightly.

"Congratulations!" Plato said, and found himself smiling as broadly as Ridge. "Something to write home about, that's for sure."

Someone yelled, the sound muffled by the wind and the fog, and Plato turned and saw Don waving from the tenth tee. "We're good to go!" He motioned for Plato and Rudy to rejoin their foursome.

"Keep it up!" Plato said to Ridge, and followed Rudy back to their tee.

"Everything okay?" Don asked.

Plato nodded. "Ridge eagled number one. That'll make the whole trip for him."

Don grinned. "Now all he needs is a hole-in-one and there'll be no living with the man."

Plato nodded in agreement, but truly, he hoped all his friends had a hole-in-one on this trip. That would be awfully special.

The fog lifted completely by the fourteenth hole, but the wind was now a constant challenge. Patrick was feeling the effects, and was lying four over, but Rudy was truly struggling. As they stood on the seventeenth tee, Plato did a mental count and realized his friend was looking at twelve over for the round.

"The book says it's two-oh-eight to the front of the green," Don said. "Wind from left to right, but with us a bit, as well."

"Looks like the flag is in the front," Patrick said.

Rudy wiggled, waggled, and swung. The ball shot off the face of the club and headed straight for the middle of the green.

"Sit down! Sit down!" Plato yelled, thus surprising himself and causing Patrick and Don to laugh.

"Well, Rude," Patrick said. "You're finally boldly going where many a man has gone before!"

"Look at that darn ball shoot across the green," Rudy said. "There's no stopping that baby."

The four of them laughed together, and Don had to step away from his teed ball and compose himself. The other three continued to chuckle.

"Hey, hey," Don said. "I'm trying to win a tournament here. Do you mind?"

Rudy waved toward the green. "By all means, whack away."

Don took a deep breath, set, leaned in to his left side, and swung. The ball left the ground and a strong gust of wind grabbed it and shoved it right.

"No, no, not over there!" Patrick said. "Get away from that bunker!"

They watched as the ball dropped like a stone, neatly into the bunker to the right of the green.

Don hummed and a lopsided grin creased his face. He waggled a finger at Patrick. "You had to say it, didn't you. You had to remind it there was sand."

Patrick grinned and shrugged. "You've been torturing that poor ball all round. It's time it had a soft landing." He hit, and his ball landed obediently in the middle of the green and spun back toward the hole.

Plato placed his neatly on the front edge. He did another mental calculation – Don had a two stroke lead after the first day's round on the Old Course, and he was two over for this round, while Patrick was five over. Plato knew he, himself, would have to birdie this hole and the eighteenth to have a chance at winning the Championship. He wondered how Chris and Vandeweghe were doing.

When they arrived at the green, Don moaned. Plato walked over and looked in the bunker. Don's ball was buried not two feet from the front lip, which was at least four feet tall.

"Hit it back out onto the fairway," Plato said. "You'll never make it out over that edge."

Don pursed his lips, took a few practice swings with his wedge, then stepped into the bunker. To Plato's dismay, the man faced the green, blade wide open but his left foot only inches from the bunker face. Plato bit his lip to keep from making a comment, then shrugged and walked away. If anyone could get out of that bunker, it was Don.

Rudy and Patrick joined Plato at the front edge of the green. Hands stuffed into pockets or crossed under armpits, they watched as Don made a mighty swing. Sand flew in the wind, and the ball ricocheted off the front edge, back toward Don's legs. Don leapt into the air to avoid getting hit. Plato shook his head slightly as his own frustration mounted.

Don knocked the sand off his wedge and reset himself over the ball, again facing the green.

"Why doesn't he just hit out the other way?" Rudy whispered. "There's no lip."

Patrick sighed, then again trying to sound like Captain Kirk, said, "There are certain things men must do to remain men."

Plato shot him a questioning look and Rudy rolled his eyes.

"What?" Patrick said. "The Ultimate Computer episode. Don't tell me you don't remember that one?"

Don swung and, again, the ball hit the peat and bounced back into the sand. Again, a thoughtful address, a good swing, and the same result. Plato could see Don's face becoming red, and his shoulders sagging. Immediately, Don addressed the ball for the fourth time and whacked at it; yet another time, the ball refused to leave the bunker, though this time – at least – it had landed further away from the lip.

Don exited the bunker, banged his wedge on the ground twice to dislodge the sand, and stood with his back facing Plato, Rudy, and Patrick. None of them said a word, though Plato felt Don's agony. What a way to ...

"Winterhalter!" Plato called. "Hit it again."

Don turned and looked directly into Plato's eyes. "I'm already two over on this hole," he said, and Plato could hear the carefully controlled anger in his voice.

"Hit it again," Plato said and smiled. "You haven't lost yet."

Don cocked his head to the side, brow furrowed. Then the realization of what Plato was communicating hit him. A big grin crossed his face.

"Maximum triple bogey net," Don said. "Does it apply to the Stroke Championship, as well?"

Plato smiled broadly, then feigned surprise. "Are you nuts?" he joked. "No, it doesn't apply to this. But hit it again, anyway."

Don shook his head and continued to grin. Still smiling, he set himself in the sand, swung, and sent the ball sailing softly over the lip. It landed five feet from the pin and rolled to a stop, mere inches from the hole.

"Hey hey!" Rudy yelled. "Nice shot!"

"Good thing you had all those practice swings," Patrick said.

Plato returned Don's nod of accomplishment, and moved to his own ball. Unless Patrick birdied the next two holes, Don would still win the Championship. Either way, a friend would win, and he'd be happy.

Plato stood at the edge of the eighteenth green, leaning on his putter. Patrick had birdied seventeen, as had Rudy, and it looked like all four of them were going to make par on eighteen. Nice way to end, Plato decided. This round had been more difficult than anticipated, a fact he attributed to the fog and wind. Ah, well – Scottish sunshine indeed. They'd been lucky with the weather during most of the trip. No whining.

Don completed his round by dropping a four-foot putt for par, and Plato was almost certain Don had won the Stroke Play Championship. Unless one of the guys in the other foursome had played lights out – not a great possibility, with the weather – Don's first round on the Old Course had secured him the win, even with that debacle in the bunker on seventeen.

Plato smiled slightly. "Nice putt," he said to Don, who moved beside him and leaned on his putter.

"Thanks," Don said. "Hope it was enough."

Plato nodded. "I think it will be."

They agreed to wait for the other Gang members and, soon enough, four balls graced the green. Vandeweghe, Charlie, Ridge, and Chris hoofed it up, trolleys in tow. Plato noticed that Charlie looked particularly sore and tired.

Putts were dropped and handshakes were given all around, and the Gang headed for the parking lot to stow their bags in the van. Plato walked silently, listening to tales of birdies missed by mere inches, bunkers tackled with various degrees of success, and drives that resembled the proverbial fish stories – getting longer by the telling. As he loaded his bag into the van, Plato realized this part of the round was almost as much fun as the part that generated it; the personality of the man was revealed by the retelling. Exuberant, considerate, lavish, or reserved, the manner of delivery was as individual as the golfer.

"Lunch?" Ridge said. "I'm near to famished."

Patrick patted his own considerable belly and said, "You're no nearer to being famished than I am. But yes, I could use some grub."

"Let's go eat at the Links Clubhouse," Vandeweghe said, and all agreed.

The Links Clubhouse was charming and inviting, Plato decided, but nothing out of the ordinary. The food, however, was excellent, and Plato was delighted when Vandeweghe treated the whole Gang to a dessert of cognac, coffee, and a cheese and chocolate platter. It seemed the perfect conclusion to their time in St Andrews.

Plato found himself becoming nostalgic and dispirited at the idea of leaving. He either wanted to stay here for the next two days, or leave Scotland altogether and head home. These past three days had seemed like the culmination of the trip. What better way to end than at the birthplace of golf? Anywhere else would seem anticlimactic.

"Plato! Hey, Pro!"

The sound of his name pulled him from his reverie. He blinked and looked up.

"I thought we lost you there," Patrick said. "Were you replaying the round in your dreams?"

Plato nodded. "Something like that."

"So we're heading to the golf shop for a little shopping," Chris said.

"Towels and head covers, shirts and hats," Patrick added. "Stuff like that."

"Do you want to come?" Chris said. "Take home a memento?"

Plato sighed. The memories of the rounds with his buddies were enough of a memento for him, but he nodded enthusiastically. "Sure, let's go."

Inside the shop, he listlessly fingered a few shirts, caps, and sweaters, but nothing struck his fancy. He noticed Don near the books and crossed to him.

"Anything interesting?" He glanced at the book Don held in his hand. "*St Andrews Golf Links. The First 600 Years.*" Then he noticed the author. "Tom Jarrett?"

Vandeweghe joined them. "Jarrett, the old Trustee? I saw him this morning. He might be hanging out at the caddy shack. He was a caddy for several years, you know."

Don grabbed two books and hummed. "Excellent. Carlo asked me to bring home a signed copy, if at all possible. I'll see you guys at the van. I'm going to go get these signed."

Plato considered following him, then decided he wasn't that intrigued by the book, beautiful as it was. He was more interested in present day experiences on the Old Course, not in its history.

"Here you go, pro," Vandeweghe said, and handed him another book. It was the same size as the Jarrett book, and had a similar cover.

"*St Andrews. How to Play the Old Course*," Plato read. He flipped it open and perused the pages. Now this was more like it.

"You can replay your rounds," Vandeweghe said. "I have this at home and I really like the aerial photos."

Plato felt his spirits lift. He patted the book. "Thanks, Gooch. This is perfect. I can show Lynea the course, as well."

Vandeweghe nodded. "Lasts longer than a sweater, too. Unless you accidentally drop it in the washer."

Plato noticed Vandeweghe held a round cardboard tube in his hand. "And what are you taking home that you don't already have?"

Vandeweghe grinned mischievously. "Just a little something. A surprise." He tucked the tube under his jacket and headed toward Charlie and Ridge, who were trying on sweaters.

Plato wondered, but only briefly. A rack of women's items had caught his attention. It was time to find something Lynea would appreciate.

Laden with treasures, the Gang of Eight headed to the van. Ken was busy organizing clubs and suitcases, and he waved at them from inside the trailer.

"Almost done," he said, hefting Vandeweghe's bag into place.

Clearly reluctant to leave, the Gang hovered around the van, chatting and glancing back toward the course. Don showed off the signatures he'd procured from the author of his books, and Patrick was showing his father the small Scottish dolls he'd found for his daughters.

Ken stuck his head out of the trailer and waved them away. "Go on," he said, "get in the van, will ya? I've a surprise for ya."

The Gang exchanged bewildered and curious looks, and filed into the van. Inside the vehicle they found a gift basket filled with fruit, candies, and homemade Scottish butter cookies. They also found two trays of steaming coffee.

"Whoa! Ken!" Rudy said. "Did you do something naughty?"

Ken grinned. "Oh, aye, sir," he said, and Plato couldn't miss the mischief in his eyes.

With a wicked grin, Patrick asked, "And where did you stay these past few days, my friend? Hmmm?"

Ken just chuckled and slid into the driver's seat. "I think ye'll be likin' the cookies, gents. They're made 'specially for you."

"Took a baking class, did you?" Chris bit into a cookie. He nodded in pleasure. "Wow, this is great. What's the secret ingredient?"

Ken turned the key and the van began to rumble. "That'll n'er be told, sir," he said, then yelled loudly, "Secure yer coffees, gents! Off we go!"

Plato settled into his seat and watched St Andrews disappear as the van rolled on to their next destination. He wrinkled his brow. What was their next destination? He didn't even remember. He turned to Don. The man was staring intently out the window, a look of soft sadness on his face. Plato glanced at the rest of the Gang and they, too, looked dispirited. Even Patrick was quiet for once, holding his coffee between both hands and watching the scenery flash by.

This just wouldn't do. What would lift the cloud? He thought for a few moments, then a smile creased his face. He began to hum, softly at first, trying to clearly remember the song Lynea had played on their stereo the night the Gang came over for dinner and a planning meeting. They had played it over and over, singing with abandon. What was the songwriter's name? He squinted. Cross, that was it. Mike Cross. He smiled. He'd learned the lyrics, partially because he liked the song, but mostly because it was about Scotland.

He hummed a few more bars, then took a breath and burst into song. "A Scotsman clad in kilt left the bar one evening fair ... And one could tell by how he walked he'd drunk more than his share." Fearing what he'd see, Plato avoided looking at the Gang, but glanced up at the rearview mirror and saw Ken smiling broadly.

With a curt nod, Ken joined in, robustly.

"He stumbled on until he could no longer keep his feet, then he staggered off into the grass to sleep beside the street!"

Patrick let out a yelp of joy and joined in as the refrain was chanted, and one by one the other Gang members began to clap in time. As the song progressed, each Gang member joined in where they could. Plato continued to sing, joined loudly by Ken and Patrick, and as he did so he looked at each of his friends – now smiling and laughing and clapping in time.

"Later on two young and lovely girls just happened by … And one says to the other with a twinkle in her eye … You see yon sleeping Scotsman so strong and handsome built? I wonder if it's true what they don't wear beneath the kilt!"

Rudy let out a yip of delight and sang the refrain with gusto, as did Patrick, Ken, and now Ridge. Plato noticed that Vandeweghe was laughing so hard tears wet his cheeks.

Plato took a breath and continued with the verse, "They creeped up to the sleeping Scotsman quiet as could be … lifted up his kilt above the waist so they could see … And there behold for them to view beneath his Scottish skirt, was nothing but what God had graced him with upon his birth!"

"Woohoo!" Patrick and Chris yelled simultaneously. "Sing it boys!"

And all nine men rocked the van with the refrain. "Ring-dine deedle deedle di-de-o! Ring di deedle-o do! Was nothing but what God had graced him with upon his birth!"

Then it was just Patrick, Ken, and Plato again, as they sang the next lines. "They marveled for a moment then one said 'we'd best be gone' … But let's leave a present for our friend before we move along … So as a gift they left a blue silk ribbon tied into a bow, around the bonny star of the Scots' kilt lifting show!"

Plato motioned for all of them to join as, again, the now familiar refrain was sung. "Ring-ding deedle deedle di-de-o! Ring di deedle-o do! Around the bonny star of the Scots' kilt lifting show!"

As the song concluded, Plato grandly motioned for Patrick and Ken to continue, and he continued to clap with the others.

"The Scotsman woke to nature's call and stumbled toward the trees ... Behind a bush he lifts his kilt and he gawks at what he sees ... Then in a startled voice he says to what's before his eyes ..."

Plato motioned grandly for a halt to all the sound then pointed toward Ken, who sang the concluding line alone, his brogue thick, "My friend I don't know where you been but I see you won first prize!"

The Gang burst into raucous yells and altogether sang the last refrain, "Ring-ding deedle deedle di-de-o! Ring di deedle-o die! My friend I don't know where you been but I see you won first prize!"

They held the last word for as long as breath would allow, then burst into hoots, hollers, and laughter. Plato wiped a tear from his eyes and looked around. The van was bursting with joy. Chris and Patrick began singing another song they'd learned on their night out in St Andrews, coffee cups raised high.

Rudy and Don began exchanging stories about their best shots on the Old Course, and Vandeweghe and Charlie were shuffling a deck of cards. Ridge was in the back of the van, humming as he made use of his porta-potty gas can.

Plato settled into his seat with smug satisfaction. They were ready for the next adventure, which was ... ah yes, Carnoustie.

All was right with the world again. At least in the world of the Gang of Eight, and in this particular moment in his life, that's what counted.

CHAPTER 41

September 6, 1998

Don Ridge and Patrick Quinn

"That's like the doctor up in the city," Ridge said in his special 'I'm telling a joke now' voice. "He's talking to a patient and the patient tells him, 'you know, when I move my arm it makes a noise.' And the doctor shakes his head and says, 'I can treat anything but a noise.'"

Ridge pulled his beard and chuckled. He was delighted by the guffaws and light banter given in response by the other Gang members. He knew his jokes were always appreciated by this group. It made them worth the telling.

"Gents," Ken called from the driver's seat of the van, "I give you Letham Grange."

Ridge looked out the window, and whistled. "Now there's a sight for sore eyes. Are we staying here tonight?"

"Last stop," Don said. "We'll be here for three nights, then it's home."

Ridge wrinkled his brow. "But I thought we were heading to Carnoustie."

Vandeweghe nodded. "Carnoustie is just a few miles away. The accommodations here are, for my money, better."

"And we know your money's always better than anyone else's," Ridge joked.

The van pulled around a group of tall trees and came to a stop at the entrance. Ridge, who always chose to sit in the back of the van so he could easily reach his gas can, was the last to exit. The Gang was standing in a small clump, gawking.

"Wow, this is really beautiful," Patrick said. "How'd you find this place?"

"Through the magic of Tony and Paula at the travel agency," Don said.

Charlie rubbed his chin. "There's a golf course here, too, isn't there?" He pointed through the trees. "I see a green."

"Aye, there be two," Ken said. "The Old 'n the New."

Chris chuckled. "Where have I heard that before?"

"The Scots must lack any sense of imagination," Rudy said. "They can't seem to come up with other names for their courses."

"Well, the Old Course here doesn't live up to its name," Plato said. "It was built in the late eighties."

Charlie shrugged. "That's more than a hundred years old, now."

Plato shook his head. "Nineteen-eighties. Not eighteen-eighties."

The Gang entered the Victorian mansion, now turned hotel, and Ridge was instantly impressed by the interior. He had the feeling he'd just stepped into another century, but as he looked around carefully, he realized everything was in perfect condition – not a rip or rub or crack anywhere. The place was immaculate and gorgeous. He sighed with contentment.

Ten minutes later they exited the building, room keys in hand. Ridge paused outside the front door and tapped Chris as he passed. "Hey Chris, can you take my picture? I think Nellie would like to see this place."

Chris nodded, took the camera, and stepped back. Vandeweghe walked through the doors, saw Chris with the camera, and jumped aside. "Oh, sorry. I didn't mean to barge into your photo."

Ridge waved for Vandeweghe to join him. "Come on, come on, get in the picture. No one wants a shot with just my ugly mug. Not even Nellie."

Chris framed the shot and pushed the button. Patrick and Rudy walked up and began to giggle.

Ridge frowned. "What are you laughing at?" He ran his hands over his beard. "Do I have potato chips in my beard again?"

"No, no!" Rudy said. "You two, standing together..." He started laughing again and motioned for Patrick to finish his sentence.

"You're the Royal and Ancient!" Patrick said. "The embodiment of Scotland!"

Vandeweghe waived and walked away. "You guys…"

Ridge chuckled. "Well, which one am I? Royal, or ancient?"

Rudy, Chris, and Patrick broke into full-force laughter. Chris handed the camera back to Ridge, and followed the others toward the van.

Ken piled their suitcases outside the trailer, made arrangements to pick up the Gang the next morning, then sped off, dust flying, trailer bouncing.

"Ugh," Vandeweghe groaned. "There go our clubs. I'll be amazed if any of us have a full set with him tossing them around like that."

Chris grinned and elbowed Patrick. "What's your bet he's heading back to St Andrews?"

Patrick nodded. "For more cookies, no doubt."

"You think?" Don said. "They were awfully good cookies. Hope he brings more back with him."

They made their way to their rooms. Ridge followed Vandeweghe through the door, dropped his bags, and began to chuckle.

Vandeweghe looked around, confused. "What's so funny? Something wrong?"

Ridge motioned toward the room. There was one king bed in the middle, and a small couch associated with a crowded seating area.

"Are you planning on sleeping on that?" he asked, pointing at the couch. "Because I certainly won't fit."

Vandeweghe surveyed the problem, harrumphed, and picked up his bag. "Well, come on." He moved toward the door. "They obviously made a mistake."

The lovely woman at the front desk was nearly mortified by the situation, and Ridge wondered how she'd handle a truly difficult problem, should one arise. Yet, within minutes, she had them moved into a different room, though further away and on the second floor. Ridge was about to complain when she handed them the key and said, "Tis th' Queen's Suite, sir." She shrugged. "Though, in truth, the Lady has ne'er visited."

"Not much of a golfer, is she?" Ridge said. "Doesn't know what she's missing."

"Aye, sir," the woman said, and bobbed her head in dismissal.

The Queen's Suite lived up to its name, with two separate, though small, rooms adjoining a center living area. For Ridge, the best were the expansive windows that displayed a view of the golf course. He wished Nellie were with him. She would have known how to thoroughly enjoy this place.

At seven, they all convened in the lobby for dinner. Ridge had noticed the large dining room when they arrived, and was surprised when the hotel manager led them to an adjoining, private dining space. The room was warmed by dark wood paneling, and enhanced by several grand windows, guarded by rich, brocade ceiling-to-floor drapes. Through them, Ridge could see a flower garden, a fairway, and a green.

The food was excellent, and Ridge was happy to hear the chef used only local produce and meats. Somehow the knowledge made the food taste even better. After dessert, Plato stood and rapped his wine glass with his butter knife. The chatter at the table grew quiet.

"Lads, I have the results of our Scottish Stroke Play Championship. It was a difficult tournament, with many a memorable shot –"

"And some very unmemorable," Charlie said. "In fact, ones we hope to quickly forget."

Plato waited for the chuckles to die before continuing. "However, a finer group of golfers has never graced the Old and New courses at St Andrews, and I'm proud to announce the winners."

Plato pulled a folded piece of paper from his pocket, flattened it, and ceremoniously held it before him. Ridge grinned in anticipation. He had no hopes of being at the top of that list, but he long ago realized this was always the best moment of any tournament – off the course, anyway. This moment when all is possible, hope still thrives, and nothing is known for certain.

Then Plato spoke, and the moment was gone.

"Fifth place Gross, with a total score of 155, is..." Plato smiled sheepishly and shrugged, "...me." He waived off the smattering of applause and continued. "Fourth place Gross, also with 155 but with a better score on the punishing back nine of the Old Course, is none other than our Burger Deluxe, Mr. Chris Clark."

"Hey, hey!" Chris called, and threw his hands in the air. "If only I hadn't found the Road Hole!"

"Or the road itself," Patrick teased. "That's hard on a score."

Plato proffered a neatly folded piece of paper to Chris, who dramatically flipped it open. "Seventeen dollars and fifty cents! My grand winnings."

Charlie chuckled. "That'll pay for your glass of wine tonight."

"Maybe," Vandeweghe said.

Ridge bristled a bit. The wine had been an issue with him the entire trip. "Well, Gooch, if you didn't always order the most expensive bottle on the menu."

Vandeweghe looked crestfallen. He glanced around the table. "I'm sorry. Are the rest of you upset at my choices? I just figured we might as well enjoy ourselves."

A small cacophony went up in his defense.

"No, no, it's been great," Rudy said, while Charlie raised his empty glass and said, "Fabulous!" and Don nodded and added, "Here, here!"

Patrick belted out, "Gooch, you almost converted me from beer to wine on this trip."

Charlie chuckled. "And that's saying something." He patted Patrick on the back. "Your mother would be pleased if something positive came out of this trip."

Patrick smiled at his father. "Other than how much fun we've had together?"

Ridge pursed his lips tightly, then leaned on the table and looked directly at Vandeweghe. "I'm not saying I didn't like the wine. I'm just saying it would've been nice if you'd taken into consideration the fact that not all of us at this table are millionaires."

There was an uncomfortable silence, and Ridge sighed. "That's all I'm saying," he whispered.

Vandeweghe tilted his head. He looked at Ridge and said, softly, "I haven't forgotten." He looked at each man sitting at the table, and there was sorrow in his eyes. "I haven't forgotten who my buds are."

Ridge suddenly felt shabby. He hadn't meant to hurt Vandeweghe; Heaven Above knew how much Ridge adored the blue-blooded oaf. But sometimes the guy just forgot the realities of life.

Plato cleared his throat and rattled his paper. "And so I am proud to announce that third place Gross goes to our esteemed leader, Tried & True – Mr. Gary Vandeweghe."

The applause was hearty, and Ridge joined in with gusto. Vandeweghe accepted the award from Plato. He held out thirty dollars for all to see.

"For the wine!" Vandeweghe said and winked at Ridge. "At least for tonight."

Laughter filled the room and Ridge relaxed back in his chair.

"Second place, with 152, goes to the Mission Prince, Mr. Patrick Quinn." Plato handed the award letter to the young man. "And now, drum roll, maestro." Plato motioned to Patrick, who promptly thrummed the thick table. Plato paused for dramatic effect, then grandly said, "Our winner, by one stroke, is the slick Silver Cloud, Mr. Don Winterhalter."

Applause filled the room, and Don pumped his fist in the air. "Thank you, Mr. Plato, for instigating that triple bogey net rule! I wouldn't be here without it."

Patrick laughed. "No, no you wouldn't, Winner-halter. You'd still be in that bunker!"

Plato waved for silence and pulled another paper from his pocket. "We now have the awards for Net. Third place, and an award large enough to buy a ball marker, goes to our Seamus McDuff, Mr. Rudy Staedler."

Rudy stood, took a bow, and accepted the paper upon which was written his name and "$10.00."

Rudy laughed. "I think I'll frame it and put it up in my office. This was the most difficult ten dollars I've ever earned."

"Second Net goes to the solid Stone Hinge," Plato said. "Congratulations, Mr. Charlie Quinn!"

With a sedate nod and a wonderfully crooked grin, Charlie rolled the award letter into a funnel, then held it aloft as if it was the Claret Jug.

The Gang erupted in applause.

Plato raised his voice and said, "And our final winner for the evening goes to the man who resembles one of golf's most decorated personalities, Old Tom Morris." Plato held out his left hand in the direction of Ridge. "Mr. Don Ridge!"

Ridge patted his belly and nodded in acknowledgment of the accolades provided by the other Gang members. He stood, took the letter which had been handed down the table, and glanced at the notation. He'd won twenty dollars, and since they'd all put in twenty-five, he'd almost broke even. He glanced around at his clapping friends. It wasn't the money that made his heart swell with joy; despite his frustration over the wine issue, he really wasn't concerned about money. No, what was important to him was this feeling of camaraderie; of being appreciated by men he admired; of feeling equal. To his utmost chagrin, Ridge felt his eyes dampen with emotion.

"Speech! Speech!" Patrick hollered.

Ridge shook his head and waved dismissal. Then he remembered Nellie's humorous imitation of Sally Fields' Academy Award acceptance speech. Ridge pressed the letter to his chest and, in a high-pitched voice, said loudly, "You like me! You really, really like me!"

Laughter filled the room. Suddenly, all the libations he'd consumed hit him, and Ridge excused himself to find the "loo." He tucked his award letter into his pocket and trotted from the dining room. A gentleman at the front desk directed him to the men's room, but when Ridge returned to the dining room, he found it empty, the table strewn with used crockery, the candles extinguished.

Ridge stood for a moment, suddenly feeling very empty. They'd left him. He felt silly and childish. He grunted with disgust at his own emotional response, and turned to leave. In the main dining room, Chris stood, waving.

"Ridge! Over here!"

Ridge followed Chris into a small, comfortably overstuffed living room and found the rest of the Gang spread over couches, chairs, and on the floor. The manager was bent over a television, wiggling wires and twisting knobs.

Ridge flopped into a large, wingback reading chair. "What's happening?"

"We're trying to get the Forty-Niner game," Rudy said. "It's the season opener, they're at home, and playing the Jets."

"Agh!" The Manager moaned and stood. "I know we kin get th' game. But I think we're missin' th' part to connect. I'll just head t'the shop 'n be right back."

He scooted from the room with a flurry of calls to his staff. Ridge blinked and looked at Rudy. "It's after nine. Where's he gonna find a store open?"

"It's Scotland," Rudy said. "He probably owns the shop, too." He flopped onto the couch. "Might as well get comfortable. We could be here a while."

Charlie, Plato, and Vandeweghe decided to return to their rooms to change, and the others settled in with a magazine to wait. Ridge crossed to the small window and looked outside. Night was finally settling in, and he could make out two faint stars in the sky. He smiled. Nellie could be looking at those same stars. The thought made him a bit homesick. Maybe it was a good thing they were here for only a few more days.

Just as Patrick was about to give up and return to his room, the manager entered with a small box and a collection of screw drivers. One of the restaurant staff delivered a tray with coffee, tea, and a decanter of what Patrick soon discovered was excellent brandy. As the Gang shared stories of that morning's round on the New Course, the manager tinkered with the television. Finally he flipped the "on" switch.

"All right!" Vandeweghe said at the sight of a clear picture.

"Now, ye said th' game's with a club called th' Forty-Niners, aye?" the manager said, as he flipped channels. "'Tis football?"

"American football, not soccer," Patrick said. "You know, helmets and shoulder pads –"

"And no one touching the ball with their feet," Chris joked.

Candlestick Park field flashed across the screen.

"There! There it is!" Rudy said. "Ah. Home sweet home."

The manager fiddled with a few more wires and knobs, and the picture popped out clear and crisp. He stood back and, with obvious delight, surveyed the results of his work. "So, you laddies enjoy the game, 'n let Agnes know if there be anything ye're wantin'."

Patrick took over the couch, motioning for his pop, who joined him. He watched as the other Gang members settled in: Ridge refreshed his brandy and settled into a wingback chair; Don snagged a pillow from the couch and flopped onto the floor, punching the pillow into a comfortable position under his head. Rudy followed suit, and Vandeweghe sprawled over another wingback chair, his left leg thrown over an overstuffed arm. Plato drug in a chair from the dining room and positioned himself beside the cold fireplace. Chris disappeared for a moment, then returned with a young Scotsman in tow, arms laden with wood.

"Now there's an excellent thought," Plato said, and made way so the two men could get to the large fireplace.

"Good plan, Chris," Don said.

Chris helped the young man place the wood on the grate. "Well, I, for one, am tired of being chilled. That fog this morning went right through to my bones."

Patrick nodded in agreement. He, too, had yet to warm up from the chilly round.

The fire caught immediately, and the young Scotsman quickly placed a screen to keep the snapping embers from exiting the fireplace. With a wave and a smile, he trotted from the room.

Chris motioned to Vandeweghe. "Hey, Gooch, throw me one of your cushions."

Patrick reached behind his back and retracted an oblong pillow. "Here, I've got one." He tossed it at Chris, who then sat on the floor with his back against the end of the couch, the pillow wedged behind him.

Ridge nudged Chris with a foot. "You want to sit here? I'm not likely to watch the whole game."

Chris shrugged. "Naw, you keep the seat. You deserve it."

Patrick slid his eyebrows upward. "What, after kicking your butt on the course these past few days?"

Chris nodded and smiled at Ridge. "Yeah, a soft seat on your backside is your big prize."

Patrick's attention returned to the game as Garrison Hearst carried the ball thirty-seven yards, getting the Niners inside the red zone. He watched as the Niners then failed several attempts at a touchdown, causing moans and groans and muttered admonitions to be issued from the Gang.

Patrick switched from brandy to coffee and wondered if the bar was open, and if they had a decent beer. The Jets intercepted the ball and ran half the field for a touchdown, and Patrick forgot about alcohol. Half way through the second quarter, the Jets called a time-out, and the station switched to commercials. Patrick stretched.

Ridge shifted in his chair. "So, you guys know the top signs you're too old to play golf?"

Charlie looked over. "You're under ground?"

"In a box," Patrick added.

"Or you're inducted into the Hall of Fame," Rudy said, "posthumously."

The Gang laughed. Ridge said, "One, your bones make so much noise that the marshal asks you to leave the course. Two, you need a step stool to get in and out of the cart. And three, your body has more dimples than a golf ball."

Patrick joined the guys in a good chuckle, then became silent as the game resumed. Within minutes, the Jets scored and another commercial came on. Ridge leaned forward. "Did I tell you guys my Arnold Palmer joke?"

"I don't think so, Ridge," Patrick said. "Tell us now."

Ridge sat upright. "Palmer is playing this tournament and he comes to a long par three, about two-twenty. He ponders a moment, then pulls a two-iron and hits the ball over the flag onto the back of the green. It then backs up to about two feet from the pin. Some sandbagger says, 'Mr. Palmer, how'd you get your two-iron to spin back like that?' Ol' Arnie asks, 'Sir, do you own a two-iron?' The guy nods. 'And how far do you hit it?' Arnie asks. 'Maybe a hundred 'n seventy yards,' the guy says. Palmer looks him in the eye and says, 'Well, why the hell would you want it to back up?'"

"Hey, I resemble that remark," Rudy said amidst the laughter.

On the television, a referee was explaining a penalty. A Jet walked up and clearly flipped off the referee.

"Oh ho!" Chris said. "Now that's not smart."

"Well, that's the difference between golf 'n football," Ridge said. "We don't tell the marshals to engage with themselves in a physically impossible act."

Charlie chuckled. "Better than engaging with the mascot."

"Especially when it's a guy with an oversized, stuffed head and helmet," Plato said.

Vandeweghe stretched his long legs. "There's always the cheerleaders."

"Aahhh," crooned Rudy. "And you would know, after your years on the basketball court."

"How do you think he met Barbara?" Patrick said, then realized he didn't actually know how Vandeweghe had met his wife.

Vandeweghe flipped his hand in the air. "Barbara wouldn't have been caught dead in a cheerleader's outfit."

"Don't know why not," Charlie said. "She looks pretty good in a golf skort."

Patrick shot his pop a look of surprise, then the crowd noise on the television drew his attention. "Oh oh oh!" he yelled and pointed at the screen. "Loose ball! Ah, come on Niners!"

"There he goes!" Don said. "End of story. Touchdown, Jets."

"Ugh," Plato groaned. "Twenty-seven, seven. Is it safe to call this a romp?"

"It's only half time," Chris said. "Give it another quarter."

Patrick switched back to brandy, and the other men refilled their glasses and mugs with their beverage of choice as the half time show played. The third quarter began, and the Gang settled in to watch. The Jets scored a field goal. Patrick got up to stoke the fire. He paused, and looked closely at Don.

"Hey guys," he said quietly. "Winterhalter's out."

Rudy looked over at the sleeping Don, and grinned. "He's not drooling, is he? 'Cause if he's drooling I'll have to go get my camera."

Chris chuckled. "Probably not drooling, but give him a moment and he'll start snoring."

As if on cue, snores played under the sound of the football game. Patrick, Chris, and Rudy exchanged looks.

"Is that Don?" Rudy asked.

Patrick leaned closer to Don. "Nope. Quiet as a church mouse." He looked around then threw back his head and moaned. "It's Pop! Oh, the humiliation of it all. My own father. In public."

He stoked the fire and returned to the couch, careful not to disturb Charlie. The game continued. The fire snapped. The coffee turned cold. The fourth quarter began with the score thirty to fourteen. Patrick stretched and thought to make a cynical comment about the Forty-Niner's season, then realized the room had grown very still. He checked his friends. All of them were asleep, passed out on the floor or in their chair. Charlie continued to snore occasionally.

Patrick checked his watch. It was nearly one in the morning. The sound of crowd excitement drew his attention back to the television. Jerry Rice caught a long pass and ran nearly the length of the field for a touchdown. Patrick yelped in joy, then looked around in guilt. Don shifted on the floor, but that was the only response to his outburst.

The game clock read ten minutes, thirty-two seconds. The score was now thirty to twenty-one. Patrick contemplated going to bed, then decided to have one more brandy. He reached for a glass, then picked up a mug. He poured an inch of brandy, crossed to the fireplace, and held the mug over the smoldering fire. He held it as long as he could stand the heat. More cheering made him turn, and he saw Garrison Hearst make another amazing run, nearly taking the ball into the end zone. One play later, the score was thirty to twenty-eight.

Patrick sunk into the couch and sipped his warmed brandy. Through the window, the moon shone brightly, and on the television, the Forty-Niners provided fireworks. With only two minutes and twenty seconds left to the game, the Jets had the ball, and Patrick was consoling himself to a loss. Suddenly, Foley threw a wobbler. The Niners intercepted and got the ball back on their own twenty-two yard line.

Patrick sat up, nearly spilling the remainder of his brandy. "Hey guys. Guys!" He nudged Chris. "Chris, wake up."

Chris woke with a start. "What?" He sat up and scratched his head. "Game still on?"

"It's a great game," Patrick said. "We're down by two and we just got the ball back on an interception."

Chris nudged Don and Vandeweghe. "Hey fellas, time to wake up. The game is finally becoming interesting."

One by one, the Gang woke as Steve Young led his team down the field, firing bullets to Jerry Rice and Terrell Owens. One minute and ten seconds left to go, and they were on the Jet's thirty yard line.

Patrick perched on the edge of the couch. "Come on, just kick the field goal! That's all you need!"

To his chagrin, the kicking unit stayed on the sidelines. Young took the snap, dodged a sack, ran sideways – "Throw it!" "Get rid of it, you moron!" "Unleash the ball!" – ran forward, and finally threw the ball ... off the field and out of bounds.

"Aw! Jeez!" Rudy yelled. "You had to throw a lemon?"

"Pretty exciting game," Don said.

Patrick gripped his mug. "Too exciting. Why don't they just kick a field goal?"

"Too much time left," Vandeweghe said. "They're playing the Jets, not the Browns."

Finally, the kicking unit trotted onto the field. Patrick blew a sigh of relief. "About time."

"Watch out," Vandeweghe said. "That place kicker has an arm."

True to Vandeweghe's words, the kicker received the ball, then dropped back and tossed the ball sideways to Roger Craig.

Patrick jumped to his feet. "Go! Go!" His fellow Gang members echoed the sentiment.

Craig zigzagged his way toward the end zone, dodged one last Jet defender, and tossed himself in for the touchdown.

A rousing cheer filled the room. Patrick swallowed the last of his brandy and sat down, exhausted. "Crimany, I feel like I just ran thirty yards."

Charlie gave him a crooked smile. "You smell like it too."

Patrick chuckled. As Steve Young trotted onto the field, he hollered at his team on the television. "What are you doing?"

"Going for two points," Vandeweghe said. "I guess, anyway."

Sure enough, the Forty-Niners lined up in front of their quarterback. Patrick placed his cup on the ground and tossed his hands in the air.

"Here we go!" Ridge said, and the snap was taken.

"Oh! Oh!" Rudy yelled.

"Find your man!" Plato said. "There!"

Young threw, and the ball found Jerry Rice. "Two point conversion!" the commentator on the television announced. "And the Forty-Niners take the lead, thirty-six to thirty with less than a minute to go!"

"Plenty of time," Chris said. "The defense has their work cut out for them."

Patrick nudged Chris with his foot. "Hey. Don't be talking like that about our team."

To his utmost joy, San Francisco hung on and won the game. As the teams jogged onto the field to pat backs and shake hands, the Gang stood as one and stretched.

"What time is it?" Charlie asked. "It feels late."

"Early," Patrick said, glancing at his watch. "Like one-fifteen early."

Vandeweghe groaned. "We have a nine a.m. tee time, ladies. Breakfast at seven, for those of you who won't still be in your beds."

Patrick said goodnight to the others, including his father, then perched on the arm of the couch and watched the commentators make their closing comments. On a whim, he poured a last splash of brandy into his mug, and tossed it down. The moon had moved out of sight, and the dark through the window was complete.

He looked around the room. This was such a beautiful spot, but if these walls could talk, what would they say? He smiled as his imagination conjured images of knights and damsels in distress, trysts, and political intrigues. He shrugged. He wasn't prone to fantasies.

Then again, he was living one, wasn't he? He yawned. Tonight, a good dream on a soft pillow would be enough.

CHAPTER 42

September 7, 1998
Charlie Quinn

Charlie downed his third cup of coffee in hopes of shaking loose the mild hangover left from the night before. Outside the tall windows that lined the dining room, gray fog concealed the lovely grounds surrounding the castle. Insult to injury – he felt like garbage, and he was going to freeze as well.

Plato pinged his orange juice glass, and Charlie turned his attention back to the warmth of the room.

"Gentlemen, today we'll play the first round of the Scratch Match Championship. We'd thought to play the Championship tomorrow here at Letham Grange and then at Edzell, but there's a good chance we'll cancel at least one of those rounds, so we'll start the Matches today, on Carnoustie."

"You afraid we'll all drop from exhaustion?" Rudy said.

Charlie looked at his compadres, all of whom were leaning heavily on their elbows, and said, "Gee, what gives you that idea?"

"Could be the snoring coming from the end of the table," Plato jested. He pointed at Patrick. "This is your fault, young man. I hold you responsible for any disasters that happen on the course today."

Patrick raised his water glass. "I hereby acknowledge my behavior last night as a act of treason against the mother ship, Gang of Eight."

The table went quiet. Charlie peered at Patrick. "What did you just say? Because none of us understood a word you said."

"Just as well," Patrick said. "Since I couldn't repeat it if I tried."

Don and Ridge entered the room, and Charlie realized, just then, much to his consternation, that they hadn't been at the table for breakfast. How could he have missed them?

"Where you been?" he asked.

Don hummed. "Out putting. It's foggy, but the putting green is terrific."

Ridge dropped into a chair and reached for the coffee pot. "It's not too bad out, once you get acclimated. And if Winner-halter here putts on the course the way he putted on this little practice green, y'all better leave your wallets at home."

Don poured a cup of coffee, took a swallow, then grimaced. "Ack, that's colder than the air outside." He wiped his mouth with a napkin, then tossed it on the table. "So, you guys ready to head to Carnoustie?" Charlie joined the others in a round of moans and groans. Don hummed and gave that little smile Charlie knew so well, then said, "Suck it up, ladies, and let's go play some golf."

"Here, here," Plato said. "The Championship awaits."

Ken was waiting for them when they arrived in the parking lot. He, too, looked bushwhacked, and grumbled when Patrick mentioned cookies.

"Must not have gone as planned last night," Ridge whispered to Charlie.

The ride to Carnoustie was silent and Charlie dozed off.

"Pops. Pops, we're here. Time to join the world."

Charlie opened his eyes, and swore under his breath. The fog was even heavier here, since they were along the coastline. And it was cold, as well; bone-chilling cold. From the van, he retrieved both a sweater and a jacket. He may look like the Michelin Man, but he wouldn't catch pneumonia.

Plato led the Gang to the clubhouse. Across the parking lot, construction cluttered the grounds.

Charlie nudged Patrick. "Must be building something fancy for The Open next year."

Patrick rolled his eyes. "Of course! I completely forgot they were holding The Open here in '99. No wonder Don and Vandeweghe were so keen to play it."

"It won't be set up as it will be for the tournament," Plato said, holding open the door to the small building and ushering the men inside. "They can make this place impossible when they want to."

Rudy rubbed the bridge of his nose. "Today, anything beyond miniature golf will be impossible."

Twenty minutes later, they stood around the first tee. Charlie was paired with Vandeweghe, which was good since he would need someone with length off the tees. He bounced his wood on the grass and wondered if he'd be able to swing it at all. His leg was throbbing, probably more from the cold than from anything else, and his head was starting to do the same. Damn. He just wanted to go back to bed.

Plato stepped onto the tee and addressed the Gang. "Gentlemen, we have arrived at the famous Carnoustie Championship course. In a moment, you will be chasing your ball down the same fairways as did Player, Watson, and of course, Ben Hogan. May your swings be as free and your putts as true. Tee it high and let it fly!"

Charlie leaned on his driver and watched as Chris and Patrick, then Don and Ridge teed off on the first hole. Amazingly enough, they all managed to find the fairway, and walked off in a jovial mood.

Water ran the length of the fairway along the left.

"It doesn't really come into play," Plato said. "I wouldn't worry about it."

"On a normal day, I wouldn't worry," Charlie said. "Today, I have no idea where this ball might go."

Through the fog, Charlie could see the first foursome had made the green, and Plato motioned for Vandeweghe to hit. "You're up, Gooch. Show us the line!"

To Charlie's delight, Vandeweghe sent his ball sailing straight and true, landing in the middle of the narrow throat of the fairway.

"Thanks for taking the pressure off me," Charlie said. He swung, and his ball also flew straight, albeit much shorter than his partner's.

"Glad to oblige," Vandeweghe said. "But you didn't really need me."

Rudy and Plato also landed their first shots in the fairway, and Charlie sighed in relief. Maybe it wasn't going to be such a long day, after all. They walked through the fog, which had lifted enough to see the surrounding area, but still clung to the coastline in dogged persistence.

"So who knows how many Open Championships have been played here?" Rudy said, then quickly added, "Besides you, Pro."

"And you, I warrant," Vandeweghe said. "Or you wouldn't ask the question."

Charlie pursed his lips. "I know Watson won it in '75, but when did Player win his? Sixty-something?"

Rudy nodded, and the motion made Charlie's head pound.

"Sixty-eight," Rudy said. "Two shots over Nicklaus and nearly ten shots over Arnie."

"Was that the Open when Doug Sanders was given the wrong score card on the first round?" Vandeweghe asked.

"Yes!" Rudy said. "Can you believe? They gave him a card to some other course by mistake, and neither he nor his caddy discovered the mistake until half way through the first round. They'd been basing their decisions on the wrong yardages for nine holes."

"If I remember right, it was a card from Panmere," Plato said. "Where we're supposed to play this afternoon."

Charlie grunted. "I'll only be playing that round in my dreams this afternoon."

Vandeweghe chuckled, then pointed at a ball resting softly on the grass. "Start dreaming, my friend. That perfect lie is yours, I believe."

They all made par on the first hole, and Charlie left the green feeling a little less muddy. After driving their balls into the fairway on two, Rudy began his history lesson again.

"So we never answered the question," Rudy said. "How many Opens have been here?"

Vandeweghe wrinkled his forehead. "We ended with Player in '68, right?" He tilted his head and squinted. "So let me think ... Hogan before that, or did he win his at the Old Course?"

Plato shook his head. "No, he won it here, and I'm thinking it would have been in '53."

Rudy smiled. "You are so correct, my friend. Fifty-three it was. And he set the course record at sixty-eight, which still stands, I think."

Charlie scratched his cheek. "He only played in one Open, right?"

Again, Rudy bobbed his head up and down and Charlie wanted to reach over and stop the motion. "Yep, only played in one, and won it going away," Rudy said. He stopped and looked at the ball at his feet. "Which is not what I'm going to do, given this lie."

Charlie glanced at the ball. It lay deep in an old divot, resting against the front lip. "Just gives you a chance to be a star."

"On what? The Cosby Show?" Rudy said, and addressed his ball. "'Cause this is going to be a laugh." He swung and ripped the ball from the earth.

"It's going left," Plato said. "But I think you're short of that front bunker."

"Ha, ha," Vandeweghe said. "And that's all the laugh you're getting."

Charlie was pleased for his friend. "Nice shot, Rude."

They found Rudy's ball just short of the bunker, and Charlie realized he and Vandeweghe, who had both made the green on their second shot, had a chance to go one up. He marked his ball and stepped off the green, waiting for Rudy to chip.

Rudy wiggled, looked at the pin, and swung. For a brief moment, Charlie thought the ball was heading over the back of the green, then it dropped and spun back toward the hole.

"Go in, you little brat!" Rudy yelled.

Vandeweghe vigorously waved his left hand. "Get out, get out! Get away from that hole!"

"It's going in!" Plato said.

And in it went. Vandeweghe groaned, but was smiling broadly. Rudy jumped up in the air and ran around in a little circle, hooting his delight. Charlie grinned and shook his head. You'd think Rudy had just won the Claret Jug.

"Now that's a great shot, Rudy," Vandeweghe said. "You're gonna make it tough on us." He placed his ball before his marker. Charlie estimated it was at least twenty feet. Vandeweghe settled in over the ball, checked his line, and stroked.

Charlie held his breath – it was going to be close.

"Stay on the line!" Vandeweghe said. It did, but came to rest just short of the hole. Charlie joined the others in a groan of disappointment.

"I wanted to see you make that, Gooch," Rudy said.

Vandeweghe tapped in the ball. He made a face, half joking, half serious. "No you didn't. You're the biggest competitor amongst us."

Charlie joined Plato and Rudy in disputing the comment, simultaneously saying, "Get outta here!" and "You're kidding, right?" and "Bull pucky!"

Vandeweghe shrugged his shoulders. "Okay, okay. So, maybe I'm just a little competitive."

Charlie rolled his eyes and placed his ball.

"You're gonna make this putt, right?" Vandeweghe said. "'Cause if you do, we stay even."

Charlie glared at his partner.

"I'm just saying, this would be a good time to sink a putt," Vandeweghe said.

Charlie glared harder. Maybe the guy would get the point.

"Otherwise, you know, we go one down," Vandeweghe said, grinning.

Charlie sighed. Then again, maybe not.

He lined up the putt then gave it a good roll. It swung left, swung right, straightened out, and skimmed the cup by millimeters. A collective "ah!" went up from his three friends.

"Pick it up, Charlie," Plato said. "That's good."

Charlie laughed. Of course he could pick it up. This was match play. "Thanks, pro. Most generous of you."

Once again, as they walked down the third fairway in pursuit of their drives, Rudy piped up. "So, how many Opens? Hm? Anyone?"

Charlie took a deep breath and exhaled loudly. "Well, we left off in– what'd we say? Fifty-three? With Hogan."

"So before that would have been..." Plato paused and squinted. "Gosh, I want to say '35. Maybe '36."

"Close!" Rudy said. "Thirty-seven, with Harry Cotton taking home the trophy."

"Hm," Charlie hummed. "Right on the edge of the Second World War."

Plato nodded briskly. "They only played two more Opens before the war broke out in earnest. There wasn't another championship until '46."

"Well, we know what they did with the courses during the war," Charlie said. "Gosh, it feels like a lifetime ago we played Turnberry."

Vandeweghe pointed at his ball, and Charlie saw it sported a large, gaping gash. "That poor soldier can be retired."

"Replace it," Plato said. "And we'll give it a sea burial in Jockie's Burn, up ahead."

To Charlie's delight, he and Vandeweghe were playing steadily. They gained the lead on six, then lost it on seven, but remained only one down for the next seven holes. Until they stood on the fourteenth tee, he felt they had a chance to win. Now, looking down the narrow fairway, crowded by tall humps, gorse, and ugly bunkers, he had his doubts. His head had cleared about the same time as the fog, but now the wind was a factor, blowing hard from the ocean.

"You're up," Plato said to Charlie. "Just take a little fade around those trees and you'll be fine."

Charlie nodded and set his ball on its tee. He swung, and then watched as the ball sailed to the right, toward a particularly thick patch of gorse.

"Hook!" Vandeweghe yelled.

Charlie puffed his cheeks and blew out a short blast of air. In answer, the wind gusted, and the ball moved off its line, dropping into the rough just off the fairway.

Rudy smiled. "Woohoo! A little love from Lady Luck." He then stepped onto the tee, waggled, and sent his ball screaming into a bunker left of the fairway.

"And that's what you get for disparaging her," Charlie said. "The equivalent of her middle-finger wave."

The men laughed, and headed toward their shots.

"Okay," Rudy said, and Charlie sighed. He just knew they hadn't finished the history lesson, though it hadn't been brought up since the third hole.

"We left off with the 1953 Open, but there's one more," Rudy said.

"Ah!" Vandeweghe moaned. "You just gave away the answer."

"No I didn't," Rudy said.

Vandeweghe pointed at him. "Yes you did, at least to your original question, which was how many Opens have been played at Carnoustie. So now we know there have been five to date."

"Spoken like a true attorney," Rudy said. "So I'll utilize my prerogative to change the question."

"Which is spoken like a true woman," Plato teased, and Charlie laughed along with the others.

"Barbara would take offense at that comment," Vandeweghe said. "And rightfully so."

Charlie chuckled. "Like Dawn wouldn't? Or any of our wives, for that matter."

"The new question," Rudy said, clearly changing the subject, "is when was the first Open played here at Carnoustie? And who won it?"

"That's two questions," Vandeweghe said, then – in response to the moans received – added, "but who's counting."

"You are!" said Charlie and the others in unison, and they all laughed.

Vandeweghe threw his head back in mock disgust. "All right, all right, let's get this over with." He paused and thought, then said with great authority, "Thirty-two, with Tommy Armour winning."

Rudy opened his mouth as if to say "right!" then dropped his head in dismay. "Right and wrong."

"Well, which is which?" Vandeweghe said. "The year or the guy?"

"You figure it out," Rudy said. "That's part of the game."

"The year," Plato said. "I'm betting it's the year."

Charlie decided to take a stab. "Thirty-one, not thirty-two. Am I right?"

"That you are, my fine friend!" Rudy said. "It was in 1931, and yes, Tommy Armour won."

Charlie nodded in pleasure. He wasn't a huge golfing history fanatic, but he remembered a few things from the books he read. "Wasn't Armour a Scot?"

Plato shrugged. "He was born in Scotland, but he'd been in the States most of his life, I think, and he played under the American flag."

"That must have burned the Scots a little," Charlie said.

Vandeweghe chuckled. "It might have, but he wore a kilt to the awards ceremony, in honor of his heritage." He shot a sideways look at Rudy and added, "That much I do know for certain."

The four golfers reached their destination.

"Just like I know for certain you're in the bunker," Vandeweghe said, and headed for his own ball on the right edge of the fairway.

By some miracle, all four of them evaded the gigantic "spectacles" bunkers, though, as they passed them, Rudy couldn't refrain from jumping into the one on the left, just to discover what he could see.

"And what do you see?" Vandeweghe asked.

Rudy laughed. "A whole lot of sand, and a damn big wall in my face. Awfully glad I was in there, and not my ball."

Vandeweghe tossed Rudy the rake, and walked away muttering to himself about "goons."

As they left hole fourteen, Charlie was relieved they had maintained the status quo. On fifteen, he struggled and posted a double-bogey, but so did Rudy and Plato, much to everyone's surprise. Vandeweghe walked to sixteen with a bounce in his step, as he'd birdied the hole, bringing the match to even. Charlie rubbed his aching leg. This course was kicking him, in more ways than one.

Rudy stood beside Charlie on the tee as Plato prepared to drive.

"You feeling okay, Charlie?" Rudy asked. "I noticed you were rubbing your back and leg."

Charlie grunted. "I feel like someone ran over me with cart. An American cart, not one of these little pull numbers." He threw a lopsided grin at his friend. "We're almost done. I'll be fine."

Rudy patted him gently on the shoulder. "This is the toughest course I've ever played. I sure wouldn't want to play it hurting."

"Neither would I," Charlie said, "so I'm just going to forget I am."

At seventeen, the wind really picked up, and the four men agreed the smartest play was laying up in the fairway between the ribbon of Barry Burn, which crossed the hole not once, but twice. Charlie watched his friends do just that with varying success, but when he stood over his tee shot, he knew he was in trouble. The pain in his leg was almost excruciating.

He gritted his teeth and swung. It took monumental control not to cry out in pain as the club swung through the ball, and he blinked to clear the stinging tears from his eyes.

"Sit!" Vandeweghe called out, and Charlie looked for a bench.

"Not you, Charlie," Vandeweghe said. "Your ball." He waved toward the burn. "It's in the water."

Charlie sighed. "I'm not surprised. But if you do find a bench, let me know. Or maybe even a stretcher."

He literally chipped his way to the green in an effort to avoid the pain in his back. Vandeweghe won the hole for them by making par, while both Plato and Rudy struggled, ending with bogeys. Charlie moaned as they stepped up to the last tee. It was formidable, even on a good day, and he wasn't having a good day.

"So it's Miller time!" Rudy said, and pointed to the right of the fairway. "Those bunkers down there, beyond the second crossing of the burn ..." He paused for the men to acknowledge the bunkers, then said, "That's where Johnny Miller lost the '75 Open."

Vandeweghe pulled his driver from his bag. "For all that I'd like to follow Miller on many a round, I think I'll try to avoid those." He then drove his ball cleanly down the middle, landing just to the left of the first bunker.

"Almost found them," Charlie said. "Good shot, Gooch."

Knowing his partner was sitting pretty, Charlie pulled an iron and aimed for the pickle-shaped fairway between the two twists of the burn. He was sure the other guys were wondering what he was doing, but he knew he wouldn't be able to drive over both threads of water, at least not without killing himself with the pain. He took in a deep breath and swung. The ball left the blade and arched high over the first section of burn. It flirted with the wind, then dropped safely into the fairway.

Plato pursed his lips and bopped his head in agreement. "Nice lay up, Charlie."

Charlie nodded. They were one up, and all he wanted to do was get to the end of that fairway without passing out in pain, or becoming permanently immobilized.

Vandeweghe found the green on his second shot, and Plato contemplated the clubs in his bag for several moments before selecting one. He addressed his ball, checked his line, then backed off the ball. He started to chuckle.

"Rats, this hole has me stumped," the pro said. "This wind…" He finally settled on a three wood and readdressed the ball. He swung, and Charlie cringed. Plato had hit it fat.

In silence the four watched the ball sail directly into the burn. Plato slapped the ground with the three wood, and stuffed it back into the bag. Rudy crossed to his ball and, also with a three wood, swung. The ball flew true for a few seconds, then got caught by the wind and came down in the vicinity of the bunker that guarded the green to the right.

The foursome trudged up the fairway, pausing only for Charlie to slap his ball just short of the burn with a seven iron. They then paused again for him to pitch it onto the green.

"There in four," Charlie said to Vandeweghe as they crossed the flat bridge to the green. "Do us a favor and make par, will you?"

"Not if I can help it," Vandeweghe said, then smiled. "I plan on making birdie."

Vandeweghe's plan worked as he dropped a twelve-foot putt for the bird, and he won the hole, putting them two up. Charlie joined the other three as they left the green and headed for the van.

"Wow," Rudy said as they watched Ken put their clubs into the trailer. "That was some course, all right."

Vandeweghe grinned mischievously. "Not so hard."

Plato shook the score card. "How'd a duffer like you make par on the Championship course? Seventy-two, Gooch. Heck of a round."

Vandeweghe waved it off, but Charlie couldn't help but notice the happy gleam in his eye.

"I don't want to know what I shot," Charlie said. "Just keep it to yourself."

Plato chuckled and Rudy said, "You didn't bogey every hole, Charlie. Just the ones that were difficult."

"Anyone else hungry?" Charlie said. "I need sustenance."

"I wonder where the other guys are," Rudy said. "Ken, did they say anything to you about where they were going?"

Ken hefted the last bag into the trailer. "I think they were headed t' lunch. Though I dinna know where they were goin'."

"Let's head to the Carnoustie Golf Club," Vandeweghe said. "I'm guessing that's where they're at."

"If not shopping," Charlie said drolly. "I forgot to confiscate Patrick's credit card before we started."

The four men waved goodbye to Ken, then crossed the street to the small, quaint Carnoustie Golf Club. They entered the dining area and, to Charlie's pleasure, found their other companions, seated with drinks in hand.

"Hey, what happened to you guys?" Chris said. "We lost you after, like, four or something."

"My back is what happened to us," Charlie said. "I slowed us down a bit."

Plato made a face. "No, you did not. We had a few – shall we say – delicate shots that took some time to negotiate."

"Delicate?" Rudy said. "Deviant would be a better word."

They chatted about their rounds, exchanging stories, and offering both condolences and congratulations. Food was ordered and consumed, and Charlie felt his sore body relax a little. At least his leg had stopped throbbing.

"So any new landmarks renamed during your round?" Patrick said. "We almost had another Winterhalter Burn on ten."

Don rolled his eyes. "Hey now. This was nothing like the debacle at Barassie. I merely rolled a ball to the edge of the burn. A single ball, mind you, not several." He glanced at his watch. "Well, gents, we have a tee-time at Panmere in less than an hour. I suggest we get going if we're going to make it."

Charlie motioned for the waitress across the room. "I suggest we have another drink and skip Panmere."

The waitress, a cute young woman with sassy red hair, stopped by Charlie, her hand on the back of the chair. "What kin I get you, sir?" she said.

"Another of these," Charlie said, tapping his now empty wine glass. "And a restraining order for these hackers."

She looked confused. "Sir?"

The Gang laughed lightly.

"He means he wants you to restrain us from going on to our next location for another round of golf," Ridge said.

The waitress bounced her curls vigorously. "Oh, absolutely, sir." She graced the entire table with her smile. "Ye no want'a be leavin' us so soon. We've the best drinks in the land."

"And the best waitresses," Patrick said. "But do you have the best beer, lassie?"

The curls bounced again. "Aye, sir, that we do. Over ninety-five, to be sure."

Patrick's eyebrows rose. "Ninety-five beers?" he said. "On tap?"

"No, sir," the waitress said, and tipped her head to the side. "In bottles, mostly. I'll get ye th' list, if ye please."

Charlie grunted. "He'll please."

Don tapped the table with his fingers. "So I take it we're not playing Panmere?" he said, clearly disappointed.

There was a pause, then Plato broke the silence. "I think some of our illustrious Gang of Eight have hit the wall. In all honesty, I don't think I could swing another driver."

"How about we have one last drink, then head back to Letham Grange," Patrick said. "I'll bet we could get a walk-on at one of their courses. I'd play with you, Don, if you want."

That seemed to mollify Don, who nodded and settled back into his chair. "Sounds good to me," he said, and proceeded to order a lemonade from the redheaded waitress.

Charlie sipped his chardonnay and adjusted his seat to relieve his back. He was glad they weren't pushing to go to Panmere. He'd heard a lot of good things about the course, but he knew he couldn't put in another eighteen. Not today, at least. And maybe not tomorrow, either. He sighed. Could this round be his last in Scotland for this trip? The thought saddened him, and he resolved to play tomorrow, no matter the pain.

Heck, it was only pain, and this, after all, was Scotland.

It was five-fifteen before Charlie woke from his nap and headed down to the lobby at Letham Grange. He found Chris lounging in a chair that faced the huge windows overlooking the course.

"Winterhalter and P.Q. are out on the New Course," Chris said. "Or, the Glens Course, as it's really called."

Charlie nodded and lowered himself into a chair. "Good. That'll take some of the wind out of Patrick. Maybe he'll sleep tonight."

"Keeping you awake, is he?" Chris asked.

Charlie chuckled. "Yeah, he's a bit like a golden retriever. You have to wear him out during the day, or he just wants to play all night. Why do you think I keep sending him out with you?"

Chris grinned and went back to his magazine. Charlie watched a few golfers come up the eighteenth fairway and play the green, which sat behind the castle hotel. "Where are the rest of the guys?"

Chris looked up, thought for a moment, then said, "Plato's giving Rudy a lesson on the driving range, Vandeweghe is reading in the library, and Ridge is still sleeping, I assume."

Charlie was surprised. "Rudy's getting a lesson? Here?"

Chris nodded. "What better place to have one than in Scotland? I'm just sorry I didn't think of it myself."

"Pops!"

The sound of his son's voice caused Charlie to turn. Patrick and Don were entering the lobby, all smiles and ruddy, wind-braced skin.

"How'd it go?" Charlie asked.

"Good course," Don said. "Short but interesting. It's a parkland course, but kind of a nice change after this morning."

"It was great fun, Pops," Patrick said, his enthusiasm apparent. "There's a little bit of everything, and it really makes you think. You can't just hammer the ball around the course."

"Well, I'm glad you liked it," Charlie said, pleased at his son's ardor. He chatted with Don and Patrick, and within a few minutes the rest of the Gang arrived. Vandeweghe arrived with a cardboard tube tucked under his arm.

"Gents, I have a request to make," he said, and popped open the tube. He unrolled several posters, and Charlie smiled his most crooked smile.

"You dog!" Rudy said. "You bought posters of St Andrews!"

"That I did, my friend," Vandeweghe said. "There are nine here – one for each of us to take home, and one to put in the men's locker room at San Jose."

Exclamations of surprised delight filled the room. Vandeweghe pulled several Sharpie pens from his pocket. "Here, you can use these to sign them."

"Oh, even better," Ridge said. "I was afraid we were just gonna take home a boring poster."

Vandeweghe bristled slightly. "Even without our signature, a poster of St Andrews is hardly 'boring'."

Ridge cocked his head and leaned in toward Vandeweghe. "Now I didn't mean anything negative by it. But it is just a poster."

Charlie signed the posters, delighted at the prospect of taking one home, framing it, and hanging it in his study.

When the last poster was signed, Vandeweghe rolled all nine back into the tube. "I'll keep these in here so they don't get damaged. When we get home, I'll make sure you each get one."

The Gang hung around the hotel living room, exchanging pleasantries and stories, and then dinner plans were made.

"But no football tonight," Plato said. "I don't want to see a bunch of hungover sandbaggers at the breakfast table again."

Vandeweghe cocked his head and grinned. "Speak for yourself."

"I am," Plato said. "Now let's go clean up and get some grub."

Charlie walked beside Patrick, his hand resting on Patrick's shoulder. "I'm glad you came along. This would never have been as much fun without you."

Patrick slung his arm around his father's shoulders, and hugged him. "Thank you, Pops," he said, and Charlie recognized the honest emotion in his son's voice.

In their room, Patrick quickly headed for the shower, tossing his clothes like bread crumbs throughout the room as he went.

Charlie rolled onto his bed to wait for his turn in the shower. His mind drifted through memories of the trip, pictures and moments melting into one another. Tomorrow was their last day in Scotland, and while he was definitely ready to go home, he knew he'd want to come back, sooner than later. With Patrick, absolutely, and with the Gang of Eight, certainly.

His mind floated back to the years they'd all spent together. The games on the course, the celebrations – weddings and christenings and graduations – and the hard times they'd overcome. So much had happened, and yet so much had not happened that could have. They were a lucky bunch, and Charlie felt a wave of fervent gratitude wash over him.

"Your turn, Pops," Patrick said as he crossed the room, a towel wrapped around his waist. "Water's nice and hot."

Charlie grunted and headed for the bathroom, pretending, as he went, that he was rubbing his eyes because of exhaustion.

CHAPTER 43

September 8, 1998
Chris Clark

Chris pulled on his rain gear, then his shoes. Outside, the weather was miserable and the rain beat a steady drumbeat against the window. Chris quietly swore. He wanted this last round in Scotland to be good, and this rain was anything but.

"Dumpin' dole," Chris muttered, remembering Ken's words from Barassie. Yes, it was dumpin' dole, and it was cold, as well.

He rubbed his forehead. He hadn't shown it at breakfast – Pro would have kicked him – but Chris had a slight headache, probably left over from the two cigars he'd smoked with Patrick last night after dinner. During the whole trip, they'd routinely snuck away after the rest of the Gang had retired for the evening, and smoked a cigar. He doubted anyone noticed – it was just the two of them, he and Patrick, hanging out around the hotels and resorts, chewing the fat and gaining a little perspective on the day.

He sighed. Well, now his perspective was skewed by this ridiculous headache. He rummaged through his suitcase and found a bottle of Tylenol. He shook out two, paused, then shook out a third and tossed the bottle back into his suitcase.

Don exited the bathroom and grabbed his jacket. "Ready, Chris?"

Chris tossed the pills into the back of his mouth and gulped down a glass of water.

"Headache?" Don asked, eyebrows raised, an impish smile on his face.

Chris nodded. "Yea, but don't tell Plato." They exited their room and headed for the parking lot. "I'll never hear the end of it."

Don hummed. "You and Patrick shouldn't have had that second cigar last night."

Chris's jaw nearly dropped. His first impulse was to deny the allegation, then he shrugged. It wasn't as if they were kids any longer.

"So, I take it we haven't been hiding it very well," he said with a chuckle.

Don shook his head and smiled. "Rather hard to hide the smell, especially when I wake up to it in the morning."

"Shit, I'm sorry," Chris said. "I didn't mean for it to be a bother."

Don placed a hand on Chris's shoulder. "Don't," he said adamantly. "You're never a bother, and luckily cigar smoke smells pretty good, even before breakfast."

They reached the van and found the rest of the Gang pulling their clubs from the trailer, umbrella's held close. Ken was nowhere in sight.

"Where's our illustrious driver?" Chris asked.

"Probably sleeping it off," Vandeweghe said. "He left the keys with the front desk and sent a note up to our room saying he was not to be disturbed, except for an emergency."

Chris nodded. That was fair; they only paid him to drive, not to baby-sit their possessions.

Four caddies shuffled toward them. They were much younger than any of the other caddies they'd encountered, and the young men appeared uncertain. Of course, they could just be wondering why anyone would want to play in this steady downpour. Chris smiled a little. If they only knew the kind of weather the Gang had endured thus far.

"You gents the ones who need caddies?" one of them asked, and Chris was surprised by the lack of brogue. He almost sounded American.

"Aye," Patrick said, as if trying to make up for the missing brogue.

"Well," another caddy said, "we're them. What kin we do for ye?"

The Gang exchanged glances. Oh boy, Chris thought, young and inexperienced.

"You can start by taking our clubs," Vandeweghe said. "Are there only four of you? Can you each carry two bags?"

"I dunna think we had to, sir," one of them said. "We were told two of ye would be usin' a buggy."

"Buggies?" Ridge said. "They have buggies?"

Vandeweghe shrugged. "I guess so." He turned to the caddies. "Okay, where are they? The buggies."

The smallest of the caddies pointed. "We'll be gettin' 'em at the clubhouse, sir."

"Okay," Vandeweghe said, "that still leaves two of you to carry a double bag."

The caddies looked from one to another and shrugged. The two largest caddies wordlessly shouldered one bag on each arm.

"All right, then," Vandeweghe said. "Off we go."

The pairings had been based on yesterday's rounds, handicapped, so Chris and Patrick were to play Charlie and Vandeweghe for the Championship, while Don and Ridge played Plato and Rudy for the consolation third and fourth places. Chris was actually excited. His headache was still hanging around, but he really wanted to go home and tell Hally he'd won against the Gang. At least once.

The course was, indeed, parkland, with trees lining most of the fairways, and lush groomed grass making up the fairways. They weren't considerably wide, nor were they long, but the conscientious placement of bunkers, and the occasional water hazard made the course anything but easy ... as Chris quickly discovered, bogeying the first three holes, with Patrick not doing much better. On the second hole, a short par three, Chris actually dumped two balls into the water, which essentially comprised the "fairway," as it stretched the entire length from tee to green.

"At least it's match play," Patrick said after the second one splashed down.

Chris's head began to pound again. On the third hole, he was sure he could make up some ground, then watched in horror as his drive hooked, slammed into a tree trunk, and ricocheted backwards. Patrick found the right bunker off the collar of the green, duffed the exit, and together they posted a double-bogey. Vandeweghe was also struggling a bit, while Charlie, on the other hand, was steadily chipping away at par, managing, somehow, to stay out of trouble. Chris attributed it to the buggy, which gave Charlie a chance to sit between shots, and saved him from walking too much. At any rate, Chris and Patrick found themselves down by three going to the fourth tee.

"So where am I aiming on this hole?" Vandeweghe asked his caddy, who had won the coin toss between he and the other caddy, and was only carrying Vandeweghe's bag.

The caddy glanced at his associate, who shrugged in response. "Sir?" he said. "Aren't ye t'aim at the hole?"

Vandeweghe expelled an expletive that would have had him tossed off most courses, then yanked his driver from his bag. "No, you *don't* always aim for the hole," he snapped. "Do you even *play* golf?"

The caddies sniffed, rubbed their noses almost in unison, and stared everywhere else but at the tall man fuming before them. Chris turned away to hide a grin. This might actually be good for their game. An angry Vandeweghe wasn't bound to play well.

Sure enough, Vandeweghe yanked the drive, sending it deep into the heavy grass on the left. He spat another expletive, shoved the driver into the bag, and hovered under his umbrella. Charlie ignored the tirade and somehow managed to sail his drive right down the middle of the soggy fairway. Watching him, Chris wasn't sure how the guy was playing golf – Charlie could barely turn and every motion looked painful. The wet weather couldn't be helping.

"You're up, Burger Man," Patrick said.

Chris nodded. He teed his ball, waggled, then looked down the fairway. A large pond beckoned on the right side of the fairway. Chris looked back down at his ball. This one had to remain in the fairway. He took a deep breath. Focus, he thought, then proceeded to pound his drive a solid three hundred yards down the left side of the fairway. He wanted this hole.

"Jeez!" Patrick said. "What was in your cigar last night?"

Patrick also hit a great drive, but Chris knew it lagged behind by at least twenty yards. They spent five minutes looking for Vandeweghe's ball, only to find it nesting in the rough – "It must'a hit a rock, sir" – then watched as Charlie jerked his iron shot into a front bunker. Patrick's ball was, indeed, many yards behind Chris's, but Chris wasn't gloating; he didn't care which one of them birdied the hole, as long as one of them did.

As it turned out, it was Chris who sunk the birdie putt, on a soaked green, water trailing behind the ball as it swam toward the hole nine feet from where he stood.

"Two down," Patrick said as they walked to five. "Lots of golf left to play."

"Kick ass," Chris said, and slid his driver from his bag.

The fifth hole was another par four, and Chris thought it looked pretty straight forward. No water, no fairway bunkers, just wet grass and dripping trees along the right. Again, he pounded his drive, and although the ball leaked to the right a little, he knew he was safe. Just to torture Vandeweghe, Chris turned to the caddies and said, "What's under those trees, to the right?"

The caddies exchanged another befuddled look. Vandeweghe rolled his eyes and sighed loudly. He went to the tee muttering, which amused Chris. It always amused him to see Vandeweghe rattled.

Chris, alone, made the green in two, as the other three were either short, long, or left. "Another chance," Patrick said, and pointed at Chris's ball. "Go get 'em, tiger."

The rain had diminished to a drizzle, but it was still steady, and the morning's deluge had left the greens ridiculously soupy. Chris tried to shovel out two small puddles with his putter, then gave up and went to his ball. It was just water, after all. Probably slow down a ball, but it shouldn't turn it much.

He lined up, checked and rechecked, then stroked. The ball muddled its way through the puddles, slid a little left, then hovered on the edge of the cup.

"Dive in!" he said, knowing the cup was filled with rainwater. "You can swim!"

The ball teetered, then dropped with a little splash.

Patrick yelped with joy. "Great putt, Chris!" He gave his partner a high-five.

Vandeweghe picked up his and Charlie's markers and gave Chris a thumbs-up. "That was great, Chris. Right through the muck and mire. Those swimming lessons back at two must have helped."

Chris nodded, but kept his attention on the next hole. They were still down by one.

The sixth hole was a two-hundred yard par three, straight over a long patch of gorse onto a decent sized green guarded by two bunkers on the right. Chris pulled his two iron from the bag, then choked down on it a bit. Under normal circumstances, this would probably put him over the green, but between the rain and the soggy ground, Chris felt confident it would stay below the flag.

He was wrong. The minute the ball left the club face, he knew he was in trouble. "Sit, sit!" he yelled. "Get down you mangy dog!"

The caddies looked around, as if expecting a mongrel to trot up, and Chris chuckled, despite his frustration at overshooting the green by a mile. Patrick landed short of the green, while dependable Charlie thwacked his ball directly into the middle of it, and Vandeweghe landed on the back and stayed there, the ball apparently plugged in the soft ground.

Vandeweghe wheeled on his caddy. "I thought you said the green was slanted from back to front?" He slammed his iron into the bag. "Do you know this course at all? Because if you don't, just say so and I'll stop asking for advice."

"So, P.Q., seen any good movies lately?" Chris said.

Patrick gave him a funny look, then caught on. "Oh, movies! Yes, movies, of course. Um, nothing since we arrived, unless you count the underwater reel we saw at Barassie."

Charlie chuckled, then said, "Or the romance picture we saw at Machrihanish, when we all fell in love with the place."

"Not the wedge, you imbecile!" Vandeweghe spat. Chris looked over in time to see the tall man shake the club in caddy's face. "This is a wedge, not a putter. I need the *putter*."

The poor caddy appeared to be about to cry, or maybe he already was crying, Chris thought. Hard to tell since the poor kid was soaked with rain.

The caddy fumbled to get the correct club, then dropped Vandeweghe's bag onto the soggy grass. Vandeweghe tossed his hands in the air.

"Okay, okay!" Vandeweghe said. "Give me the bag, I'll carry it myself."

He reached for the bag and the caddy, shorter and younger, snatched it off the ground and slung it back on his shoulder. He squared off with a very surprised Vandeweghe.

"No sir," the caddy said tightly. "I'll be carryin' yer bag, for I'll not learn any other way."

Vandeweghe stared at the young man for a beat, then said, "You'll learn?"

"Aye, sir."

The wind seemed to go out of Vandeweghe's sails. "How long have you been doing this, young man?"

The caddy pulled his sleeve up and looked at his watch. "About an hour, sir."

Vandeweghe shook his head. "Not how long have we been on this round," he sputtered. "How long have you been working as a caddy? And I use the word 'working' loosely."

The caddy blinked but, to his credit, he remained stoic. "They be the same, sir."

Vandeweghe took a deep breath and gazed out into the rain. For what felt like an eternity, the tall man and his caddy stood there, facing off. Chris watched, both bemused and surprised at his friend's reaction to this feisty young caddy. Finally Vandeweghe relaxed, his shoulders dropping as he sighed.

"Do you want to do this kind of work?" Vandeweghe asked. The caddy nodded emphatically. "Okay, then." Vandeweghe looked at the other caddy, who was hiding behind Chris and Patrick. "You, there –" Vandeweghe beckoned for the young rascal to step forward. "Are you new at this, as well?"

The second caddy pondered his response, and his shoulders sagged. "Aye, sir," he said quietly. "That I am."

"Oh for Pete's sake!" Vandeweghe exploded. The caddies stepped back a pace, and Chris wasn't sure they weren't going to drop their bags and run for cover. He knew he would have.

Vandeweghe turned to the two caddies. "Fine, fine!" He looked at Chris, Patrick, and Charlie. "Looks like we've landed in a training camp. You guys up for this?"

"Of course!" "No problem." "Absolutely!" were the responses, and the caddies relaxed.

"Okay, let's go," Vandeweghe said. "We're wasting daylight standing around gumming ourselves to death." He pointed at the putter in his bag and, with more kindness in his voice than Chris had ever heard from him, said, "That's the putter, young man. You hand that club to me, or any golfer, as we approach the green. Got it?"

The caddy smiled broadly, and Chris was pleased to see the young man had all his teeth. At least for now.

"Aye, sir, yes, sir!" the caddy said, and whipped the putter from the bag. He handed it to Vandeweghe.

"Now that we have that straightened out, let's go play golf," Vandeweghe said, and strode toward his ball.

Over the next few holes, Chris found himself everywhere but in the center of either fairways or greens. He bogeyed eight, nine, and ten, made par on eleven, then bogeyed twelve and thirteen. Yet, while he was hopeless, Patrick was cleaning up around him. The guy couldn't miss a putt, and his fairway shots were consistent and true. Charlie still chugged along, and Vandeweghe seemed to relish his new role as teacher. It settled him and he played solid through the thirteenth hole, but it was Patrick who was playing real golf on this course, while the rest of them were along for a stroll under their umbrellas.

Chris walked beside Patrick down the fifteenth fairway, a decent par five with trees waving at them along the right. They were up by three, and Patrick had, once again, carved the fairway down the middle with his drive.

"We should be playing this game at night," Chris said. Patrick shot him a look of confusion, to which he clarified, "You're a star, partner, shinin' bright!"

Patrick moaned. "That the corniest thing I've ever heard you say."

"Well, my brain is waterlogged, or still foggy with smoke. Take your pick."

Patrick grabbed his three wood and stood behind the ball. "Think I can make it?" he asked Chris.

Chris stood beside him and eyeballed the remaining yards to the green. It was at least two-fifty to the green. "Sure." He hoped he sounded confident. "Go for it."

Patrick addressed the ball, shifted his feet a few times, then settled and swung. The ball screamed into the air.

"It's on the flag," Chris said, watching. "It's all over the flag!"

The ball dropped, rolled, and came to rest close to the pin. How close was hard to tell from this distance, but Chris was sure it would be flirting with a birdie, if not an eagle.

"Nice shot, hotshot!" Vandeweghe called from his location on the edge of the fairway. "You want to come hit mine, as well?"

Knowing Patrick was safe, Chris rushed a bit and sent his bleeding right, somewhere toward the sixteenth tee. Neither Charlie nor Vandeweghe would make the green in two, and he was hopeful that Patrick would, at the very least, birdie the hole and they could all go back to the hotel and get dry. The incessant drizzle was beginning to wear on him.

Charlie and Vandeweghe both dropped their third shots near the pin. When they arrived at the green, Chris knew the door was closed.

"Holy mackerel!" he said. "P.Q., you're not two feet from the hole!"

Patrick smiled broadly and marked his ball. "I knew it would be good, but I didn't think it was that good."

"It's no gimme," Vandeweghe said, "but you'd have to do something really stupid to miss it."

Chris sent his caddy to go look for his ball, sure it wouldn't be located, and just as sure it wouldn't matter. He stood by Patrick as Vandeweghe and Charlie putted, both knocking it close, but not making their birdie putts. They both made par, and Chris felt himself swell with joy. Patrick would most certainly put their opponents to bed on this hole.

"Stop with the Cheshire grin," Vandeweghe said to Chris. "He still has to make this, you know."

Chris held up two fingers. "In two, Gooch," he jested. "He has two strokes to close the door on you guys." He waved his fingers in the air and mouthed, silently, "Two!"

Charlie rolled his eyes and leaned on his putter. "Well, get on with it, will you. I'd like to see which Quinn brings home the bacon today."

Patrick placed his ball, read the line briefly, then settled into his stance. Within a breath he sent the ball rolling, and Chris's heart skipped a beat. The damn ball was going to slide by the hole! Then it found a small indent, turned, and dropped politely into the cup.

Patrick grinned from ear to ear. "See it and weep! Eagle on fifteen!"

"Heck, I'm not weeping," Chris said. "I'm ecstatic! We won, Patrick! We won!" He thrust his hand out, grasped Patrick's, and pumped vigorously. "You did it, pal! We're the Scottish Champions!"

From the edge of the green, the caddies clapped and hooted in appreciation.

"Congratulations, you two flat bellies," Vandeweghe said, and shook both Patrick's and Chris's hands firmly. "You beat us four and three. Couldn't be more pleased. Good game, P.Q."

"Yeah, thanks for carrying me on your back," Chris said.

Patrick feigned pain in his lower back and teased, "You're awfully heavy though. Next time, walk yourself, will ya?"

"Shall we head in?" Vandeweghe said. "Or play on?"

Chris was about to suggest they head in, but he paused. "Hey, no rain." He held out both hands, palms up. "Play on?"

"I'd like to finish the course," Charlie said. "It's our last round, after all. And for once I don't have to walk."

The all agreed to continue, and Chris thoroughly enjoyed playing the last three holes. Vandeweghe seized the moment to play full professor to the fledgling caddies, gesturing as he lectured on the rules of etiquette and the caddy's responsibilities. Charlie was clearly in less pain, turning more easily in his backswing and driving as if he didn't have a care in the world. And Patrick was making birdies like cotton candy, sweet and easy. Heck, Chris wasn't even upset when he duffed his drive on eighteen and landed in the back left fairway bunker, a mere two hundred yards up from the tee. Sure, he would have liked a great "last drive" in Scotland, but he had plenty of good ones to remember.

When they approached the eighteenth green, they found the other members of the Gang huddled, waiting.

"Wow, are you guys going all the way to the end?" Ridge asked. "We were done on fifteen."

"So were we," Chris said, barely able to contain himself, "but we decided to finish out the round for the hell-of-it."

Don hummed and his eyes shone as he looked at Plato, Rudy, and Ridge. "I told you they'd finish out, regardless. Aren't you glad we did the same?"

A golden silence descended as Chris's foursome completed their putting. When his ball fell into the hole – for a bogey, unfortunately – Chris felt a pang of disappointment. They were scheduled to play another course at two-something, and for some weird reason, Chris wanted this to be the concluding round.

"Congratulations, again," Charlie said, and patted Chris on the back. "You deserved it."

"Patrick deserved it, not me," Chris said. "But I'm awfully happy he was my partner." He slung an arm loosely over Charlie's shoulders. "We'll be gloating about this for years to come, you know."

Charlie grinned and his eyes shone beneath his heavy eyelids. "Don't I know it. There'll be no living with Patrick."

The Gang mingled on the edge of the eighteenth green, apparently reluctant to end the round.

"So?" Plato said, looking from Charlie to Patrick and from Vandeweghe to Chris. "What's the verdict?"

Chris thrust his hand toward Patrick, "Put it there, partner. We're the Champions!"

"Well, well!" Plato vigorously shook both Patrick's and Chris's hands. "Congratulations!"

Charlie chuckled. "Took 'em long enough to figure out how to beat a couple of old farts." He motioned between Don and Ridge, and Plato and Vandeweghe. "And what about you guys? Who's the third place winner?"

Don wiggled his index finger in the air. "That would be us."

"And well earned, indeed," Plato said. "Ridge played better than he has all trip."

"Which isn't saying much," Ridge joked.

Plato drifted toward the castle hotel, and the Gang followed, still sharing stories. Before Chris understood why, they were standing in the parking lot near the van. The caddies dropped their bags and were paid – with a hefty tip to all four from Vandeweghe, along with a few last-minute lessons. Ken arrived and began loading the golf bags.

"Hey Ken," Don said, "leave mine out. I'll need to pack it."

Ken looked confused for a moment, then nodded. "Oh, aye, Mr. Winterhalter, but ye've the round at Edzell, no?"

Chris looked at the faces of his friends. It appeared no one was anxious to play another round. "I suggest we have lunch and call it a day," he said. "Anyone want to second the motion?"

"Here, here," Ridge said, and raised his hand. "I'll second that. I'm done for the day. Beating these two jokers has taken its toll."

"Just as well, laddies," Ken said. "We're in for more weather, so I'm told." He pulled Don's bag from the trailer and stood it up, alone. "There ye are, sir."

The Gang grew silent. It was the sudden stillness that came with the announcement of impending doom, and Chris felt a lump jump into his throat.

Don looked around. "Jeez, fellas. I'm just heading to Paris. No one's died."

Chris forced a laugh and, even to his ears, it sounded hollow. "He's heading to Paris! Is the guy spoiled or what?"

Don waved dismissively. "Come on, let's eat. I'm starved."

Chris and Patrick hung back, and neither said a word until they entered the castle hotel.

Finally, Patrick broke the silence between them. "Well, we did it," he said, his voice rushed and pitched just a little too high. "I had my doubts for a few holes, but –"

"Hey, I don't want this to end, either," Chris said. "At least we're ending on a winner's note."

Patrick nodded and looked down. When he looked back up, Chris noticed his eyes were shiny.

"No point in getting all choked up," Patrick said.

Chris shook his head, trying to dislodge his own lump. "Heck, we're flying home with the Gang." He smiled weakly. "Well, maybe not with Don, but we'll see him soon enough."

"Yo! Champions!"

Ridge beckoned them from the dining room. "Coming anytime soon?" He planted his hands on his hips. "Or are you waiting for the red carpet? 'Cause you'll be waiting a long time, if that's the case."

Chris joined Patrick in laughter, and the lump in his throat dissolved, quickly replaced by a deep rumble from his stomach. Winning a championship sure made a man hungry. Gee, maybe he'd have a burger.

CHAPTER 44

September 8, 1998

Don Winterhalter

In an effort to prolong the camaraderie, the Gang had lingered over lunch longer than they should have, and Don found himself scrambling to pack in time to leave. Chris hovered like a baby chick, trying to be helpful but, inevitably, getting in the way. Finally, Don assigned him the job of packing his golf bag, and Chris assumed the responsibility with gusto.

Suddenly, there were no more clothes to pack, no more shoes to stow, no more trinkets to tuck into pockets of space. Don looked around the hotel room.

"I think I have everything. Do you see anything I've forgotten?"

Chris's eyes swept the room. "Nope. I think that's it."

A knock on the door announced the arrival of the bellhop. He pushed in a cart, loaded Don's luggage and golf bag, and lumbered out of the room. Don checked his watch.

"I have forty minutes before Ken drives me off in that stinky van," Don said. "Let's get the guys and meet downstairs for one more pop."

Chris agreed and trotted off to collect the rest of the Gang from their rooms. Don opened drawers and closets, and made one more sweep of the bathroom. Satisfied he'd left nothing behind, he shouldered his camera bag and exited the room. The sound of the door closing brought a knot to his stomach. He pursed his lips. There was no point in getting all sentimental.

In the bar, he sat in one of the corner chairs. No one else was there, and he counted seats to make sure there'd be enough for the eight of them. Laughter and familiar voices announced the imminent arrival of his friends, and they swooped in loudly.

"Hey Winner-halter," Ridge said, "did you hear ol' Chris here dumped not one, but two balls into the water at two?"

Don nodded. "Yep, I heard all about it while I was packing. Every – single – shot."

"Aaahh, heck," Chris wailed. "Was I boring you? 'Cause if I was boring you, I deeply apologize."

Don hummed. Chris wouldn't know how to bore him; the "kid" was always fascinating. With a start, he realized he'd known Chris for over twenty years. How time had flown …

The Gang situated themselves in a ramshackle circle, and Don waved for the bartender. He looked at the guys. "What are you all having? I only have about half an hour, so don't order something that requires a Ph.D. in bartending."

"You buying?" Vandeweghe asked. "You shouldn't be buying. You're leaving, for Pete's sake."

"I'm buying, I'm buying," Don said, and tossed his credit card onto the bartender's tray. "Stop your complaining."

Orders were taken, and the bartender, sensing the urgency of the moment, called for backup help. The drinks were disseminated within minutes, and Don raised his Manhattan in a toast. The Gang grew silent, all waiting.

"Here's to the best pals a guy could ever ask for," Don said. He looked squarely into the eyes of each of his friends. "Thank you," he said, emphatically. "You have no idea how much this has meant to me."

"Cheers!" Plato said, a little too loudly, and the rest of the Gang echoed the sentiment.

Don took two deep swallows of his drink, letting the alcohol warm his gut. He took a deep breath and steadied himself. He was surprised by how emotional he felt.

"So when do you land in Paris?" Charlie asked, rousing Don from his reverie.

"A little after ten tonight. Penny's already there. She left a message at the front desk saying she'd arrived safely and was at the hotel."

Charlie nodded. "You'll have a great time."

Don took another swallow of his drink. He knew he'd have fun in Paris, and it would absolutely be wonderful to see Penny. He'd missed her, and often had wished she'd been there to share in the sights. But long ago Don realized his life revolved around golf. Penny was always accusing him of putting family second to the game, and as much as Don tried to make her believe that wasn't true, it probably was.

As the Gang chatted on around him, he ruminated. He'd once told his eldest daughter to "find something about which you can be passionate, and don't let go." He'd meant it. Humans were built with passion, and they were meant to be passionate; it was just in their genes. Penny's passion was her social work – Girl Scouts and Welcoming Wagon and committees at the Club. Darby's passion was horses, and Judy's had been gymnastics and dance, and was now her young son. In the midst of the everyday tedium of life, he hoped they wouldn't lose their passion for the things that brought them joy. In honesty, he was sorry neither of them had developed a passion for golf, but at least they'd found something. And Penny enjoyed golf enough to occasionally join him.

"Winner-halter!"

Don looked up. Vandeweghe had his wine glass raised.

"Here's to Scooter!" Vandeweghe said. "May you travel safe, stay away from the Louvre – 'cause it'll suck you in for days – and return to Terravita with a renewed sense of love for this silly game we all play." He hefted his glass over his head. "To you, Don – the reason this whole trip was conceived!"

Loud cheers were voiced, and Don acknowledged them with a smile and the raising of his own glass. He drained it and contemplated a second, then decided against it. He hated flying drunk, and in his current state of mind, he'd get intoxicated quickly.

Ken appeared at the entrance to the bar. He motioned to Don, and tapped his watch. Don nodded. It was time to go.

He stood and a quick hush descended upon the room. Even the bartender stopped clanking glasses together.

"Okay, fellas, time for me to jettison this joint," he said. "Try not to drink the place dry in one night, and fly home safe to California."

He wanted to say more – so much more – but he knew if he even tried to convey how much this all had meant to him, he'd start blubbering like a school kid, and embarrass everyone. Worse yet, he had a feeling they'd all break down, too, and that would just be too much.

Don crossed the room, quickly shaking hands as he went. He reached Ken at the door before the bartender caught his attention with a loud whistle.

"Mr. Winterhalter! Your card!" The bartender waived Don's credit card.

"Oh shit!" Don muttered, and trotted back to the bar amidst laughter from his pals. He signed the tab and tucked the card in his wallet. "I'd be in trouble without this."

"Now get outta here, Scooter," Plato said, "before we kidnap you, send notice to all our wives, and stay another week!"

Don grinned. "You'd all have to stay here forever if you tried that stunt. Because your wives would throw you all out on your ears!" He waved, and bolted for the door. It wouldn't do to stay another minute, for several reasons, not the least of which is he might be tempted to take Plato up on his silly scheme.

Several calls of farewell followed Don out of the castle. Ken jumped into the van and closed the door.

"Are ye ready, sir?" Ken said, glancing at Don through the rearview mirror. "Ye've got all your goods?"

Don nodded, not trusting his voice to speak. The van ground into gear and lurched into motion. Behind him, something bounced and rolled in the van. Ridge's gas can had tipped and was lodged under the last seat.

Don smiled, then began to laugh, continuing for several moments. Ken chuckled in response, and began to hum a Scottish tune. They turned out of town and rumbled onto the highway toward Edinburgh. Don relaxed and watched the landscape roll past him, recognizing several landmarks from their travels.

They'd covered quite a bit of ground in eleven days. They'd played fourteen courses and seen a bit of the countryside. He sighed. How many drives had he taken? How many putts?

The van rocked gently as it sped down the highway. He tried to recount the rounds they'd played, then gave up. Maybe someday he'd figure it out. Right now, he just wanted to sleep.

He closed his eyes and let the sound of the tires on the pavement lull him to sleep. He'd seen enough of Scotland for one trip.

CHAPTER 45

September 9, 1998
Gary Vandeweghe

The alarm went off at five a.m. Vandeweghe reached over and batted at it several times before knocking it to the floor and stopping the racket. Ridge was showering, so he rolled over and closed his eyes. Just a minute or two more...

"Gucci. Gooch, get up," Ridge said, nudging his foot.

He sat up and shook his head, trying to clear the cobwebs from his brain. "Jeez, I must have fallen back asleep. What time is it?"

"Five-twenty-eight," Ridge said. "We gotta leave in half an hour."

Still half asleep, Vandeweghe showered and shaved, somehow managing not to cut himself in the process, then pulled on clothes. Thank heavens he'd packed the night before and had only to drop his dopp kit and pajamas into his suitcase.

He followed Ridge down to the dining room. The rest of the Gang, minus Don of course, sat hunched around the table, silently nibbling on toast and sipping hot coffee.

"Does anyone remember last night?" Vandeweghe said. He reached for a mug and poured himself coffee. "I certainly am fuzzy about it."

Patrick grinned. "Then you don't remember dancing with the bartender's wife and singing *Mack the Knife*?"

Vandeweghe felt a pang of panic, and noted his friends' expressions. "You had me going, P.Q. Very funny."

Patrick shrugged. "It was worth that look on your face. Even if it was fleeting."

Vandeweghe finished his coffee, took two bites from a piece of toast, then joined the rest of the men as they returned to their rooms. He was pleased to see Ken had collected his luggage, along with Ridge's, in their absence. The only thing remaining was his briefcase. He paused to take one last look at the comfortable room. He liked this place. Maybe he'd return with Barbara.

Ken had the van warmed up, and he waved the Gang in with a happy smile. Vandeweghe was sure the guy was ready to be done with all of them, and didn't blame him. They hadn't been a difficult bunch, but they hadn't been easy, either.

"Hey! My porta-potty!" Ridge said, dislodging the gas can from under the seat. He opened the cap and gingerly sniffed. "Oh good, it's clean. I can pack it in my suitcase when we get to the airport."

Plato turned in his seat and looked at Ridge. "You're not going to take that home with you, are you? It's just a plastic gas container."

"Waste not, want not," Ridge said. "Besides, I might need it during the trip home."

Chris chuckled. "We have gas stations every ten miles back home. The limo can stop if you need to pee."

Ridge just snuffled and tucked the gas can beside him on the seat. Vandeweghe was sure it was going home with them. He smiled at the thought of security trying to figure out what it was doing in some guy's suitcase.

"That better not set off any bomb sensors," he called over his shoulder. "If we get stuck on the tarmac waiting for a bomb squad, I'm throwing you off the plane."

"Fair enough," Ridge said.

The van grew quiet and Vandeweghe looked out the window. It had been dark when they left, but now the sun's first rays crossed the fields and hamlets. It was beautiful, tranquil, and so vastly different from San Jose and San Francisco that it almost felt like a different planet. He smiled. Sometimes that Scottish brogue was so thick, it sounded like a different planet, as well.

They arrived at Glasgow with plenty of time to spare, and he almost asked Ken to take them back into town for a proper breakfast. But the driver had leapt from the van and was unloading their bags from the trailer before Vandeweghe could organize his thoughts, so he gave up and stood aside, letting Ken finish.

Ken slammed the trailer closed and turned to the men. "Well, gents, it's been a lovely trip. Ye travel safe t' your homes now, and let me know next time you're in Scotlan'."

He shook the Gang's hands, one after the other, and Vandeweghe was pleased that he looked them all directly in the eye as he did so.

Chris pulled an envelope from his pocket and handed it to Ken. "Here, this is a little something from the Gang." He pressed the envelope into Ken's hands. "With our thanks."

Ken opened the envelope flap and peeked inside. His eyes flew wide and his eyebrows shot up. "By th' grace!" He stuffed the envelope deep into his pocket. "Thank ye." He smiled at each of the men. "Thank ye very much."

To Vandeweghe's surprise, Chris then pulled a wad of bills from his pocket and handed those over, as well. "And this is from me," Chris said with a wry smile and a tip of his head toward the Gang. "You saved me from taking directions from these know-it-alls."

A porter shuffled up, cart in tow. "Kin I take yer bags, gentlemen?" His brogue was so thick Vandeweghe had to squint to understand it.

"That sounds good to me," Ridge said. "I don't fancy carrying them to the counter myself."

The rest of the Gang agreed, and the bags were loaded, then disappeared into the building. Vandeweghe had a fleeting thought this would be the last time he'd see his golf clubs.

"Breakfast, anyone?" Rudy said. "I don't know about you guys, but the six a.m. toast has left me."

Charlie grunted. "More information than I need to know."

Rudy rolled his eyes and chuckled. "I didn't mean it that way, Charlie."

They hoofed it into the small airport and found a cafe, settled into several adjoining tables, and ordered. Vandeweghe realized this was the first time in nearly two weeks they weren't sitting at the same table. It was a bit disconcerting.

Rudy scanned the menu, then dropped it on the table. "I can't wait to get back to the States and be able to order a decaf coffee."

"You and your decaffeinated coffee," Vandeweghe said. "What's the point?"

Plato chuckled. "I imagine that's what the folks at Starbucks think about the coffee Lynea orders – a latte, decaf, no fat. Non, non, non kind of thing. One of Lynea's girlfriends called it a 'why bother'."

Thirty minutes later, the Gang wandered to the ticket counter, checked in, made sure their luggage had been accounted for, then shuffled to the gate. Vandeweghe stood by the window, watching the few planes come and go. It wasn't a large airport, and there weren't many flights, but more than he had anticipated.

A small biplane landed and he had a sudden memory of their flight to Machrihanish. He turned to his pals.

"Hey guys," he said, pointing at the tarmac. "They're missing something."

Rudy strained to look past Vandeweghe. "What?"

Vandeweghe grinned. "The fire engine."

The men dutifully chuckled. Twenty minutes later they were boarding the plane. Vandeweghe waited until the last possible moment, continuing to look out the window at the landscape surrounding the airport. He'd been to Scotland numerous times before, and would return many more, he knew. But this time had been special, and he was loath to let it go.

"Last call for flight forty-eight, thirty-five to Heathrow!"

Vandeweghe sighed and turned from the window. It was time to go home.

The flight from Glasgow to Heathrow had been bumpy, then their flight from Heathrow to San Francisco had been delayed by three hours. Vandeweghe, much to his surprise – and he was sure to the surprise of everyone else – took the delays in stride and remained unruffled. He wasn't in a rush to get home, and there were plenty of good eating establishments at

Heathrow. He simply ushered the other Gang members to a darkly paneled pub, plopped down at the nearest table, and ordered fish and chips and a beer. A soccer game played on the television over the bar, and Vandeweghe watched, mildly amused. Soccer had never been his game; there seemed to be an awful lot of running around, for very little reward.

Finally, they boarded their United flight back to the States. He had made arrangements for an upgrade to Business, as had Charlie, and they waved to the rest of their compadres as they turned left toward their seats. They both settled in, and Charlie was asleep before they taxied from the gate.

Vandeweghe took advantage of the complimentary beverages, then put on his earphones and listened to the commercials and banter before the start of the movie. The movie didn't interest him when it did come on, so he tried to sleep. It evaded him, however. He tossed and fussed, got up, went to the bathroom, ordered a glass of wine, tried to sleep again. No luck. His head was filled with memories, his body filled with a desire to hit a golf ball across a windswept links fairway.

It was going to be a long flight.

The wheels touched down with a dull thud, and Vandeweghe looked up from his magazine with a start. He hadn't slept a wink, while Charlie snored throughout the entire flight. He wondered how the guys in coach had fared. It was even harder to sleep back there, between the crying babies and the cramped leg room.

"Come on, Charlie," Vandeweghe said, and nudged the dozing man. "Time to go home."

Charlie started, then grunted. "We still have three hours left to this excursion. Don't make me wake up too much."

Vandeweghe smiled and led the way off the plane. They waited in the lobby for the rest of the Gang. Finally, after half the plane had disembarked, he saw them.

"How was your flight?" he asked in jest. "Mine was pretty nondescript."

A small bundle of energy charged past him.

"Daddy! Daddy!" the bundle screamed, his voice declaring him male, and young.

Chris leaned down and swooped up the charging child. "CJ!" Chris said, and began ferociously nuzzling the young boy.

Hally kissed her husband, then turned to the rest of the Gang. "Hi fellas. Nice to see you all home, safe and sound."

"Well, not all," Patrick said, a little defensively, Vandeweghe thought. "Don's still in Europe, gallivanting around Paris with Penny."

Hally smiled and sighed. "Ah, the joys of having grown children." She turned to Chris. "Someday we can travel the world, as well."

Chris planted a kiss on her lips then said, "You bet. We'll go around the world one of these days."

As a group, they walked to the luggage area, waited for their bags, and piled them up as they arrived. To Vandeweghe's delight, none were missing.

"Gee," Ridge said, hefting his suitcase onto a luggage cart, "Here I have all the underwear I need, and they manage to get my luggage to me on time."

Hally gave him a confused look, and the men laughed.

"I'll explain on the drive home," Chris said. "It's a long story."

"Not that long," Ridge said. "Lost luggage. End of story."

Vandeweghe laughed. He'd forgotten about the lost luggage. It seemed so very long ago.

Ridge sniffed his luggage.

"What's up?" Vandeweghe asked. "Dirty underwear?"

"Ah, heck," Ridge said. "I think my bottle of Scotch broke. I can smell it."

Vandeweghe raised his eyebrows. "You packed a bottle of Scotch in your suitcase?"

Ridge nodded. "I didn't want to carry it all over the globe." He sighed. "Oh well, I'll have sweet smelling laundry when I get home. Nellie's gonna love me."

As they exited the building, Rudy pointed. "Well lookee there. That's our guy."

Vandeweghe turned to see an older man in a tux standing on the curb beside a stretch limo, holding a sign that read "Gang of Eight." Vandeweghe felt a tightness in his chest. There would only be six of them in the limo going home, but it was still the Gang of Eight in spirit.

He gave Chris a quick hug. "So long, Burger boy. Been nice knowing ya."

Chris laughed. "Yeah, I'll bet you're done with me after the past few weeks. Unfortunately, you have a tournament with me in ten days, so don't get too comfortable in my absence."

Vandeweghe wrinkled his brow. A tournament?

"The Spyglass Member-Guest, you oaf," Chris said, feigning heartbreak. "Gosh, how quickly they forget."

"Oh, right, right!" Vandeweghe said. "Yeah, okay, I'll see you at the club!" He waved at Hally, who was carrying CJ, then ducked into the limo. Patrick, Charlie, Ridge, Rudy, and Plato were already in their seats. He noticed the champaign bottle had already been popped.

He motioned with his hand. "Okay, you guys, pass me a glass of that bubbly."

Patrick grinned. "Good thing Hally showed up or Chris would have to walk home. There's no room in the trunk for another briefcase, let alone a suitcase and golf bag."

Vandeweghe shrugged. "We'd just put it in the front seat," he said.

Patrick pointed over his shoulder. The front seat sported two golf bags, standing upright. Vandeweghe smiled. "I guess our bags expanded," he said to Patrick, and sipped his champaign.

As if the past eleven days had not happened, the men's conversation turned to items local – San Jose Country Club, the men's group, possible renovations. Vandeweghe joined occasionally, but for the most part he closed his eyes and tried to block out the moment. He was still savoring Scotland.

"Hey, Gooch, you asleep?" Ridge asked.

Vandeweghe opened one eye. "If I was, you made sure I didn't stay that way."

Ridge laughed. "We were trying to remember who it was that had the shot over the burn with the bunny. You know, they landed near the rabbit and it took off running, and then ran into the flag stick, and knocked it out of the hole, and someone – we don't remember that either – yelled 'rabbit in the hole!' and we all broke up laughing."

Vandeweghe shrugged. "Seems you remember it well enough. What's the question?"

"Well who was it? Who was there?" Ridge said.

"We all seem to remember," Patrick said. "But only four of us could have actually been there, you know?"

Vandeweghe sat up. He began to laugh, and his glass shook. Infectious as it always is, the laughter spread to the other men, and within seconds, the limo was rocking.

"What are we laughing about?" Patrick gasped.

Vandeweghe waved his hand, unable to speak. But he knew why they were laughing. The Gang of Eight had developed a collective consciousness. They were a strange bunch of individuals, different in so many ways. Yet they were first and foremost a tight-knit bunch of golfers, so close, in fact, that they sometimes shared memories and thoughts, especially about golf.

He gained enough control to finally speak. "It doesn't matter who was actually there for the rabbit incident." He wiped the tears from his face. "We were all there in spirit."

"That's the most esoteric thing I've ever heard you say, Gooch," Ridge said.

"Stick around," Vandeweghe said. "You might hear more."

Ridge tugged at his beard. "I'm not going anywhere. And neither are you."

Vandeweghe nodded. The man was right. None of them were going anywhere – well, except home.

The limo sped down highway 280 toward San Jose, and the Gang became comfortably quiet. Vandeweghe closed his eyes again. Ridge's words echoed through his mind.

"I'm not going anywhere ... and neither are you."

The Gang of Eight: two Garys, two Dons, two Quinns, a Rudy, and a Chris. Eight individuals, one group ... and a whole lot of golf courses in the world to explore.

He wriggled into the seat, and the sensation of the wheels on the pavement could be felt. Motion. Travel.

Yep. Ridge was right – and wrong. The Gang of Eight wasn't going anywhere, but they were going places. Many places.

Of that, he was certain.

www.ingramcontent.com/pod-product-compliance
Lightning Source LLC
Chambersburg PA
CBHW022102290426
44112CB00008B/521